Pocket Book of
British Ceramic Marks

Also by J. P. Cushion
(in collaboration with W. B. Honey)

HANDBOOK OF POTTERY AND
PORCELAIN MARKS
(fourth, revised edition)

POCKET BOOK OF
BRITISH
CERAMIC MARKS

including
Index to Registered Designs
1842–83

compiled by

J. P. CUSHION, FRSA
Former Senior Research Assistant
of the Department of Ceramics
Victoria and Albert Museum,
London

FOURTH EDITION

faber and faber

First published in 1959
by Faber and Faber Limited
3 Queen Square London WCIN 3AU
as Pocket Book of English Ceramic Marks
Second edition 1965
Second impression 1967
Third impression 1969
Fourth impression 1970
Fifth impression 1972
Third enlarged edition, revised and reset 1976
First published in Faber Paperbacks in 1983
Reprinted in 1986 and 1988
Fourth enlarged edition, revised and reset 1994
Photoset by Datix
Printed in England by
Clays Ltd, St Ives plc

© 1959, 1965, 1976, 1994 John Patrick Cushion

A CIP record for this book
is available from The British Library

ISBN 0-571-16364-5

4 6 8 10 9 7 5

CONTENTS

MARKS

Acknowledgements for Fourth Edition

It is now over thirty-five years since the author's first *Handbook of Pottery and Porcelain Marks* was published in collaboration with the late W. B. Honey, Keeper of the Department of Ceramics at the Victoria and Albert Museum. Since that time the search for the answers to elusive ceramic marks has continued, with the help of many people who have kindly passed on information 'for the next edition'.

To make rash claims as to the completeness of a book of this type would be foolish; in fact, with so much current research taking place in the ceramic field to-day, almost every book written on ceramics lacks some new information or discovery that came to light during the period it was in the hands of the printer.

Without doubt the author is especially indebted to the staff of the Ceramic Department of the City Museum and Art Gallery, Stoke-on-Trent, and the recent invaluable catalogue of the 1990 exhibition, Dynamic Design: *The British Pottery Industry 1940–90*, by Kathy Niblett, Senior Assistant Keeper of Ceramics, which so clearly and competently tells us of the numerous changes that have taken place in ownership – in take-overs and mergers, etc – in the British pottery industry over recent years.

A further source of information has been the 'Potteries Jotteries' which has appeared in the quarterly Newsletters of the Northern Ceramic Society by Rodney Hampson, who over the past ten years has kept the members up to date with current potteries news and told them what changes have been taking place in the industry, gleaning material from local newspapers, local radio and trade magazines. In the issue of December 1990, Mr Hampson tells us that according to

vii

the 'Yellow Pages' there were some three hundred and fifty separate firms still operating in Stoke; but with the industry going through a very difficult period due to the current recession and growing foreign competition, this number is constantly changing.

Information on the marks of many factories and individual potters has been gathered from the many published monographs on specific factories, such as Minton, Spode, Worcester, Sunderland Ware, and Grays Pottery, all of which appear in the recommended bibliography.

Preface: Scope and Arrangement
of the Book
Fourth Edition

This pocket-book of ceramic marks has been produced specially to answer the requirements of the collector and dealer who is in need of such a guide when on 'pot-hunting' expeditions. In order to restrict the bulk of the volume the marks recorded have been confined to those of Great Britain and Ireland; Continental and Far Eastern marks are dealt with in the author's larger *Handbook of Pottery and Porcelain Marks*.

The marks recorded here are restricted to factory or potter's marks which by their frequent occurrence, or in other ways, are of actual use in helping to identify the place and period of manufacture of a marked ceramic item.

Unlike in previous editions, the arrangement is now in alphabetical order by either the potter or the name of the factory; and where only initials, a monogram or a device is used, such as a bird, castle or anchor, these are also included alphabetically.

As far as practicable the marks are shown in facsimile (space has not permitted full-scale reproduction in all cases), the chief exception being those numerous modern marks consisting of the names or initials of the maker, or of the place of manufacture, which are reproduced by using printers' type, as has so often been done in the marks themselves on the actual wares.

To help the enquirer, an approximate date or period is given for every mark together with the name of the principal proprietor where of interest, and a word or two about the type of ware on which the mark is generally found.

The *Pocket Book of British Ceramic Marks* includes that part of the Class IV Design Index which relates to pottery and porcelain

(Appendix B, p. 421). It is included by kind permission of the Public Record Office and will enable readers not only to date their wares by using the tables on pages 421–525, but also to determine the name of the manufacturer, person or firm who initially registered the design to protect it from 'piracy' over a restricted period.

Historical Note and Methods
of Marking

The practice of marking ceramic wares as a guide to the manufacturer is a very old one and was carried out by the Romans on their red-wares, but it is not until the sixteenth century in Europe that the soft-paste Italian 'Medici' porcelain appears with a fully developed factory-mark, i.e. the sketch of the dome of Florence Cathedral in underglaze blue.

It was not until 1723 that the Meissen (Dresden) factory in Saxony adopted as a regular factory-mark the crossed swords of the arms of Saxony; this mark was invariably painted in underglaze blue on the base of the article in the Chinese manner. Other European porcelain and faience factories quickly followed the lead of Meissen and in 1766 the porcelain makers of France were required by law to use a mark which had been previously registered with the police authorities.

The practice of marking was never regularized throughout the eighteenth century with the result that factories which were proud of their reputation used a recognized mark, whilst the less important factories either left their wares unmarked in the hope that they would be mistaken for those factories whose style they were copying, or alternatively, used a mark similar enough to a famous one to be mis-taken for genuine. The crossed swords of Meissen were used on numerous imitations and quite openly copied on Bow, Derby, Worcester and Lowestoft.

Many of the marks encountered on ceramics are merely those of painters or workmen and are not a sure guide to the place of manu-facture even when identified, for these people were of a very nomadic nature and often worked in many different factories in the course of their career. The throwers and 'repairers' (a term used for the workers who assembled the various parts of figures, etc) invariably used a mark scratched in the body prior to the biscuit firing. These marks when under the glaze can safely be treated as genuine, but otherwise they should be closely examined for the burr or raised edge which is unavoidable when scratching soft clay, to ensure the mark has not been ground in after firing in order to deceive.

Painters and gilders generally used one of the colours in their palette or gilt, to mark the wares upon which they worked; this information was probably solely for the benefit of the management and for purposes of payment, which was often on a piecework basis.

Not to be confused with the names of potters are those of London dealers, who during the eighteenth and nineteenth centuries had goods made and decorated to their specific orders.

The marks used on English wares were applied in several different ways, including the incising (or scratching) on the unfired clay we have mentioned above. The other marks impressed in the body at this stage are also a reliable guide and usually were names of the factory, place or proprietor, made up of printers' type and stamped in one operation.

Painting or transfer-printing under the glaze in blue (also in green after 1850) was a most common method of marking wares and may be accepted as genuine, at least as far as knowing the piece was marked at the time of manufacture.

The practice of marking by painting, transfer-printing, or stencilling over the glaze in enamel-colours, are methods which are always liable to be fraudulent, as it is possible to add this type of mark at any time after the piece has been made.

The beginner should approach all marks with caution and it is important to learn to detect the difference between the various materials (i.e. earthenware, hard-paste porcelain, soft-paste porcelain and bone-china, etc); this would enable him immediately to realize that a neat gold anchor on a Chelsea-type figure cannot possibly be of that factory if the body is a hard continental paste and not the soft-paste as used at Chelsea. Finally do remember that many nineteenth-century factories include the date of their establishment in their mark and those early dates do not signify that the piece in question was made at that date, and also, that grandmother, who died at the ripe old age of one hundred and one, did not necessarily acquire the piece of china she has passed down to you at her birth.

Notes on Wares Made in
Great Britain and Ireland

The English late-medieval wares are not only of great artistic interest, but historically important as the direct ancestors of the Staffordshire wares. Little is known of the places of their production, the finer specimens perhaps being made in monasteries, and though of coarse materials the jugs and pitchers are often of great beauty of form and bear simple but effective decoration.

In the fifteenth and sixteenth centuries smaller neater jugs appear with a rich copper-green glaze together with a hard red pottery with dark brown or black glaze sometimes decorated with trailed white slip or with applied pads of white clay.

A rare and distinct class of sixteenth-century English pottery comprises cisterns, stove-tiles and candle-brackets finely moulded in relief and covered with a green or yellow glaze.

English pottery tradition before the industrial period was rooted in the medieval use of lead-glazed earthenware. The sixteenth-century Cistercian pottery was the immediate forerunner of the Tickenhall and Staffordshire slip-wares, and the tradition of the last in turn gave vitality to the 'Astbury' and 'Whieldon' wares made in the same district in the eighteenth century.

The impulse towards refinement, which had been inspired by the Elers brothers (who made fine red wares in the Chinese style) and by the vogue of porcelain, also led to the making of a fine white salt-glazed stoneware in Staffordshire, where the industrializing process was finally carried through by Josiah Wedgwood. His cream-coloured ware was immediately imitated at numerous neighbouring potteries as well as at Leeds, Liverpool, Bristol, Swansea, Sunderland, Newcastle, Portobello and elsewhere, quickly securing a world-wide market.

Aside from the main English tradition are the decorative stonewares of Wedgwood, products of the neo-Classical enthusiasm.

Tin-glazed ware, largely inspired by Italian, Dutch and Chinese models, was made at London, Bristol, Liverpool, Dublin and Glasgow, but had little effect on the main current of the English tradition as represented by the wares of Staffordshire, where delftware (as this is called) was never made. English delftware was painted in high-temperature colours; overglaze enamels were used only on very rare examples and were probably the work of Dutch independent enamellers.

The seventeenth-century stoneware of Fulham, inspired at first by the Rhenish and Chinese wares, produced the isolated phenomenon of Dwight's admirable figures; that of Nottingham, though typically English, was of minor importance, reflecting latterly something of the Staffordshire style.

English porcelain of the eighteenth century is remarkable for its variety of composition. Soft-pastes of French type were made at Chelsea, Derby and Longton Hall; soapstone pastes at Worcester, Caughley and Liverpool; and hard-paste at Plymouth and Bristol. From about 1750 onwards for several decades Derby was a most productive factory and a large proportion of the surviving English porcelain figures were made there. At Bow the use of bone-ash from 1747 heralded the type of porcelain which towards the end of the eighteenth century became and still remains the English standard body; this last was a hybrid porcelain in which some part of the kaolin was replaced by bone-ash. At Nantgarw and Swansea a belated soft-paste was made in the period 1813–22.

None of the factories enjoyed royal or princely protection or subsidy and most were short-lived. Chelsea, and possibly Worcester, alone reached the standard set by the chief manufacturers of France or the many establishments supported by the rulers of small states in Germany; the porcelain of the first-named, however, ranks with the best ever made in Europe. The unsophisticated charm of Bow and Lowestoft is of a different order and typically English.

Due to the absence of marks, many English porcelains are difficult to identify, but recent excavations in Vauxhall and Limehouse have enabled the wares made at these two important factories to be recognized, whilst the porcelain, if any, made at other London factories, such as Greenwich and Kentish Town, has yet to be revealed.

The ceramic art of the nineteenth century suffered no less than others from misdirected effort and mistaken enthusiasms. While the early part of the century lived largely on the artistic capital of the preceding period, the later part was chiefly occupied with the deliberate revival of former styles.

Yet in spite of unfavourable conditions the native genius of the English potters did succeed in producing wares which are both beautiful and of permanent value; the simple 'cottage china' and lustre wares of the New Hall type and its kindred earthenware; Worcester, Derby, Spode, Coalport and other porcelains which were its opulent contemporaries and successors, the charming blue-printed ware, and the entirely English brown stonewares of the Midlands and Lambeth. A singular use of glazed Parian is to be noted in the wares of Belleek in Co. Fermanagh, Ireland, where a pottery was started in 1863. Vases in naturalistic shell-forms were especially characteristic.

At the end of the century the revival of handicraft makes its appearance with De Morgan and the Martin Brothers, heralding the studio pottery of the present day.

The Marks

A

A, stylized   *see* Wornell, G.

A. B.   *see* Briglin Pottery

A. Bros.   *see* Ashworth Bros. Ltd., G. L.

A. & Co.   *see* Asbury & Co., Edward

A. B./Shelton*   *see* Adams & Bromley

A. & B.   *see* Adams & Bromley

A. B. & Co.   *see* Allman, Broughton & Co.
        A. Bullock & Co.
        North British Pottery

Abbey, Richard Abbey, Richard (*b.* 1754, *d.* 1819)
  ABBEY   Engraver & printer, 1773–*c.* 1785
  LIVERPOOL   probably a potter from *c.* 1790 in Liverpool
 R. Abbey, sculp.

Abbott Potter Andrew Abbott *Lane End, Staffs*
  impressed   1781–3, earthenware

Abbott Andrew *see* Turner, John (Abbott probably
        only London agent for John Turner)

Abbott & Mist *Lane End, Staffs*
 impressed or painted 1787–1809, earthenware

* Note: a stroke between initials and a name indicates 'written above':

            A. B.
            SHELTON

ABD   *see* Barrett-Danes, Alan

A.B.J. & Sons   *see* Jones & Sons, Ltd., A. B.

Ablitt, John   *Shepton Mallet, Soms.*

c. 1968–, studio-potter producing burnished wares

Absolon, William   *Yarmouth, Norfolk*

1784–1815, independent enameller of earthenware and glass.

A. & C.   *see* Adams & Cooper

Ackerley, Tim   *see* Della Robbia Co. Ltd.

A C S monogram   *see* Caiger-Smith, Alan

Adams, Benjamin   *Tunstall, Staffs*
B. ADAMS   c. 1800–20, earthenware & stoneware
impressed

Adams & Bromley   *Hanley, Staffs.*
A & B   1873–94, earthenware, stoneware & Parian

A & B
SHELTON   ADAMS & BROMLEY
printed or impressed

Adams & Cooper   *Longton, Staffs*
A. & C.   1850–c. 1879, bone-china
printed

4

Adams & Co., Harvey   *Longton, Staffs.*
      H. A. & CO.   *c.* 1869–87, earthenware & bone-china
      over crown   printed

Adams & Co., John   *Hanley, Staffs.*
     J. ADAMS & CO.   *c.* 1860–73, earthenware, stoneware & Parian
     ADAMS & CO.   printed

Adams & Sons (Potters) Ltd., William   (*b.* 1772)
                   William Adams III Master Potter from 1804,
                   factories at *Greengates*, *Tunstall* & *Stoke*,
                   earthenware and various types of porcelain.

   ADAMS & CO.   ADAMS   W. ADAMS & CO.
   1769–1800   1787–1864   *c.* 1815
              all impressed

 W. ADAMS & SONS   ADAMS   W. ADAMS
    printed in a variety of backstamps, *c.* 1820–63

  printed 1804–40   impressed, 1810–25 impressed, 1845–55
  W. A. & CO.   or full name, printed in a variety of
                  backstamps
                  1893–1917, 'ENGLAND' included after 1891

ADAMS
ENGLAND
printed, 1879–

printed from 1896, with
'TITIAN WARE', 'IMPERIAL STONE WARE', etc.

ADAMS
ESTBD 1657
TUNSTALL
ENGLAND

impressed on Wedgwood-type
jasperwares from 1896
with confusing establishment
date

ESTᴮ 1657
ENGLAND

printed 1914–40

W. Adams & Sons
printed under crown

Calyx Ware

1950–, later marks include
full name

Taken over by Josiah Wedgwood & Sons Ltd., 1966

Adams, W. & T. *Tunstall, Staffs*
  W. & T. ADAMS 1866–92, earthenware
   TUNSTALL
printed under Royal Arms

Adderley Floral China Works *Longton, Staffs*
      1945– , taken over by Ridgway Potteries
      in 1949

printed on decorative bone-china
Part of the Royal Doulton Group
from 1973

Adderley, J. Fellows   *Longton, Staffs.*
      J.F.A.   *c.* 1902–5, bone-china
              printed trade mark, and initials

Adderley, William Alsager   *Longton, Staffs.*

c.1875–1905, earthenware and bone-china

W.A.A.   printed or impressed c.1875

W.A.A. & CO.   from 1886–1905

printed trade-mark

Adderleys Ltd.   *Longton, Staffs.*

1905–47, bone-china
printed mark 1905–26, later marks
include name of firm.
Purchased by Lawleys 1947, now
part of Doulton Group

A.F. & S.   *see* Fenton & Sons, Alfred

A.G.R.   *see* Richardson, Albert G.

A.G.H.J.   *see* Jones, A. G. Harley

ah   *see* Heaps, Alan

A H monogram   *see* Bullers Ltd.
                                      Hoy, Anita

Ainsworth, W. H. & J. H.   *Stockton-on-Tees, Cleveland*
                                      1865–1901, earthenware
impressed

A J monogram   *see* Ablitt, John

A J G stylized monogram   *see* Griffiths A. J.

A. J. M. in Staffs knot   *see* Mountford, A. J.

A L B trade-mark   *see* Alcock, Lindley & Bloor

Albion Pottery   *see* Ouseburn Bridge Pottery
                                      Bourne & Leigh Ltd.

Albion Works   *see* Dimmock & Co., J.

Alcock & Co. Ltd., Henry   *Cobridge, Staffs.*
        H.A. & CO.   1861–1910, earthenware,
                                      printed in a variety of backstamps 1861–80.
                                      Full name & 'Cobridge' with Royal Arms,
                                      printed 1880–1910, 'Ltd' added 1900

Alcock Pottery, The Henry   *Stoke, Staffs.*
                                      1910–35, earthenware, printed mark with
                                      'Royal Arms'
        SEMI-PORCELAIN/HENRY ALCOCK POTTERY/ENGLAND

8

Alcock, John   *Cobridge Staffs.*

   JOHN ALCOCK   *c.* 1853–61, earthenware and probably
     COBRIDGE   bone-china
  name printed in a variety of backstamps

Alcock, John & George   *Cobridge, Staffs.*

   J. & G. ALCOCK   1839–46, earthenware and probably
     COBRIDGE   bone-china

    ORIENTAL
     STONE   marks impressed
   J. & G. ALCOCK

    J. & G.A.   initials impressed or printed in a
                variety of backstamps

Alcock Junior, John & Samuel   *Cobridge, Staffs.*

               c. 1848–50, earthenware & bone-china
  J. & S. ALCOCK JR. printed or impressed

Alcock, Lindley & Bloor Ltd.   *Hanley, Staffs.*

    A L B   1919–, earthenware, 'Ltd' from 1931
   trade-mark   a subsidiary of Swinnertons Ltd.
             1965, acquired by Allied English
             Potteries, since 1973 are part of
             Royal Doulton

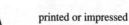

             printed or impressed

Alcock & Co., Samuel   *Cobridge & Buslem, Staffs.*

               c. 1828–59, earthenware, china and Parian.
  SAM^L ALCOCK & CO. *c.* 1828–53
     COBRIDGE

SAM^L ALCOCK & CO. BURSLEM	printed, impressed or moulded *c.* 1830–59

SAM^L ALCOCK & CO.   S.A. & CO.   S. ALCOCK & CO.
printed, painted or impressed in a wide range of backstamps. Royal Arms used without initials, name, etc. on some Alcock wares

Aldridge & Co.   *Longton, Staffs,*
                                  1919–49, earthenware

ALDRIDGE & CO. LONGTON	impressed

Aldwych China   *see* Beswick, John
                                     Bridgett & Bates

Aller Pottery   *see* Phillips & Co., J.

Aller Vale Art Potteries   *Newton Abbott, Devon*

AV	1887–1902, earthenware incised from *c.* 1895
Aller Vale Devon	incised or painted
ALLER VALE H. H. & CO.	impressed *c.* 1897–1902 for Messrs Hexter, Humpherson & Co.

Allerton & Sons, Charles   *Longton, Staffs.*

C. A. & SONS	1860–1911, earthenware & bone china
CHAS. ALLERTON & SONS ENGLAND.	printed or impressed *c.* 1890– 1942, many later marks include full name.

Allertons Ltd.   *Longton, Staffs.*
    'A' within   *c*. 1912–42, earthenware & bone-china
     wreath   printed from *c*. 1929–42
     over
  ALLERTONS LTD.

Allsup, John   *London retailer only*
   JOHN ALLSUP   1832–58, printed
 ST. PAUL'S CHURCH-
   YARD, LONDON

Alpha Ware   *see* Hulme, William

Alton China Co. Ltd.   *Longton, Staffs*
    ALTON   *c*. 1950–57, bone-china
  BONE CHINA   printed mark

Alton Towers Handcraft Pottery (Staffs) Ltd.   *Stoke, Staffs.*
               1953–, earthenware

               TOWERS CRAFT WARE

               printed or impressed

A M   *see* McGarva, Andrew

A M   *see* Mackee, Andrew
L

Amison & Co. Ltd., Charles *Longton, Staffs.*

C.A.
L.

c. 1889–1962, bone-china
'& Co.' from *c.* 1916, 'Ltd.' from *c.* 1930;
later trade-names: 'STANLEY BONE CHINA'
c. 1949–53, 'FLORAL BONE CHINA' 1951–62

printed 1906–30

Anchor & Castle *see* Ainsworth, W.H. & J.H.

Anchor Porcelain Co. *Longton, Staffs.*

A.P.CO. 1901–16, bone-china

A.P.CO.L. impressed initials 1901–16

  anchor impressed or printed
1901–16

trade-name: Royal Westminster China used with
initials and anchor in printed mark

Annfield *see* Thompson & Son, John

Anton Potteries Ltd., Jon *Longton, Staffs.*
c. 1968–75, earthenware and bone-china

12

A P monogram   *see* Ault, William
                            Caiger-Smith, Alan
                            Partridge, Judith
                            Phillips, A.
                            Powell, Alfred & L.

apple-tree   *see* Dick, Peter & Jill

Arbeid, Dan   *Saffron Walden, Essex*
                          1956–, studio-potter

    D.A.   ARBEID   painted or impressed

A R F   *see* Fuchs, Annette

Aristocrat Florals & Fancies   *Longton, Staffs.*
                        c. 1958–73, bone-china decorative
                        wares. Part of Wedgwood Group
                        from 1973

                        printed

Arkinstall & Sons Ltd.   *Stoke, Staffs.*
                        c. 1904–25, mostly crested bone-
        A & S   china. Taken over by Cauldon Ltd.
     printed in   in 1925. Cauldon Potteries Ltd.
    various marks   purchased by Pountney of Bristol
                        1958

      ARCADIAN
                        trade-names used in marks
   ARCADIAN CHINA

Arnup, Mick   *Holtby, Yorks.*
                        c. 1972–, studio-potter working in stoneware

Arnup

written signature

Art Pottery Co.   *Hanley, Staffs.*
ART POTTERY CO.   1900–11, earthenware
  ENGLAND   (see also Cooper's Art Pottery Co.)
(with crown)
    printed

A S   *see* Samuel, Audrey

A.S. & Co.   *see* Smith & Co., Ambrose

A.S/B   *see* Stanyer, A.

Asbury & Co., Edward   *Longton, Staffs.*
              c. 1875–1925, bone-china

  ASBURY   also printed with above trade-mark
  LONGTON

  A. & CO.   printed in a variety of marks

Ashby Potters' Guild   *Woodville, Derbys.*
              1909–22, earthenware. Tunnicliffe,
   Pascoe. (Ault & Tunnicliffe from
              1923)

  impressed

14

Ashstead Potteries Ltd, *Ashstead, Surrey*

1926–36, earthenware (some figures designed by P. Stabler)

printed

Ashworth & Bros. Ltd. *Hanley, Staffs.*

ASHWORTH	1862–1968, earthenware. Re-named
impressed	1968 to Mason's Ironstone China Ltd.
1862–80-	1973 taken over by Wedgwood Group
	re-named Mason's Ironstone

A. BROS   printed in a variety of marks
G.L.A. & BROS.   1862–*c*. 90

Royal Arms
over   printed from *c*. 1862
IRONSTONE CHINA

From 1862 Ashworths used 'MASON'S PATENT IRONSTONE CHINA' mark sometimes adding 'ASHWORTHS' 'ENGLAND' added from *c*. 1891

printed mark from *c*. 1880

LUSTROSA   printed trade-name on some wares from 1932

15

printed from *c.* 1957

Astbury   *Shelton, Staffs.*
    ASTBURY   mid-18th century, earthenware

    incised or   there were many potters of this
    impressed   name active in Staffs at this period

Astbury, Richard Meir   *Shelton, Staffs.*
                   1790, earthenware
    R.M.A.   impressed

Aston, Christopher S.   *Elkesley, Notts.*
                   studio -potter working in stoneware

                   applied label

Athlo Ware   *see* Price Bros (Burslem) Ltd.

Atkinson & Co.   *Sunderland, Tyne & Wear*
    ATKINSON & CO.   1788–99, Southwick Pottery, earthenware
    impressed or
    printed
Atlas, holding globe   *see* Chapmans & Sons, David

Atlas Bone China   *see* Grimwade Ltd.

Atlas China Co. Ltd.   *Stoke, Staffs.*

printed

1906–10, bone-china. Name revived by
Grimwades Ltd. in 1910 as Atlas
Bone China. Taken over by Coloroll
c. 1978 as part of Howard Pottery
Group

Ault, William   *Swadlincote, Staffs.*

printed or
impressed

1887–1923, earthenware (Ault Faience)
c. 1910, Ault's English Art Pottery
1922, amalgamated with Ashby Potters'
Guild
1923 Ault & Tunnicliffe
1937– Ault Potteries Ltd.

The wares of this pottery sometimes bear the
signature of the designer Christopher Dresser, 1891–6

c. 1964 taken over by Pearson Group
(Allied English Potteries), 1973
merged with Royal Doulton

printed, 1887–1923

Austin   *see* Phillips, J.

Avon Art Pottery Ltd.   *Longton, Staffs.*
1930–69, earthenware, merged with
Elektra Porcelain Co. 1962

printed or impressed   printed, 1947–
1930–39

A W   *see* Wallwork, A.

A.W./L   *see* Wood, Arthur

Aylieff, Felicity   *Bath, Avon*
c. 1976– , studio-potter,
earthenware with inlaid decoration

Aynsley & Co., H.   *Longton, Staffs.*
1873– earthenware
H. AYNSLEY & CO.   H.A. & CO.
LONGTON   L
printed in a variety of marks,
'Ltd.' from *c.* 1932

Aynsley, John   *Lane End, Staffs.*
AYNSLEY   *c.* 1790– *d.* 1829, enameller & engraver.
LANE END   1796–1802, earthenware & probably china

I. AYNSLEY   J. AYNSLEY   JOHN AYNSLEY
LANE END   LANE END   LANE END
signatures with on-glaze prints

Aynsley & Sons, Ltd, John *Longton, Staffs.*

AYNSLEY   1864–1971, bone-china. Part of
impressed   Waterford Glass Co. Ltd. Eire from
                   1970, then purchased by Aynsley
later marks   Group PLC in 1987, who then
include name   purchased names and patterns of
AYNSLEY with   Hammersley China Ltd. & Palissy
'England' from   Pottery Ltd. 1989
1891. 'Ltd.'
from 1933

B

B   *see* Baddeley, John & Edward
        Barlow, Thomas
        Barlow & Sons Ltd., T.W.
        Barron, Paul
        Blair & Co
        Bow
        Bristol
        Worcester

B, in crescent   *see* Booths Ltd.

B+   *see* Bristol

B. & Co.   *see* Birks & Co., L.A.
                      Bodley & Co.
                      Boulton & Co.

B. & Co./L   *see* Boulton & Co.

B. Ltd.   *see* Barlows (Longton) Ltd.

B & Son   *see* Bodley & Son

Babbercombe Pottery Ltd.   *Torquay, Devon*
                      1952– , earthenware

stamped

B.A. & B.   *see* Bradbury, Anderson & Bettaney

Baddeley, John & Edward   *Shelton, Staffs.*
                      1784–1806, earthenware

B	I.E.B.	I.E.B.
	impressed marks	w

Baddeley, Ralph & John   *Shelton, Staffs.*
                      1759–95, earthenware & unidentified
BADDELEY   porcelain

R. & J.   initials impressed
BADDELEY

                    1759–61 Reid, Baddeley & Co.
                    at Liverpool
                    1761–75 J. Baddeley & Fletcher
                    1775– R. Baddeley (son) & Fletcher

Baddeley, Thomas   *Hanley, Staffs.*
   T.BADDELEY   1800–34, engraver of copper plates
   HANLEY   for printing & enameller
printed signature

Baddeley, William   *Hanley, Staffs.*
   EASTWOOD   1802–22, Wedgwood-type wares
badly impressed mark to deceive

Baggerley & Ball   *Longton, Staffs.*
   B. & B.   1822–36, earthenware & bone-china
     L
printed in cartouche with 'Opaque China'
bone-china as yet unidentified

Baguley, A. & I.   *see* Rockingham & Mexborough (*Mexbro*)

Bailey, C.J.C.   *Fulham, London*
   BAILEY   1864–89, stoneware, *terra-cotta*
   FULHAM   & porcelain from *c.* 1873

   C.J.C. BAILEY   1891, Fulham Pottery &
  FULHAM POTTERY   Cheavin Filter Co.
    LONDON

              FULHAM   FULHAM POTTERY
            c. 1889–1920   *c.* 1948
                  impressed

From *c.* 1956, Fulham Pottery only supplier of
ceramic materials and wares made to order.

Bailey & Batkin   *Longton, Staffs.*
                                    1814–26, enamellers, gilders &
                                    lustrers only

Bailey & Batkin   Bailey & Batkin, Sole Patentees
                                    rare impressed or moulded marks on 'blanks'
                                    made to order for decoration, gilding, etc.

Bailey & Harvey   *Longport, Staffs.*
                                    1832–35, earthenware & bone-china
BAILEY & HARVEY   impressed

Bailey & Sons, William   *Longton, Staffs.*
                                    1912–14, earthenware

                                    printed

Bailey Potteries Ltd.   *Fenton, Staffs.*
                                    1935–40, earthenware
BEWLEY POTTERY   printed in a variety of marks
MADE IN ENGLAND

Bairstow & Co., P.E.   *Shelton, Staffs.*
                                    1946– present, earthenware & bone-
        BAIRSTOW   china

FANCIES FAYRE   trade-name
Name changed in *c.* 1979 to BAIRSTOW MANOR POTTERY LTD.

Baker, Bevans & Irwin   *Swansea, Wales*
                        1813–38, earthenware

BAKER, BEVANS
   & IRWIN

B. B. & I.

printed or impressed in a variety of marks

Baker & Co., W.   *Fenton, Staffs.*
                        1839–1932, earthenware
W. BAKER & CO.   BAKER & CO.
printed or impressed, 'Ltd.' added 1893

Bakewell Bros. Ltd.   *Hanley, Staffs.*
                        1927–43, earthenware & stoneware
BAKEWELL BROS.
      LTD.   printed

Balaam, W.   *Ipswich, Suffolk*
                        1870–81, slipwares
      W. BALAAM
ROPE LANE POTTERY   impressed
      IPSWICH

Balfour China Co. Ltd.   *Longton, Staffs.*
                        c. 1947–52, bone-china
      BALFOUR
ROYAL CROWN   printed under crown
      POTTERY
(Known as Trentham Bone China until 1957)

Ball Brothers   *Sunderland, Tyne & Wear*
                        1857–1918, earthenware at Deptford Pottery

COPYRIGHT	rare printed mark of late
BALL BROS,	19th century
SUNDERLAND	

Bare, Ruth (Mrs R. Baier)   *see* Della Robbia

Barker, John, Richard & William   *Lane End, Staffs.*
<blockquote>
c. 1800– early 19th C.
</blockquote>

BARKER	earthenware & stoneware
impressed	

Barker Bros. Ltd.   *Longton, Staffs.*

B.B.	1876–1981, earthenware & china
impressed	
c. 1876–1900	

B.B.LTD   or full-name in a variety of marks
trade names: MEIR CHINA (1912–30), MEIR WARE (1930–37),
TUDOR WARE (1937–), ROYAL TUDOR WARE (1937–)
Purchased by Alfred Clough in 1959, sold to
John Tams Ltd. 1982, works demolished

Barker Pottery Co.   *Chesterfield, Derbys.*
<blockquote>
1887–1957, stoneware
</blockquote>

printed or impressed, 1928–57

Barkers & Kent Ltd.   *Fenton, Staffs.*

B. & K.	*c.* 1889–1941, earthenware & china

B. & K.L.   B. & K.LTD.
printed or impressed in a variety of marks
'Ltd.' added 1898

Barlow, Thomas (*d.* 1864)   *Longton, Staffs.*
earthenware & china wares not identified with
certainty, but firm continued in Barlow's name
to 1884

Barlow & Son Ltd., T.W.   *Longton, Staffs.*
B   1882–40, earthenware

B & S   rare impressed marks
'CORONATION WARE' included in printed or
impressed marks 1928–40

Barlows (Longton) Ltd.   *Longton, Staffs.*
1920–52, earthenware
B.LTD.   1920–22, Barlows Ltd.
1923–52, Barlows (Longton) Ltd.
impressed
1920–
Later marks include trade-name: 'MELBA WARE'

Barn Pottery Ltd.   *Paignton, Devon*

1964– , earthenware
trade-name: Barn Ware

Barnard, H.   *see* Wedgwood & Sons, Ltd., J.

Baron, W.L. & son Frederick   *Barnstaple, Devon*
     1899–1930, earthenware
BARON. BARNSTAPLE   incised writing, 1899–1939
 BARON DEVON   impressed, 1905–38
     absorbed in 1939 by C.H. Brannam's

Barr, Flight & Barr   *see* Worcester

Barrett-Danes, Ruth & Alan   *Abergavenny, Gwent*
     active in 1989, studio-potters in
     porcelain

Barrett's of Staffordshire Ltd.   *Burslem, Staffs.*
     1943–1987, earthenware. Taken over
     by Queensway Guarantee Corporation
     Operating under own name 1990
     trade-name: 'DELPHATIC' 1957–

Barton Pottery   *Torquay, Devon*
     c. 1922–1937, earthenware
BARTON POTTERY LTD.
  TORQUAY stamped

Bates & Bennett   *Cobridge, Staffs.*
  B. & B. 1868–95, earthenware
 printed or impressed in a variety of backstamps

Bates, Brown-Westhead & Moore   *Hanley, Staffs.*
    B.B.W.& M.   1859–61, earthenware & bone-china
printed or impressed in a variety of backstamps

Bates, Gildea & Walker   *Burslem, Staffs.*
    B.G. & W.   1878–81, earthenware & bone-china
printed in a variety of backstamps

Bates, Walker & Co.   *Burslem, Staffs.*
    B.W. & CO.   1875–8, earthenware, stoneware &
                             bone-china

  BATES, WALKER
    & CO.   initials or name printed in a
                         variety of backstamps

Bathwell & Goodfellow   *Burslem & Tunstall, Staffs.*
                     1818–23 Burslem, earthenware
  BATHWELL &   1820–22 Tunstall, earthenware
  GOODFELLOW   impressed

Batkin, Walker & Broadhurst   *Lane End, Staffs.*
    B.W. & M.   1840–5, earthenware & stone-china
printed in a variety of backstamps

Baxter, John Denton   *Hanley, Staffs.*
    I.D.B.   1823–7, earthenware
    J.D.B.   printed in a variety of backstamps

Baxter, Rowley & Tams   *Longton, Staffs.*
    B.R. & T.   *c.* 1882–5, bone-china
impressed

Bayer, Svend   *Beaworthy, Devon*

studio-potter, active in producing
stoneware in 1989

Bayley, Michael   *Temple Ewell, Devon*

studio-potter, active in producing
stoneware in 1989

Bayley, Murray & Co.   *Glasgow, Scotland*
B.M. & CO.   1875–84, earthenware
SARACEN POTTERY   known as Saracen Pottery Co.
                     from 1884–1900

B.B.   *see* Bancroft & Bennett
            Barker Bros.
            Minton

B.B.B. under crown   *see* Booth Ltd.

B.B./B.   see Bridgett, Bates & Beech

B. & B.   *see* Baggerley & Ball
               Bates & Bennett
               Blackhurst & Bourne
               Bridgett & Bates

B.B. & I.   *see* Baker, Bevans & Irwin

B.W.W. & M.   *see* Bates, Brown-Westhead &
                  Moore

B C, stylized monogram   *see* Colls, Barbara

B. & C.   *see* Bridgwood & Clarke

B.C.Co.   *see* Britannia China Co.

B.C.G.   *see* Godwin, B.C.

B. & E.   *see* Beardmore & Edwards

Beard, Peter   *nr Sittingbourne, Kent*
    P F B   1985– studio-pottery

Beardmore & Edwards   *Longton, Staffs.*
    B. & E.   1856–8, earthenware
printed in a variety of marks

Beardmore & Co., Frank   *Fenton, Staffs.*
    F.B. & CO.   1903–14, earthenware
      F   impressed or printed in a variety of
                marks

Beaumont, Annie   *see* Della Robbia

Bednall & Heath   *Hanley, Staffs.*
    B. & H.   1879–99, earthenware
printed in a variety of marks

Beech & Hancock   *Tunstall, Staffs.*
    BEECH & HANCOCK 1857–76, earthenware

B. & H.   printed in a variety of backstamps

Beech, James   *Tunstall, & Burslem, Staffs.*
                   1877–89, earthenware

J.B.   printed

Beehive   *see* Burgess & Leigh Ltd.

Belfield & Co.   *Prestonpans, Scotland*
  BELFIELD & CO.   *c.* 1836–1941, earthenware
  PRESTONPANS
impressed or printed

Bell China   *see* Shore & Coggins

Bell-Hughes, Terry   *Gwynedd, N. Wales*
                      c. 1967– , studio-potter
                      producing high-fired domestic
                      wares

Bell, J. & M.P.   *Glasgow, Scotland*
       J.B.   1841–*c.* 1910 (continuing as
    printed or   merchant until 1941)
    impressed   earthenware, Parian and from *c.* 1870
                  bone-china
 J. & M.P. BELL & CO.   J. & M.P.B. & CO.
  printed in a variety of marks, 'Ltd.' from 1880.
  impressed or printed bell, with 'B' or 'J.B.'

Belle Vue Pottery   *see* Hull Pottery

Bells, A.E.   *see* Della Robbia

Belleek   *Co. Fermanagh, Ireland*

> BELLEEK   *c.* 1863– , earthenware, stoneware,
> CO. FERMANAGH   Parian & porcelain
>   McBirney, David & Armstrong, R.
>
> FERMANAGH
> POTTERY   impressed, *c.* 1863–90

rare impressed mark, 1862–90

early version of printed mark
1863–91

The post–1891 version of this mark includes
'IRELAND' and 'CO. FERMANAGH' to comply with
the U.S.A. McKinley Tariff Act.
Sold to Erne Heritage in 1990

Belper Pottery   *nr Derby, Derbys.*

>   1809–34, stoneware
> BELPER
>
> BELPER & DENBY
>   BOURNES   (transferred to Denby, 1834;
>   POTTERIES   *see* Bournes)
>   DERBYSHIRE
>   impressed

Benham, Tony   *Wateringbury, Kent*

1958, studio-potter (now at Preston)

written or incised with year

Bennett & Co., George   *Stoke, Staffs.*
G.B. & CO.   1894–1902, earthenware
impressed or printed

Bennett & Co., J.   *Hanley, Staffs.*
J.B. & CO.   1896–1900, earthenware
printed or impressed

Bennett (Hanley) Ltd., William   *Hanley, Staffs.*
W.B.   1882–1937, earthenware
H
WILLIAM BENNETT
HANLEY   printed or impressed, 'LTD.'
from 1922

Bentley & Co. Ltd., G.L.   *Longton, Staffs.*
G.L.B. & CO.   *c.* 1898–1912, bone-china
LONGTON   'LTD' added from 1904

Bentley, Wear & Bourne   *Shelton, Staffs.*
1815–33, printers & enamellers
BENTLEY, WEAR   'BENTLEY & WEAR' from 1823
& BOURNE
ENGRAVERS &
PRINTERS   name with printed decoration
SHELTON
STAFFORDSHIRE

Beswick Ltd., John   *Longton, Staffs.*
   BESWICK/WARE   *c.* 1927, earthenware & bone-china
   printed *c.* 1936– 'Ltd.' added 1938
   Trade-names: Beswick Ware, Warwick China
   & Aldwych China
   Taken over in 1969 by Doulton & Co. Ltd.
   trading as John Beswick Studio of Royal Doulton

Beswick & Son   *Longton, Staffs.*
      B. & S.   *c.* 1916–30, bone-china
   printed or impressed in a variety of marks

Bevington & Co., T. & J.   *see* Swansea Pottery

Bevington, John   *Hanley, Staffs.*

                      c. 1860–92, earthenware, stoneware,
                      Parian & bone-china
                      painted in under-glaze blue, 1872–92

   This mark was obviously adopted to imitate that
   of Meissen and used on 'Dresden style' wares.
   Reproductions were also made of some major
   English factories, including Derby, Chelsea, etc.

Bevington & Co., John   *Hanley, Staffs.*
      J.B. & CO.
         H.   printed in a variety of backstamps

Bevington, James & Thomas   *Hanley, Staffs.*
      J. & T.B.   *c.* 1865–77, Parian & bone-china
   impressed on Parian, bone-china as yet unidentified

Bevington, Thomas   *Hanley, Staffs.*
c. 1869–91, earthenware, Parian &
bone-china

T.B.

initials printed in a variety
of marks

Bewley Pottery Ltd.   *see* Bailey Potteries Ltd.

B F   *see* Floyd, Benjamin

B.F.B.   *see* Worcester, Barr, Flight & Barr

B.G.   *see* Godwin, Benjamin

B.G.P.Co. (or as monogram)   *see* Brownfields Guild
Pottery Society Ltd.

B.G. & W.   *see* Bates, Gildea & Walker

B. & H.   *see* Bednall & Heath
Beech & Hancock
Blackhurst & Hulme
Bodley & Harrold

Billinge, Thomas   *Liverpool, Merseyside*
1766–1800, engraver employed by
BILLINGE SCULP.   Sadler & Green
LIVERPOOL

Billingsley, William   *Mansfield, Notts.*
c. 1799–1802, painter & gilder

BILLINGSLEY   probably only decorating
MANSFIELD   'blanks' made elsewhere
rare written signature

Billington, Dora May   *various addresses*
                           1912–68, studio-potter

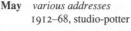

                           painted on Bernard Moore wares
                           1912–15

                           incised or painted, 1920–

Biltons (1912) Ltd.   *Stoke, Staffs.*

                           1900– , earthenware
                           name changed to Biltons Tableware
                           Ltd. Purchased in 1986 by
                           Coloroll Ceramics, renamed Coloroll
                           Biltons

Bingham, Edward (*b.* **1829)**   *Castle Hedingham, Essex*
                           Hedingham Art Pottery, 1864–1901,
                           reproductions in earthenware of
                           Medieval & Tudor-type wares

                                   E. BINGHAM
                               CASTLE HEDINGHAM
applied in relief   ESSEX
                               incised signature

1901– taken over as
ROYAL ESSEX ART POTTERY
       incised

Birch, Edmund John   *Shelton, Staffs.*
    BIRCH   1796–1814, earthenware &
                      stoneware

       E.I.B.
   impressed marks

Birch & Whitehead   *Hanley, Staffs.*
    B. & W.   *c.* 1796, earthenware & stoneware
   impressed

bird, a   *see* Wondrausch, M.
           Wren, R.

Birks Brothers & Seddon   *Cobridge, Staffs.*
                1877–86, earthenware & stoneware
  IMPERIAL IRONSTONE
      CHINA
 BIRKS BROS. & SEDDON printed under Royal Arms

Birks & Co., L.A.   *Stoke, Staffs.*
              c. 1896–8, bone-china

                  BIRKS   B. & CO.
                impressed   printed

        printed

Birks, Rawlins & Co. Ltd.   *Stoke, Staffs.*
              c. 1898– 1932, bone-china
    B.R. & CO.
   printed on above 'Vine' mark
   trade-names: Roseate Porcelain, Carlton China,
             Savoy China & Birks China

36

Bishop   *see* Bishop & Stonier

Bishop & Stonier Ltd.   *Hanley, Staffs.*

                       1891–1939, earthenware & bone-china

     B. & S.

  printed or impressed in a variety of marks

"Bisto"   "BISTO"   BISHOP ENGLAND

other marks include 'BISHOP/ENGLAND' printed or impressed

Bishops Waltham Pottery   *Bishops Waltham, Hants.*
    BISHOPS   1866–7, decorative earthenware
    WALTHAM   in Greek Revival form
                  printed

Bisto   *see* Bishops & Stonier Ltd.

B. & K.   *see* Barkers & Kent Ltd.
B. & K. L.
B. & K. Ltd.

B L monogram   *see* Leach, Bernard

B. & L.   *see* Burgess & Leigh

Blackhurst & Co. Ltd., John   *Cobridge, Staffs.*
    J. BLACKHURST   1951–9, earthenware
      ENGLAND   printed

Blackhurst, Jabez   *Tunstall, Staffs.*

JABEZ BLACKHURST   1872–83, earthenware
printed in a variety of
backstamps

Blackhurst & Bourne   *Burslem, Staffs.*

B. & B.   1880–92, earthenware
printed

Blackhurst & Hulme   *Longton, Staffs.*

B. & H.   *c.* 1888–1932, bone-china
printed in a variety of marks *c.* 1888–1914

THE BELGRAVE
   CHINA   printed 1914–
   B & H
    L
  ENGLAND

Blackhurst & Tunnicliffe   *Burslem, Staffs.*

B. & T.   *c.* 1879– earthenware
printed in a variety of marks

Blackie, Sebastian   *Farnham, Surrey*

mark   studio-potter, active in 1989–
a 'finger-print' in clay

Blackman, Audrey   *Boars Hill, Oxford*

A. Blackman   1949–*d.* 1990,
signature, dated   studio-potter, abstract
& numbered   sculpture in stoneware

Blades, John   *London*

BLADES, LONDON   *c.* 1800–30, retailer only

Blairs (Longton) Ltd.   *Longton, Staffs.*

B (in diamond)   *c.* 1879–1930, bone-china
                       impressed or printed 1879–1900

BLAIRS CHINA
ENGLAND   impressed or printed, 1900–

                       'Ltd.' added 1912
                       'Longton' added *c.* 1923

                       printed 1900–

Blakeney Art Pottery   *Stoke, Staffs.*
                       1968–, earthenware
'Flow Blue Victoria' printed ware
Kent Staffordshire figures & floral art
containers. M.J. & S.K. Bailey

                       printed backstamp
                       in brown 'M.J.B.'
                       (Michael J. Bailey)

                       similar backstamp
                       used with:
                       FLO BLUE
                       T.M. STAFFORDSHIRE
                       ENGLAND

IRONSTONE
STAFFORDSHIRE
ENGLAND

Similar Royal
Arms mark used,
with 'Romantic'
pattern

Note the lion and harp
in coat-of-arms are in
reverse positions to the
authentic version

FLO BLUE
T.M. STAFFORDSHIRE
ENGLAND

printed backstamps in under-glaze blue

Blue John Pottery Ltd. *Hanley, Staffs.*

1939–, earthenware

variety of printed marks including 'BLUE JOHN'

Blue Mist *see* Booths & Colclough Ltd.

Bluestone Ware *see* Winterton Pottery (Longton) Ltd.

Blyth Porcelain Co. Ltd. *Longton, Staffs.*
B.P.CO.LTD. *c.* 1905–35, bone-china
printed in a variety of marks in diamond-form under crown
'DIAMOND CHINA' with initials from *c.* 1925–35

B M monogram *see* Moore, Bernard

B.M. & Co. *see* Bayley, Murray & Co.
(Saracen Pottery)

B.M. & T. with swan *see* Boulton, Machin & Tennant

B.N. & Co. *see* Bourne, Nixon & Co.

Bodley & Co. *Burslem, Staffs.*

1865, earthenware

Bodley & Co., Edward F. *Burslem, Staffs.*
1862–81, earthenware

E.F.B. & CO.   printed in a variety of
                backstamps

E.F.B.

SCOTIA POTTERY   impressed

Bodley & Son, E.F. *Longport, Staffs.*
E.F.B. & SON.   E.F.B. & S.
printed or impressed on earthenware
1881–98
trade-mark: 1883–98

Bodley & Son *Burslem, Staffs.*
B. & SON   1874–75, bone-china
printed in Staffordshire knot

Bodley, E.J.D. *Burslem, Staffs.*
E.J.D. BODLEY   1875–92, earthenware & bone-china
E.J.D.B.
printed or impressed in a variety of marks
'E.J.D.B.' as monogram with 'TRADE MARK BURSLEM'

Bodley & Harrold *Burslem, Staffs.*
B. & H.   1863–65, earthenware
BODLEY & HARROLD
printed in a variety of backstamps

Boote Ltd., T. & R. *Burslem, Staffs.*
                1849–1963, Parian, tiles &
                earthenware

T. & R. B.   T. & R. BOOTE
T. B. & S.

printed or impressed in a variety of marks

Merged with Richards Tiles in 1963

Booth & Son, Ephraim   *Stoke, Staffs.*
  E.B. & S.   *c.* 1795, earthenware
  impressed

Booth, Frederick   *Bradford, Yorks.*
  F.B.   *c.* 1881, earthenware

Booth, G.R.   *Hanley, Staffs.*
                1829–44, earthenware
  PUBLISHED BY
  G.R. BOOTH & CO.   '& CO.' added *c.* 1839
  HANLEY
  STAFFORDSHIRE   impressed & dated

Booth & Sons   *Lane End, Staffs.*
  BOOTH & SONS   *c.* 1825–35, bone-china
  impressed
    B & S   (within wreath under lion)

43

Booth & Co., Thomas   *Burslem, Staffs.*
    T B & CO.   1868–72, earthenware
  printed in a variety of backstamps

Booth & Son, Thomas   *Tunstall, Staffs.*
    T.B. & S.   1872–6, earthenware
  printed in a variety of marks

Booth, Thomas G.   *Tunstall, Staffs.*

                 1876–83, earthenware

                 printed with name of pattern
                 on strap

Booth, T.G. & F.   *Tunstall, Staffs*
    T.G. & F.B.   *c.* 1883–*c.* 93, earthenware
  printed in a variety of marks

Booths Ltd.   *Tunstall, Staffs.*

                 1898–1948, earthenware

                 'Ltd.' from 1898

                 printed, *c.* 1898–1906

                 1948 purchased Colclough China Ltd.
                 1948–53 Booths & Colcloughs Ltd.
  painted or printed   1954 renamed Ridgway, Adderley,
  on reproductions of Booths & Colclough Ltd.
  Worcester porcelain 1955 renamed Ridgway Potterie Ltd.
  1905–

printed 1912–   printed 1930–

part of Royal Doulton group since 1972

Booths & Colcloughs Ltd.   *Hanley, Staffs.*

1948–54, earthenware & bone-china
various marks include 'Colclough'
or trade-names: 'Blue Mist', 'Royal
Swan' & 'Malvern China ware'

printed 1950–54

Bott & Co.   *Lane End, Staffs.*

BOTT & CO.   *c.* 1810–11, earthenware
impressed

bottles (three stoneware)   *see* Kennedy & Sons

Boulton & Co.   *Longton, Staffs.*

B. & CO.   *c.* 1892–1902, bone-china
printed

B. & CO.   printed or impressed in shield
L

Boulton, Machin & Tennant   *Tunstall, Staffs.*
1889–99, earthenware

45

 printed or impressed

Bourne, Charles   (*d.* 1836)   *Fenton, Staffs.*
    <u>CB</u>   *c.* 1807– earthenware
pattern no.   *c.* 1817–30 earthenware & bone-china

initials written over pattern number approx.
numbering 1–*c.* 1017

Bourne, Edward   *Longport, Staffs.*
   E.BOURNE   1790–1811, earthenware
   impressed

Bourne & Son Ltd., Joseph   *Denby, Derbys.*
   BOURNES   1809–, stoneware
   WARRANTED   impressed

  BOURNES POTTERIES
  DENBY & CODNOR   impressed, 1833–61
       PARK
   DERBYSHIRE

  J. BOURNE & SON
  DENBY POTTERY   impressed, 1850–
   NEAR DERBY

Later marks include the name 'DENBY'

Bournes taken over by Coloroll 1987
and sold again by receivers in 1990

Bourne & Leigh Ltd.   *Burslem, Staffs.*

     B. & L.   1892–1941, earthenware

   E.B. & J.E.L.   E.B. & J.E.L.   E.B.J.E.L.

                   B

initials included in a variety of marks
trade-name 'LEIGHTON POTTERY' from *c.* 1930

Bourne, Nixon & Co.   *Tunstall, Staffs.*

     B.N. & CO.   1828–30, earthenware

printed in a variety of marks

   BOURNE, NIXON   impressed
       & CO.

Bourne, Samuel   *Hanley, Staffs.*

     S.BOURNE   *c.* 1803–13, earthenware figures
     impressed

Bournemouth Pottery Co.   *Hanley, Staffs.*

   1945–52 at Bournemouth, Dorset, 1952– Hanley

   BOURNEMOUTH   earthenware
     POTTERY
     ENGLAND   printed or impressed, 1945–51

   BOURNEMOUTH   printed or impressed in circle,
     HANLEY   1952–57
     POTTERY CO.

Bovey Pottery Co. Ltd.   *Bovey Tracey, Devon*
                       1894–1957, earthenware

printed or impressed
c. 1937–49   1949–56

   E II R BOVEY   printed, 1954–7
POTTERY CO. LTD.
    1952
printed to commemorate coronation of Elizabeth II

Bovey Tracey Pottery Co.   *Bovey Tracey, Devon*
   B.T.P.CO.   1842–94
   printed or impressed

Bow China Works (New Canton)   *Stratford, Essex*
                              c. 1747–1774, bone-porcelain
   early marks *c*. 1750
   incised

   presumably 'repairers'   R   AF
   marks 1750–60, incised

               impressed   B
   probably mark of 'repairer'
   John Toulouse   T• T

   marks on blue-painted   ⅂B   G
   wares 1750–70

underglaze
blue

on figures and wares
of the 'anchor & dagger'
period, *c.* 1762–74
probably mark
of an outside
decorator

in red

in underglaze blue & red enamel

in red

in underglaze blue

underglaze blue
and red

underglaze blue

on blue-and-white
cups, underglaze blue

underglaze blue

Bowers & Co., G.F. *Tunstall, Staffs.*

G.F.B.

c. 1841–71, earthenware & bone-china
printed

G.F.B.B.T.   printed in a variety of marks

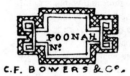

Bowker, Arthur   *Fenton, Staffs.*
                          1948–58, bone-china

STAFFORDSHIRE
FINE BONE CHINA   (printed under
OF   crown)
ARTHUR BOWKER

Boyle & Sons, Zachariah   *Hanley & Stoke*
                          1823–50, earthenware & bone-china
    BOYLE
impressed, 1823–50

    Z.B.   Z.B. & S.
printed, 1823–8   printed, 1828–50
these marks are on earthenware; bone-china
as yet unidentified

B.P. Co. monogram   *see* Brownhills Pottery Co.

B.P.Co. Ltd.   *see* Blyth Porcelain Co. Ltd.

B.P.Co. Ltd. monogram with anchor   *see* British Anchor
Pottery Co. Ltd.

B.P.Ltd.   *see* British Pottery Ltd.

B.R. & Co.   *see* Birks, Rawlins & Co.

Bradbury, Anderson & Bettaney   *Longton, Staffs.*
    B.A. & B.   1844–50, earthenware, Parian
printed in a   and bone-china
variety of marks, sometimes with Royal Arms

Braden, Norah   *St. Ives, Cornwall & Coleshill, Wilts.*

various incised or impressed monograms
on studio-pottery, 1924–36

Bradley, F.D.   *Longton, Staffs.*
    BRADLEY   *c.* 1876–96, bone-china
impressed

Bradley & Co., J.   *London*
  J. BRADLEY & CO.   *c.* 1813–20, independent decorator
                       and retailer
  J. BRADLEY & CO.   Painted or printed
    47 PALL MALL   on wares decorated by
      LONDON   J. & T. Bradley

Bradleys (Longton) Ltd.   *Longton, Staffs.*
                         c. 1922–41, bone-china

BRADLEYS   printed with crown
LONGTON
MADE IN   trade-names: 'CLARENCE' or
ENGLAND   'CROWN CLARENCE'

Brain & Co. Ltd., E.   *Fenton, Staffs.*
E.B. & CO.   1903–61, bone-china
F
impressed, wide variety of marks with name,
initials, including 'FOLEY CHINA'
1958 E. Brain purchased Coalport
1963 all their productions called Coalport
1967 taken over by Wedgwood Group
'HARJIAN', trade-name from 1903

Brameld, John Wager (*d.* 1851)   *London*
c. 1830–50, retailer only

I.W. BRAMELD
PICCADILLY   (previously a partner of
LONDON   the Rockingham factory)
printed

Brannam Ltd., C.H.   *Barnstaple, Devon*
1879– earthenware &
C.H. BRANNAM   art ware from 1882
BARUM
incised signature, 1879–

C.H. BRANNAM   C.H.BRANNAM LTD.
impressed, 1879–1913   1913–

CASTLE WARE   20th C. trade-name
ROYAL BARUM WARE

C.H.BRANNAM   C.H.BRANNAM
LTD.   BARUM DEVON
BARNSTAPLE

impressed 1930–
'Made in England' sometimes added. In hands
of family until 1979. 'BARUM' early Roman name
for Barnstaple

Braunton Pottery Co. Ltd.   *Braunton, N. Devon*
1910–*c.* 1972, earthenware

printed or impressed, *c.* 1947–

Breeze   *Tunstall & Cobridge, Staffs.*
BREEZE   *c.* 1802–12, bone-china
incised or painted. Other potters named Breeze were operating
from late 18th C. – *c.* 1830, with varying christian names, John,
Jesse and William, making certain identification impossible

Bridge, A (impressed)   *see* Cardew, Seth

Bridge, A. (stylized)   *see* Watson, Dorothy

Bridgett, Bates & Beech   *Longton, Staffs.*
B B   *c.* 1875–81, bone-china
B   printed in shield

Bridgett & Bates   *Longton, Staffs.*
B & B   *c.* 1881–1915, bone-china
printed or impressed

trade -name 'ALDWYCH CHINA' printed on ribbon
used from *c.* 1912

Bridgwood & Clarke   *Burslem & Tunstall, Staffs.*

B. & C.	1857–64, earthenware
B. & C.	BRIDGWOOD &
BURSLEM	CLARKE
printed	impressed

Bridgwood, Sampson   *Longton, Staffs.*
                         c. 1822–1984, earthenware & china
                         from 1854

BRIDGWOOD & SON   S. BRIDGWOOD &
                                                SON

impressed mid-19th C.
'Son' added to title from 1854. 'Ltd.' from 1933
1963 purchased by James Broadhurst & Sons Ltd.
1984 renamed Churchill Hotelware

S.B. & S.	other various printed marks
printed under	include full-name or 'S.B. & S.'
armorial crest	usually with anchor

Parisian Granite mark
printed *c.* 1870–

Briglin Pottery Ltd.   *London*
BRIGLIN   1947– earthenware
impressed

Bristol   *Bristol, Avon*

yᵉ 1ˢᵗ: Septᵗ 1761

Bowen - fecit,

1650–, tin-glazed earthenware
'delftware'
mark of John Bowen, painter
apprenticed 1734

E	N
M B	J E
1760	1733
attributed to	probably John &
Michael Edkins,	Esther Niglett,
painter and wife	painter
Betty	

Lund & Miller's factory   *Bristol, Avon*

BRISTOL

BRISTOLL

c. 1749–52, soapstone porcelain
(transferred to Worcester 1752)

marks moulded in relief

Cookworthy & Champion's factory   *Bristol, Avon*

4

1770–81, hard-paste porcelain
(transferred from Plymouth)

mark for tin, underglaze-blue, blue enamel, red or gold

X   6ₓ   ✗   ×B

all in blue enamel

Bristol Pottery   *Bristol, Avon*
                          c. 1785–1825, earthenware

BRISTOL POTTERY   impressed or painted
                     from *c.* 1785
(*see also* POUNTNEY & Co. Ltd., POUNTNEY & ALLIES
POUNTNEY & GOLDNEY, POWELL & SONS. W., RING & Co.)

Britannia Designs Ltd.   *Dartmouth, Devon.*
                             1959–, decorators

                             mark on applied label
                             used from 1971

Britannia, figure of   *see* Dudson, Wilcox & Till

Britannia China Co.   *Longton, Staffs.*
       B.C.CO.   *c.* 1894–1906, bone-china
       impressed

                         printed or impressed, 1904–6
                         other full-names marks also
                         used, *c.* 1900–4

Britannia Pottery Co.   *Glasgow, Scotland*
                            1920–1937, earthenware

                            printed 1930–37

trade-name: *c.* 1925 'HIAWATHA'
(*see also*) COCHRAN R. & COCHRAN & FLEMING

British Anchor Pottery Co. Ltd.   *Longton, Staffs.*

1884–1982, earthenware
printed or impressed mark 1884–1913
other printed or impressed marks
include full-name and various trade-
names: REGENCY, MONTMARTRE, RICHMOND
HOSTESS TABLE WARE, & TRIANON.
1970 sold to group including Thomas Poole &
Gladstone China Ltd., marketed as Hostess Tableware Ltd.
1973 merged with Alfred Clough
1982 closed, works sold to Churchill

British Art Pottery Co. (Fenton) Ltd.   *Fenton, Staffs.*

1920–6, bone-china

printed or impressed

British Crown Ware   *see* Lancaster & Sons, &
Lancaster, Sandland Ltd.

British Pottery Ltd.   *Tunstall, Staffs.*

1920–6, earthenware

printed

British Pottery Ltd.   *Longton, Staffs.*
B.P.LTD   *c.* 1930–, agents only
printed

Broadhurst & Sons, James   *Longton, Staffs.*
                c. 1854–63 earthenware & bone-china
      J.B.&S.   printed

Broadhurst, James   *Longton, Staffs.*
                c. 1863–70, earthenware & probably
      J.B.   bone-china
   printed

Broadhurst & Sons, James   *Fenton, Staffs.*
                1870–1983, earthenware
      J.B. & S.   printed from 1870–
      J.B. & S.LTD.   printed from 1922
   renamed James Broadhurst Group from 1930;
   works closed in 1983, becoming part of
   Churchill Group at Longton in 1984

Broadway   *see* Creyke & Sons, G.M.

Broadstairs Pottery Ltd.   *Broadstairs, Kent*
   printed mark   1966– , stoneware

Brough & Blackhurst   *Longton, Staffs.*
   BROUGH &   1872–95, earthenware
   BLACKHURST
   printed in a variety of backstamps

Brougham & Mayer   *Tunstall, Staffs.*
                1853–5, earthenware
   BROUGHAM &
     MAYER   printed in a variety of marks

Brown & Co., Robert   *Paisley, Scotland*
                1876–1933, earthenware

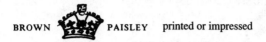

BROWN PAISLEY   printed or impressed

Brown & Steventon Ltd.   *Burslem, Staffs.*
    B. & S.   1900–23, earthenware
    printed

printed 1920–23

Brownfield, William   *Cobridge, Staffs.*
    W.B.   1850–92, earthenware, Parian and
                     bone-china from 1871

              printed, impressed or moulded
    BROWNFIELD   BROWNFIELDS
impressed with numbers for month & year
from 1860
    W.B. & S.   W.B. & SON.
            printed from 1871
    W.B. & SONS.   printed from *c.* 1876
double-globe mark with full name 1871–

Brownfields Guild Pottery Society Ltd.   *Cobridge, Staffs.*
                  1892–1900, earthenware & bone-china
    B.G.P.CO.   impressed
various printed marks with 'BROWNFIELDS'

printed monogram

Brownhills Pottery Co.   *Tunstall, Staffs.*
　　　　B.P.CO.　　　　1872–96, earthenware & bone-china
impressed or printed

painted marks of *c.* 1880–96

Brown-Westhead, Moore & Co.   *Hanley, Staffs.*
　　　　　　　　1861–1904, earthenware, Parian & bone-china
　　　B.W.M.　　　　　B.W.M. & CO.　　　printed or impressed
in a variety of backstamps from 1861–

　　　　　　　T.C.BROWN
　　　WESTHEAD MOORE　　BROWN-WESTHEAD
　　　　　& CO.　　　　　　MOORE
　　　　　　　impressed

printed or impressed, 1884–1904

Brunton, John   *Sunderland, Tyne & Wear*
    J. BRUNTON   1789–1803, earthenware
    printed

B. & S.   *see* Barlow & Son Ltd., W.
          Beswick & Son
          Bishop & Stonier Ltd.
          Brown & Steventon Ltd.

B. & S.H.   *see* Hancock, B. & S.

B. & T.   *see* Blackhurst & Tunnicliffe

B.T.P.Co.   *see* Bovey Tracey Pottery Co.

Buchan & Co. Ltd., A.W.   *Portobello, Scotland*
                      1867–, stoneware
                      trade-names: PORTOVASE, CENOLITH,
                      SENOLITH, 1920s,
                      and 1930s

                      printed 1949–

Buckler, Gwendoline   *see* Della Robbia

Buckley, Heath & Co.   *Burslem, Staffs.*
                      1885–90, earthenware

                      printed or impressed

Buckley, Wood & Co.   *Burslem, Staffs.*
    B.W.& CO.   1875–85, pottery
    printed or impressed

Bullers Ltd.   *Hanley, Staffs.*
>   BULLERS MADE   *c.* 1934–52, earthenware & porcelain
>   IN ENGLAND
>   several painted or incised marks include 'BULLERS'
>   A H monogram is that of their designer & decorator
>   Agnete Hoy, *c.* 1940–52

Bullock & Co., A.   *Hanley, Staffs.*
>   A.B.& CO.H.   1895–1915, earthenware, including
>   A.B.& CO.   majolica
>   printed or impressed

Burgess Bros.   *Longton, Staffs.*
>   'BURCRAFT'   1922–39, earthenware
>   BURGESS BROS
>   MADE IN ENGLAND   BURGESS WARE
>   printed   printed under crown

Burgess, Henry   *Burslem, Staffs.*
>   H.B.   1864–92, earthenware
>   printed or impressed under Royal Arms
>   HENRY BURGESS   printed or impressed as above

Burgess & Leigh   *Burslem, Staffs.*
>   B. & L.   1862–, earthenware
>   printed in a variety of marks

'L B' monograms printed or impressed, 1862

'ENGLAND' added 1891
'LTD.' added *c.* 1919

printed 1862–   1930–

Burgess, Thomas   *Hanley, Staffs.*
1903–17, earthenware

printed or impressed
mark of previous partnership, Harrop & Burgess
continued to be used

Burleigh   *see* Burgess & Leigh

Burlington   *see* Shaw & Sons (Longton) Ltd.

Burmantofts   *Leeds, Yorks.*
BURMANTOFTS   1882–1889 art pottery
   FAIENCE

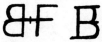   impressed

Bursley Ware   *see* Wood, H.J.

Burslem Pottery Co. Ltd.   *Burslem, Staffs.*
1894–33, earthenware

63

printed

Burslem School of Art. *Burslem, Staffs.*

1935–41, earthenware figures, etc.
in 'Astbury' style

impressed

Burton, Samuel & John *Hanley, Staffs.*
S. & J.B.   1832–45, earthenware
rare impressed mark
'IMPROVED STONE CHINA' printed or impressed
in hexagonal frame

Burton, William *Codnor Park, Derbys.*
W.BURTON   *c.* 1821–32, stoneware
CODNOR PARK

WM.BURTON   impressed

Butterfield, W. & J. *Tunstall, Staffs.*
W. & J.B.   1854–61, earthenware
printed

B. & W.   *see* Birch & Whitehead

B.W. & B.   *see* Batkin, Walker & Broadhurst

B.W. & Co.   *see*   Bates, Walker & Co.
                        Buckley, Wood & Co.

B.W.M. (B.W.M. & Co.)   *see* Brown-Westhead, Moore & Co.

Byers, Ian   *Croydon, Surrey*
                 c. 1970– , studio-potter in low-
                 fired *Raku* ware.

C

C   *see* Caughley
       Constantinidis, Joanna

C. & C.   *see*   Calland & Co.
                      Clokie & Co.
                      Cope & Co.
                      Stanley Pottery Ltd.

C.A. & Co. Ltd.   *see* Ceramic Art Co. (1905) Ltd.

C.A./L.   *see* Amison, Charles

C.A. & Sons   *see* Allertons & Sons, Charles

Cadborough Pottery   *nr. Rye, Sussex*
                         1807–71, earthenware

OLD SUSSEX WARE	RYE POTTERY	MITCHELL
RYE		M

incised marks

owners: James Smith (1807–40), William Mitchell
(1840–59), Mitchell & Sons, W. (1859–69),
Mitchell, F. & H. (1869–71)

Caiger-Smith, Alan   *Aldermaston, Bucks.*

1955–1993, studio-potter, specializing in tin-glazed earthenware.
Assisted in 1989 by Edgar Campden, Julian Bellmont, Andrew Hazelden, Mary O'Gorman, Ursula Waechter & Michael Willey

Calland & Co., J.F.   *Swansea, Wales*

C. & CO.   1852–6, earthenware
CALLAND SWANSEA   J. F. CALLAND & CO.
printed or impressed   LANDORE POTTERY

Caluwé, Madame Marianne de   *see* Della Robbia

Calvert, James & Lovatt   *Langley Mill, nr Notts.*

1865– , salt-glazed stoneware
see Lovatt & Lovatt from 1895–

Cambrian Pottery   *see* Swansea Pottery

Cambrian Ceramic Co. Ltd.   *Llandudno, Wales*

CAMBRIAN   1958– , earthenware of studio-
STUDIO   pottery type
WARE   printed or impressed

Campbellfield Pottery Co. Ltd.   *Glasgow, Scotland*

1835–1899, earthenware & stoneware
CAMPBELLFIELD   C.P.CO.   printed or impressed
'LTD.' added 1881

printed *c.* 1884–1899

'Springburn' with
thistle over C.P.CO.LTD.
from *c.* 1884

printed, *c.* 1884. Original factory closed 1889

Candy & Co. Ltd.   *Newton Abbott, Devon*
             1882– , earthenware
    C   printed or impressed in a variety of
   N A   marks from *c.* 1900

   CANDY WARE   20th C. trade-name
   CANDY TILES LTD   took over Art Tile Co. of
Etruria in 1988

Capper & Wood   *Longton, Staffs.*
    C. & W.   1895–1904, earthenware
printed or impressed in a variety of marks

C A R   *see* Richards, C. A.

Cara China Co.   *Longton, Staffs.*
   CARA CHINA   *c.* 1945– , bone-china
printed in a variety of marks

Cardew, Michael   *Cornwall, Winchcombe & Wenford Bridge, Glos.*

studio-potter *b.* 1901 – *d.* 1982

1923–26, with Bernard Leach at
St. Ives, Cornwall

1926–39	with partner R. Finch at Winchcombe Pottery
1939–42	at Wenford Bridge, then in Ghana and elsewhere until 1948; back to Wenford Bridge for two years, then returning to Nigeria; returning to Cornwall & Wenford Bridge in 1965

Cardew, Seth   *Wenford Bridge Pottery, Bodmin, Cornwall*
(son of above)   1971–, studio-potter
                             working in wood-fired stoneware

Cardigan Potteries   *Wales*
   CARDIGAN   *c.* 1875–90, earthenware
   POTTERIES

               printed in a variety of marks
WOODWARD & CO.
   CARDIGAN

Carey, Thomas & John   *Lane End, Staffs.*
              c. 1826–42, earthenware & bone-china
   CAREYS   impressed & printed

Carlton China   *see* Birks, Rawlins & Co. Ltd.

Carlton Ware   *see* Wiltshaw & Robinson

Carlton Ware Ltd.   *Stoke, Staffs.*
              1958–, earthenware & bone-china

mark used by Wiltshaw & Robinson cont.

 printed

purchased by A. Wood & Son (Longport) Ltd.
1966
1987 purchased by County Properties PLC and re-named
CARLTON & KENT. 1989, name, books and moulds
purchased by GROSVENOR CERAMIC HARDWARE LTD.
Relaunched 1990, under trade-name: CARLTON WARE

Carnegy, Daphne *London*

 1980–, studio-potter, tin-glazed domestic
ware

Carr, John *N. Shields, Northumberland*

J.CARR & CO. *c.* 1845–1900, earthenware
printed '& Co.' added *c.* 1845
'& Son' added *c.* 1854
'& Sons' added *c.* 1861

Carrig Ware *see* Carrigaline Pottery

Carrigaline Pottery Ltd. *Cork, Ireland*

CARRIG WARE 1928–, earthenware

CARRIGALINE printed marks
POTTERY

Carr's Hill Pottery *see* Warburton, J.

Carter, Stabler & Adams   *see* Poole Pottery Ltd.

Cartledge, John   *Longton, Staffs.*
                         c. 1800– , earthenware figures
  JOHN CARTLEDGE   rare incised mark

Cartledge & Co., F.   *Longton, Staffs.*
                         1889–1904, bone-china
       F.C.   '& Co' from 1892
   F.C. & CO.   printed or impressed in a variety
                         of marks

Cartwright & Edwards   *Longton, Staffs.*
                         1858–1988, earthenware & bone-china
   C. & E.   from *c.* 1912. 'LTD.' from *c.* 1926.
   printed   c. 1982 earthenware division purchased
     or   by Cartwright of England & Alfred
  impressed, 1880 Clough Ltd. 1987, bought by Coloroll
                       Housewares Group. 1988, productions
                       transferred to Coloroll Ceramics, Meir.
                       Former premises sold

printed mark from *c.* 1912. Trade names: Norville & Baronian

C A S monogram   *see* Aston C.S.

Casson, Michael & Sheila   *Ross-on-Wye, Herefs.*
studio-potters, earthenware, stoneware
& porcelain, 1953–

current   current

castle, enclosing C   *see* Castle Wynd Potteries

Castlecliffe Ware   *see* Westminster Pottery Ltd.

Castle Wynd Potteries   *Inverdruie, Scotland*

1950– , earthenware & stoneware printed marks

trade-names: CASTLE WYND AVIEMORE

moved to Gifford in 1954 and to Fort William in 1974

Caughley Works (Salopian)   *nr. Broseley, Salop*

c. 1772–99, soapstone porcelain
and probably hard-paste porcelain from c. 1796.
Taken over by John Rose of Coalport, 1799

TURNER   GALLIMORE TURNER   TURNER GALLIMORE
SALOPIAN

rare impressed marks

Salopian   SALOPIAN
impressed

not to be confused with Salopian Art Pottery Co.,
Benthall, near Broseley, who made earthenware
c. 1882–c. 1912

printed or painted in underglaze-blue

Cauldon   *see* Brown-Westhead, Moore & Co.
                         (previous owners)

Cauldon Ltd.   *Hanley, Staffs.*
    CAULDON   1905–62, earthenware & porcelain
  CAULDON-ENGLAND   CAULDON POTTERIES LTD from 1920
    Purchased by Pountney & Co Ltd., Bristol in 1962
    for production of earthenware
                         Cauldon Bristol Potteries
                         Ltd. Redruth, Cornwall
    1985 'CAULDON POTTERIES LTD.' part of Perks Ceramic Group,
    Yorkshire

Cauldon (under crown)   *see* Brown-Westhead, Moore
                                          & Co. & Cauldon Ltd.

Caverswall China Co. Ltd.   *Stoke, Staffs.*

                  1973–, bone-china
                  1984/5 acquired by Thomas Goode,
                  London retailer
                  1986 acquired by Bullers PLC
                  1990 trade-name: Caverswall

C.B.   *see* Bourne, Charles
                   Collingwood Bros.
                   Christie & Beardmore

C.B./F.   *see* Christie & Beardmore

C. & B.   *see* Christie & Beardmore
                     Cotton & Barlow

C.C. & Co.   *see* Cockson & Chetwynd

C.D.   *see* Coalport Porcelain Works
             Davies, Clive

C. & D.   *see* Cooper & Dethick

C. & E.   *see* Cartwright & Edwards
             Cork & Edge

C. & E. Ltd.   *see* Cartwright & Edwards

C. E. & M.   *see* Cork, Edge & Malkin

Cenolith   *see* Buchan & Co. Ltd., A.W.

Ceramic Art Co. (1905) Ltd.   *Hanley, Staffs.*
  C.A. & CO. LTD.   1905–19, earthenware
  printed or impressed in a variety of marks

C. F. monogram   *see* Ford, Charles
  (sometimes with swan)

C.F. or C.F/G.   *see* Cochran & Fleming

C.H. or C.H. & S.   *see* Hobson, Charles

C. & H.   *see* Cockson & Harding
             Coggins & Hill
             Cumberlidge & Humphreys

Challinor & Co., C.   *Fenton, Staffs.*
                    1892–6, earthenware
  C. CHALLINOR & CO.   printed in a variety
      ENGLAND   of marks

Challinor, Edward   *Tunstall, Staffs.*
      E.C.   1842–67, earthenware
   E.CHALLINOR   printed in a variety of marks

Challinor & Co. E.   *Fenton, Staffs.*
                 1853–62, earthenware
  E. CHALLINOR & CO.   printed in a variety of marks

Challinor, E. & C.   *Fenton, Staffs.*
    E. & C.C.   1862–91, earthenware & stoneware
  E. & C. CHALLINOR
    FENTON   printed in a variety of marks

Chamberlain   *see* Worcester

Chambers & Co.   *see* South Wales Pottery

Chambers, John (*d.* 1751)   *Dublin, Ireland*
                   c. 1735–*c.*45, tin-glazed earthenware
  'DUBLIN 1735'   inscribed

Champion, G.H. & E.E.   *Rustington, Sussex*
                1947– , studio-potters

Chanticleer   *see* Soho Pottery

Chapman & Sons, David   *Longton, Staffs.*
               c. 1889–1906, bone-china

printed 'Atlas' mark 1889–1906

Chapmans Longton Ltd.   *Longton, Staffs.*
                          c. 1916–69, bone-china
STANDARD CHINA
     (crown)   printed *c.* 1916–30
     ENGLAND   various other marks from *c.* 1930
include trade-names: 'Royal Standard' & 'Royal
Mayfair'; 1947, merged with T.C.Wild & Sons Ltd.
but run separately
Since 1973 part of Royal Doulton Group

Chelsea   *Chelsea, London*
                          c. 1744–69, soft-paste porcelain
owned by Nicholas Sprimont, taken over by
William Duesbury of Derby factory and referred
to as Chelsea-Derby until final closure in 1884

rare incised mark on
'triangle' period
1745–*c.* 1749

usual triangle mark

rare mark of 'crown   incised
and trident', 1745–*c.*
1750 in underglaze blue

75

'raised-anchor' mark
c. 1749–52, latterly
picked out in red

in applied relief

'red-anchor' mark
1752–*c.* 1758
occasionally painted in
blue or purple

c. 1750–56
painted in underglaze blue

'gold anchor' mark
c. 1756–69
(also seen on Chelsea-
Derby wares as late
as 1775)

in gold

rare 'repairers' mark
(not Roubiliac)

impressed

The 'gold-anchor' mark is frequently
used on Continental hard-paste reproductions
and Chelsea-type wares

Chelsea-Derby   *Chelsea, London, and Derby,*
                    Derbys.
        1770–74, soft-paste porcelain

painted in gold

Chelsea Pottery   *Chelsea, London*

1952– , earthenware
Rawnsley Academy Ltd.

CHELSEA POTTERY incised
impressed or incised

Chelsea or Royal Chelsea   *see* New Chelsea
Porcelain Co. Ltd. & New Chelsea China Co. Ltd.

Chelson   *see* New Chelsea Porcelain Co. Ltd.

Chesworth & Robinson   *Lane End, Staffs.*
  C. & R.   1825–40, earthenware
printed, but same initials used by Chetham
& Robinson

Chetham & Son   *Longton, Staffs.*
                   1814–21, earthenware
  CHETHAM   CHETHAM & SON
               impressed

Chetham, Jonathan Lowe   *Longton, Staffs.*
  J. L. C.   1841–62, earthenware and probably
  printed   bone-china until *c.* 1854

Chetham, J.R. & F.   *Longton, Staffs.*
  J.R. & F.C.   1862– *c.* 69, earthenware
printed in a variety of marks

Chetham & Robinson (& Son)   *Longton, Staffs.*
  C. & R.   1822–40, earthenware & bone-china
printed (Robinson's son a partner from 1834)

Chetham & Woolley   *Lane End, Staffs.*
 CHETHAM &   1796–1810, earthenware
 WOOLLEY
 LANE END   incised

Chew, John   *Longton, Staffs.*
  J. C.   1903–4, bone-china
  L   impressed in diamond

Chieftan Ware   *see* Govancroft Potteries Ltd.

Christie & Beardmore   *Fenton, Staffs.*
  C.B.   1902–3, earthenware
        printed in a variety of marks

  C. B.
  F

Churchill   *Longton, Staffs.*

1984– , earthenware & bone-china
Group renamed Churchill Hotelware, 1984;
comprising: Bridgwood & Son Ltd.,
Sampson (1805–1984), Broadhurst & Son
Ltd., James, (1847–1984) & Wessex Ceramic
(1970s). Trade-names: Churchill China
(1976), Churchill Tableware (1984),
Churchill Hotelware (1984)

C i   *see* Jenkins, C.

C J monogram   *see* Clarke, Jenny

C.J.W.   *see* Wileman, James & Charles

78

Clare China Co. Ltd.   *Longton, Staffs.*

1951–*c.* 61, decorators of porcelain

BONE CHINA   possibly taken over by Taylor & Kent

CLARE

MADE IN ENGLAND   printed

Clark, Henry   *Cheam, Surrey*

HENRY CLARK   1869–1880, red earthenware

CHEAM POTTERY   impressed or incised

Clark & Nephews, Uriah   *Lower Dicker, Sussex*

U.C. & N.   1843–59, earthenware

THE DICKER   marks found impressed on

SUSSEX   reproductions of earlier Sussex
                     wares

DICKER WARE   1933–   Dicker Potteries Ltd.

MADE IN ENGLAND   1946–59

Clarke & Co., Edward   *Burslem, Longport & Tunstall*

EDWARD CLARKE   1865–87, earthenware

(over town)   Tunstall, *c.* 1865–77
                     Longport, *c.* 1878–80
                     Burslem 1880–87

EDWARD CLARKE &

CO. (town)

ROYAL SEMI-   impressed or printed *c.* 1877–

PORCELAIN

Clarke, Jenny   *Bristol, Avon*

   c. 1965– , studio-potter in domestic
stoneware
working in Bristol since '74

Clarkson, Derek   *Bacup, Lancs.*
1980–, studio-potter, porcelain & stoneware
raku & lustre

impressed seal with year symbol since
1987

Clementson Bros.   *Hanley, Staffs.*
CLEMENTSON BROS.   1865–1916, earthenware & stoneware
printed under Royal Arms, *c.* 1867–80
various full-named printed marks with phoenix
from 1870– . 'LTD.' added 1910

printed 1913–16

Clementson, Joseph   *Hanley, Staffs.*
J.C.   *c.* 1839–64, earthenware

J. CLEMENTSON   printed in a variety of marks

Clementson & Young   *Hanley, Staffs.*
1845–7, earthenware

CLEMENTSON & YOUNG   impressed or printed in a
variety of marks

Clementson, Young & Jameson   *Hanley, Staffs.*
C.Y. & J.   *c.* 1844, earthenware
printed

Clews & Co. Ltd., George *Tunstall, Staffs.*

1906–61, earthenware

printed with name or pattern title
on band

trade-name: Chameleon Ware 1906

Clews, James & Ralph *Cobridge, Staffs.*

1815–34, earthenware and probably
New Hall type porcelain

impressed on blue-printed wares

Cliff   *see* Dimmock & Co., J.

Clinton, Margery *Haddington, E. Lothian*

c. 1976, studio-potter of porcelain
& white stoneware
dated marks

Clive, J.H. *Tunstall, Staffs.*

CLIVE   1802–11, earthenware
impressed

Clive, Stephen *Tunstall, Staffs.*

S.C.   1875–80, earthenware
                  '& CO.' from 1876–
S.C. & CO.   printed in a variety of marks

Clokie & Co. *Castleford, Yorks.*

1888–1961, earthenware

CLOKIE & CO.
1864–1901
'LTD.' from 1940–

printed in a variety of marks with name or initials

Clokie & Masterson   *Castleford, Yorks.*
1872–1887, earthenware
CLOKIE & MASTERSON   C. & M.
printed or impressed in a variety of marks

Close & Co.   *Stoke, Staffs.*
1855–64, earthenware
CLOSE & CO. LATE
W.ADAMS & SONS   printed or impressed in
STOKE-UPON-TRENT   a variety of marks

Clough's Royal Art Pottery   *Longton, Staffs.*
1961–69, earthenware
ROYAL ART POTTERY
    ENGLAND   printed
  (with crown)
(started in 1913 as Alfred Clough Royal
Art Pottery) 'Ltd.' from 1932

Clowes, William   *Burslem, Staffs.*
c. 1783–96, earthenware &
W. CLOWES   stoneware
impressed

Clulow & Co.   *Fenton, Staffs.*
CLULOW & CO.   *c.* 1802, earthenware & stoneware
FENTON   moulded

Clyde Pottery Co. Ltd. *Glasgow, Scotland*
    CLYDE   1816–1900, earthenware

    GREENOCK   James & Andrew Muir, 1816–41

    T.S. & CO.   Thomas Shirley & Co., 1841–59

    G.C.P.CO.   Clyde Pottery Co. Ltd., 1859–63

  C.P.CO.   C.P.CO.   Clyde Pottery Co., 1863–1900
                 G
    printed or impressed marks in a variety of styles
           'Ltd.' from 1895–1900

C.M. *see* Cardew, Michael
            Casson, Michael
            Manzoni, Carlo
            Meigh, Charles

C. & M. *see* Clokie & Masterson
             Cumberlidge & Humphreys

C.M. & S. *see* Meigh & Son, Charles

C.M.S. & P. *see* Meigh, Son & Pankhurst, Charles

Coalbrook Potteries *Hanley, Staffs.*
                 1937– , earthenware
    COALBROOK
    MADE IN   printed from *c.* 1948–
    ENGLAND

Coalport Porcelain Works   *Coalport, Shrops.*
John Rose & Co.   *c.* 1795– porcelain. Moved to Stoke-
                        upon-Trent *c.* 1926

rare early mark in red   **COALBROOKDALE**

1815–25 on many wares
decorated in Swansea
style

                                                         impressed

c. 1810–25, in underglaze
blue

underglaze blue mark
c. 1810–20

                                                         C. B. DALE

marks used from *c.* 1820

1830–50

JOHN ROSE & CO.
COALBROOKDALE
SHROPSHIRE

c. 1851–61, painted or gilt

c. 1861–75,
'c' Coalport, 's',
Swansea, 'n', Nantgarw

painted or gilt

printed mark c. 1870–80
incorporating Patent
Office Registration
mark

c. 1875–81, printed or
painted
late marks c. 1881–
'England' added 1891
'Made in England'
c. 1920

COALPORT A.D. 1750

wares made for London
dealer A. B. & R. P.
Daniell c. 1860–1917

large size anchor mark
on Coalport copies of
Chelsea, also on
Continental wares
without 'c'

COALBROOKDALE   1960–, painted on floral
BY COALPORT   encrusted wares
MADE IN ENGLAND

1920   purchased by Cauldon Potteries Ltd.
c. 1930–   Cauldon purchased George Jones & Sons Ltd.
1936   Coalport, Cauldon & Jones trading as
       Crescent Potteries
1950   Jones trading as Coalport
1958   Coalport & Jones purchased by E. Brain
       Cauldon purchased by Pountney of Bristol
1963   Coalport & Jones wares called Coalport
1967   Now part of the Wedgwood Group

Coates, Russell   *Frome, Somerset*

active 1989–, studio-potter
in Japanese enamelled porcelain style

Cochran & Co., R.   *Glasgow, Scotland*
                     1846–1918, earthenware, stoneware &
R.C. & CO.   bone-china to *c.* 1856
                     impressed, 1846–

R. COCHRAN & CO.   over Royal Arms & 'Glasgow'

Cochran & Fleming   *see* Britannia Pottery, Glasgow

Cochran & Fleming   *Glasgow, Scotland*
C. & F.   1896–1920, earthenware
         printed or impressed

C. & F.   ROYAL
G.   IRONSTONE CHINA

                              COCHRAN & FLEMING
1896–1920   GLASGOW BRITAIN
printed   1900–20

                      PORCELAIN OPAQUE
impressed   GLASGOW. BRITAIN
1900–20   FLEMING

Cockson & Chetwynd   *Cobridge, Staffs.*
                          1867–75, earthenware
COCKSON & CHETWYND   C. C. & CO.
printed in a variety of marks

Cockson & Harding, W.M. & J.B.   *Shelton, Staffs.*
                          1856–63, earthenware at Hanley
C. & H.   bone-china at Cobridge

C. & H.   printed or impressed in
LATE HACKWOOD   a variety of marks
Charles Cockson continued bone-china production
from *c.* 1863–66, but marks are unrecorded

Cockson & Seddon   *Cobridge, Staffs.*
                          1875–7, earthenware

87

IMPERIAL IRONSTONE   printed under
      CHINA   Royal Arms
COCKSON & SEDDON

Coggins & Hill *Longton, Staffs.*
      C. & H.   1892–7, bone-china
printed or impressed in a variety of marks

Coke, John *see* Pinxton

Colclough & Co. *Longton, Staffs.*
                    c. 1887–1928, earthenware &
ROYAL STANLEY WARE   bone-china
    (with crown)
    printed 1903–19

    printed 1919–28

Colclough, H.J. *Longton, Staffs.*
                    c. 1897–1937, earthenware & bone-china
    H.J.C.
      L   printed in a variety of marks
trade-names: 'VALE CHINA' or 'ROYAL VALE CHINA' from 1908
    COLCLOUGH
    LONGTON   printed 1935–7
    ENGLAND
    BONE CHINA

Colclough China Ltd. *Longton, Staffs.*
                    c. 1937–48, bone-china

Colclough
GENUINE
BONE CHINA

printed from *c.* 1945 in a variety
of marks including England or
Made in England. Trade-name:
'VALE' also used

Purchased in 1948 by Booths Ltd., now part
of Royal Doulton Group

Coldrum   *see* Wells, Reginald

Collard, C.   *Honiton, Devon*
1918–47, earthenware

COLLARD HONITON
ENGLAND   impressed

Colley & Co. Ltd., A.   *Tunstall, Staffs.*
1909–14, earthenware

printed or impressed

Collier Ltd., S. & E.   *Reading, Berks.*
c. 1848–1957, *terra-cotta*

impressed or printed,
c. 1905–57

trade-name: 'SILCHESTER WARE', impressed

Collingwood Bros. Ltd.   *Longton, Staffs.*
c. 1887–1957, bone-china

COLLINGWOOD   impressed, *c.* 1887–1900
   C. B.
   L   printed with crown
full-name or 'C.B.' appear in a variety of
other printed marks

Collingwood & Greatbatch *Longton, Staffs.*
   C. & G.   1870–1887, bone-china
   L   printed or impressed

printed or impressed; crown
also used alone

   C. & G.

Collinson & Co., Charles *Burslem, Staffs.*
                   1851–73, earthenware
  C. COLLINSON & CO. printed in a variety
                   of backstamps

Collis, Charles (*d.* 1967) *see* Della Robbia

Colls, Barbara *Norwich, Norfolk*

active in 1989, studio-potter
in stoneware & porcelain

Collyer, Ernest & Pamela *London*
                 1950, studio-potters
  E.C. (date)   Ernest Collyer

P.N.	Pamela Nash (*d.* 1987)
	(maiden name)

compass & globe   *see* Green & Clay

Cone Ltd. Thomas   *Longton, Staffs.*

T.C.	1892–1967, earthenware
L	printed in a variety of marks
	1892–1912
T.C.	'T.C.' monogram, printed 1912–35
LONGTON	

'Alma Ware' printed under crown, 1935–
'ROYAL ALMA' printed with crown, 1946
acquired by Coloroll Ceramics, *c.* 1945

Constantinidis, Joanna   *Chelmsford, Essex*
active in 1989, studio-potter
in stoneware & porcelain

Conway Pottery Co. Ltd.   *Longton, Staffs.*

CONWAY	1930–57, earthenware
POTTERY	
ENGLAND	printed from *c.* 1945

trade-name: 'CONWAY' from 1948 as part
of Collingwood China Ltd., who in turn
were acquired by Coloroll Ceramics

Cooke & Hulse   *Longton, Staffs.*

COOKE & HULSE	1853–57, bone-china
printed	

Cookson, Delan   *Penzance, Cornwall*

 c. 1964, studio-potter working
mostly in porcelain

Cookworthy, William   *see* Plymouth Porcelain Works

Cookworthy & Champion   *see* Bristol Porcelain

Coombes   *Bristol, Avon*

 1775–1805, china-mender

Coombs & Holland   *see* S. Wales Pottery

Cooper & Dethick   *Longton, Staffs.*
C. & D.   1876–88, earthenware
printed in a variety of marks

Cooper, Emanuel   *London*

 c. 1965– studio-potter, working
mostly in porcelain

Coopercraft   *see* Summerbank Pottery Ltd.

Cooper China Ltd., Susie   *Longton, Staffs.*
1950–58, bone-china, part of
Wedgwood Group from 1959–

Cooper & Co., J.   *Burslem, Staffs.*
                        1922–25, earthenware

J. COOPER & CO.
   ENGLAND   printed or impressed
DUCAL WORKS   in circle, 1922–

Cooper Pottery, Susie   *Burslem & Tunstall, Staffs.*
                        c. 1929– , earthenware & china
renamed Susie Cooper Ltd. in 1958, following
partnership with R.H. & S.L. Plant Ltd.,
who in 1966 were taken over by Wedgwood Group,
who in 1989 re-named factory Royal Tuscan

   printed from *c.* 1932

Coopers Art Pottery Co.   *Hanley, Staffs.*
                        c. 1912–58, earthenware

ART POTTERY CO.
   (over crown)   (*see also* Art Pottery Co.)

COOPER ENGLAND   printed *c.* 1936–58

Co-operative Wholesale Society Ltd.   *Longton, Staffs.*

1922–71, earthenware
from *c.* 1946, bone-china from *c.* 1922

printed *c.* 1946–

printed on earthenware
c. 1946
earthenware trade-names: Balmoral,
Crown Clarence
bone-china trade names: Windsor,
Clarence Bone china

From 1971, Jon Anton Ltd. 1975, buildings
acquired by Churchill

Cope & Co., J.H.   *Longton, Staffs.*
      C. & CO.   1887–1947, bone-china
printed or impressed, 1887–
    J.H.C. & CO.   printed in a variety of marks
                        from *c.* 1900
trade-names: WELLINGTON CHINA with crown 1906–,
WELLINGTON CHINA with profile of Duke *c.* 1924–

Copeland & Garrett, Copeland, W.T., etc.   *see* Spode

Coper, Hans   *London, & Welwyn Garden City, Herts, & Somerset*

HC

              1946–*d*, 1981, studio-potter
              1946–58 with Lucie Rie in London
impressed   1958–69 in Welwyn
or incised   1969–81 London & Somerset

Cork & Edge   *Burslem, Staffs.*
     C & E.   1846–60, earthenware
printed with full-name or initials in
a variety of backstamps

Cork, Edge & Malkin   *Burslem, Staffs.*
     C.E. & M.   1860–71, earthenware
printed in a variety of designs

Corn, W. & E.   *Longport & Burslem, Staffs.*
     W. & E.C.   1864–1904, earthenware
     W.E.C.   printed in a variety of marks
                   on late wares
full-name usually included in 20th C.wares

Coronation Pottery Co.   *Stoke, Staffs.*
                    1903–54, earthenware

                    'Ltd.' from 1947

                    printed or impressed

Coronation Ware   *see* Barlow & Son Ltd., T.W.

Corre, Gilles Le   *Oxford, Oxon.*
                    1982, studio-potter, stoneware

Cotton & Barlow   *Longton, Staffs.*
     C & B.   1850–57, earthenware

Cotton Ltd., Elijah   *Hanley, Staffs.*
                    1880– , earthenware

various full-named printed marks from *c.* 1913
and trade-names: NELSON WARE, LORD NELSON WARE

Cowlishaw, W.H.   *Letchworth, Herts.*
                    1908–14, earthenware
    ICENI WARE   impressed

C.P.   *see* De Morgan

C.P. monogram   *see* Thorpe, O.

C.P. monogram stylized   *see* Pearson, C.

C.P.Co.   *see* Campbellfield Pottery Co.
              Clyde Pottery Co. Ltd.

C.P.Co.G.   *see* Clyde Pottery Co. Ltd.

C.P.P.Co.   *see* Crystal Porcelain Pottery Co. Ltd.

C. & R.   *see* Chesworth & Robinson
             Chetham & Robinson

Craven Dunnill & Co. Ltd.   *Jackfield, Shrops.*
                    1872–1951, tiles
    CRAVEN & CO.   JACKFIELD
                    CRAVEN DUNNILL
      impressed   & CO. JACKFIELD
        marks   SALOP

Creigiau Pottery   *nr. Cardiff, S. Wales*
                    1947–, earthenware in copper lustre

CREIGIAU
POTTERY
WALES

Southcliffe, R.G. & Co. Ltd.

'Creigiau'

SOUTHCLIFFE
POTTERY
CREIGIAU
impressed or printed

SOUTHCLIFFE
CREIGIAU
WALES

Crescent Pottery   *see* Cauldon Potteries Ltd.

Creyke & Sons, G.M.   *Hanley, Staffs.*
     G M C   1920–48, earthenware
(or as monogram), printed or impressed
in a variety of marks from 1920–

trade-name: Broadway (from *c.* 1935)

Crisp, John   *Dublin, Ireland*
      C   *c.* 1745–*c.* 1748, tin-glazed wares
    I E
    1748   painted, probably John & Elizabeth
               Crisp

Croft   *see* Govancroft Potteries

Crotty, Peter   *Strathpeffer, Ross &*
               Cromarty IV
               c. 1945–, studio-potter, stoneware
               birds and animals, (*see also*
               Rosemary Wren)

crossed-swords   *see* Worcester

Crown Chelsea China   *see* Morris, Thomas

Crown China Crafts Ltd.   *Stoke, Staffs.*
1946–58, earthenware & bone-china

Crown Clarence or **Clarence**   *see* Co-operative
Wholesale Society Ltd.

Crown Devon   *see* Fielding & Co. Ltd., S.

Crown Dresden Ware   *see* Lancaster & Sons
Lancaster & Sandland Ltd.

Crown Ducal Ware   *see* Richardson & Co. Ltd., A. G.

Crownford   *see* Ford & Sons

Crown Pottery   *Glasgow, Scotland*
M. & Y.   *c.* 1875–80, earthenware
with crown   MILLER & YOUNG
                  CROWN POTTERY
marks printed   GLASGOW
or impressed

Crown Staffordshire Porcelain Co. Ltd.   *Fenton, Staffs.*
1889–1948, bone-china

printed 1889–1912

later printed marks include Crown Staffordshire
Ltd. (from 1903). Renamed Crown Staffordshire
China Co., Ltd. (1948).
1973 taken over by Wedgwood Group. Trade-names:
Crown Staffordshire or Crown Staffs only rarely used

Crystal Porcelain Pottery Co. Ltd.   *Cobridge, Staffs.*
                                        c. 1882–6, porcelain & pottery
    C.P.P.CO.   tiles, etc.
printed or impressed, sometimes with flying dove

C S monogram   *see* Cardew, Seth

Cumberlidge & Humphreys   *Tunstall, Staffs.*
    C. & H.   1886–95, earthenware

    C. & H.   printed or impressed in a
    TUNSTALL   variety of marks

Cunningham, Alice Maud   *see* Della Robbia
  (from 1899, Mrs Harold Rathbone)

Cutts, James   *Shelton, Staffs.*
    J. CUTTS   *c.* 1834–70, designer & engraver
  signature on prints

99

C.V.   *see* Vyse, Charles

C W monogram, stylized   *see* Whyman, C.

C. & W.   *see* Capper & Wood

C.W.Ltd. or as monogram   *see* Waine & Co. Ltd., Charles

C. & W.K.H. (or Harvey)   *see* Harvey, C. & W.K.

C.Y. & J.   *see* Clementson, Young & Jameson

Cymro Stone Ware   *see* Swansea Pottery

Cyples, Joseph (& family)   *Longton, Staffs.*

CYPLES   *c.* 1780–1850, earthenware, stoneware & china from *c.* 1828

I. CYPLES   impressed   Marks of various members of this family were rarely used

Cyples & Barker   *Longton, Staffs.*

CYPLES & BARKER   1846–47, black earthenware & bone-china
impressed

D

D.   *see* Derby Porcelain Works
             Dimmock & Co., T.
             Leach, David
             Swansea Pottery

D. & Co.   *see* Swansea Pottery

D.A.   *see* Arbeid, Dan

Dakin, Thomas   *Shelton, Staffs.*
early 18th C., earthenware

THOMAS DAKIN
MADE THIS CUP   slip-trailed
1710

Dale, John   *Burslem, Staffs.*
early 19th C., earthenware figures

J. DALE   I. DALE
BURSLEM   BURSLEM
impressed

Dalmeny   *see* McNay & Sons, C.W.

Dalton, William B.   *London*
1900–, studio-potter, earthenware,
stoneware & porcelain
emigrated to the U.S.A. 1941
printed or painted

Daniel & Cork   *Burslem, Staffs.*
DANIEL & CORK   1867–9, earthenware
printed

Daniel & Son   *Stoke, Staffs.*
c. 1822–6, bone-china
rare marks: CHINA/DANIEL & SON/
STOKE/STAFFORDSHIRE

Daniel, H. & R.   *Stoke, Staffs.*
c. 1826–46, earthenware & bone-china

H. & R. DANIEL	printed on rare
Stoke upon Trent	ornately engraved
STAFFORDSHIRE	mark

Daniel, John   *Cobridge, Staffs.*

     c. 1770–*c.* 86, earthenware

JOHN DANIEL   incised signature

Daniell, A.B. & R.P.   *London*

     c. 1825–1917, retailer only

     mark seen on Coalport wares
     made to order

Dart Pottery   *Dartington Hall, S. Devon*

     (site of Bernard Leach's original
     pottery in 1920)
     Stephen Course & Peter Cook
     Janice Tchalenko, designer

Dartmouth Pottery   *Dartmouth, Devon*

     1947– , earthenware

     printed

Davenport & Co., W.   *Longport, Staffs.*

     c. 1791–1887, earthenware, stoneware
     and porcelains
     impressed anchor, *c.* 1794–1820

earthenware & stoneware:

Davenport
impressed with or without anchor
c. 1798–1820

similar impressed mark with 'DAVENPORT' in
caps, *c.* 1830–60

the numerals alongside anchor
denote year, 1839 is a rare
date

early printed stone china
mark, *c.* 1812–30

common stone-china mark
c. 1815–*c.* 75

the term 'Opaque China' with anchor marks
c. 1850–*c.* 85
porcelain:
'LONGPORT' painted over anchor, *c.* 1806
'LONGPORT' written, 1805–10

common standard mark from *c.* 1812
to the late years, the enamel
marks are early, the underglaze
blue, post– *c.* 1845

DAVENPORT	DAVENPORT
LONGPORT	LONGPORT
	STAFFORDSHIRE

printed marks,
1812–40, the later versions are with crown

Davenport, Banks & Co.   *Hanley, Staffs.*

1860–73, earthenware,

D.B. & CO.   including, majolica

printed in a variety of marks

DAVENPORT   impressed or printed in

BANKS & CO.   various backstamps

ETRURIA

Davenport, Beck & Co.   *Hanley, Staffs.*

1873–80, earthenware including

D.B. & CO.   majolica

printed in a variety of marks

Davidson, John   *Truro, Cornwall*

c. 1960, studio-potter in
domestic stoneware & porcelain

Davies & Co.   *Newcastle upon Tyne, Tyne & Wear*

1833–51, earthenware, including lustreware.

DAVIES & CO.   Tyne Main Pottery

impressed

Davies, Clive   *nr. Harleston, Norfolk*

active in '89, studio-potter in
stoneware

Davis, Derek M.   *Arundel, W. Sussex*

active in '89, studio-potter in
stoneware & porcelain

Davis, Harry & May   *Praze, Cornwall*

1946–62, studio-potter
emigrated to N. Zealand

Crowan Pottery

impressed

Davis, J. Heath   *Hanley, Staffs.*

J.H. DAVIS   1881–91, earthenware
HANLEY   printed in a variety of marks

Davison & Son, Ltd.   *Burslem, Staffs.*

c. 1898–1952, earthenware

early wares were apparently
unmarked, printed 1948–52

Dawson, John (*d.* 1848)   *Sunderland, Tyne & Wear*

c. 1799–1864, earthenware

DAWSON   I. DAWSON   DAWSON & CO.

printed or impressed in a variety of marks.
Sons joined pottery, Thomas (1796–1839)
John (1798–1832); after death of founder was
taken over by grandsons, under whom the
factory failed in 1864

DAWSON & CO.   J. DAWSON & CO.   J. DAWSON
LOW FORD   LOW FORD   SOUTH HYLTON

titles included in a variety of printed marks
usually within decoration

Day, George   *Longton, Staffs.*

1882–9, earthenware
printed under 'STAFFORDSHIRE'

Day & Pratt *Longton, Staffs.*
DAY & PRATT *c.* 1887–8, bone-china
printed or impressed

D.B. & Co. *see* Davenport, Banks & Co.
Davenport, Beck & Co.
Dunn, Bennett & Co.

D C monogram *see* Clarkson, Derek
Cookson, Delan

D C *see* Carnegy, Daphne
Dixon & Co., R.F.

D D monogram *see* Derby Porcelain Works
Dimmock & Co., T.

D.D. & Co. *see* Dunderdale & Co.

D E see Emms, D.
Eeles, D.

Deakin & Son *Lane End, Staffs.*
1833–41, earthenware

printed

Dean & Sons, Ltd., Thomas *Tunstall, Staffs.*
1789–1947, earthenware

acquired in 1948 by Lawley Group; renamed in 1964 Allied English Potteries, becoming Royal Doulton in 1973

printed

Dean, S.W.   *Burslem, Staffs.*
1904–10, earthenware

printed

Deans (1910) Ltd.   *Burslem, Staffs.*
1910–19, earthenware

DEANS (1910) LTD.
BURSLEM
ENGLAND   printed

Decoro Pottery Co.   *Longton, Staffs.*
1933–49, earthenware

TUSCAN   (owned by R.H. & S.L. Plant Ltd.)
DECORO
POTTERY   printed in a variety of marks

d f monogram   *see* Frith, David

Delamain, Captain Henry (*d.* 1757) *Dublin, Ireland*
1752–*c.* 1771, tin-glazed earthenware

printed

107

Della Robbia Co. Ltd.   *Birkenhead, Merseyside*

1894–1900, earthenware, tiles, etc.
1900–1906 Della Robbia Pottery
& Marble Co. Ltd.

(founded by H.B. Rathbone & Conrad Dressler)

c. 1894–1900 incised mark
with initial 'C' for Charles
Collis, decorator

Recorded marks of Della Robbia decorators:

Ackerley, Ted		De Caluwé, Madame Marianne	
Bare, Ruth		Fletcher, W. Harry	
Beaumont, Annie		Ford, Jack	
Bell, A.E.			
Buckler, Gwendoline		Fogo, John	
		Furniss, May	
Collis, Charles		Hall, Tom	

| Hughes, James | *JH* | Seddon, George | *JS* |

Jones, Annie

Jones, Alice
Louise

Jones, Hannah

Manzoni, Giovanni
Carlo

Pearce, Harry

Peirce, Aphra

Rathbone, Alice

Rathbone, Harold

Rope, Ellen
Mary

Russell, Gertrude

Seddon, George

Shirley, C. J.   *Cecil John Shirley*

Smith, Annie

Woodhouse,   *Violet*
Violet

Walker, Cassandia   *C.A.W–*
Annie

Warwick, William   *·W·*

Watkins, Frank   *FW*

Wilkins, Liz   *LW*

Williams, Annie   *W*

Williams, Billy   *W*

Wood, E.M.   *FMW.*

De Morgan, William   (*b.* 1839; *d.* 1917) *Chelsea, London*
Chelsea, 1872–82
Merton Abbey, 1882–88
Fulham, 1888–98
Fulham, 1898–1907 primarily
decorating only

decorator of earthenwares made to order
from other factories, and own wares
impressed mark, 1882–
'& Co.' added after 1888

marks used at Merton Abbey, 1882–88
made own tiles from *c.* 1879,
and wares from 1882

impressed or painted
1882–

Sands End Pottery, 1888–97
(period of partnership with
Halsey Ricardo)

1898–1907, partnership with
Frank Iles, Charles & Fred
Passenger at Fulham

impressed

decoration continued until 1911, four years
after De Morgan retired

D.I.P. De Morgan, Iles & Passenger 1898–1907
partners from *c.* 1898–*c.* 1911
individual decorators:

F.P. – Fred Passenger	M.J. – M. Juster
C.P. – Charles Passenger	J.J. – Joe Juster
J.M. – Jim Hersey	H.R. – Halsey Rocardo

earthenwares were decorated
in De Morgan style at
Mrs. Ida Perrin's studio,
Bushey Heath, 1921–33
by Fred Passenger

Denaby Pottery   *see* Wardle & Co., J.

Denton China (Longton) Ltd.   *Longton, Staffs.*
1945–68, bone-china

DENTON   Purchased by Aynsley Group PLC (1969)
CHINA   who in turn were purchased by
printed   Waterford Glass Co. Ltd., Eire. (1970)
& renamed Aynsley China Ltd., but were
bought back by Aynsley Group PLC in 1987

Derby Porcelain Works   *Derby, Derbys.*

Derby   *D*
1750

c. 1750–1848
soft-paste porcelain   incised
early marks of Planché
period *c.* 1750–56

Derby Porcelain Works
1756–1848
'William Duesbury &
Co.' c. 1760

incised

rebus mark on wares decorated with on-glaze transfer-prints
engraved by Richard Holdship

c. 1764–9

painted on wares made in imitation of Chinese
porcelain, probably to depict a *ting* (incense-
burner), c. 1765–80

'N' seen on dishes, etc.
c. 1770–80

incised

'Chelsea-Derby' marks
c. 1770–84

in gold

c. 1770–82, in blue or
purple

incised model numbers
on figures, c. 1775–
early 19th century

common Derby mark
1782–, incised, purple
blue or black
c. 1800–25 in red
enamel

mark of Isaac
Farnsworth 'repairer'

mark of Joseph Hill
'repairer'

'size' mark

'Duesbury & Kean',
c. 1795
in blue, crimson or purple

blue-painted mark in
imitation of Meissen
c. 1785–1825

Robert Bloor Period

printed in red
c. 1820–40

printed in red
c. 1830–48

113

mark in imitation of
Sèvres, *c.* 1825–48
in blue enamel

Locker & Co., King Street factory
c. 1849–59

similar marks used also
by:
Stevenson Sharp & Co.
1859–61
'Courtney late Bloor'
1849–63

Stevenson & Hancock
1861–1935, this mark
also used after 1935
when King St. factory
was taken over by Royal Crown Derby
Porcelain Co. Ltd.

Derby Crown Porcelain Co. Ltd. Est. 1876
c. 1878–90, together
with year mark as
shown in table on next
page

printed

Derby

impressed

Royal Crown Derby Porcelain Co. Ltd.
1890–

printed mark of *c.* 1890
'England' from 1891
'Made in England'
added from *c.* 1920
together with year
mark
(Part of Royal Doulton Tableware Ltd. from 1973)

TABLE OF DERBY YEAR-MARKS,
1882–

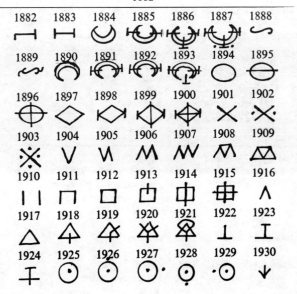

1931	1932	1933	1934	1935	1936	1937
⚓	⚓	⚓	⚓	⚓	⚓	⚓
1938	**1939**	**1940**	**1941**	**1942**	**1943**	**1944**
I	II	III	IV	V	VI	VII
1945	**1946**	**1947**	**1948**	**1949**	**1950**	**1951**
VIII	IX	X	XI	XII	XIII	etc.

Devon Silverine   *see* Fielding & Co. Ltd., S.

Devonshire Potteries Ltd.   *Bovey Tracey, Devon.*
1947–*c.* 1980, earthenware

printed 1947–
TRENTHAM
ART WARE
MADE IN DEVON
printed on label 1959–

Dewes & Copestake   *Longton Staffs.*
D & C   *c.* 1893–1915, earthenware & bone-china
L   printed in a variety of marks on
               earthenware, bone-china as yet
               unidentified

Diamond China   *see* Blyth Porcelain Co. Ltd.

Diamond Pottery Co. Ltd.   *Hanley, Staffs.*
D.P.CO.   1908–1935, earthenware

D.P.CO. LTD.   printed in a variety of marks

Diane Pottery Co.   *Longton, Staffs.*
1960–, now closed, bone-china

DIANE
POTTERY   printed in a variety of marks
LONGTON
STAFFORDSHIRE

Dick, Peter & Jill   *Coxwold, Yorks.*
1965–, studio-potters in
stoneware & earthenware

Dicker Pottery   *see* Clark, Uriah

Dillon, Francis   *Cobridge, Staffs.*
DILLON   1834–43, earthenware
impressed
F.D.   printed in a variety of marks

Dillwyn & Co.   *see* Swansea Pottery

Dimmock & Co., J.   *Hanley, Staffs.*
J.D. & CO.   1862–1904, earthenware

       printed in a variety of marks
taken over *c.* 1878 by W.D. Cliff
who used a wide range of marks
including: CLIFF, ALBION CHINA or
ALBION WORKS

Dimmock (Junr) & Co., Thomas   *Shelton & Hanley, Staffs.*
        D   1828–59, earthenware
    printed in a variety of marks, including
    'KAOLIN WARE' & 'STONEWARE'

   impressed or printed
double 'D' monogram.
Similar to mark used at
Derby from 1877

Dimmock & Smith   *Hanley, Staffs.*
        D. & S.   1826–33 & 1842–59, earthenware
    printed in a variety of marks

Dinky Art Pottery   *Longton, Staffs.*
        MADE IN   1931–47, earthenware
    DINKY WARE
        ENGLAND   printed

Dixon & Co.   *see* Phillips, J.

Dixon & Co., R.F.   *Longton, Staffs.*
        D.C.   1916–1929, ceramic retailers
                          & importers
    initials included in marks on wares made to order

D L monogram   *see* Jones, David, H.,

D.L.&Co. or D.L. & Sons   *see* Lockhart & Arthur

D.M.   *see* De Morgan, William

D M   *see* Miller, D.

D.M.& S.   *see* Methven & Sons, David

Dodd, Mike   *Wigton, Cumbria*

studio-potter, active in 1989

Doe & Rogers   *see* Worcester

Doherty, Jack   *Ross-on-Wye, Heref.*

studio-potter in porcelain,
active in 1989

Don Pottery   *Swinton, Yorks.*

DON POTTERY
impressed
1801–34

printed
1810–34

impressed
c. 1805–34

c. 1801–1893, creamware & white
earthenware
John Green (*d.* 1815)
Greens, Clark & Co. 1801–1817
John & William Green & Co. 1817–1835
Samuel Barker, 1839–*c.* 1851
Samuel Barker & Son, *c.* 1851–*c.* 1882
continued under same name until
closure in 1893

    Don Pottery
written, *c.* 1807

DON, on embossed tablet,
c. 1820–34

S.B. & S. *c.* 1860–93, printed
on a variety of backstamps

Donovan & Son, James   *Dublin, Ireland*

DONOVAN
c. 1770–1829, decorator of English
pottery & porcelain

DONOVAN
DUBLIN   painted

door, a   *see* Barn Pottery Ltd.

Dorothy Ann Floral China   *Stoke, Staffs.*
1946– , bone-china
floral jewellery

Dorothy Ann
STOKE ON TRENT   printed
ENGLAND

double-cross   *see* Corre, Gilles Le

Doulton & Watts   *Lambeth, London*
1820–54, salt-glazed stoneware &
DOULTON & WATTS   *terra-cotta*

impressed, moulded
or incised marks c. 1827–
c. 1858

DOULTON&WATTS
LAMBETH POTTERY
LONDON

DOULTON
LAMBETH

Doulton & Co. c. 1858–c. 1910
'ENGLAND' added after 1891
impressed on Lambeth wares

impressed on decorated
salt-glazed stoneware, *c.* 1869–
c. 72. Dates are frequently added
in centre of this form of mark

  impressed or printed on
Lambeth wares from *c.* 1873–
1914, 'ENGLAND' denoting made
after 1891

 impressed or printed on
earthenware (Faience)
c. 1873– *c.* 1914

 impressed or printed on
decorated stoneware
c. 1879–*c.* 1902. 'England'
added 1891 and sometimes
year date

Production started at Nile St., Burslem, *c.* 1882
for the manufacture of earthenware; china being
added in 1884

 'DOULTON BURSLEM' from
c. 1882, 'crown' added *c.* 1885–
c. 1902

DOULTON
LAMBETH impressed on stonewares
ENGLAND *c.* 1891–1956

impressed or printed on
'Impasto' wares made at Lambeth
c. 1879–1906

impressed or printed on
'Crown Lambeth' wares
c. 1891–*c.* 1900

DOULTON & SLATERS   impressed or printed
PATENT   additional mark on some
Lambeth & Burslem wares
involving designs in raised gold, *c.* 1886–*c.* 1911

impressed or printed on
Lambeth 'Marqueterie'
earthenware, *c.* 1887–1906

impressed on Lambeth
'Carrara' stoneware,
c. 1887–*c.* 1896

 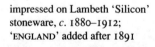

impressed on Lambeth 'Silicon'
stoneware, *c.* 1880–1912;
'ENGLAND' added after 1891

new trade-mark on all Doulton
wares, including the word 'Royal'
1902–22 & 1927–32; also on
some Burslem wares (1922–7)

printed on Burslem wares,
c. 1922–7

printed or impressed on
Lambeth wares, 1922–56,
the lion was at times omitted

impressed or printed on
Lambeth stoneware jugs,
figures, etc., c. 1912–56

Lambeth 'Persian' style wares
printed or impressed
c. 1920–7

'BONE CHINA' added to standard mark 1932–59
'ENGLISH FINE BONE CHINA' from 1959
'ENGLISH TRANSLUCENT CHINA' on new body
introduced 1960

The following are decorators, designers and
painters employed at Lambeth, who marked their
work with initials or monogram, many other

artists signed their work in full

Aitken, Margaret, 1882

Arding, Helen A., *c.* 1878–*c.* 1884

Arding, Mary M., *c.* 1879–*c.* 1883

Atkins, Elizabeth, *c.* 1876–*c.* 1882

Baigent, Agnes E.M., *c.* 1901–9

Banks, Eliza S., *c.* 1876–*c.* 1884

Barker, Clara S., 1882

Barlow, Arthur B., 1871–8

Barlow, Florence E., 1873–1909

Barlow, Hannah B., 1871–1913

Barlow, Lucy A., 1884

Barnard, Harry, *c.* 1880–1890

Baron, W., 1883

Bearne, George W., *c.* 1881–*c.* 1890

Beere, Arthur, *c.* 1877–*c.* 1881

Bishop, Ernest R., 1882

Broad, John, *c.* 1873–1919

Bryon, A., *c.* 1870–*c.* 1874
(mark unrecorded)

Budden, Alice E., *c.* 1879–*c.* 1882

Butler, Frank A., 1872–1911

Butterton, Mary, *c.* 1874–*c.* 1894

Callahan, James E., 1883–1936
(mark unrecorded)

Capes, Mary, *c.* 1876–*c.* 1883

Challis, Margaret M., *c.* 1878–*c.* 1883

Collins, F.M., *c.* 1878–80

Cowper, Joan, 1936–9

Crawley, Minna L., *c.* 1878–*c.* 1885

Cruikshank, James R., *c.* 1881–*c.* 1888

Davis, Louisa J., *c.* 1873–*c.* 1895

Denley, M., *c.* 1889–1894

Dennis, Ada, *c.* 1881–*c.* 1894

Dunn, W. Edward, *c.* 1883– *c.* 1895

Durtnall, L. Imogen, *c.* 1880–*c.* 1890

Edwards, Emily J., *c.* 1872–*c.* 1886

Edwards, Louisa E., *c.* 1873–*c.* 1890

Eggleton, Edward W.G., 1927–56

Ellis, Herbert, *c.* 1879–1928

Eyre, John, *c.* 1884–97

Fisher, Elizabeth, *c.* 1873–*c.* 1888

Gandy, Walter, 1800–1932

Gillman, Emily J., *c.* 1898–1913

Green, Alberta L., *c.* 1878–*c.* 1882

Hall, Alice, 1882

Harding, J.B., 1902

Harradine, Arthur Leslie, 1902–14

Hastings, W., *c.* 1885–*c.* 1890

Haughton, Lizzie, 1882

Hoy, Agnete, 1952–56

Hubert, Eliza L., 1879–82

Huggins, Vera, 1923–50

Hunt, Florence L., 1882

Huskisson, John, 1882

Johnson, Doris 1922–56

Keen, Rosa, *c*. 1875–*c*. 1890

Kemp, Percy, *c*. 1880–1890 (mark unrecorded)

Lee, Francis E., *c*. 1875–*c*. 1890

Lewis, Esther, *c*. 1880–*c*. 1895

Lewis, Florence E., *c*. 1875–*c*. 1897

Lewis, Isabel, *c*. 1876–*c*. 1898

Linnell, Frances M., *c*. 1880– *c*. 1885

Lupton, Edith D., *c*. 1876–*c*. 1889

McLellan, John Henry, *c*. 1880– *c*. 1910

Marshall, Alice, *c*. 1897–1914

Marshall Mark V., 1879–*c*. 1912

Mitchell, Mary, *c*. 1874–*c*. 1887

Mott, Joseph H., 1880–1950

Neatby W.J., *c*. 1892–*c*. 1907

Nunn, W.J.W., late 19th C.

Parker, William, *c.* 1880–*c.* 1892

Pearce, Arthur E., 1873–1934

Pope, Francis C., 1880–1923

Rhead, Geroge Wooliscroft, 1882

Rix, Wilton P., 1870–97 (unrecorded)

Roberts, Florence C., *c.* 1879–1930

Rogers, Edith, 1882

Rogers, Kate, *c.* 1880–*c.* 1892

Rogers, Martha M., 1882

Rowe, William, 1883–1939

Shelley, Alice, *c.* 1877–*c.* 1882

Simeon, Harry, 1894–1936

Simmance, Elise, *c.* 1873–1928

Smallfield, Katherine B., *c.* 1882–1912

Smallfield, Mildred B., 1882

Stable, Fanny, 1880–3

Sturgeon, Katherine, 1880–3

Tabor, George Hugo, c. 1878–c. 1890

Thatcher, Euphemia A., 1879–82

Thompson, Margaret E., c. 1900–20

Tinworth, George, 1866–1913

Vigor C., c. 1880–c. 1885 (mark unrecorded)

Viner, Emily M., 1882

Watt, Linnie, c. 1880–c. 1886

Wilson, Edgar W., c. 1880–c. 1895

Youatt, Bessie J., c. 1873–c. 1890

From 1877 Doulton was in partnership with
Pinder, Bourne & Co. at Burslem until 1882.
In 1898 Doulton became a Limited Company,
and was granted a Royal Warrant in 1901.
The Lambeth works were closed in 1956.
In 1984 the company was renamed Royal Doulton
Limited and in 1990 the following trade-names
were in use: Royal Doulton, Royal Albert,
Royal Crown Derby, Minton, Royal Doulton
Crystal, Bunnykins, Colclough, Expressions,
Goss, Images, John Beswick, Lambethware,
Paragon, Queen Anne, Reflections, Ridgway,
Royal Adderley, Royal Kent, Royal Knight, & Shelley

D P monogram   *see* Dick, Peter

D P stylized monogram   *see* Dart Pottery

D.P. & Co.   *see* Phillips, J.

D.P. & Co. Ltd.   *see* Diamond Pottery Co., Ltd.
                                    Dresden Porcelain Co.

D R   *see* Roberts, D.

dragon (Welsh)   *see* Creigiau Pottery

Dresden Floral Porcelain Co. Ltd.   *Longton, Staffs.*
                          c. 1945–56, bone-china

                         printed with 'ENGLAND'

Dresden Porcelain Co.   *Longton, Staffs.*
D.P. CO.   *c.* 1895–1904, bone-china

    D.P.CO.
      L

                         printed marks

Dresser, Dr. Christopher   *see* Linthorpe Pottery

Dreydel & Co., Henry   *London*
                     late 19th C. retailer of imported

and English porcelain
made to order

D.S.   *see* Scott, D.

D. & S.   *see* Dimmock & Smith

d T e   *see* Trey, M. de

Duchess   *see* Finney & Sons, Ltd., A.T.

Duckworth, Ruth   *Kew, Surrey*

$$\begin{matrix} R \\ W \\ D \end{matrix}$$

1956– , studio-potter.
To the U.S.A. in 1960s.

printed or incised

Dudson Bros Ltd.   *Hanley (now in Tunstall)*
1898– , earthenware & stoneware

DUDSON
ENGLAND

DUDSON BROTHERS   impressed or printed
ENGLAND

printed, 1936–45

Dudson, James *Hanley, Staffs.*

DUDSON

impressed

1838–88, earthenware, including
many Spaniels, Poodle-like
dogs, & Wedgwood-type stoneware

Dudson, J.T. *Hanley, Staffs.*

1888–98, earthenware & stoneware

J.DUDSON   J.DUDSON
                                                      ENGLAND

impressed, 'ENGLAND' added from 1891

Dudson, Wilcox & Till Ltd. *Hanley, Staffs.*

1902–26, earthenware
printed or impressed
figure of Britannia also
used within double-ring, with
full name & address of firm

Duke & Nephews, Sir James *Burslem, Staffs.*

c. 1860–4, bone-china, Parian
and earthenware

mark impressed

Dunderdale & Co., David *Castleford, Yorks.*

c. 1790–1820, earthenware &
stoneware

D.D. & CO.	D.D. & CO.	D.D. & CO.
CASTLEFORD	CASTLEFORD	
POTTERY		CASTLEFORD
CASTLEFORD	POTTERY	

all impressed marks

Dunmore Pottery Co.   *Airth, Scotland*
1860–*c.* 1911, earthenware.
'CO' added from 1903.

PETER GARDNER
DUNMORE POTTERY   DUNMORE

Dunn, Bennett & Co.   *Burslem, Staffs.*
1875–1983, earthenware & bone-
D.B. & CO.   china ('LTD' added 1907)

printed in a variety of marks
c. 1875–1907

DUNN, BENNETT & CO. LTD.   under crown
    BURSLEM
    ENGLAND   printed 1937–
1968, taken over by Doulton & Co.
1983, renamed Goss China Co. Ltd.
    now part of Royal Doulton

Dunn, Mrs Constance   *Billingham, Durham*
c. 1933–, artist-potter in stoneware,
teaching previously

incised

Dunn, John   *Brighton, Sussex*

studio-potter, specializing in
raku wares, active in 1989

Dura Porcelain Co. Ltd.   *Hanley, Staffs.*
1919–21, bone-china

printed, trade-name:
SYLVAN CHINA

Durham China Co. Ltd.   *Gateshead, Tyne & Wear*
1947–57, bone-china & earthenware

printed or impressed

Dwight, John   *Fulham, London*
patented salt-glazed stoneware
in 1672, but no recorded marks

E

E, within circle   *see* Cooper, Emanuel

eagle, an   *see* Grosvenor & Son, F.

Eardley & Hammersley   *Tunstall, Staffs.*
E. & H.   1862–6, earthenware, printed mark

134

Eastop, Geoffrey   *Newbury, Berks.*

                        c. 1958–, studio-potter in
                        stoneware & porcelain

Eastwood   *see* Baddeley, William

E.B. & B.   *see* Edge, Barker & Barker

E.B. & Co.   *see* Brain & Co., Edward

E. & B.   *see* Evans & Booth

E.B.F.   *see* Fishley

E. & B.L.   *see* Edwards & Brown

E.B. & S.   *see* Booth & Son, Ephraim

E.C.   *see* Challinor, Edward
             Collyer, Ernest

E. & C.C.   *see* Challinor, E. & C.

Edge, William & Samuel   *Lane Delph, Staffs.*
     W. & S.E.   1841–8, earthenware
printed in a variety of marks

Edge, Barker & Barker   *Fenton, Staffs.*
     E.B.& B.   1836–40, earthenware
printed in a variety of marks

Edge, Barker & Co.   *Fenton, Staffs.*
    E.B. & CO.   1835–6, earthenware
  printed in a variety of marks

Edge & Grocott   *Tunstall, Staffs.*
                         c. 1830, earthenware figures
  EDGE & GROCOTT   rare impressed mark

Edge, Malkin & Co.   *Burslem, Staffs.*
                         1871–1903, earthenware
  E.M. & CO.   'LTD' from 1899

    E.M. & CO.   EDGE MALKIN
      B   & CO.
    printed   impressed

                       printed mark registered
                       in 1873

Edwards & Son, James   *Burslem, Staffs.*
    J.E. & S.   1851–82, earthenware

    STONE CHINA   EDWARDS
    JAMES EDWARDS   D.H.
    & SON. DALE HALL
  printed or impressed in a variety of marks

Edwards & Co., John   *Longton & Fenton, Staffs.*
                         1847–53 Longton

1853–1900 Fenton, earthenware
      J.E.   and unmarked porcelain
                    '& Co' added *c.* 1873
      J.E. & CO.   impressed or printed marks
                    in a variety of patterns
trade-marks: WARRANTED IRONSTONE CHINA &
                      PORCELAINE DE TERRE from
                      c. 1880

Edwards, James & Thomas *Burslem, Staffs.*
    J. & T.E.   1839–41, earthenware

   J. & T. EDWARDS   EDWARDS
      B
printed or impressed in a variety of marks

Edwards & Brown *Longton, Staffs.*
    E. & B.L.   1882–1933, bone-china
printed or impressed in a variety of marks
trade-name: 'DUCHESS CHINA' from 1910–

Eeles, David *Beaminster, Dorset,*

                      Shepherd's Well Pottery.
                      1955–, studio-potter in stoneware,
                      earthenware & porcelain

                      D. E.   impressed marks

E. & E.W. *see* Wood & Sons, Enoch

E.F.B. & Co. or **E.F.B.** *see* Bodley & Co., E.F.

E.G. monogram   *see* Eastop, G.

E.G. & C.   *see* Everard, Glover & Colclough

E. & G.P.   *see* Phillips, Edward & George

E. & H.   *see* Eardley & Hammersley

Ehlers, A.W.G.   *Bovey Tracey, Devon*
                                    1946–55, studio-potter

                                    incised or painted

E.I.B.   *see* Birch, Edmund John

E.J.   *see* Jones, Elijah

E.J.D.B. or as monogram   *see* Bodley, E.J.D.

E.K.B.   *see* Elkin, Knight & Bridgwood

E.K. & Co.   *see* Elkin, Knight & Co.

E.L.   *see* Lowenstein, Eileen

Elektra Porcelain Co. Ltd.   *Longton, Staffs.*
      Zanobia Ware   1924–71, earthenware
          c. 1924
      Vulcan Ware   *c.* 1940– , both printed

Elgin Pottery   *Glasgow, Scotland*
                    1860–*c*. 75, earthenware
ELGIN POTTERY C.P.   J. Johnson & Co. 1860–65
      c. 1865   Charles Purves 1865–70
      impressed   Thomas Purves 1870–*c*. 75

Elizabethan   *see* Ford & Sons
                  Rosina China Co. Ltd.

Elkin, Knight & Bridgwood   *Fenton, Staffs.*
        or
Knight, Elkin & Bridgwood
                    c. 1827–40, earthenware & bone-china
        E.K.B.   K.E. & B.   printed in a variety
                                      of marks

Elkin, Knight & Co.   *Fenton, Staffs.*
      E.K. & CO.   1822–6, earthenware
    ELKIN, KNIGHT
        & CO.   printed or impressed in a
                      variety of marks

Elkin & Newbon   *Longton, Staffs.*
        E. & N.   1845–56, earthenware
    printed in a variety of marks

Elkin, Samuel   *Longton, Staffs.*
        S.E.   1856–64, earthenware
    printed in a variety of marks

Ellgreave Pottery Co. Ltd.   *Burslem, Staffs.*
                    1921– , earthenware
    trade-names: Lottie Rhead Ware & Heatmaster

Ellis, Unwin & Mountford   *Hanley, Staffs.*
    E.U. & M.   1860–61, earthenware
  printed in a variety of marks

Elsmore & Forster   *Tunstall, Staffs.*
                          1853–71, earthenware & Parian
  ELSMORE & FORSTER
  printed in a variety of marks

Elsmore & Son, Thomas   *Tunstall, Staffs.*
    ELSMORE & SON   1872–87, earthenware
       ENGLAND   printed

Elton, Sir Edmund Harry (*d.* 1920)   *Clevedon, Avon*
                          1879–1930, art pottery

Elton   cross added to same signature
                    after death of founder. Continued
  by George Masters (*d.* 1921) and Sir Ambrose Elton (son).

Elton & Co. Ltd., J.F.   *Burslem, Staffs.*
                  1901–10, earthenware
    J.F.E.CO.LTD.
      BURSLEM   also printed or impressed
  as a monogram

Emberton, Thomas, Isaac & James   *Tunstall, Staffs.*
    T.I. & J.E.   1869–82, earthenware
  initials printed under circular garter bearing
  name of pattern, full-name and initials also used

Emberton, William   *Tunstall, Staffs.*

      W.E.   1851–69, earthenware
printed in a wide variety of marks

Embosa Ware   *see* Fell & Co., J.T.

E.M. & Co.   *see* Edge, Malkin & Co. Ltd.

Emery, Francis J.   *Burslem, Staffs.*
      F.J.EMERY.   *c.* 1878–93, earthenware
included in a wide range of printed marks

Emery, James   *Mexborough, Yorks.*

                c. 1837–*c.* 1886, brown earthenware
                Emery, James *c.* 1837–74
                Emery, James & Peter 1841–
                Emery, James, Peter & Alfred

                rare incised mark

Emms, Derek   *Stone, Staffs.*

                1955–, studio-potter, porcelain &
                stoneware, specializing in
                celadon glazes from iron-oxide
impressed mark

Empire Porcelain Co.   *Stoke, Staffs.*
                1896–1967, earthenware
                'LTD.' added *c.* 1963
                (1958–67, part of Qualcast Group)

                printed mark, *c.* 1896–1912
                trade-names in 1930s: 'Shelton Ivory',
                'EMPIRE WARE'

wide variety of marks including 'EMPIRE'
used until closure

 printed during 1960s

E. & N.   *see* Elkin & Newbon

E.P.Co. or as monogram   *see* Empire Porcelain Co.

ERA Art Pottery Co.   *Stoke, Staffs.*
1930–47, earthenware

printed *c.* 1936, ERA or ERA WARE
were used in a variety of marks

ermine mark   *see* Minton

Essex Art Pottery   *see* Bingham, Edward

E.U. & M.   *see* Ellis, Unwin & Mountford

Evans & Booth   *Burslem, Staffs.*
E. & B.   1856–69, earthenware
printed in a wide variety of backstamps

Evans & Co.   *see* Swansea Pottery

Evans & Glasson   *see* Swansea Pottery

Everard, Glover & Colclough   *Lane End, Staffs.*
c. 1847– , earthenware & bone-china

continued as Glover & Colclough
to 1854, but the wares have not been
E.G.&C.   identified

initials probably used on wares of *c.* 1847

Everett, Raymond R.   *Rye, Sussex*
1963– , studio-potter

painted mark, full-name printed or
impressed mark also used

Everson, Ronald   *Stoke d' Aberton, Surrey*
1953– , porcelain & bone-china

mark in form of a dated signature

E.W.   *see* Wood, Enoch

E.W. & S.   *see* Wood & Sons, Enoch

Exeter Art Pottery   *Exeter, Devon*
1892–96, art pottery

impressed mark including
incised pattern number

F

F. & Sons Ltd.   *see* Ford & Sons

Falcon Ware   *see* Lawrence (Longton) Ltd., Thomas
                     Weatherby & Sons Ltd.

Fancies Fayre Pottery   *Hanley & Shelton, Staffs.*
                            c. 1946– , earthenware
Changed name to Bairstow Manor Pottery Ltd., 1979.

F ANCIES AYRE	NICK K NACKS	STAFFORDSHIRE
ENGLAND	ENGLAND	F.F. ENGLAND

printed or impressed:
    1946–   1949–   1950–

F.B.   *see* Booth, Frederick

F.B.B.   *see* Worcester

F.B. & Co.   *see* Beardmore & Co., Frank
   F

F. & B.   *see* Worcester

F.C. or F.C. & Co.   *see* Cartlidge & Co., F.

F. & C. or F.C.&Co.   *see* Ford, Challinor & Co.

F.D.   *see* Dillon, Francis

Featherstone Potteries   *Stoke, Staffs.*
        F.P.   1949–50, earthenware
                        printed or impressed in a
        F.N.P.   variety of marks

Federated Potteries Co. Ltd.   *Tunstall & Fenton*
                              1982– , earthenware & bone-china
   trade-name: FPC, Grindley, Royal Tudor, Salisbury Bone China
   Subsidiary of United Kingdom Provident Inst.
   1987, Grindley sold to Royal Stafford & then
   to Churchill
   1987, Cartwright & Edwards sold to Coloroll
   1990 trade-name of 'Grindley' in use
   1991 in hands of receivers

Feibleman, Dorothy   *London*
                              studio-potter in various clays combined
                              with precious metals, active in 1989

Fell & Co., J.T.   *Longton, Staffs.*
                              1923–57, earthenware
   EMBOSA WARE   printed or impressed

Fell & Co. Ltd., Thomas   *Newcastle upon Tyne, Tyne & Wear*
                              1817–1890, earthenware
                              'LTD.' from 1869
            FELL   impressed, 1817–30

   impressed:

   F. & CO.   T.F. & CO.   T.FELL & C.
   impressed or printed in a variety of marks
   names of patterns included in backstamps:
   Wild Rose, Dragon, The Bosphorus, Corinth,
   Willow, Lasso and Berry

Fenton & Sons, Alfred   *Hanley, Staffs.*
    A.F.&S.   1887–1901, earthenware & bone-china
impressed or printed initials in a variety
of marks

Fenton Stone Works   *see* Mason, G.M. & C.J.

Fermanagh Pottery   *see* Belleek

Ferrybridge Pottery   *nr. Pontefract, Yorks.*
                    1793– , earthenware
  TOMLINSON & CO.   impressed, 1793–8
  WEDGWOOD & CO.   impressed, 1798–1800
(Tomlinson, Foster, Wedgwood & Co.)
    FERRYBRIDGE   impressed, 1801–70
    B.T.& S.F.B.   on crown, Benjamin Taylor
               & Son, Ferrybridge, *c.* 1845–50
    R. & T.   Reed & Taylor, 1832–*c.* 38
    L.W.   Lewis Woolf, 1851–*c.* 77; trade-name:
OPAQUE GRANITE CHINA also used by B. Taylor
& Son and Lewis & Sydney Woolf, *c.* 1845–84
    S.W.   Sydney Woolf, *c.* 1860–87

    P.B.   P.BROS.   POULSON BROTHERS
impressed or printed initials used on a wide
variety of marks by POULSON BROS., 1884–95
      S.B.   printed or impressed by Sefton & Brown,
      F.B.   1895–1919

      T.B.&S.   impressed by Thomas Brown & Sons
      F.B.   Ltd., 1919–

F.F.   *see* Fancies Fayre Pottery

F.H.   *see* Holland, W. Fishley

F.H. monogram stylized   *see* Hamer, F.

F. & H.   *see* Forester & Hulme

Fieldhouse, Murray   *see* Pendley Potteries

Fielding & Co.Ltd., S.   *Stoke, Staffs.*

	1879–1982 earthenware including
FIELDING	majolica. 'LTD.' from 1905
	impressed, 1879–
S.F.& CO.	printed in a variety of marks
	1880–1917

name changed to Crown Devon in 1905;
purchased by a Liverpool company in 1976 and
company closed in 1982. Manufacturing equipment
purchased first by Caverswall China Co. Ltd. in
'83 and in 1984 by Thomas Goode & Co., London
retailer. Works demolished in 1987

Fife Pottery, The   *see* Heron & Son, R.

Fifield, William (*d.* 1857)   *Bristol, Avon.*

	c. 1810–55, independent painter
W. FIFIELD	on Bristol pottery
W.F.	W.F.B.

painted signature or initials

Finch, Ray   *Cheltenham, Glos.*

studio-potter at Winchcombe since 1946

working in wood-fired
stoneware, with son and
assistants

Fine Arts Porcelain Ltd.   *London*
                     1948–52, earthenware

finger-print, a   *see* Blackie, Sebastian

Finney & Sons Ltd., A.T.   *Longton, Staffs.*
                     c. 1922– , bone-china
     trade-name of 'DUCHESS' included in a wide
     variety of printed marks
     Sold to John Tams in February, 1989

fish, stylized & W.   *see* Walter J.

Fishley, George (*b.* 1771, *d.* 1865)   *Fremington, Devon*
                     domestic and decorative earthenwares,
                     late 18th C. – early 1930s
Fishley, Edmund (*b.* 1839 *d.* 1861)
     earthenware harvest-jugs with sgraffito
        Edmund Fishley Maker,   incised with date
     FISHLEY, EDWIN BEER (*b.* 1861 *d.* 1911)
        E.B.F./FREMINGTON/N.DEVON   incised
     HOLLAND, WILLIAM FISHLEY (*b.*, 1889 *d.* 1970)
     earthenware harvest-jugs, 1902–12,
     after which he went to Braunton & Clevedon,
     factory continued by Staffordshire firm

Five Towns China Co. Ltd.   *Middleport, Staffs.*
                             1957– *c.* 1967, bone-china

FIVE TOWNS CHINA
     CO. LTD   printed in a variety of marks
     ENGLAND

Flacket, Toft & Robinson   *Longton, Staffs.*
    F.T.& R.   1858, earthenware
initials printed in a wide variety of marks

Fletcher, Harry   *see* Della Robbia

Fletcher, Thomas   *Shelton, Staffs.*
                         c. 1795–1820, printer & decorator on
                         other potters' wares, known as
                         'black-printer'
  THOS. FLETCHER   T. FLETCHER   signatures
    Thos. Fletcher & Co. Shelton

Flight & Barr   *see* Worcester

Flight, Barr & Barr   *see* Worcester

Floral China Co. Ltd.   *Longton, Staffs.*

                     1940–51, bone-china
                     various printed marks with
                     either 'FLORAL' or 'FLORETTA'

Floyd, Benjamin   *Lane End, Staffs.*
      B F   *c.* 1843, earthenware
initials printed in a variety of marks

Floyd & Sons, R.   *Stoke, Staffs.*

1907–30, earthenware

printed or impressed

F.M. or F.M. & Co.   *see* Morley & Co., Francis

Fogo, John   *see* Della Robbia

Folch, Stephen   *Stoke, Staffs.*

c. 1819–28, earthenware, stone-china
& possible bone-china (unmarked)

FOLCH'S GENUINE
STONE CHINA   impressed

FOLCH & SONS
(Royal Arms)
NEW CAMBRIAN CHINA

Foley China   *see* Wileman & Co.

Ford & Sons Ltd.   *Burslem, Staffs.*

c. 1893–1938, earthenware & bone-china
'FORD & SONS (CROWNFORD) LTD.'
from 1938

F. & S.   F. & S.   S. & SONS LTD.
                          B

printed in a variety of marks including:
CROWN FORD or CROWNFORD
1987, Elizabethan Fine Bone China Ltd. &
The Rosina China Co. merged, known by 1988

as Crownford Holding Ltd. Known in 1989 as
Crownford China Company Ltd. Trade-names in
1990: Queen's and Elizabethan

Ford, Charles   *Hanley, Staffs.*
                         c. 1874–1904, bone-china

printed or impressed   *c.* 1900–04
1874–1904

Ford, Jack   *see* Della Robbia

Ford, Challinor & Co.   *Tunstall, Staffs.*
        F.C.   1865–80, earthenware
        F.C. & CO.   initials printed in a variety of marks

Ford & Pointon Ltd.   *Hanley, Staffs.*
                         1917–36, bone-china
                         printed *c.* 1920–36
                         (absorbed by Cauldon Group, *c.* 1921)

Ford Pottery   *see* Dawson, J.
                         Maling, C.T.

Ford & Riley   *Burslem, Staffs.*
        F. & R.   1882–93, earthenware
        printed in a variety of backstamps, often
        with name of pattern

Ford & Co., Samuel   *Burslem, Staffs.*

1898–1939, earthenware
printed mark also used by Smith
& Ford, previous owners
trade-name: Samford Ware *c.* 1936–9

Ford, Thomas   *Hanley, Staffs.*

1860–75, bone-china
printed or impressed marks,
numerals indicate month &
year of manufacture,
e.g. June (6) 1872

Ford, T. & C.   *Hanley, Staffs.*

T. & C.F.   *c.* 1854–71, bone-china
printed or impressed marks

Fordy & Patterson   *Newcastle upon Tyne, Tyne & Wear*
1824–1892, earthenware, including lustre
1824–27, J. Fordy & Co.
1827–29, Fordy, Patterson & Co.
1830–47, Jackson & Patterson
1847–51, Thomas Patterson
1851–92, George Patterson

FORDY, & PATTERSON.N.CASTLE. SHERIFF
HILL POTTERY
printed in circular form

J. & P.   Jackson & Patterson, 1830–47

G.P.   a wide range of printed marks including
the initials or full-name of George Patterson,
1851–92; backstamps often with name of pattern
including 'Grecian', 'Willow' or 'Albion'

Forester & Hulme   *Fenton, Staffs.*

1887–93, earthenware

printed

Forester & Co., Thomas   *Longton, Staffs.*

c. 1888, earthenware

printed

Forester Son & Co., Thomas   *Fenton, Staffs.*

1884–1959, earthenware & bone-china

'LTD.' added *c.* 1891
'T.F. & S. LTD.' in a variety of marks,
some with trade-names: PHOENIX
CHINA or PHOENIX WARE

printed 1891–12

Forster & Hunt   *Honiton, Devon*
F.H.   1915–18, earthenware
Honiton   incised mark

153

Foster's Pottery Co.   *Redruth, Cornwall*
    FOSTER'S   1949– , earthenware
    POTTERY
    REDRUTH   stamped mark

Fours, Sylvia Des   *Leatherhead, Surrey*

    studio-potter, working in
    stoneware & porcelain

Fowler, Thompson & Co.   *Prestonpans, Scotland*
    c. 1820–40, earthenware
  FOWLER & THOMPSON
    & CO.   printed or impressed

Fowke, Sir Frederick   *Lowesby, Leics.*
    LOWESBY   *c.* 1835–40, earthenware

    impressed

F.P. or F.N.P.   *see* De Morgan, William
              Featherstone Potteries

F. & R. or F. & R./B   *see* Ford & Riley

fretted square in blue   *see* Worcester

Frith, David   *Denbigh, N. Wales*
          1963– , studio-potter working in

154

stoneware & porcelain
(working with wife, Margaret)

F. & R.P.   *see* F. & R. Pratt Co. Ltd.
F. & R.P.Co.

Fry, Roger   *London*

       c. 1913–19, tin-glazed earthenware
(founder of Omega Workshop)

F.S.   *see* Smith F.

F.S. monogram stylized   *see* Smith, F.

F. & S. or **F & S.**   *see* Ford & Sons
     B

F.T. & R.   *see* Flacket, Toft & Robinson

Fuchs, Annette   *Henley-on-Thames, Oxon.*

       1965– , studio-potter in earthenware,
stoneware & porcelain

Fuchs, Tessa   *Kingston-on-Thames, Surrey*

       1961– studio-potter, working in
high-fired earthenware

Fulham Pottery & Cheavin Filter Co.   *see* Bailey, C.J.C.

Furniss, May   *see* Della Robbia

Furnival & Co., Jacob   *Cobridge, Staffs.*
    J.F. & CO.   *c.* 1845–70, earthenware
  printed in a variety of backstamps

Furnival, Jacob & Thomas   *Hanley, Staffs.*
                    c. 1843, earthenware
  STONE CHINA
    J. & T.F.   printed under Royal Arms

Furnival & Co., Thomas   *Hanley, Staffs.*
    T.F. & CO.   *c.* 1844–6, earthenware
  printed in a variety of marks

Furnival & Sons, Thomas   *Cobridge, Staffs.*
                    1871–90, earthenware

                    'T.F. & SONS' printed in a
                    wide range of marks as a
                    monogram

Furnivals Ltd.   *Cobridge, Staffs.*
                    1890–1968, earthenware

                    'LTD.' added *c.* 1895

                    printed, 1905–13
                    name changed to FURNIVALS
                    (1913) LTD. in 1913–

  Taken over by Barratt's of Staffordshire in
  1967; closed 1968

Futura Art Pottery Ltd.   *Hanley, Staffs.*
                         1947–56, earthenware
   Futura/ART POTTERY LTD.   printed

F.W. & Co. or as monogram   *see* Winkle & Co. Ltd.

G

G. Bros, within star & circle   *see* Grimwade Bros.

G. & Co.   *see* Worcester (Grainger)

G. & Co.   *see* Gallimore & Co. Ltd.
   L

Gallimore & Co. Ltd.   *Longton, Staffs.*
                         1906–34, earthenware

   ⟨ G. & CO. ⟩
        L

                         impressed or printed

Gallimore, Robert & Ambrose   *Longton, Staffs.*
                         1832–37, earthenware, unidentified
                         (then Robert Gallimore alone until 1841)

Galloway & Atkinson   *see* Ouseburn B.P.

Gant, Tony & Janet   *Southfields, London*
                         1957, studio-pottery, stoneware
   TONY GANT   JANET S. GANT   T.G.
     (date)   (date)
   marks incised or painted

Garner, Robert   *Fenton, Staffs.*
       R.G.   late 18th C. earthenware jugs, etc.
rare moulded mark

Gater, Hall & Co.   *Burslem & Tunstall, Staffs.*
    G H & CO   1895–1943, earthenware
initials printed in a wide range of marks, 1895

  printed   printed
   1914–   1914   1936–43
Moved to Burslem in 1907 & taken over by
Barrett's of Staffordshire 1943–: some
earlier marks continued, other marks include
full name of Barrett's. Trade-name:
DELPHATIC (from 1957)

G.B. (with globe)   *see* Grimwades Ltd.

G. & B.   *see* Goodwin & Bullock

G.B. & B.   *see* Griffiths, Beardmore & Birks

G.B.H.   *see* Goodwin, Bridgwood & Harris

G.B.O.   *see* Goodwin, Bridgwood & Orton

G. & C.J.M.   *see* Mason G.M. & C.J.

G.D. monogram   *see* Day, George

G.& D. or G.& D.L.   *see* Guest & Dewsbury
  L

G. & E.   *see* Goodwin & Ellis

Geddes & Son, John   *Glasgow, Scotland*
                        1820–1918, black basalt, earthenware
                        and porcelain in 1830s & 40s.
JOHN GEDDES,   Verreville Pottery was under
Verreville   various ownerships: John Geddes
Pottery   & Son (1824–7), R. A. Kidson,
printed   Robert Cochran & Son. Sold
c. 1820–   in 1918 by Conrad Cochran
       R.A.K. & CO.   R.C. & CO.
      printed *c.* 1845   printed *c.* 1865

Gelson Bros.   *Hanley, Staffs.*
                   1867–76, earthenware
GELSON BROS.
  HANLEY   printed in a variety of marks

Gem Pottery Ltd.   *Tunstall, Staffs.*
                   1961– insolvent 1993, earthenware

                   printed

Genders, Carolyn   *Crawley, Sussex*
                   1980– , studio-potter

G.F.F. or G.F.B.B.T.   *see* Bowers & Co., G.F.

G.F.S.   *see* Smith, George F.

G.H.C. monogram   *see* Rustington Pottery

G.H. & Co.   *see* Gater, Hall & Co.

G. & H.H.   *see* Godwin & Hewitt

Gibson, John & Solomon   *Liverpool, Merseyside*
JOHN GIBSON   early 19th C. earthenware
LIVERPOOL   S. Gibson was a well-known
(date)   Liverpool sculptor whose ceramic
                   models were sometimes fired at
SOLOMON GIBSON   the Herculaneum factory
(date)

Gibson & Sons Ltd.   *Burslem, Staffs.*

1885–1970s, earthenware
trade-names: Albany & Harvey or Royal
Harvey. Transferred to Howard Pottery
Co. Ltd. (1965), Coloroll Ceramics Div.
(1986), Coloroll Ceramics (1990)
printed *c.* 1904–9

Gildea, James   *Burslem, Staffs.*
1885–8, earthenware,

printed mark with pattern name

Gildea & Walker   *Burslem, Staffs.*
G. & W.   1881–5, earthenware
printed initials in a wide variety of marks

Gildea & Walker

$$\frac{4}{82}$$

impressed marks with date,
(April, 1882)
printed trade-mark

Gill, William   *Castleford, Yorks.*

	1858–1929, earthenware
W.G.	1858–mid–70s George Gill
printed	mid–70s–1928, under William
	Gill & William Gill & Sons.
	1928–9, William Gill (Potters) Ltd.

Gimson & Co., Wallis   *Fenton, Staffs.*

	1884–90, earthenware
WALLIS GIMSON &	printed with a beehive & name
CO.	of pattern

Ginder & Co., Samuel   *Fenton, Staffs.*
S. GINDER & CO.   1811–43, earthenware
printed in a variety of backstamps

G.L.A. & Bros.   *see* Ashworth & Bros. Ltd., G.L.

Gladstone China   *see* Proctor & Co. Ltd., George

Gladstone China (Longton) Ltd.   *Longton, Staffs.*
GLADSTONE   c. 1939–52, bone-china
BONE CHINA
MADE IN ENGLAND   printed with crown from 1946–61
Continued as Gladstone China from c. 1952–70
later marks all include Gladstone Bone China

Glass, John   *Hanley, Staffs.*
                              c. 1784–1838, earthenware & stoneware
   GLASS HANLEY   J. GLASS HANLEY
   marks impressed, but initials also apply to
   three other Hanley potters around same period

Glass, Joseph   *Hanley, Staffs.*
                              late 17th C. to early 18th .
                              slipware
   JOSEPH GLASS   name applied in slip

Globe Mark   *see* Clews & Co., George

Globe Pottery Co. Ltd.   *Cobridge, Staffs.*
                              1914– , earthenware
   1932 purchased Ridgways and moved to Shelton
   1948 Globe & Ridgway owned by Lawleys Ltd.
   1952 Lawley Group taken over by S. Pearson & Son
   1964 renamed Allied English Potteries
   1971 Allied English Potteries acquire Doulton
   1973 renamed Royal Doulton Tableware Ltd.
   1984 renamed Royal Doulton Ltd.

G.M.C. (or as monogram)   *see* Creyke & Sons, G.M.

Goddard Ltd., Elaine   *Bruton, Som.*

1939, earthenware

printed label

Godwin, Benjamin E.   *Cobridge, Staffs,*
          B.G.   1834–41, earthenware
initials printed in a wide range of backstamps

Godwin, B.C.   *Burslem, Staffs.*
          B.C.G.   *c.* 1851–
initials printed in a variety of marks

Godwin &Hewitt   *Hereford, Heref.*
1889–1910, tiles

          printed or impressed during life of
          factory

Godwin, John & Robert   *Cobridge, Staffs.*
          J. & R.G.   1834–66, earthenware
initials printed in a variety of marks

Godwin, Rowley & Co.   *Burslem, Staffs.*
          G.R. & CO.   1828–31, earthenware & stone
                              china
initials printed in a wide range of marks

Godwin, Thomas   *Burslem, Staffs.*
          T.G.   1834–54, earthenware

THOS. GODWIN	THOS GODWIN	OPAQUE CHINA
BURSLEM	NEW WHARF	T. GODWIN
STONE CHINA		WHARF

printed or impressed in a wide range of marks

Godwin, Thomas & Benjamin   *Burslem, Staffs.*

    T. & B.G.   *c.* 1809–34, earthenware

     T.B.G.

initials printed in a variety of marks

T. & B. GODWIN

  NEW WHARF   impressed

Goldscheider (Staffordshire) Pottery Ltd.   *Hanley, Staffs.*

                   c. 1950–59, earthenware &

                   bone-china

  printed ✓

Goode & Co., Thomas   *London retailer*

                   c. 1840– offered for sale 1991.

                   'LTD' from 1918

The retailing firm of Thomas Goode & Co. &
Minton had a very close relationship, and from
c. 1840 Minton was Goode's main supplier of
wares which were appropriately marked

Goodfellow, Thomas   *Tunstall, Staffs.*

                   1828–54, earthenware & possibly
                   bone-china

  T. GOODFELLOW   name printed in a variety of marks

Goodwin, Bridgwood & Harris   *Lane End, Staffs.*

     G.B.H.   1829–31, earthenware

printed in a variety of marks

Goodwin, Bridgwood & Orton   *Lane End, Staffs.*

     G.B.O.   1827–9, earthenware

     G.B.& O.   initials printed in a variety of marks

Goodwin & Bullock   *Longton, Staffs.*
  G. & B.   1857–59, bone-china
 initials printed with Staffordshire knot

Goodwin & Ellis   *Lane End, Staffs.*
  G. & E.,   1840, earthenware
 initials printed in a wide range of marks

Goodwin, Stoddart & Co.   *Longton, Staffs.*
  J.G.S. & CO. 1898–1940, bone-china
 initials printed on globe

Goodwins & Harris   *Lane End, Staffs.*
  GOODWINS & *c.* 1831–8, earthenware
  HARRIS   impressed mark

Gordon's Pottery   *Prestonpans, Scotland*
  GORDON   early 19th C.–1832, earthenware
  impressed   G.G. printed, all marks rare

Gordon. William   *nr. Chesterfield, Derbys.*
         1939: 1946–56, salt-glaze stoneware

         incised or impressed mark

Goss W.H.   *Stoke, Staffs.*
  W.H.G.   1858–44, bone-china & Parian

         1931 acquired by H.T. Robinson and
         retitled GOSS CHINA LTD., after
         purchase from Cauldon Potteries.
         1956 production materials purchased
         by Lawley Group and name & trade-mark
  printed   revived by Royal Doulton Ltd., 1985

Govancroft Potteries Ltd. *Glasgow, Scotland*

1913– earthenware & stoneware

trade-names: CROFT, HAMILTON, LUNAR, & CHIEFTAN

CROWN   GOVAN

printed or impressed, 1913–49

Gp *see* Greta Pottery

G.P. & Co. or **G.P.&Co./L.** *see* Proctor & Co. Ltd.

G.R. *see* Richardson, George

G.R. & Co. *see* Godwin, Rowley & Co.

Grainger, George *see* Worcester

Grainger, Lee & Co. *see* Worcester

Grainger, Wood & Co. *see* Worcester

Gray & Co. Ltd., A.E. *Hanley & Stoke, Staffs.*

c. 1912–61, earthenware

Purchased by Portmeirion Potteries Ltd. in 1959. Taken over by Crown Winsor 1990

1912–

printed 1914   printed 1930–45

Gray & Sons Ltd., W.A.   *Portobello, Scotland*
                             c. 1857–1931, earthenware & stoneware
   W.A.GRAY   '& SON' added 1870
   printed   'LTD.' added 1926

Greatbatch, William (*d.* 1813).   *Fenton, Staffs.*
                             c. 1760–80, earthenware potter,
   GREATBATCH   modeller & printer
   full-name, etc., on late printed creamwares

Green & Clay   *Longton, Staffs.*
                        1888–91, earthenware

                        printed or impressed

Green & Co., J.   *London, retailer*
                        1834–*c.* 74
                        (at St. Paul's Churchyard until *c.* 1842)
                        '& SONS' added *c.* 1841
   JAMES GREEN
   UPPER THAMES ST.   printed marks include various
   & 62 CORNHILL   London addresses after 1842
   LONDON

Green & Co., M.   *Fenton, Staffs.*
                        1859–76, earthenware & bone-china
   M. GREEN & CO.   various printed marks including
                        full name
Green, Stephen   *Lambeth, London*
                        c. 1820–58, stoneware

STEPHEN GREEN	STEPHEN GREEN
LAMBETH	IMPERIAL
	POTTERIES
S. GREEN LAMBETH	LAMBETH

all marks, impressed, incised or in relief

Green, Thomas   *Fenton, Staffs.*

T. GREEN   1848–59, earthenware & bone-china
FENTON POTTERIES   printed marks on
earthenware, porcelain
rarely marked

Green, T.A. & Co.   *Fenton, Staffs.*

              c. 1876–89, earthenware & bone-china
T.A. & S.G.   printed in Staffordshire knot &
other various forms of mark
From 1889 this firm became known as the
CROWN STAFFORDSHIRE PORCELAIN CO. In 1973
were take over by Wedgwood Group, who only
rarely use the trade-name of CROWN STAFFORDSHIRE

Green & Co., T.G.   *Church Gresley, Derbys.*

              c. 1864– , earthenware & stoneware

printed, 1888   printed 1930s
a wide variety of other printed marks all
including name, initials or drawing of the church

168

Greene, John   *(d. 1686) Wrotham, Kent.*
       I.G.   *c.* 1670, slipware
  applied in slip

Greenock   *see* Clyde Pottery Co. Ltd.

Greenock Pottery   *Glasgow, Scotland*
    GREENOCK   *c.* 1820–60, earthenware
    POTTERY   printed or impressed in a variety
                     of marks

Greenwood, S.   *Fenton, Staffs.*
                 c. 1790, black basalt
  the full-name impressed is very rare

Grenville Pottery Ltd.   *Tunstall, Staffs.*

                1946– , earthenware

Gresley   *see* Green & Co., T.G.

Greta Pottery   *Stoke, Staffs.*
     G   1938–41, earthenware
      P   printed or painted

griffin, a   *see* Williamson & Sons, H.M.

Griffiths, Arthur J.   *Walton-Le-Wolds, Leics.*

             1949, on own 1983–, studio-potter in
             stoneware & porcelain

             impressed

Griffiths, Beardmore & Birks   *Lane End, Staffs.*
    G.B. & B.   1830–, earthenware
    printed

Grimwade Bros.   *Hanley & Stoke, Staffs.*
                1886–1900, earthenware, majolica
    G. BROS   & bone-china
    printed on star, within a circle

Grimwades Ltd.   *Hanley & Stoke, Staffs.*

                1900–1970s, earthenware & bone-china
                many various fully-named marks
                including: WINTON (1906–), VITRO
STOKE POTTERY HOTEL WARE, ROYAL WINTON, ATLAS BONE
    printed *c.* 1900–   CHINA, *c.* 1934–9
    trade-names: RUBIAN ART (1906), IVORY, (1930),
    & ATLAS. 1978 taken over by Staffordshire
    Potteries Ltd. 1986, bought by Coloroll, 1990
    and sold by receivers to Flowergrove

Grindley Hotel Ware Co. Ltd.   *Tunstall, Staffs.*

                1908–, earthenware
                printed mark
                1987, purchased by Churchill
                Tableware Ltd from Royal Stafford

Grindley & Co. Ltd., W.H.   *Tunstall, Staffs.*

                1880–, earthenware.
                'LTD.' from 1925; 1960 purchased by
                Alfred Clough Ltd; renamed 1978:
                GRINDLEY OF STOKE (CERAMICS) LTD.
    printed   1982, FEDERATED POTTERIES CO. LTD.
    1880–1914   1988, re-purchased by W.H. GRINDLEY

printed 1914–25   printed *c.* 1954–
1991 in hands of receivers. Taken over by Woodlands Pottery,
1991

Grosvenor & Son, Frederick   *Glasgow, Scotland*

1869–*c.* 1924, stoneware & earthenware
'& SON' added in *c.* 1899
'GROSVENOR & SON' printed or impressed
in a variety of marks
First known as Bridgeton Pottery
then changed to Eagle Pottery
GROSVENOR GLASGOW impressed *c.* 1880

Grove & Stark   *Longton, Staffs.*
      G. & S.   1871–85, earthenware & bone-china
initials printed in a variety of marks
   GROVE & STARK
      LONGTON   full-name printed or impressed

Groves, Lavender   *London*
                       1952– , studio-potter

$Groves$

impressed or painted

G.S. monogram *see* Standige, G.

G. & S. (or as monogram)   *see* Grove & Stark

G.S. & Co.   *see* Skinner & Co., George

G.S. & S.   *see* Shaw & Sons Ltd., G.

G.T.M.   *see* Mountford, G.T.

G.T. & S.   *see* Turner & Sons, G.T.

Guernsey Pottery Ltd., The   *Guernsey, C.Is*

1961– , red ware &
studio-pottery

Guest & Dewsbury   *Llanelly, Wales*
G. & D.L.   1877–1927, earthenware
G.D.   initials printed in a variety of marks
L

G.W. or G.W. & S. Ltd.   *see* Warrilow & Sons. Ltd.

G. & W.   *see* Gildea & Walker

G.W.T.S., G.W.T. & S. or G.W.T. & Sons.   *see* Turner & Sons,
G.W.

H

H   *see* Hughes & Co., E.
         Hulme, William

H. & Co.   *see* Hackwood & Co.
                  Hammersley & Co.
                  Hill & Co.,

H. Ltd.   *see* Hoods, Ltd.

H.A. & Co.   *see* Adams & Co., Harvey
                    Alcock & Co. Ltd., Henry
                    Aynsley & Co. Ltd.

H. & A.   *see* Hammersley & Asbury
                  Hulse & Adderley

H. & A. (with ship)   *see* Hulse & Adderley

Hackwood & Co.   *Hanley, Staffs.*
   H. & C.   1807–27, earthenware & stoneware

   HACKWOOD & CO.   impressed marks

Hackwood & Keeling   *Hanley, Staffs.*
   H. & K.   1835–6, earthenware
   printed in a variety of backstamps

Hackwood, William   *Hanley, Staffs.*
   W.H.   1827–43, earthenware
   HACKWOOD   printed or impressed

Hackwood & Son, William   *Shelton, Staffs.*
   W.H. & S.   1846–9, earthenware

W.H. & S.   printed in a variety of backstamps

Hadley & Sons, James   *see* Worcester

Haines, Batchelor & Co.   *London retailers*
H.B.   1880–90
initials printed with name of pattern on
earthenware & bone-china manufactured to
their order

Haile, T.S. (*d.* 1948)   *Dartington, Devon*

c. 1936–43: 1945–8, studio-potter
who also worked in the U.S.A.
impressed mark

Hales, Hancock & Godwin Ltd.   *London*
1922–60, ceramic retailers
H.H.& G.Ltd.   printed in various marks on
wares made to their order

Hall & Sons, John   *Burslem, Staffs.*
I. HALL   1814–32, earthenware
HALL   I. HALL & SONS
printed or impressed in a variety of marks

Hall, Ralph   *Tunstall, Staffs.*
R. HALL   1822–49, earthenware
printed, 1822–41   R. HALL & SON
printed, *c.* 1836
R. HALL & CO.   R.H. & CO.
printed or impressed   printed
1841–9   1841–9

Hall, Samuel   *Hanley, Staffs.*
    HALL   *c.* 1841–56, earthenware figures
rare impressed mark

Hall & Read   *Hanley, Staffs.*
                1882–8, earthenware
  HALL & READ   H. & R.
  HANLEY
printed in a variety of marks

Hall, Tom   *see* Della Robbia

Hallam & Day   *Longton, Staffs.*
    H. & D.   1880–83, bone-china
printed, often with Royal Arms

Hamer, Frank & Janet   *Pontypool, Gwent.*

                1952, studio-potters, working in
                reduced stoneware

Hamilton   *see* Govancroft Potteries Ltd.

Hamilton, Robert   *Stoke, Staffs.*
  HAMILTON   1811–26, earthenware
  STOKE   printed in a variety of marks

Hamilton, Robert   *see* Wolfe, Thomas

Hamlyn, Jane   *nr. Doncaster, Yorks.*
                studio-potter in salt-glazed
                stoneware

Hammersley & Co.   *Longton, Staffs.*

       1827– , bone-china

H. & C.   1932–74 Hammersley & Co. (Longton) Ltd.

       1970, purchased by Spode Ltd., &

       renamed Hammersley China Ltd.,

       this name being taken over by

       Palissy Pottery Ltd. in 1982; until

       1988, when Palissy was demolished;

       Hammersley trade-name purchased by

       Aynsley China Ltd. in 1989.

Many later fully-named marks used.

Hammersley & Asbury   *Longton, Staffs.*

  H. & A.   *c.* 1870–75, earthenware & bone-china

printed, sometimes with Prince of Wales feathers

Hammersley, J. & R.   *Hanley, Staffs.*

  J.R.H.   1887–1917, earthenware & bone-china

  J. & R.H. printed in a variety of marks

Hammersley & Son, Ralph   *Burslem & Tunstall, Staffs.*

  R.H.   1860–1905, earthenware

  printed in a variety of marks, 1860–83

  R.H. & SONS printed 1884–1905

'ENGLAND' added from 1891

Hammond, Henry   *Farnham, Surrey*

       1934–1989 (*d*), studio-potter

       working in stoneware

incised impressed

Hampson & Broadhurst   *Longton, Staffs.*
      H. & B.   1847–54, earthenware
   printed in a variety of marks
   HAMPSON/LONGTON   probably the mark of
   Peter Hampson Jnr. alone from 1854–58

Hampton Ivory   *see* Swinnertons Ltd.

Hancock, Benjamin & Sampson   *Stoke, Staffs.*
      B. & S.H.   1876–81, earthenware
   printed in a variety of marks

Hancock & Co., F.   *Stoke, Staffs.*
                1899–1900, earthenware

              printed

Hancock, Robert   *see* Worcester

Hancock & Sons, Sampson   *Stoke, Staffs.*
             1858–1937, earthenware & possibly
    S.H.   bone-china (moved from Tunstall 1870)
  S. HANCOCK   printed in a variety of marks
  1858–91

  S.H.&S.   S.H. & SONS   printed 1891–1935

             printed 1900–06

printed 1906–12

trade-name: from 1911– 'DUCHESS CHINA'
1935–7 known as S. HANCOCK & SONS (POTTERS) LTD.

Hancock & Whittingham & Co. *Burslem, Staffs.*
    H.W. & CO.   1863–72, earthenware
printed in a variety of patterns

Hancock, Whittingham *Stoke, Staffs.*
    H. & W.   1873–9, earthenware
printed in a wide range of marks

hands, clasped *see* Buckley, Heath & Co.

Hanley China Co. *Hanley, Staffs.*
    H   *c.* 1899–1902, bone-china
    C C^O   printed in crowned Staffordshire knot

Hanley Porcelain Co. *Hanley, Staffs.*
    c. 1891–8, bone-china

  printed

Harding & Cockson *Cobridge, Staffs.*
    COBRIDGE   *c.* 1834–61, earthenware & bone-china
    H. & C.
printed in a variety of marks
HARDING & COCKSON   impressed on bone-china

Harding, Joseph *Burslem, Staffs.*
    J. HARDING   1850–51, earthenware
  printed in a variety of marks

Harding, W.J. *Shelton, Staffs.*
                  1862–72, earthenware
    W. & J.H.   printed in a variety of marks
                  which at times include pattern

Harley, Thomas *Lane End, Staffs.*
                  1805–8, earthenware
  HARLEY   T. HARLEY   T. HARLEY
      impressed   LANE END
                                printed or written

harp, Irish *see* Belleek

Harrison, George *Lane Delph & Fenton, Staffs.*
                  c. 1790–5, earthenware
  G. HARRISON   impressed mark

Harrison & Phillips *Burslem, Staffs.*
    H. & P.   1914–15, earthenware
    BURSLEM
  printed in various marks

Harrop & Burgess *Hanley, Staffs.*
                  1894–1903, earthenware

                  printed

Hart & Son   *London*
      H. & S.   1826–69, ceramic retailers
printed on wares manufactured to order

Hartley, Greens & Co.   *see* Leeds

Hartleys (Castleford) Ltd.   *Castleford, Yorks.*
                          c. 1898–1960, stonewares &
   HARTROX   earthenwares, art wares from 1953
mark on later decorative wares

Hartrox   *see* Hartleys (Castleford)

Harvey, Bailey & Co.   *Lane End, Staffs.*
    H.B. & CO.,   1833–5, earthenware
printed in a variety of marks

Harvey, C. & W.K.   *Longton, Staffs.*
                     1835–53, earthenware, & bone-china
                     made up to 1847
  C. & W.K.H.   C. & W.K.HARVEY   HARVEY
        printed   impressed

Harwood, J.   *Stockton-on-Tees, Cleveland*
   HARWOOD   c. 1849–77, earthenware

   HARWOOD   marks, impressed
   STOCKTON

Hawkins & Son, John   *Henley-on-Thames, Berks.*
                  1867–c. 1935, dealers in glass &
                  ceramics

'FAMOUS HENLEY CHINA'
Est. 1867
HAWKINS
HENLEY-on-THAMES

Hawley Bros.   *Rotherham, Yorks.*

	1868–1903, earthenware
H.B.	'LTD.' added 1897
HAWLEY BROS	marks printed include name or initials

printed mark registered in
1898 and continued by
Northfield Hawley Pottery
Co. Ltd. to *c.* 1919

Hawley & Co., J.   *Foley, Staffs.*

| HAWLEY | 1842–87, earthenware |
| HAWLEY & CO. | marks impressed |

Hawley, W. & G.   *Rotherham, Yorks.*

| | 1863–68, earthenware |
| W. & G. HAWLEY | impressed or printed in a variety of marks |

Hawley, Webberley & Co.   *Longton, Staffs.*

1895–1902, earthenware

printed

H.B.   *see* Burgess, Henry
               Haines, Batchelor & Co.
               Hawley Bros.
               Hines. Bros.

H.B. monogram   *see* Hawley Bros.

H. & B.   *see* Hampson & Broadhurst
                  Heath & Blackhurst
                  Hibbert & Boughey

H. & B. (on pennant)   *see* Burgess, Thomas
                              Harrop & Burgess
H.B. & Co.   *see* Harvey, Bailey & Co.
               Heath, Blackhurst & Co.

H.C. monogram   *see* Coper, Hans

H. & C.   *see* Hammersley & Co.
               Harding & Cockson
               Hope & Carter
               Hulme & Christie

H. & C./F.   *see* Hulme & Christie

H.C. & Co.   *see* Hanley China Co.

H. & D.   *see* Hallam & Day

Heaps, Alan   *Newtown, Powys*
        a h   1973, studio-potter

Heath, Job   *Stoke, Staffs.*
>   JOB HEATH   early 18th C. earthenware
>   slip-trailed

Heath, John   *Burslem, Staffs.*
>   *c.* 1810–22, earthenware, &
>   HEATH   porcelain which is not as yet
>   impressed   identified

Heath, Joshua   *Hanley, Staffs.*
>   *c.* 1740– , earthenware
>   JOSHUA HEATH   incised

Heath, Joseph   *Tunstall, Staffs.*
>   J. HEATH   1845–53, earthenware
>   name printed in a variety of backstamps

Heath & Co., Joseph   *Tunstall, Staffs.*
>   J.H. & CO.   1828–41, earthenware
>   I.H. & CO.   printed in a variety
>   J. HEATH & CO.   of marks

Heath, Thomas   *Burslem, Staffs.*
>   T. HEATH   1812–35, earthenware
>
>   T. HEATH   impressed or printed in a
>   BURSLEM   variety of marks

Heath, Blackhurst & Co.   *Burslem, Staffs.*
>   H. & B.   1859–77, earthenware
>   H.B. & CO.
>   printed in a variety of marks, often with
>   name of pattern included

Heath & Greatbatch   *Burslem, Staffs.*
    H. & G.   1891–93, earthenware
      B   printed or impressed in lozenge

Heath & Son   *Burslem, Staffs.*
   HEATH & SON   *c.* 1800, earthenware
    impressed

Heathcote   *see* Williamson & Sons, H.M.

Heathcote & Co., Charles   *Lane End, Staffs.*
                      c. 1818–24, earthenware, & probably
                      unmarked china
  C. HEATHCOTE & CO.   printed in a variety
                      of marks

Heatmaster   *see* Ellgreave Pottery Co. Ltd.

Hedingham Art Pottery   *see* Bingham, Edward

Hepworth, Joan   *nr. Dorking, Surrey*
                      studio-potter in earthenware &
   full signature   porcelain

Herculaneum Pottery   *Liverpool, Lancs.*
                      c. 1793–1841, earthenware &
  HERCULANEUM   porcelain
 impressed or printed, *c.* 1796–1833

                      impressed or printed under
                      Worthington, Humble & Holland
                      1794–1806

impressed or printed marks, *c.* 1796–1833
HERCULANEUM   impressed mark from *c.* 1822
POTTERY

usually printed in   'Liver' bird printed
red, 1833–36, by   or impressed, *c.* 1836–41
Thomas Case &
John Mort

Heron & Son, Robert *Kirkcaldy, Scotland*

c. 1827–1929, earthenware
better known as 'WEMYSS WARE'
from late 19th C.
The date of 1820 in mark is
that of an earlier pottery
taken over by Heron

printed   'R.H. & SON.' printed in a variety
1920–9   of marks, as also 'R.H.F.P.'
                    (Robert Heron Fife Pottery)

In 1930 Bovey Tracey Pottery Co. purchased
rights to Wemyss ware designs

Hewitt & Leadbeater   *Longton, Staffs.*

1907–1919, bone-china &
Parian

printed mark continued until 1926 by Hewitt Bros.

H.F.   *see* Hughes & Co. E.

H.F.W. & Co. Ltd.   *see* Wedgwood & Co. Ltd., H.F.

H. & G.   *see* Holland & Green

H. & G./B.   *see* Heath & Greatbatch
                         Hollinshead & Griffiths

H H monogram   *see* Hammond, Henry

H.H. & G. Ltd.   *see* Hales, Hancock & Godwin Ltd.

H.H. & M.   *see* Holdcroft, Hill & Mellor

H.I.   *see* Ifield, Henry

Hibbert & Boughey   *Longton, Staffs.*
        H. & B.   1889–90, bone-china
    printed under crown

Hicks & Meigh   *Shelton, Staffs.*
                        c. 1803–22, earthenware & bone-china
        HICKS & MEIGH   impressed or printed on
    earthenware, china not as yet identified with certainty. 'Stone
    China' and Royal Arms, also used in printed marks

Hicks, Meigh & Johnson   *Shelton, Staffs.*

H.M.J.   1822–35, earthenware & bone-china
H.M. & J.   printed in a variety of marks
Royal Arms with 'Stone China' also used
The bone-china has not as yet been clearly
identified

Hilditch & Sons, William   *Lane End, Staffs.*
                1819–35, bone-china

                printed marks

Hilditch & Hopwood   *Lane End, Staffs.*
                1835–59, bone-china

Hill & Co.   *Longton, Staffs.*

H. & CO.   1898–1919, bone-china
impressed or printed in a variety of marks

Hill Pottery Co. Ltd.   *Burslem, Staffs.*
                c. 1861–67, earthenware & bone-china
HILL POTTERY   printed in a variety of marks
BURSLEM   often with pattern name

'J.' with 'S.H.' monogram included in some marks

Hines Brothers   *Fenton, Staffs.*
　　　　　　H.B.　　　　　　　1886–1907, earthenware
　　impressed
　　'HINES BROS.' printed in mark with 'OPAQUE
　　PORCELAINE MANUFACTURERS' on ribbon

H.J. or as monogram   *see* Jones, A.G. Harley

H.J. monogram (also on globe)   *see* Holdcroft, J.
　　　　　　　　　　　　　　　　　　　　　　Haile, T.S.

H.J.C.   *see* Colclough, H.J.

H.J.W.   *see* H.J. Wood, Ltd.

H. & K.   *see* Hackwood & Keeling
　　　　　　Hollinshead & Kirkham Ltd.

H.M.   *see* Matthews, Heber

H.M. with lion rampant   *see* Hudson & Middleton Ltd.

H.M.J. or H.M. & J.   *see* Hicks, Meigh & Johnson

H.M.W. & Sons   *see* H.M. Williamson & Sons

H.N. & A.   *see* Hulse, Nixon & Adderley

Hobson   *see* Hobson, George
　　B

Hobson, Charles   *Burslem, Staffs.*
 C.H.   1865–80, earthenware
 C.H. & S.   initials printed in variety
                                     of marks, 's' added *c.* 1873–5

Hobson, George   *Burslem, Staffs.*
                                     1901–23, earthenware

                                     mark printed or impressed

Hobson, G. & T.   *Burslem, Staffs.*
 HOBSON'S   1883–1901, earthenware
 printed

Holdcroft, Joseph   *Longton, Staffs.*
                                     1865–1940, earthenware & Parian

                                     printed or impressed, 1865–1906

                                     printed 1890–1939
                                     Holdcroft Ltd. *c.* 1906 &
                                     later Cartwright & Edwards,
                                     until closure. Cartwright & Edwards
                                     earthenware productions was sold
                                     to Alfred Clough in 1955

Holdcroft & Co., Peter   *Burslem, Staffs.*
 P.H.& CO.   1846–52, earthenware
 mark printed in a variety of styles

Holdcroft, Hill & Mellor   *Burslem, Staffs.*
 H.H. & M.   printed 1860–70, earthenware

Holdsworth, Peter   *see* Ramsbury

Holland, George Fishley   *Clevedon, Som.*
       1955–9, art pottery

printed, painted or impressed

Holland, John   *Tunstall, Staffs.*
  J. HOLLAND 1852–4, earthenware
 full-name printed in backstamp

Holland, William Fishley   *Clevedon, Som.*
       c. 1921– , earthenware

          I. HOLLAND
 HOLLAND, ISABEL FISHLEY, (daughter)
 1929–42, mark   I. HOLLAND signature

Holland & Green   *Longton, Staffs.*
      1853–82, earthenware & probably
  H. & G.   bone-china
  LATE HARVEY   HOLLAND & HARVEY
 printed or impressed in a variety of marks

Hollins, Samuel   *Shelton, Staffs.*
  S. HOLLINS *c.* 1781–1813, earthenware & stoneware
  HOLLINS   full-names impressed
 Samuel Hollins was a partner of the New Hall China Works

Hollins, T. & J.   *Shelton, Staffs.*

	c. 1785–1820, earthenware &
T. & J. HOLLINS	stoneware
impressed	

Hollins, Thomas, John & Richard   *Hanley, Staffs.*

	c. 1818–22, earthenware & stoneware
T.J. & R. HOLLINS	mark impressed

Hollinshead & Griffiths   *Burslem, Staffs.*

1890–1909, earthenware

printed mark

Hollinshead & Kirkham   *Tunstall, Staffs.*

H. & K.	1870–1956, earthenware
H. & K.	
TUNSTALL	variety of printed or impressed marks, 1870–*c.* 1900
H. & K.	
LATE WEDGWOOD	*c.* 1890– , impressed

printed Unicorn mark from
c. 1890, over 'Hollinshead &
Kirkham/TUNSTALL/ENGLAND'
following take-over of
the Unicorn Pottery,
of Wedgwood & Co. Later marks all include initial
or name of Hollinshead & Kirkham in full

Holmes, Plant & Maydew   *Burslem, Staffs.*
     H.P. & M.   1876–1885, earthenware
   initials printed in a variety of marks

Holmes & Son   *Longton, Staffs.*
     H. & S.   1898–1903, earthenware
     LONGTON   impressed or printed
   other marks include full-name

Honiton Art Potteries   *Honiton, Devon.*
                  1881– , earthenware

THE HONITON	COLLARD HONITON
LACE ART POTTERY	ENGLAND
CO.	
printed or impressed	printed or impressed
1915–	1918–47
HONITON POTTERY	HONITON ENGLAND
DEVON	

         printed or impressed, 1947–

Hoods Ltd.   *Fenton, Staffs.*

          1919– now closed,
          earthenware

          'H. LTD.' printed

hooks, crossed, with JB monogram   *see* Bevington, John

Hope & Carter   *Burslem, Staffs.*
          H. & C.   1862–80, earthenware
     initials printed in a variety of marks

Hornsea Pottery Co. Ltd.   *Hornsea, Yorks.*
                         1949– earthenware

      1951–   1960–   1962   1962–
               all marks printed or impressed
     also in Lancaster, Lancs., from 1974–1987.
     1987, purchased by Peter Black Holdings PLC

     trade-mark in use in 1990:

Howard Pottery Co. Ltd.   *Shelton, Staffs.*
                         1925–1970s, earthenware

          printed 1925–

     acquired by Coloroll Ceramics *c.* 1978

Howell & James   *London*
                         c. 1820–1922, retailers & organizers
          HOWELL &   of exhibitions of amateur &
          JAMES   professional ceramic painting in
          various   the late 1870s & supplier of
          marks   painting materials

                              193

Hoy, Anita   *Acton, London*

1952– , studio-potter in various
ceramic bodies (has worked with
Bullers Ltd. & Doulton)

H.P.Co.   *see* Gibson & Sons Ltd.
              Hanley Porcelain Co.

H.P. & M.   *see* Holmes, Plant & Maydew

H. & R.   *see* Hall & Read

H.S.   *see* Swain, H.

H.& S.   *see* Hart & Son
            Hilditch & Sons
            Holmes & Son

H.T. also monogram   *see* Linthorpe Pottery

Hubble, Nicholas (*d.* 1689) *Wrotham, Kent*
                       c. 1650–1700, slipware
        N.H.   (father & son)
     applied in slip

Hudden, John Thomas   *Longton, Staffs.*
        J.T.H.   1861–*c.* 1883
       LONGTON   name or initials printed in
                         a variety of marks, sometimes
     J.T. HUDDEN   including name of pattern
       LONGTON

Hudson, William   *Longton, Staffs.*

W.H.   1889–1941, bone-china
initials printed in a wide variety of marks
other printed marks include trade-name:
'SUTHERLAND CHINA'

Hudson & Middleton   *Longton, Staffs.*

c. 1941–75, bone-china

both marks were previously used by Hudson
& Middleton prior to merger

Huggins, John   *Swindon, Wilts.*

studio-potter in *terra-cotta*
active in 1989–

Hughes & Co., Elijah   *Cobridge, Staffs.*

1853–67, earthenware
E. HUGHES & CO.   impressed

Hughes & Co., E.   *Fenton, Staffs.*

H   1882–1953, bone-china
impressed, 1882–98

H.F.   impressed or printed in square, 1898–1905
renamed HUGHES (FENTON) LTD. in 1939
trade-names: FENTON CHINA, PALADIN CHINA,
EUSCANCOS. Purchased by Lawleys Ltd., 1948

printed mark of *c.* 1908–12

variety of other marks with
trade-name on globe from
1914–41

Hughes, James   *see* Della Robbia

Hughes, Thomas   *Burslem, Staffs.*
                    1960–94, earthenware
THOMAS HUGHES
IRONSTONE CHINA   impressed mark

Hughes & Son Ltd., Thomas   *Burslem, Staffs.*
THOS. HUGHES &   1895–1957, earthenware & china
SON   mark impressed or printed
ENGLAND   'LTD.' added *c.* 1910

Hull Pottery   *Hull, Humberside*
                    c. 1826–41, earthenware
                    William Bell, Belle Vue Pottery

impressed

printed

Hulme & Christie   *Fenton, Staffs.*
                    1893–1902, earthenware

printed

Hulme & Sons, John   *Lane End, Staffs.*
                    1827–31, earthenware
HULME & SONS.   printed in a variety of marks

Hulme & Sons, Henry   *Burslem, Staffs.*
      W. & H.   1906–32, earthenware
      B   impressed or printed (W. & H.
continued from previous partnership of
Wood & Hulme)

Hulme, William   *Burslem, Staffs.*
                         1891–1941, earthenware

                         from 1925–, William Hulme (Burslem) Ltd.
                         trade-name from 1936: ALPHA WARE

Hulme, William   *Cobridge, Staffs.*
                         1948–58, earthenware

                         printed

Hulse & Adderley   *Longton, Staffs.*
                         1869–74, earthenware & bone-china

                         printed

   H. & A.

Hulse, Nixon & Adderley   *Longton, Staffs.*
    H.N. & A.   1853–68, earthenware & bone-china
  printed in a variety of marks

H.W. & Co.   *see* Hancock, Whittingham & Co.

H.W. & Co. monogram   *see* Hawley, Webberley & Co.

H.W.M. & Sons   *see* Williamson & Sons, H.M.

I

I.B. monogram   *see* Byers, Ian

Iceni Ware   *see* Cowlishaw, W.H.

I.D.B.   *see* Baxter, John Denton

Iden Pottery   *nr. Rye, Sussex*

               1961– , studio pottery, earthenware
               & stoneware by D. Townsend & J.H. Wood
               (moved from Iden to Rye in 1963)

I.E.B. or **I.E.B.**   *see* Baddeley, John & Edward
        W

Ifield, Thomas, Henry & John.   *Wrotham, Kent*
    T.I.   *c.* 1621–1676, rare slipware

    H.I.   initials of above applied in slip

    I.I.

I.G.   *see* Greene, John

I.H.   *see* Heath, J.

I.I.   *see* Ifield, John

I.K.   *see* Kishere, Joseph

I.L.   *see* Livermore, John

IMP. CHINA with lion   *see* Poole, Thomas

Improved Stone China   *see* Burton, S. & J.

Indeo Pottery   *Bovey Tracey, Devon*
               c. 1772–1841, earthenware
    INDEO   impressed

Ingleby & Co., Thomas   *Tunstall, Staffs.*
    T.I.& CO.   *c.* 1834–5, earthenware
  printed in a variety of marks

Ions, Neil   *Moreton-in-Marsh, Glos.*
               studio-potter, earthenware
               musical instruments & sculpture

  signature and date

I.P. monogram   *see* Pirie, I.

Isle of Man Potteries   *Isle of Man*
               1963– , earthenware

Isleworth Pottery *Middx.*
                    c. 1760–1825, earthenware

SHORE & CO.

             Note: 's. & G.' seen on

S. & G.   Wedgwood-type wares are
             usually by Schiller &

S. & G.   Gerbing, Bodenbach, Bohemia
ISLEWORTH

J

J'S, two *see* Doherty, J.

J.A. monogram *see* Ablitt, John

J. & Co. *see* Jackson & Co., J.

Jackson & Co., Harry Fletcher *Torquay, Devon*
                  1921–26, earthenware
H.F. JACKSON & CO. The Mayville Pottery
TORQUAY   impressed

Jackson & Co., J. *Rotherham, Yorks.*
J.J. & CO.   1870–87, earthenware
J. & CO.   initials printed in a variety of marks

Jackson, Job & John   *Burslem, Staffs.*
                               1930–35, earthenware
    J. & J. JACKSON
      JACKSON'S   impressed or printed
     WARRANTED   in a variety of marks

Jackson & Gosling Ltd.   *Longton, Staffs.*
                           c. 1866–1961, bone-china
      J. & G.   'LTD.' from 1928
                   impressed or printed in a
      J. & G.   variety of marks, many including
        L   full name or trade name:
                   'GROSVENOR CHINA'

Jackson & Patterson   *Newcastle upon Tyne, Tyne & Wear*
      J. & P.   1830–45, earthenware
  initials printed in a variety of marks

J.B.   *see* Bell & Co., J. & M.P.

J.B. with swan   *see* Beech, James

J.B. monogram with crossed hooks   *see* Bevington, John

J.B. & Co.   *see* Bennett & Co., J.
                  Bevington & Co., John

J.B. & S.   *see* Broadhurst & Sons, James

J.B.W.   *see* Wathen, James B.

J.C. *see* Clementson, Joseph

J.C./L. *see* Chew, John

J. & C.W. *see* Wileman, James & Charles

J.D. monogram *see* Davidson, John

J.D.B. *see* Baxter, John Denton

J.D. & Co. (or in monogram form) *see* Dimmock & Co., J.

J.E. or J.E. & Co. *see* Edwards, John

J.E.J. *see* Jones, Josiah Ellis

Jelfs, John *Bourton-on-the-Water, Glos.*
1973–, studio-potter, stoneware & porcelain
J.J.   a swan   Bourton on the Water
various marks used

Jenkins, Chris *Huddersfield, Yorks.*
1957– , studio-potter in stoneware

Jersey Potteries Ltd. *Jersey, C.Is*
1946–   1946– , earthenware

1951–

J.E. & S.   *see* Edwards & Son, James

J.F.A.   *see* Adderley, J. Fellows

J.F. & Co.   *see* Furnival, Jacob

J.F.E.Co.Ltd.   *see* Elton & Co. Ltd., J.F.
or as monogram 'Co.F.J.E.LTD.'

J.F. & C.W.   *see* Wileman, James & Charles

J.F.W.   *see* Wileman, James F.

J.G.   *see* Gildea, James

J. & G.   *see* Jackson & Gosling Ltd.

J. & G.A.   *see* Alcock, John & George

J.G.S. & Co.   *see* Goodwin, Stoddart & Co.

J.H.   *see* Huggins, John

J.H. monogram   *see* Hamlyn, J.

J.H.C. & Co.   *see* Cope & Co. Ltd., J.H.

J.H.L. monogram   *see* Leach, John

J.H.R. & Co. monogram   *see* Roth & Co., J.H.

J.H.W.   *see* Walton, J.H.

J.H.W. & Sons.   *see* Weatherby & Sons, J.H.

J.J.   *see* De Morgan
            Jelfs, J.

J.J. & Co.   *see* Jackson & Co., J.

J.K. or **J.K.L.**   *see* Kent, James

J.L.   *see* Leach, Janet

J.L.C.   *see* Chetham, Jonathan Lowe

J.M.   *see* Meir, John

J.M. monogram   *see* Macintyre & Co. Ltd.,J.

J.M.& Co.   *see* North British Pottery
I.M.& Co.   *see* Maudsley & Co.,J.
J.M.Co.   *see* Macintyre & Co.,J.

J.M./F   *see* Mayer, John

J. & M.P.B. & Co.   *see* Bell & Co. Ltd.,J. & M.P.

J.M. & S.   *see* Meir & Son, John
J.M. & Son.
I.M. & S.

Johnson Bros (Hanley) Ltd.   *Hanley, Staffs.*
1913–   1883– , earthenware

other fully named marks include:
'ROYAL IRONSTONE CHINA' 1883–1913
'CARNIVAL' 1955– , taken over by
Wedgwood Group, 1968

Johnson & Co., J.   *see* Elgin Pottery

Johnson, Joseph   *Liverpool, Merseyside*
late 18th– 19th C., engraver of copper-
plates

| I.JOHNSON | JOSEPH JOHNSON |
| LIVERPOOL | LIVERPOOL |

signatures appearing on printed decoration

Johnson Ltd., Samuel   *Burslem, Staffs.*
S.J.   1887–1931, earthenware

S.J.B.   initials printed in a variety of marks

S.J.B.LTD.   'LTD.' added from *c.* 1912
'BRITANNIA POTTERY' from *c.* 1916

JoIoW (on outline of Isle of Wight)   *see* Lester, Jo

Jones & Sons, A.B.   *Longton, Staffs.*
c. 1876–1971, earthenware & bone-china.
A.B.Jones until 1900, then
A.B.Jones & Sons Ltd. 1900–1971
A.B.J. & S.   printed in a variety of marks
A.B.J. & SONS   from 1900
trade-names: 'GRAFTON' & 'ROYAL GRAFTON'
Purchased in 1971 by Crown Lynn Potteries Ltd.
renamed CROWN LYNN CERAMIC (U.K.) LTD.
1985, again changed hands and renamed RGC LTD.
with production under trade-names: ROYAL
GRAFTON CHINA & MARLBOROUGH BONE CHINA

Jones (Longton) Ltd., A.E.   *Longton, Staffs.*
1905–46, earthenware

printed or impressed, 1908–36
PALISSY POTTERY LTD. from *c.* 1930, other
marks included name of Palissy. Taken over
in 1946 by Royal Worcester, until 1982,
when taken over by Hammersley China Ltd.,
who used trade name until 1988.
Palissy Pottery demolished in 1989

Jones, A.G. Harley   *Fenton, Staffs.*
1907–34, earthenware
H.J.   or as monogram
A.G.H.J.   printed in a variety of marks
other initialled marks include trade-names:
FENTONIA WARE, PARAMOUNT, WILTON WARE

Jones, Alice Louisa   *see* Della Robbia

Jones, Annie   *see* Della Robbia

Jones, David Howard   *Leamington Spa, Warwicks.*
studio-potter, *raku* ware

Jones, David Lloyd   *Fulford, Yorks.*
1962– , studio-potter,
stoneware & porcelain

Jones, Elijah   *Cobridge, Staffs.*
1831–9, earthenware

fully named impressed marks and date on
moulded jugs, etc.
'E.J.' printed, but could apply to other
potters of the period

Jones & Co., Frederick   *Longton, Staffs.*
1865–86, earthenware
F.JONES LONGTON   impressed or printed in a
variety of marks

Jones, George   *Burslem, Staffs.*
c. 1854, earthenware
GEORGE JONES   impressed mark

Jones, George   *Stoke, Staffs.*

c. 1861–1951, earthenware & bone-china
from 1872. 'LTD.' added 1873.
'CRESCENT POTTERY' from *c.* 1907
relief, impressed or printed
mark until *c.* 1873, when '& SONS'
on a crescent was added below

Jones, Hannah   *see* Della Robbia

Jones, Josiah Ellis   *Longton, Staffs.*
1868–72, earthenware
J.E.J.   or full-name printed in a variety
of marks

Jones, Shepherd & Co.   *Longton, Staffs.*
1867–8, earthenware
J.S. & CO.   initials printed in a
variety of marks

Jones & Son   *Hanley, Staffs.*
    JONES & SON.   *c.* 1826–8, earthenware
    printed mark

Jones & Walley   *Cobridge, Staffs.*
                       1841–3, earthenware, full named
    J. & W.   impressed or moulded mark with
                       date on jugs, etc.
  initials printed in a variety of marks

Jonroth   *see* Roth & Co., John R.

J.P.   *see* Phillips, P. & J.

J.P. monogram   *see* Jersey Potteries
                         Perryman, J.
                         Pollex, J.

J.P. & Co. (L).   *see* Pratt & Co.Ltd., John

J.P./L.   *see* Proctor, John

J.P. Ltd.   *see* Pearson Ltd., James

J.R. (or J.R.& Co.)   *see* Reeves, James
                           Ridgway, Job
                           Ridgway, John
                           Rogers, J. & G.
                           Rogers & Son, J.

J.R. or J.R./F.   *see* Reeves, James

J.R./B.   *see* Robinson, J.

J.R.B. & Co. *see* Ridgway, Bates & Co., J.

J.R. & F.C. *see* Chetham, J.R. & F.

J. & R.G. *see* Godwin, John & Robert

J.R.H. *see* Hammersley, J. & R.

J.R. & S. *see* Robinson & Son, J.

J.S. *see* Solly, John

J.S. monogram *see* Smith, James

J.S. & Co. *see* Jones, Shepherd & Co.
Shore & Co., J.

J.S.H. or
J. with S.H. monogram *see* Hill Pottery, Burslem

J.S.S.B. *see* Sadler & Sons Ltd., James

J.S.S. monogram *see* Shaw & Sons (LONGTON) Ltd., J.

J.S.W. or as monogram *see* Wild Bros.

J.T. *see* Twemlow, John
Twigg, Joseph

J.T. or as monogram *see* Tams, John

J.T. or J.T.& Sons *see* Thomson & Sons, John

J. & T.B.   *see* Bevington, James & Thomas

J. & T.E.   *see* Edwards, James & Thomas

J. & T.F.   *see* Furnival, Jacob & Thomas

J.T.H.   *see* Hudden, John Thomas

J.V or **J.V. & S.**   *see* Vernon & Son., James
J.V.JUNR.

J.W.   *see* Ward, J.

J. & W.   *see* Jones & Walley

J.W.P.   *see* Pankhurst & Co., J.W.

J.W.R. or **J.& W.R.**   *see* Ridgway, John & William

J.W.& S.   *see* Wilson & Sons, J.

J.Y.   *see* Yates, John

K

K   *see* Kellam, Colin

K's, two facing enclosing O   *see* Kellam, Colin

K. & Co. or K.&Co./B.   *see* Keeling & Co.

K. & Co. (also as monogram)   *see* Kirkby & Co., W.

K. & Co. or **K. & Co./E.**   *see* Kirkland & Co.

K.B. monogram   *see* Pleydell-Bouverie, K.

K. & B.   *see* Kerr & Binns (Worcester)
                        King & Barrett
                        Knapper & Blackhurst

K.E. & Co.   *see* Knight, Elkin & Co.

K.E.B.   *see* Elkin, Knight & Bridgwood

K.E.&B.   *see* King, Edge & Barrett
                       Knight, Elkin & Bridgwood

Keele Street Pottery Co.   *Tunstall, Staffs.*
                        1916–*c.* 1958, earthenware
K.S.P.   among a group of potteries acquired
printed   by Coloroll in 1950 and renamed
                        Staffordshire Potteries Ltd; now known
                        as Coloroll Tableware Ltd. in 1990

Keeling & Sons., Anthony   *Tunstall, Staffs.*
                        1792–1795, earthenware & bone-china
A.E.KEELING   painted in a variety of marks

Keeling, Anthony & Enoch   *Tunstall, Staffs.*
                        c. 1795–1810, earthenware & bone-china
A.& E.KEELING
A.E.KEELING   painted

Keeling, Charles   *Shelton, Staffs.*
                        1822–5, earthenware & bone-china

probably only a decorator, no wares
identified as yet with certainty

Keeling & Co.Ltd.   *Burslem, Staffs.*
                                1886–1936, earthenware
    K. & CO.   K.& CO.B.   K.CO.
initials printed in a variety of marks
                                ENGLAND added *c.* 1891
                                'LTD' from *c.* 1909

                                trade-name: LOSOL WARE from *c.* 1912
                                printed trade-mark adopted
K & Cº B
LATE MAYERS   from previous partnerships

Keeling, Joseph   *Hanley, Staffs.*
                                c. 1802–8, earthenware & stoneware
    JOSEPH KEELING   impressed

Keeling & Co., Samuel   *Hanley, Staffs.*
    S.K.& CO.   1840–50, earthenware & stoneware
    S.KEELING & CO.   initials & name printed
    in a variety of backstamps

Keeling, Toft & Co.   *Hanley, Staffs.*
                                1805–26, stonewares
        KEELING, TOFT & CO.   KEELING & TOFT.
                                impressed marks

K.E. & K.   *see* Knight, Elkin & Knight

Kellam, Colin   *Totnes, Devon*
                                1969–, studio-potter, stoneware

Kelsboro Ware   *see* Longton New Art Pottery

Kennedy & Sons Ltd., Henry   *Glasgow, Scotland*

1866–*c*. 1930, stoneware for commercial
and industrial use
'LTD.' from 1910

Kennedy, James   *Burslem, Staffs.*
                  c. 1818–34, engraver for printed wares
KENNEDY   or J. KENNEDY printed signature

Kennedy, William Sadler   *Burslem, Staffs.*
                  1843–54, earthenware
W.S.KENNEDY   impressed or printed

Kennedy & Macintyre   *Burslem, Staffs.*
                  1854–60, earthenware
W.S.KENNEDY   impressed or printed
& J.MACINTYRE

Kensington Fine Art Pottery Co.   *Hanley, Staffs.*
                  1892–9, earthenware

213

printed or impressed
mark of Kensington Fine
Art Pottery Co.

Kensington Pottery Ltd.   *Hanley & Burslem, Staffs.*

1922–61, earthenware
printed mark
Price & Kensington Potteries Ltd.
from 1961 to at least 1990

Kent, James   *Longton, Staffs.*

	1897–, earthenware & bone-china
ROYAL SEMI CHINA	printed, until *c.* 1915
(Royal Arms)	'LTD.' from 1913
JAMES KENT	various printed marks include
ENGLAND	full name, 'J.K.L.' or 'J.K.'

from 1897 until *c.* 1955, when 'OLD FOLEY'
trade-name was used
1989, renamed JAMES KENT (1989) Ltd. by
new owners, using trade-name 'Old Foley' or
JAMES KENT on crowned globe
Sold by receivers to Hadida Fine Bone China,
April 1989

Kent (Porcelains) Ltd., William   *Burslem, Staffs.*

1944–62, earthenware figures
from 19th century moulds, rarely
marked and often sold as earlier

rare printed mark or 'W B K' moulded

Kerr & Binns   *see* Worcester

Keys & Mountford   *Stoke, Staffs.*
      K. & M.   *c.* 1850–53, Parian ware

      S.KEYS   impressed
  & MOUNTFORD

K.F.A.   *see* Kensington Fine Art Pottery Co.

Kidson & Co., R.A.   *Glasgow, Scotland*
                   c. 1830s–46, earthenware
                   Verreville Pottery
      R.A.K.   printed mark of *c.* 1845

King & Barrett   *Burslem, Staffs.*
                   1898–1940, earthenware &
      K. & B.   stoneware
  impressed or printed in a variety of marks

King, Ruth   *Shipton-by-Beningbrough, Yorks.*
                   1978– , studio-potter, stoneware

King, Edge & Barrett   *Burslem, Staffs.*
      K.E. & B.   1896–7, earthenware
  printed initials in a variety of marks

Kirkby & Co., William   *Fenton, Staffs.*
      K. & CO.   *c.* 1879–85, earthenware & bone-china
      W.K. & CO.   printed or impressed initials
      K. & CO.   also printed as a monogram

Kirkham, William   *Stoke, Staffs.*

           1862–92, earthenware

   W. KIRKHAM   impressed mark

Kirkhams Ltd.   *Stoke, Staffs.*

           1946–61, earthenware
Acquired in 1961 by Portmeiron
Potteries Ltd., who were formerly
A.E.Gray & Co.Ltd.

           printed

trade-name: 'Old Staffordshire Porcelains'

Kirkland & Co.   *Etruria, Staffs.*

           1892– , earthenware

   K.& CO.   *c.* 1938, KIRKLANDS (ETRURIA) LTD.

           1947, KIRKLANDS (Staffordshire) LTD.

   K.& CO.   trade-names: KIRALPO WARE

     E   EMBASSY WARE

initials or full name in a variety of
printed marks, appears to have ceased by 1969

Kishere, Joseph   *Mortlake, Surrey*

           1810–43, stoneware

KISHERE	KISHERE	KISHERE
	MORTLAKE	POTTERY
I.K.		MORTLAKE
		SURREY

all marks impressed
continued by J. Abbot & son, until being
demolished in *c.* 1868

K. & M.   *see* Keys & Mountford

Knapper & Blackhurst *Tunstall & Burslem, Staffs.*

                     1867–71 Tunstall

    K. & B.   1883–8 Burslem

                     earthenware

  KNAPPER AND

  BLACKHURST   initials or full-name in a

variety of printed or impressed marks

Knight, Elkin & Co. *Fenton, Staffs.*

                     c. 1826–46, earthenware &

    K.E. & CO.   probably bone-china

  KNIGHT ELKIN

     & CO.   full-name or initials printed

                     in a variety of marks

Knight, Elkin & Bridgwood *Fenton, Staffs.*

                     c. 1827–40, earthenware, &

    K.E.& B.   possibly bone-china

printed in a variety of marks

Knight, Elkin & Knight *Fenton, Staffs.*

    K.E.& K.   1841–4, earthenware

printed in a variety of marks

Knight, John King *Fenton, Staffs.*

    J.K.KNIGHT   1846–53, earthenware

    I.K.KNIGHT

printed in a variety of marks often

with name of pattern

Knowles & Son, Matthew *Brampton, Derbys.*

    KNOWLES   *c.* 1835–1911, earthenware & stoneware

probable mark

Koch, Gabriele   *London*
                1982– , studio-potter,
                coiled pottery
        full-signature

K.P.H. in Staffordshire knot   *see* Kensington Pottery Ltd.

K Q monogram   *see* Leach, Bernard (K. Quick)

Krusta Ware   *see* Pearson & Co.

K.S.P.   *see* Keele Street Pottery Co.

L

L +   *see* Leach, D.

L. & Sons   *see* Lancaster & Sons

L. & A.   *see* Lockhart & Arthur

Lake & Son Ltd., W.H.   *Truro, Cornwall*
                1872– , earthenware

LAKE'S CORNISH	LAKE'S HANDMADE
POTTERY TRURO	CORNISH POTTERY
	TRURO ENGLAND

        printed or impressed marks

Lakin & Poole   *Burslem, Staffs.*
                c. 1791–5, various types of
                pottery & figures

LAKIN & POOLE   L. & P.
                                        BURSLEM

POOLE, LAKIN & CO.
          all marks impressed

Lancaster & Sons *Hanley, Staffs.*
          L.S.   1900–44, earthenware
printed in a variety of marks
'& Sons' or '& S.' added 1906–
'LTD.' added 1906

LANCASTERS LTD.
HANLEY
ENGLAND
printed under crown
c. 1938–44

printed from 1920–
trade-names: Royall & Lansan 1930–
British Crown Ware, *c.* 1935–, Crown
Dresden Ware, *c.* 1935–

Lancaster & Sandland Ltd.   *Hanley, Staffs.*
                    1944–, earthenware
BRITISH CROWN WARE   1935–, 'Crown DresdenWare',
     1935– , many printed marks including full-
     name or 'SANDLAND' from 1949. Mark from 1961
     suggests bone-china was being made at that time

Lane, Peter   *Alresford, Hants.*
          1987– , studio-potter working in
                    porcelain
                    or full signature

Langdale Pottery Co. Ltd.   *Hanley, Staffs.*
    Langdale   1947–58, earthenware
MADE IN ENGLAND
    printed

Langley Ware   *see* Lovatt & Lovatt

Landore Pottery   *see* Calland & Co.,J.F.

Lawleys Ltd.   *Stoke, Staffs.*
               1921– , ceramic retailers & potters
first established in Birmingham in 1908,
Lawleys (1921) Ltd. in 1921 and renamed
Lawleys Ltd. in 1929
Began manufacturing also *c.* 1936, acquiring
North Staffordshire Pottery Co. in 1940
and by 1948 had taken over 10 companies
as Lawley Group Ltd., who were in turn taken
over by S. Pearson & Son Ltd. in 1952, who
adopted name of Allied English Potteries,
who merged with Royal Doulton in 1972

Lawrence (Longton) Ltd., Thomas   *Longton, Staffs.*

               1892–1964, earthenware
other printed or impressed
marks with Falcon Ware or
artists' palette

  printed, 1936–

L B monogram   *see* Burgess & Leigh

L & C or L.C.   *see* Lemon & Crute

L D monogram   *see* Leach, D.

Leach, C.B.E., Bernard H.   *St. Ives, Cornwall*
1921– *d.* 1979, studio-potter

  Leach Pottery marks

 personal marks of
Bernard Leach

mark of Shoji Hamada, who worked
with Bernard Leach 1920–23, 1929–
30 (*d.* 1978)

Leach, David   *Bovey Tracey, Devon*
1930 (with father Bernard
Leach until 1956) studio-
potter working in stoneware &
porcelain

 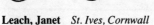

Leach, Janet   *St. Ives, Cornwall*
1956– , studio-potter, stoneware
(wife of the late Bernard Leach)

Leach, Jeremy   *London*
c. 1959– , studio-potter
    J.L.   incised or impressed

Leach, John   *nr. Langport, Som.*

1964– , studio-potter, working
with wife & family in stoneware
(grandson of the late Bernard Leach)

Leach, Margaret   *Brockweir, Monmouth, & elsewhere*

1946–56, studio-potter
impressed mark when working at
the Taena Community, Aylburton,
Glos. from 1951–

Leach, Michael   *Fremington, Devon*

1956– *d.* 85, studio-potter
(son of the late Bernard Leach)

Leadbeater, Edwin   *Longton, Staffs.*

c. 1919–24, bone-china

printed or impressed

Lear, Samuel   *Hanley, Staffs.*

LEAR
impressed

1877–86, earthenware, stoneware
& bone-china & decorator of
other potters' wares

Ledgar, Thomas P.   *Longton, Staffs.*

      c. 1898–1905, earthenware
  T.P.L.   & bone-china
printed or impressed in a variety of marks

Leeds Pottery   *Leeds, Yorks.*

      c. 1770–1881, earthenware
      & stoneware

Green Bros., 1770–   LEEDS *POTTERY
         impressed

Humble, Green & Co., 1774–76

Humble, Hartley, Greens LEEDS POTTERY
& Co., 1776–1780

Hartley, Greens & Co.
1781–1830

1800–1830

all marks impressed

1780–1810
impressed or enamelled   **LP**

Britton & Son, Richard   R.B. & S.
1872–8, earthenware   printed
initials found on variety
of transfer-printed wares

Rainforth & Co. 1800–17   RAINFORTH & CO.
Petty's Pottery, 1817–46   PETTYS & CO. LEEDS
earthenware & creamware

                    printed or impressed

Leeds Fireclay Co. Ltd.   *Leeds, Yorks.*
              L   1889–*c.* 1912, earthenware
              F.C.   production of art wares
                           ceased about this time
          LEFICO   GRANITOFTS
      registered trade-names of 1905 & 1906

Leeds Pottery Co. Ltd.   *Burslem, Staffs.*
                    1988– , 'Authentic Leeds Ware'
      transferred from Leeds by Leeds & City
      Corporation in 1988, starting at Leeds
      in 1982

Leighton Pottery Ltd.   *Burslem, Staffs.*
              1940–54, earthenware
      fully-named printed mark or 'Royal
      Leighton Ware' on banner

Lemon, William   *Weston-super-Mare, Som.*
                    1926–*c.* 1939, art pottery

                          224

T. W. Lemon + Son

Wesuma Pottery

Weston-S-Mare

Lemon, William & Crute, Harry   *Torquay, Devon.*
                                    1913–*c*. 39, art pottery

LEMON & CRUTE Tor Vale
Lemon + Crute L&C
Daison Art Pottery
         Torquay

W. Lemon left in *c*. 1926 to start Wesuma
Pottery, Weston-super-Mare, Somerset

Lessore, Emile   *see* Wedgwood & Sons Ltd., J.

Lester, Jo   *Freshwater, Isle of Wight*

1953–, studio-potter in earthenware
printed or impressed.
'Freshwater' sometimes added
to mark

Lewenstein, Eileen   *Brighton, Sussex*

c. 1950– , studio-potter in
stoneware & porcelain

L   *see* Leeds Fireclay Co.
F C

L.F.M.   *see* Matthew, L.F.

L. & H. or **L.&H.**   *see* Lockett & Hulme
L. E.

Liddle, Elliott & Son   *Longport, Staffs.*
                             1862–69, earthenware, &
          L.E. & S.   unidentified bone-china
    impressed or printed in a variety of marks

Lingard, Webster & Co. Ltd.   *Tunstall, Staffs.*
                                   1900– *c.* 71, earthenware

                             printed or impressed
                             from *c.* 1946

Linthorpe Pottery   *Middlesbrough, Cleveland*
                         1879–89, art pottery, specializing
     LINTHORPE   in glazes
     impressed   Established by John Harrison
                          Henry Tooth, manager *c.* 1880–82
                          Dr. Christopher Dresser, designer &
                          director, 1879–*c.* 84

                  impressed

lion (rampant)   *see* Adderley, J. Fellows

lion with globe   *see* Hawley Bros & Northfield Hanley Pottery

Liverpool   *Liverpool, Merseyside*
The following major potters are known to
have been producing porcelain in Liverpool
during the 18th C., but no factory-marks
or any aids to sure identification appear
to have been used: Samuel Gilbody, Richard
Chaffers, Philip Christian, Seth Pennington,
James Pennington, John & Jane Pennington,
Zachariah Barnes & W. Reid & Thomas Wolfe

Livesley, Powell & Co.   *Hanley, Staffs.*
1851–65, earthenware, Parian &
LIVESLEY POWELL   bone-china
& CO.

BEST L.P. & CO.   L.P. & CO.
impressed or printed in a variety of marks

L J   *see* Jones, D.L.

Lloyd, John & Rebecca   *Hanley, Staffs.*
c. 1834–52, earthenware & bone-
china figures, including
'shaggy' poodles
LLOYD SHELTON   LLOYD
impressed marks   SHELTON

L M   *see* Leach, Michael

Locke & Co.   *see* Worcester

Locker & Co.   *see* Derby

Lockett, Baguley & Cooper   *Hanley, Staffs.*
                  c. 1855–61, earthenware & bone-china
   Full-name only on earthenware, only Patent
   Office registration marks on some china or
   rare publishing mark with name & date

Locket & Hulme   *Lane End, Staffs.*
        L. & H.   1819–26, earthenware
          LE   printed initials in a variety of marks
   (*see also* Lockett & Shaw)

Lockett & Son, John   *Longton, Staffs.*
                  1827–35, earthenware
     J. LOCKETT   impressed
   (*see also* Lockett & Shaw)

Lockett & Shaw   *Longton, Staffs.*
                  1796–1804, earthenware & bone-china
                  from 1805 under later owners
   Lockett & Co., George, 1805–16
   Lockett, Robinson & Hulme, 1816–18
   Lockett & Hulme, 1819–26. Mark, L & H
   Lockett & Son., John, 1827–35, Mark 'J. LOCKETT'
   Lockett, John & Thomas, 1836–55, Mark
                  'J. LOCKETT & CO'.
                  'J. LOCKETT & SONS'
   Lockett, John, 1855–c. 65
   continued by Hancock, J.W. & Hancock, R.L.
   to c. 1956, then Burgess & Leigh to c. 1980

Lockett, William   *Notts.*

                        c. 1740–80, stoneware
Wm. Lockett   incised signature

Lockhart & Arthur   *Glasgow, Scotland*

                        1855–1952, earthenware & chimney
       L. & A.   piece ornaments
LOCKHART & ARTHUR   initials or name
printed or impressed in a variety of marks
1864– trading as D. Lockhart & Co.
1894– trading as David Lockhart & Sons.
continuing in family until 1952
     D. L & CO.   D.L. & SONS.
printed in various marks. Note: in
marks 'POLLOKSHAWS' is spelt 'POLLOCKSHAWS'

Lockitt, William H.   *Hanley, Staffs.*

       W.H.L.   1901–19, earthenware
         H.   printed in crescent 1901–13
DURA-WARE, with lion rampant over name
in printed mark from 1913

Longbottom, Samuel   *nr. Hull, Humberside*

       S.L.   late 19th C.–1899, earthenware
impressed

Longpark Pottery Co. Ltd.   *Torquay, Devon*

             1883–1940. & 1947–57, earthenware
             LONGPARK   TORMOHUN
             TORQUAY   WARE
             c. 1910–30   *c.* 1903–14

             c. 1885, impressed

Longton Hall   *Longton, Staffs.*

c. 1749–60, porcelain
rare marks painted in
underglaze-blue on early
wares

Longton New Art Pottery Co.   *Longton, Staffs.*

1932–66, earthenware
Kelsboro'   various printed marks include
Ware   trade-name: 'Kelsboro'

Longton Porcelain Co. Ltd.   *Longton, Staffs.*
L.P.Co.   *c.* 1892–1908, bone-china
printed in monogram form within strap

Longton Pottery Co. Ltd. *Longton, Staffs.*

1946–55, earthenware
L.P.CO. LTD.   various printed marks with
initials or full name & trade-name:
Blue Bell Ware

Losol Ware   *see* Keeling & Co.

Lottie Rhead Ware   *see* Ellgreave Pottery Co. Ltd.

Lovatt & Lovatt   *Langley Mill, nr. Nottingham*

1895– , earthenware & stoneware

c. 1900   *c.* 1931–62

LANGLEY WARE   impressed mark from *c.* 1895
Lovatt's Potteries Ltd. from 1931–
acquired by Bourne's of Denby, 1959,
but continuing under own name

Lovique Ware   *see* Lovatt & Lovatt

Lowe, William   *Longton, Staffs.*

c. 1874–1930, earthenware &
bone-china

printed or impressed, 1874–1912
other printed marks include initials or
full-name and trade-name: COURT CHINA,
or ROYAL SYDNEY WARE

Lowe, Ratcliffe & Co.   *Longton, Staffs.*

1882–92, earthenware

printed or impressed

Lowesby Pottery   *see* Fowke, Sir Frederick

Lowestoft   *Lowestoft, Suffolk*

/ 3 5
c. 1757–*c.* 1801, soft-paste
porcelain, little production
after *c.* 1799.
selection of workmen's tally-marks painted
in underglaze-blue on inner footrim, 3 & 5
being the most common, 5 usually on dated wares

marks from Lowestoft wares in Norwich
Castle Museum:

1.   2.   3.

1.   Crescent mark in imitation of Worcester hand-painted
      wares from *c.* 1770
2.   'hatched crescent' after Worcester, usually on transfer-
      printed wares
3.   'crossed-swords' sometimes applied to wares decorated
      in imitation of Meissen

L.P. monogram   *see* Lane, P.
                    Skipwith, M. & E.

L.P.Co. & as monogram   *see* Longton Porcelain Co.
                            Longton Pottery Co.

L.P. & Co.   *see* Livesley, Powell & Co.

L. & P.   *see* Lakin & Poole

L R monogram   *see* Rie, Lucie

L.R.& Co. monogram   *see* Lowe, Ratcliffe & Co.

L.S.   *see* Lancaster & Sons

L. & Sons Ltd.   *see* Lancaster & Sons

Luckock (or Lucock), John   *see* Wolfe, Thomas

Lunar   *see* Govancroft Potteries Ltd.

Lund & Miller   *see* Bristol Porcelain

Lustrosa   *see* Ashworth & Bros Ltd., G.L.

M

M   *see* Cadborough Pottery
          Maddock, John
          Maling
          Matthews, L.F.
          Minton
          Schloessingk, M.

M. & Co.   *see* Minton
               Moore & Co., Fenton
               (M) Moore & Co., Hanley

M. & A.   *see* Morley & Ashworth

Machin & Potts   *Burslem, Staffs.*
                   1833–40, earthenware & bone-china
   MACHIN & POTTS

   MACHIN & POTTS   patent for multi-colour
       PATENT   printing, 1835
   printed in a variety of marks

Machin & Thomas   *Burslem, Staffs.*
      M. & T.   *c.* 1831–2, earthenware
      printed

Macbride, Kitty   *London*

1960– , earthenware figures of
mice. Trade-name: The Happy Mice
of Berkeley Square

Kitty MacBride
England

Macintyre & Co. Ltd., J.   *Burslem, Staffs.*

1860–1928, earthenware

MACINTYRE   J. MACINTYRE

printed or impressed, *c.* 1860–7

J.M. & C.   J. MACINTYRE & CO.

printed or impressed, *c.* 1867–1928

'LTD.' added to mark from 1894

Mackee, Andrew   *Longton, Staffs.*

A. M.   1892–1906, earthenware & bone-china
L.   impressed or printed

Maddock, John   *Burslem, Staffs.*

M   1842–55, earthenware

MADDOCK   initial or name printed in a variety
of backstamps, but 'M' used by other
potters

Maddock & Sons Ltd., John   *Burslem, Staffs.*

1855–1987, earthenware of various
kinds. 'LTD.' added to title 1896,
many fully-named printed marks, including the
trade-names: Ironstone China, with '& Son'

used from *c.* 1855. Vitrified or Royal
Vitreous (1880–*c.* 96), Royal Stone China &
Royal Semi Porcelain (from 1906), Royal
Ivory (*c.* 1927–) Embassy (*c.* 1935). Late
marks include 'ENGLAND'.
Trade-name purchased by Royal Stafford
China in 1987, when factory was demolished

Maddock & Seddon   *Burslem, Staffs.*
     M. & S.   *c.* 1839–42, earthenware
printed in a variety of marks, often with
name of pattern

Madeley   *see* Randall, Thomas M.

Magson, Mal   *Scarborough, N. Yorks.*

1973– , studio-potter, specializing
in an unusual method of laminating
stoneware & porcelain

Maling, Christopher Thomas & John   *Sunderland, Tyne & Wear*
                         1762–*c.* 1848, earthenware

HYLTON POT WORKS	MALING
	impressed, early 19th C.
JOHN PHILLIPS	Maling, C.T. & J. 1762–*c.* 97
HYLTON POTTERY	Maling, J. & R. *c.* 1797–1815
	Phillips, J. 1815–*c* 1848

J. PHILLIPS
HYLTON POTTERY
  printed

Maling, C.T.   *Newcastle upon Tyne, Tyne & Wear*
                                    The Ford Pottery
        MALING   1859–1926, earthenware
          K
impressed on food containers for Keiller, with
leadless glaze

        MALING   New Ford Pottery of C.T. Maling from
           1879–
                        C.T. Maling & Sons from 1890, and taken
                        over by Frederick Hoult in 1947, closing
                        in 1963

        c. 1890

c. 1897   *c.* 1911   *c.* 1919

MALING
MADE IN
ENGLAND
c. 1937

c. 1946   *c.* 1949–63
selection of printed marks from 1879–1963

236

Malkin, Frederick   *Burslem, Staffs.*
1891–1905, earthenware

printed

Malkin, Ralph   *Fenton, Staffs.*
R.M.   1863–81, earthenware
initials printed in a variety of marks
usually including name of pattern

Malkin & Son, Ralph   *Fenton, Staffs.*
R.M. & S.   1882–92, earthenware
initials printed in a variety of marks
usually including name of pattern

Malkin, Samuel   *Burslem, Staffs.*
early 18th C. slip-trailed
S.M. or   earthenware
SAMUEL MALKIN   included in decoration

Malkin, Walker & Hulse   *Longton, Staffs.*
M.W. & H.   1858–64, earthenware
printed in a variety of backstamps, which
usually include name of pattern

Maltby, John   *Crediton, Devon*
1964, studio-potter, working in
MALTBY   stoneware

237

Malvern Chinaware   *see* Booth & Colclough Ltd.

Mann & Co.   *Hanley, Staffs.*
   MANN & CO.   1858–60, earthenware & bone-china
     HANLEY
  printed in a variety of marks often with
  name of pattern

Mansfield Works   *see* Billingsley, William

Manzoni, Carlo   *Hanley, Staffs.*
                        c. 1895–8, studio-pottery
                        joined staff at Della Robbia
                        c. 1898–99
                        incised mark including date

Manzoni, Giovanni Carlo (*d.* 1910)   *see* Della Robbia

Margrie, C.B.E., Victor   *Moretonhampstead, Devon*
                        1952, studio-potter

                        impressed

Marshall & Co.Ltd., John   *Bo'ness, Scotland*
  JOHN MARSHALL &   1854–99, earthenware
        CO.   'LTD.' added 1897
     printed

Marshall, Ray   *Stedham, Sussex*

                        1945– , studio-potter in stoneware
                        impressed or full-signature & date

Marshall, William   *St. Ives, Cornwall*

         1954–, studio-potter, former
         student of Bernard Leach

     1956–   **impressed**   incised, 1954

Martin Brothers   *Fulham & Southall, London*

         1873–1914, studio-potters
Robert Wallace *d.* 1923, Walter *d.* 1912,
Edwin *d.* 1915 & Charles *d.* 1910

   1873–5   R. W. Martin fecit

   1873–4

   1874–8

   1878–9

SOUTHALL	MARTIN
MARTIN	SOUTHALL
POTTERY	POTTERY

   1879–82

   1882–

all marks either incised or impressed together
with month and year

Martin, Shaw & Cope *Longton, Staffs.*
   MARTIN SHAW   1822–23, bone-china
     & COPE
   IMPROVED CHINA   printed

Mason, Charles James *Lane Delph, Staffs.*
                      c. 1845–8, earthenware

             printed, 1845–

Mason & Co., Charles James *Lane Delph, Staffs.*
                  1830–45, earthenware
'MASON'S CAMBRIAN ARGIL'   impressed or
'MASON'S BANDANA WARE'   printed
                      c. 1825–40

    FENTON   FENTON
   STONE WORKS   STONE WORKS
   C.J.M.& CO.   C.J.M. & CO.
   GRANITE CHINA
   printed in a variety of marks, 1830–45

Mason, G.M. & C.J. *Lane Delph, Staffs.*
                c. 1813–30, earthenware including
   G. & C.J.M.   MASON'S PATENT IRONSTONE CHINA
                & porcelain
  C.M. & C.J.MASON
    c. 1820
PATENT IRONSTONE CHINA   printed *c.* 1825

Mason, Miles   *Lane Delph, Staffs.*

M.MASON

MILES MASON
impressed

c. 1800–*c.* 1813, porcelain, both
hard-paste & bone-china
At Liverpool 1792–1800
(unmarked wares)

printed mark on 'CHINOISERIE'
patterns

(*see* Wolfe, Thomas)

MASON'S IRONSTONE now taken over by
Wedgwood Group, having been
owned by Francis Morley, *c.* 1848–62, &
G.L. Ashworth & Bros., *c.* 1862–1973

Mason, William   *Lane Delph, Staffs.*

W. MASON   *c.* 1811–24, earthenware
rare printed mark

Mason, Holt & Co.   *Longton, Staffs.*

M.H. & CO.   1857–84, bone-china
printed or impressed in a variety of marks

Mason's   *see also* Ashworth & Bros. Ltd.

Mason's Ironstone   *see* Ashworth & Bros. Ltd.

Massey, Wildblood & Co.   *Longton, Staffs.*

M.W. & CO.   *c.* 1883–6, bone-china
printed in a variety of marks

Mathews, Heber (*d.* 1958)   *Lee, Kent*

H M

1931–58, studio-potter working
in stoneware & porcelain
incised initials

Matthews & Clark   *Longton, Staffs.*

c. 1902–6, decorators only of

M. & C.   bone-china & earthenwares

L.   initials printed in ornamental frame

Matthews, John   *Weston-Super-Mare, Avon*

1871–88, *terra-cotta* ornamental
wares & tiles

JOHN MATTHEWS

"LATE PHILLIPS"   early Matthews mark

ROYAL POTTERY   including 'Royal Pottery'

WESTON-SUPER-MARE

impressed over Royal Arms

Matthews, Leo Francis   *nr. Shrewsbury, Shrops.*

·M· **'FM·**

1954– , active in '89,
sculpture, murals & pottery
painted or incised marks

Mattona Ware   *see* Price Bros. (Burslem) Ltd.

Maudesley & Co., J.   *Tunstall, Staffs.*

STONE WARE   1862–4, earthenware

J.M. & CO.

printed mark attributed to this pottery

Maw & Co. Ltd.   *nr. Jackfield, Shrops.*

c. 1850–1967, tiles, and art pottery

242

MAW   MAW & CO.   MAW & CO.
                                           BROSELEY

impressed, moulded or printed, 'Brosley'
added to mark in *c.* 1857

FLOREAT MAW   *c.* 1880. ENGLAND' after 1891
SALOPIA

Mayer, Elijah   *Hanley, Staffs.*
                     c. 1790–1834, earthenware & unidentified
                     porcelain from *c.* 1805

E. MAYER   E. MAYER & SON
impressed   impressed or printed

Mayer & Elliott   *Longport, Staffs.*

1858–60, earthenware, Parian
& bone-china

printed mark, with month & last two
numerals of year impressed, e.g.

$$\frac{6}{59} = \text{June, } 1859$$

Mayer, John   *Fenton, Staffs.*

J. M.   *c.* 1832–41, earthenware & bone-china
F   printed in a variety of marks
bone-china wares as yet unidentified

Mayer & Co., Joseph   *Hanley, Staffs.*

JOSEPH MAYER & CO.   *c.* 1822–33, earthenware
HANLEY   MAYER & CO.
impressed or printed marks

Mayer, Thomas   *Stoke, Staffs.*

	1826–35, bone-china &
T. MAYER	earthenware
T. MAYER, STOKE	printed in a variety

of marks, bone-china production as yet
unidentified

Mayer, Thomas, John & Joseph   *Burslem, Staffs.*

c. 1842–55, Parian & Pratt-type
multi-coloured printed earthenware

T.J.& J.MAYER
full name included in various printed marks

Mayer & Maudesley   *Tunstall, Staffs.*

| M. & M. | 1837–8, earthenware |
| printed | |

Mayer & Newbold   *Lane End, Staffs.*

c. 1817–32, earthenware & bone-china
M. & N.   MAY^R & NEWB^D

Mayer & Newbold

painted or printed in a variety of marks

Mayer & Sherratt   *Longton, Staffs.*

| M & S. | c. 1906–41, bone-china |
| L | |

initials printed under crown, other marks
include the trade-names: MELBA CHINA or
MELBA BONE CHINA

M.B.   *see* Bayley, Michael

M. & B.   *see* Minton (Minton & Boyle)

M.C. monogram   *see* Casson, Michael

M C over C P monogram   *see* Clinton, Margery

M. & C.   *see* Matthews & Clark
   L

McGarva, A.   *Ross-on-Wye, Heref.*
                         studio-potter, stoneware

McKenzie, Warren   *Dartington, Devon*
                         1950–, studio-potter
                         mark when with Bernard Leach

                         1950–52

                         mark at Dartington– , 1963–

McNay & Sons, Charles W.   *Bo' ness, Scotland*
                         1887–1958, earthenware

labels with 'DALMENY' trade name, 1946–

McNeal & Co.Ltd.   *Longton, Staffs.*

1894–1906, earthenware

printed

M. & E.   *see* Mayer & Elliott

Meakin Ltd., Alfred   *Tunstall, Staffs.*

1875–, earthenware and imported bone-china

ALFRED MEAKIN   ALFRED MEAKIN LTD

impressed or printed, 'LTD.' from 1897

printed mark *c.* 1875–97

printed mark
c. 1891– with
'ENGLAND'

retitled Alfred Meakin (Tunstall) Ltd. 1913–
purchased by Myott & Son Co. Ltd., trading as
Myatt-Meakin (1982) Ltd. at Hanley, with
their bone-china being produced in Pakistan.
Later marks include trade-names: BLEU DE ROI,
ROYAL IRONSTONE CHINA, ROYAL SEMI PORCELAIN

Meakin, Charles   *Hanley, Staffs.*

1883–9, earthenware

246

CHARLES MEAKIN   printed under
     HANLEY   Royal Arms

Meakin, Henry   *Cobridge, Staffs.*
   IRONSTONE CHINA   1873–6, earthenware
     H. MEAKIN   printed under Royal Arms

Meakin Ltd, J.&G.   *Hanley, Staffs.*

1851– earthenware
printed mark *c.* 1890–
numerous other marks from *c.* 1912
include full-name, IRONSTONE CHINA,
or trade-name: SOL, PASTEL
VITRESOL, STUDIO-WARE, or SOUTH SEAS
merged with W.R.Midwinter, 1968
taken over by Wedgwood Group 1970

Meanley, Peter   *Bangor, N.Ireland*
                 1987– , studio-potter specializing
     pm 88   in stoneware teapots
  initials with date

Meigh, Charles   *Hanley, Staffs.*
      C.M.   1835–49, earthenware & stoneware.
   CHARLES MEIGH   full-name or initials in
large range of impressed marks, some with
Royal Arms or name of pattern, including:
INDIA STONE CHINA, FRENCH CHINA, ENAMEL
PORCELAIN and IMPROVED STONE CHINA, which
was also used by Minton & S. & J. Burton

Meigh & Son, Charles   *Hanley, Staffs.*
     M. & S.   1851–61, earthenware
   C. M. & S.

C. MEIGH & SON   OPAQUE
                                                  PORCELAIN
MEIGH'S   printed or
(Royal Arms)   impressed
CHINA

marks printed in a variety of styles

Meigh, Son & Pankhurst, Charles   *Hanley, Staffs.*
CM.S.&P.   1850–51, earthenware
initials printed in a variety of designs

Meigh, Job   *Hanley, Staffs.*
                      c. 1805–34, earthenware & possibly
MEIGH   bone-china from *c.* 1812
impressed, 1805–
OLD HALL   impressed or printed mark, 1805–
'& SON' added from *c.* 1812

Meigh, W. & R.   *Stoke, Staffs.*
                      1894–9, earthenware

printed

Meir China or Meir Ware   *see* Barker & Son Ltd.

Meir, John   *Shelton, Staffs.*
                      late 17th – early 18th C.
JOHN MEIR   slip-trailed earthenwares
slip-trailed name & dated 1708

Meir, John   *Tunstall, Staffs.*
J.M. or I.M.   printed *c.* 1812–36, earthenware

Meir & Son, John   *Tunstall, Staffs.*

    J.M. & SON.   1837–97, earthenware

    I.M. & S.   J.M. & SON   J. MEIR & SON

                     MEIR & SON

name or initials printed in a variety of marks,
to which 'ENGLAND' is added from *c.* 1891.
Impressed numerals indicate date, e.g.

$$\frac{9}{75} \qquad = \text{September, } 1875$$

Meir, Richard   *Shelton, Staffs.*

                     late 17th – early 18th C.

                     slip-trailed earthenwares

   RICHARD MEIR   name written in slip

Melba China or **Melba Bone China**   *see* Mayer & Sherratt
                                 Melba China Co. Ltd
                                 Ridgways Potteries Ltd.
                                 H.A. Wain & Sons Ltd.

Melba China Co., Ltd.   *Longton, Staffs.*

    (crown)   1948–51, bone-china

 MELBA BONE CHINA

   GUARANTEED   printed

 MADE IN ENGLAND

Melbar Ware   *see* Barlows (Longton) Ltd.

Melbourne Works with kangaroo   *see* Forester & Co.

Mellon, Eric James   *Bognor Regis, Sussex*
                       1951–, studio-potter in stoneware

Eric James Mellon   mark of E.J.Mellon

Mellor, Venables & Co.   *Burslem, Staffs.*
  M.V. & CO.   1834–51, earthenware & bone-china
  MELLOR, VENABLES
      & CO.   impressed or printed in
                      a variety of marks
  The bone-china appears to have been unmarked

Mellor, Taylor & Co.   *Burslem, Staffs.*
                 c. 1882–1904, earthenware
  printed or impressed marks with full-name,
  crown, Royal Arms, ROYAL IRONSTONE CHINA or
  SEMI PORCELAIN.

Meon   *see* Wood, N.

Methven & Sons, David   *Kirkcaldy, Scotland*
    D.M. & S.   *c.* 1840–c. 1930, earthenware
    METHVEN   D. METHVEN & SONS   printed or
  impressed initials or names from *c.* 1875
  rubber-stamped marks on Methven sponged wares:
  AIRLIE WARE, LOMOND WARE, NISBET WARE, AULD HEATHER
  WARE

Mexborough   *see* Baguley (Alfred), Denaby Pottery,
  James Emery, Mexbro Pottery, J. & J. Reed, Rock Pottery,
  Sowter & Co., J. Wardle & Co. Wilkinson & Wardle

Mexborough (Mexbro)   *S. Yorks.*
                        1865–91, Alfred Baguley
                        decorators in Rockingham style

ROCKINGHAM WORKS
    BAGULEY   painted or printed
    MEXBRO.

M.F. monogram   *see* Morley, Fox & Co.Ltd.
                        Pendley Pottery

M.F. & Co.Ltd.   *see* Morley, Fox & Co.Ltd.

M.H. & Co.   *see* Mason, Holt & Co.

M. & H.   *see* Minton

Middlesbrough Pottery Co.   *Middlesbrough, Cleveland*
                        1834–44, earthenware

M.P.CO.   MIDDLESBRO'   MIDDLESBRO'
                        POTTERY CO.   POTTERY

                        impressed marks from 1834–44

becomes Middlesbrough Earthenware Co.
from 1844–52.   M.E.C.   impressed
anchor mark continued in use with numerous backstamps
with patterns: Cypriot Bower, Caledonia, Arabian Nights,
Granada, Rhine, Wild Rose, Devon, Caprera & Hop Pickers etc.
Taken over in 1852 by Isaac Wilson & Co.
until closure in 1887

<table>
<tr><td>I.W. & CO.</td><td>I.W. & CO.</td><td>I.W. & CO.</td></tr>
<tr><td></td><td>MIDDLESBRO'</td><td>MIDDLESBROUGH</td></tr>
</table>

other backstamps of varying designs had
initials of Isaac Walton & Co. printed

Middleton & Co., J.H.   *Longton, Staffs.*

c. 1889–1941, bone-china
other printed marks include
trade-name Delphine

Midwinter Ltd.,W.R.   *Burslem, Staffs.*
1910–1987, earthenware
1965 takes over A.J. Wilkinson & Newport Pottery
1968 above group and J. & G. Meakin merge
to form English Tableware Group
1970 Taken over by Wedgwood Group
Works closed in 1987

Millar, John   *Edinburgh, Scotland*
JOHN MILLAR   1840–82, retailer only
Name printed with address

Miller, David   *Surbiton, Surrey, & France*
studio-potter in *raku* & stoneware

Miller & Young   *see* Crown Pottery

Mills, Donald *London*

1846–55, studio-potter in
Donald Mills stoneware

or 'D.M.' with date

Mills, Henry *Hanley, Staffs.*

H. MILLS *c.* 1892, earthenware
printed with 'STONE CHINA'

Milne Cornwall & Co. *Portobello, Scotland*

c. 1830–40, stoneware

MILNE CORNWALL
& CO. impressed mark

Minton *Stoke, Staffs.*

1793– , earthenware and various types of
porcelains

Sèvres type mark used
on porcelain *c.* 1800–16
sometimes with
pattern number

in blue enamel

printed mark with
'M', 1822–1836

printed 1822–36

'M. & B.' for Minton &
Boyle partnership
1836–41, printed

'M. & Co.' Minton &
Co., 1841–73

'M. & H.', Minton &
Hollins partnership
1845–68

1862–71, 's' added   MINTON
in 1873   impressed

printed 1860–c. 69

impressed for 'BEST   B.B.
BODY' mid-19th century

'Globe-mark', 1863–72
's' added to Minton
in 1871

impressed mark with
year 1875, used from
1868–80

18
MINTON
75

printed mark from 1873,
'England' added from
1891, and 'Made in
England' about 1910
crown added in early 1880s

impressed or moulded
c. 1890–1910

MINTONS
ENGLAND

'Globe-mark', c. 1912–50

standard factory-mark
adopted in 1951

'Ermine' mark used from
c. 1845–65 to identify
wares that had been
dipped in a soft-glaze
on which painting was
to be applied

painted, incised
or printed

relief mark of *c.* 1846–52
on 'Summerly's Art
Manufacturers' made
by Minton

Solon, Marc Louis, 1870–1904
decorator

signature 'Henri Deux'   TOFT
reproductions
Mussill, W. (*d.* 1906)   W. Mussill
decorator in 1870s

YEARLY MARKS OF MINTONS LTD., 1842–1942;

✳	△	□	✕	⬭
1842	1843	1844	1845	1846
⌒	—	⋈	♣	∵
1847	1848	1849	1850	1851
V	♘	∿	✻	♀
1852	1853	1854	1855	1856
◇	♈	Ж	☖	人
1857	1858	1859	1860	1861

1862	1863	1864	1865	1866
1867	1868	1869	1870	1871
1872	1873	1874	1875	1876
1877	1878	1879	1880	1881
1882	1883	1884	1885	1886
1887	1888	1889	1890	1891
1892	1893	1894	1895	1896
1897	1898	1899	1900	1901
1902	1903	1904	1905	1906
1907	1908	1909	1910	1911
1912	1913	1914	1915	1916

257

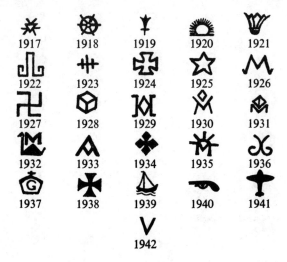

1917	1918	1919	1920	1921
1922	1923	1924	1925	1926
1927	1928	1929	1930	1931
1932	1933	1934	1935	1936
1937	1938	1939	1940	1941
		1942		

If impressed into a translucent body, these years marks are more easily read if held before a strong artificial light.

At the commencement of 1943 the system of yearly date-marks that had operated from 1842 was discontinued, being replaced by figures denoting the year of production, preceded by a number allocated to the actual maker of the article. Number one was given to the factory's leading plate-maker, and plates he produces have stamped in the clay 1–76, the last two digits representing the year.

Taken over by Doulton in 1968

Mitchell & Sons, W.   *see* Cadborough Pottery

M.J.   *see* De Morgan

M.J. & Co.   *see* Macintyre & Co., J.

M.K. monogram   *see* Marshall, Ray

M.L. & Co.   *see* Moore, Leason & Co.

M.L.S.   *see* Minton

M.M.   *see* Magson, M.

M. & M.   *see* Mayer & Maudesley
                  Price Brothers

M. & N.   *see* Mayer & Newbold

M.N. & Co.   *see* McNeal & Co.Ltd.

Moorcroft Ltd., W.   *Burslem, Staffs.*

MOORCROFT
BURSLEM

1913– , earthenware printed or impressed 1913– signatures of William Moorcroft (*d.* 1945) & initials of son, Walter. Associated with Churchill 1984–6. 1986–70% owned by Mr & Mrs R. Dennis & Hugh Edwards. Modern wares: 'MOORCROFT' over 'Made in England'

Moore, Bernard   *Stoke, Staffs.*

c. 1905–15, earthenware &
porcelain, with *flambé*
glazes
painted initials

painted or printed

Moore Bros.   *Longton, Staffs.*

              c. 1870–1905, porcelain

MOORE   impressed or printed, *c.* 1870–1905

MOORE BROS.   impressed *c.* 1872–1905

MOORE,   printed over globe, *c.* 1880–

MOORE BROTHERS/ENGLAND   impressed 1891–1905

printed, 1902–5

1905, works sold to
Wild & Co., & Bernard Moore
transferred to Stoke

Moore & Co., Samuel   *Sunderland, Tyne & Wear*

              1803–4, earthenware

S.MOORE & CO.   S.M. & CO.

SUNDERLAND   impressed or printed

1803–31 Samuel Moore & Peter Austin

1831–47 Charles Moore

1847–52 Charles & George S. Moore

1852–61 George S. Moore

1861–74 Ralph Seddon (manager)

Moore & Co.   *Fenton, Staffs.*
     M. & CO.   1872–92, earthenware
impressed or printed initials in a variety
of designs, but are common to other factories

(M) Moore & Co.   *Hanley, Staffs.*
     M. & CO.   1898–1903, earthenware
impressed or printed in a variety of
marks, but also apply to Minton & Moore & Co.

Moore, Leason & Co.   *Fenton, Staffs.*
     M.L. & CO.   1892–6, earthenware
printed in a variety of backstamps

Morgan, Wood & Co.   *Burslem, Staffs.*
     M.W. & CO.   1860–70, earthenware
printed in a variety of marks

Morley & Ashworth   *Hanley, Staffs.*
     M. & A.   1859–62, earthenware, including
    MORLEY &   Ironstone
    ASHWORTH   impressed or printed in a variety
    HANLEY   of designs

Morley & Co., Francis   *Hanley, Staffs.*
    F.M.   1845–58, earthenware
    F.M. & CO.   printed or impressed in
   F. MORLEY & CO.   a variety of marks

Morley, Fox & Co. Ltd.   *Fenton, Staffs.*
                1906–44, earthenware
    M.F. & CO.   or M.F. & CO. LTD. printed in a
variety of designs

other printed marks include
full-name, initials or trade-name:
HOMELEIGH WARE or CROWN MANOR WARE

Morley Ware   *see* Morley, Fox & Co. Ltd.
Morley & Co. Ltd, W.

Morley & Co. Ltd.,William   *Fenton, Staffs.*

1944–57, earthenware
printed, other printed marks
include MORLEY WARE/ENGLAND
or MADE IN ENGLAND

Morris, Thomas   *Longton, Staffs.*

c. 1898–1903, bone-china

impressed or printed, at
times with 'T.M.'

Morris, Thomas   *Longton, Staffs.*

c. 1892–1941, bone-china
printed mark of c. 1892– ,
trade-name of CROWN CHELSEA
CHINA used from c. 1912

Mortlock, J.   *London*

1746–c. 1930, major retailer

MORTLOCKS   early written mark

MORTLOCK   rare impressed mark on wares made
to order, probably by Minton, who
frequently made exclusive wares for Mortlock

MORTLOCK'S   MORTLOCK'S
STUDIO LONDON   OXFORD STREET
                                         or
                                    ORCHARD STREET

wide range of printed marks with full name & address,
sometimes with mark of manufacturer

Morris, W.   *see* Ouseburne, B.P.

Mortlake Pottery   *see* Kishere, J.

Moseley, John   *Cobridge & Burslem, Staffs.*
   MOSELEY   *c.* 1802–22, earthenware
   impressed   & Wedgwood-type stoneware

Mountford, A.J.   *Burslem, Staffs.*
                     1897–1901, earthenware

                 printed

Mountford, G.T.   *Stoke, Staffs.*
   G.T.M.   *c.* 1888–98, earthenware
   STOKE   printed in a variety of marks

Mountford, John   *Stoke, Staffs.*
                     c. 1857–9, Parian ware
  J. MOUNTFORD
   STOKE   incised signature

M.P.Co.   *see* Middlesbrough Pottery Co.

M.S. & Co.   *see* Myott, Sons & Co. Ltd.

M. & S.   *see* Maddock & Seddon
                 Mayer & Sherratt
                 Meigh & Son, Charles

M. & T.   *see* Machin & Thomas

Murray & Co., Ltd.,W.F.   *Glasgow, Scotland*
                                1826–1925, earthenware & stoneware
                                The Caledonian Pottery

                                1826–41, Murray & Co.
                                1842–50, Murray & Couper
                                1850–67, Murray & Fullerton
                                1867–68, Murray & Grosvenor
                                1868–1900, Murray & Co.
impressed   1910–25, The Caledonian Pottery Co. Ltd.
or printed

Murray, William S. (*d.* 1962)   *London & Southern Rhodesia*
                                    (*Zimbabwe*)
                                    c. 1919–39, studio-potter specialising in
                                    stoneware

      W.S.MURRAY
          (date)
        LONDON
   incised or painted

Mussill,W.   *see* Minton

M.V. & Co.   *see* Mellor Venables & Co.

M.W.   *see* McKenzie, Warren

M.W. monogram   *see* Wondrausch, M.

M.W. & Co.   *see* Massey, Wildblood & Co.
                             Morgan, Wood & Co.

M.W.H.   *see* Malkin, Walker & Hulse

M. & Y.   *see* Crown Pottery

Myatt   *Lane Delph, Staffs.*
    MYATT   late 18th-early 19th C., earthenware
  impressed

Myott, Son & Co. Ltd.   *Stoke, Staffs.*
                           1898– , earthenware & imported
  M.S. & CO.   bone-china from *c.* 1982

1898–1902   printed   *c.* 1900
trade-names: IMPERIAL SEMI PORCELAIN (1907–),
ROYAL CROWN (1930–), CHINA-LYKE (*c.* 1959–),
OLD CHELSEA (*c.* 1961–), SAFARI (*c.* 1961)
Merged in *c.* 1982 with Alfred Meakin (1982) Ltd.
Since taken over by Melton Modes
Purchased by Churchill Group, 1991

N

N.   *see* Neale & Co., James

Nantgarw China Works   *Nantgarw, Wales*

NANT GARW	1813–14, & *c.* 1817–20, soft-paste porcelain
NANTGARW	factory of William Billingsley & Samuel Walker
NANTGARW C.W.	impressed marks during both periods, 'C.W.' for 'China Works'

    NANTGARW   painted or stencilled, an
unreliable mark, often on reproductions

Nautilus Pottery Co.   *Glasgow, Scotland*
1875–1948, Parian & bone-china
started as Saracen Pottery in 1875 under Bayley,
Murray and Brammer. *c.* 1896–1918, under the
ownership of J. McDougall & Sons for the
production of Nautilus Porcelain and known
from 1898–1901 as Possil Pottery Co.,
1918–48, under J. & R. Tennent for the
production of stoneware

printed 1896–1913

N.C.P.Co. monogram   *see* New Chelsea Porcelain Co.Ltd.

Neale & Co., James   *Hanley, Staffs.*
       c. 1778–92, earthenware, Wedgwood-type
   N   stoneware, & porcelain
  NEALE
  I.NEALE   I.NEALE.HANLEY   NEALE & CO.
       '& CO.' added from *c*. 1778
       all marks impressed

Neale & Bailey or Neale & Co.   *Hanley, Staffs.*
       c. 1788–1800, earthenware & bone-china
  NEALE   ceramic manufacturers agents
   &
  BAILEY   printed or impressed

Neale, Harrison & Co.   *Hanley, Staffs.*
       c. 1875–82, earthenware & bone-china
  N.H. & CO. printed in a variety of marks

Neale & Palmer   *Hanley, Staffs.*
       c. 1769–76, earthenware & stoneware
  NEALE & PALMER impressed

Neale & Wilson   *Hanley, Staffs.*
       c. 1783–92, earthenware, stoneware &
  NEALE & WILSON porcelain
  NEALE & CO. impressed

Nelson Ware   *see* Cotton Ltd., Elijah

Newcastle Pottery   *see* Wallace & Co., J.

New Chelsea China Co. Ltd. *Longton, Staffs.*

1951–61, bone-china

printed

New Chelsea Porcelain Co. Ltd. *Longton, Staffs.*

1912–51, bone-china other
various printed marks include
an anchor with various trade-names:
CHELSON (*c.* 1913), NEW CHELSEA (*c.* 1919),
ROYAL CHELSEA (*c.* 1943)

printed, 1912–

Newland, William *Prestwood, Bucks.*

W N   studio-potter, 1948–
with last two numerals of date
full signature of W.Newland & date

New Hall Porcelain Works *Hanley, Staffs.*

c. 1782–1835, hard-paste porcelain
changing to bone-china from *c.* 1814

printed only on some bone-
china. Painted pattern
numbers with 'N' or 'No.' &
number or just number on
hard-paste wares, recorded
to 1048, and 2679 on bone-china

New Hall Pottery Co. Ltd. *Hanley, Staffs.*

1899–1956, earthenware

printed mark from
c. 1930–51, after which
the printing was reversed
to white on a black ground
until 1956

Newport Pottery Co. Ltd.   *Burslem, Staffs.*
1920–87, earthenware
1964, taken over by Midwinter Ltd.W.R.
1970, taken over by Wedgwood Group
1987, works closed
various printed marks all including
full-name of pottery, & that of Clarice
Cliff on some marks from *c*. 1938

New Park Potteries Ltd.   *Longton, Staffs.*

N.P.P.LTD.	1935–57, earthenware
NEW PARK	NEW PARK
POTTERIES	initials or name printed
LONGTON	in a variety of marks

New Pearl Pottery Co. Ltd.   *Hanley, Staffs.*
1936–41, earthenware
full-named printed mark with trade-name:
ROYAL BOURBON WARE

New Wharf Pottery Co.   *Burslem, Staffs.*

N.W.P.CO.	1878–94, earthenware
N.W.P.CO.	N.W.P.CO.
B	BURSLEM

initials or full-name in a wide range
of printed patterns, often with name of pattern

N.H. & Co.   *see* Neale, Harrison & Co.

Nicholson &Co., Thomas   *Castleford, Yorks.*
    T.N.&CO.   *c.* 1854–*c.* '69, earthenware
initials included in a variety of marks,
often including name of pattern

North British Pottery   *Glasgow, Scotland*
opened in 1860 as the Armitage Pottery, earthenware
then Osley Pottery from 1860–8, under R.H.Penman,
1868–74 under J.Miller & Co., who changed name to
North British Pottery, and finally from 1874–1904
under Alexander Balfour & Co.
    J.M.& CO.   I.M.& CO.   J.M. CO.
various printed marks during Miller period.
    A.B.& CO.   in printed marks 1874–1904

North Staffordshire Pottery Co. Ltd.   *Cobridge & Hanley, Staffs.*

1940–52, earthenware
printed mark 1944–

Acquired by Lawley Group Ltd., 1940,
who were in turn taken over in 1952
by S.Pearson & Son Ltd., becoming
Allied English Potteries, 1964, who
merged with Doulton & Co.Ltd., 1972, and from
1984 known as Royal Doulton Ltd.

Northen & Co., W.   *London*
    W.NORTHEN   1847–92, stoneware
    POTTER   W.NORTHEN
    VAUXHALL   POTTER
    LAMBETH   impressed marks, '& Co' from 1887–92

Northfield Hawley Pottery Co. Ltd.   *Rotherham, Yorks.*

                                         1903–1919, earthenware
                                         impressed or printed mark

Nowell, C.D.   *Disley & Prestbury, Ches.*
                                         c. 1946–59, studio-potter
mark, full signature over name of location,
e.g. Prestbury or Disley, to Prestbury *c.* 1951

N.P.P. Ltd.   *see* New Park Potteries Ltd.

N.S.Pottery Co. Ltd.   *see* North Staffordshire Pottery Co. Ltd.

numerals, 'disguised Chinese'   *see* Worcester

N.W.P.Co.   *see* New Wharf Pottery Co.

O

O with stroke thro'   *see* Gordon, William

Odundo, Magdalene Anyango N.   *Bentley, Hants.*
                                         studio-potter, earthenware

Odundo
1988   name over date

O.H.E.C.   *see* Old Hall Earthenware Co.

O.I. monogram   *see* Castle Wynd Potteries

Oldfield & Co.   *Brampton, Derbys.*
| J.OLDFIELD | *c.* 1838–88, earthenware |
| OLDFIELD & CO. | impressed name in a variety of marks |

Old Hall   *see* Meigh, Job

Old Hall Ivory Ware   *see* Richardson & Co.Ltd.

Old Hall Pottery Co. Ltd.   *Hanley, Staffs.*

c. 1861–86, earthenware, Parian & possibly bone-china
trade-mark of 1884– , printed or impressed

a wide range of various marks with such trade-names as INDIAN STONE CHINA, OPAQUE PORCELAIN & IMPERIAL PARISIAN GRANITE

Old Hall Porcelain Works Ltd.   *Hanley, Staffs.*
1886–1902, earthenware & bone-china
The above mark was continued with the addition of 'ENGLAND' from *c.* 1891

Old Royal China   *see* Smith, Sampson

Ollivant Potteries Ltd.   *Stoke, Staffs.*
| O.P. | 1948–54, earthenware | |
| O.P.L. | OLLIVANT | OPL in shield |

various printed marks including name or initials

O'Malley, Peter   *London*

1953– , studio-potter
impressed

O.P. or **O.P.L.**   *see* Ollivant Potteries Ltd.

Opaque Porcelain   *see* Old Hall Pottery Co.Ltd.

Oriental Ivory   *see* Powell, Bishop & Stonier

Osbourne China Co. Ltd.   *Longton, Staffs.*
                                        1909–40, bone-china
OSBOURNE CHINA   printed with torch
    ENGLAND
'LTD.' from 1937. Purchased by Colclough China Ltd.
1940, & Booths Ltd. in 1948, who were retitled
Booths & Colclough Ltd. Merged with Ridgway 1953,
and are now part of Royal Doulton

Ouseburn Bridge Pottery   *Newcastle upon Tyne, Tyne & Wear*
                                        1815–75, earthenware
                                        (transferred from North Hylton Pottery)
Maling, Robert, 1815–53; Maling, C.T., 1853–59.
Works closed and reopened as Albion Pottery
1860, under Bell Bros., Isaac Bell, Galloway
& Atkinson, Atkinson, until *c.* 1871. 1871–75,
W.Morris, after which pottery closed

    M   MALING   Maling   C.T.MALING
                                SEMI CHINA
printed on transfer-printed earthenware
1815–59

printed, 1930

owl *see* Wage & Son Ltd.,G.

P

P *see* Pilkingtons
    Pountney & Allies
    Proctor & Co., J. & H.

P. & Co. see Pearson & Co.
      Pountney & Co.

P. & A. *see* Pountney & Allies

Palissy *see* A.E.Jones (LONGTON) Ltd.

Palissy Pottery Ltd. *Longton, Staffs.*
      1946–89, earthenware
Various printed marks, some previously used
by A.E.Jones (Longton) Ltd., all including
PALISSY POTTERY or PALISSY WARE, owned by
Royal Worcester from 1958 and Derby
International from 1989, who demolished
factory in August of same year

Palm Athlo *see* Price Bros. (Burslem) Ltd.

274

Palmer, Humphrey   *Hanley, Staffs.*
    PALMER   *c.* 1760–78, earthenware & stoneware

    impressed marks

Pankhurst & Co., J.W.   *Hanley, Staffs.*
    J.W.P.   1850–82, earthenware
    J.W.PANKHURST   J.PANKHURST & CO.
'& CO.' added from *c.* 1852, variety of
printed marks all including name or initials

Paragon China Ltd.   *Longton, Staffs.*
    1919–87, bone-china
formerly Star China Co.) renamed Royal Paragon China
Ltd., 1933/4. Taken over by C.Wild & Sons Ltd., 1960.
Works closed 1987. Now part of Royal Doulton
as Royal Albert.

    printed mark of 1957– ,
    all other marks include
    the name 'PARAGON'

Paragon China   *see* Star China Co.

Pardoe, Thomas (*d.* 1823)   *Bristol, Avon.*
    c. 1809–20, painter at Derby,
Worcester, Cambrian Pottery, Swansea & Nantgarw.
Independent decorator of pottery & porcelain

at Bristol, *c.* 1809–

	Pardoe	
Pardoe	28 Bath Street	Pardoe, Bristol
(date)	Bristol	
	Warranted	
	(1812–16)	

Painted signatures only on work decorated
independently, not when employed at other
potteries

Pardoe, William Henry   *Cardiff, Wales*
(son of above)   *c.* 1826–35, decorator
  PARDOE. CARDIFF   printed mark

Park Hall China Ltd.   *Longton, Staffs.*
  'ROYAL PARK'   1985–1991, bone-china
  (with crown)

Parnell, Gwendolen   *London*
                   1916–35, earthenware figures.
Modelled for the Worcester Royal Porcelain Co.
where the mark of 'G.M.P.' indicates her work
  CHELSEA CHEYNE   G.P.
  incised (with date)   (with drawing of rabbit)

Parr, Harry   *London*
                   c. 1919–48, studio-potter,
specializing in earthenware figures
            HY PARR/CHELSEA (with date)

Parrot & Co. Ltd.   *Burslem, Staffs.*
                  1921– ceased *c.* 1960, earthenware

printed trade-mark

Patent Ironstone China   *see* Mason, G.M. & C.J.

Patience, Thomas   *Bristol, Avon.*
    PATIENCE   *c.* mid-18th C., stoneware
    impressed

Patterson, George   *Gateshead, Tyne & Wear*
                       1851– *c.* 92, earthenware
   Sheriff Hill Pottery, various printed marks:

G. PATTERSON	GRECIAN
GATESHEAD ON TYNE	G. PATTERSON
	SHERIFF HILL

   some including name of pattern

Pattison, J.   *Longton, Staffs.*
                 c. 1818–30, earthenware
   figures, but as yet not identified

Payne   *Salisbury, Wilts.*
    PAYNE SARUM   *c.* 1834–41, retailer only.
   printed on wares made to order

P.B.   *see* Poulson Bros. Ltd.

P. & B.   *see* Powell & Bishop

P.B. & Co.   *see* Pinder, Bourne & Co.

P.B. & H.   *see* Pinder, Bourne & Hope

P.B.L.   *see* Plant Bros.

P.B.&S.   *see* Powell, Bishop & Stonier

P. & C.   *see* Physick & Cooper

P.E. monogram   *see* Empire Porcelain Co.

Peanco   *see* Pearson & Co.

Pearce, Alfred B.   *London*
                       1866–1940, retailer only

ALFRED B. PEARCE
39 LUDGATE HILL   printed on wares made
LONDON   to order

Pearl Pottery Co. Ltd.   *Hanley, Staffs.*

                  1894–1936, earthenware
                  printed or impressed, 1894–1912
                  'P.P.& CO.' on crowned globes 1912–

trade-names: Royal Bourbon Ware & Lynton

Pearson & Co.   *Chesterfield, Derbys.*
        P. & CO.   *c.* 1805– earthenware & stoneware

PEARSON & CO.
WHITTINGTON
MOOR
impressed
early marks   impressed or printed   *c.* 1880–

Pearson & Co., (Chesterfield) Ltd. *Derbys.*

     c. 1925– , new title of previous
entry. Trade-names: 'KRUSTA' WARE, & 'PEANCO'.
Previous 'potter's wheel' mark continued in use,
with Pearsons of Chesterfield above

Pearson, Colin *Islington, London*

     1962– , studio-potter, working in
     porcelain & stoneware

Pearson Ltd., James *Brampton, Derbys.*

  J.P.LTD.   19th C, – 1939, stoneware
impressed or printed, 1907–
Trade-name from 1920, Bramfield Ware, &
from *c.* 1930 BAKE-WELL, on domestic wares.
Merged with Pearson & Co. (Chesterfield) Ltd.
in 1939

Pellatt & Co. Ltd., Apsley *London*

     c. 1789–, retailers in ceramics
 APSLEY PELLATT & glass
  & CO.

Pellatt & Green *London*

     c. 1805–30, retailers only
 PELLATT & GREEN
  LONDON

Pellatt & Wood *London*

     c. 1870–90, retailers
 PELLATT & WOOD printed mark

Pendley Manor   *Tring, Herts.*

1949– , studio-pottery Murray Fieldhouse, now at Northfields Studio. Incised or printed marks, 'P.P.' for Pendley Pottery, 'M.F.' for Murray Fieldhouse

Perryman, Jane   *Cambridge, Cambs.*

1980– , studio-potter, in porcelain (first two years in the U.S.A.).

Peover, Frederick & Ann   *Hanley, Staffs.*

PEOVER impressed   *c.* 1818–22, bone-china, wares are rare & very rarely marked. The pottery was probably run by wife, Ann, after husband, Frederick, died in 1820

Perrin, Mrs Ida   *see* De Morgan, William

P. & F.W.   *see* Warburton, Peter & Francis

P.G.   *see* Bridgwood & Son Ltd., Sampson

P.H. monogram   *see* Ramsbury

P.H. Co.   *see* Hanley Porcelain Co.

P.H. & Co.   *see* Holdcroft & Co.,P.

Phillips, W.P.G.   *London*

c. 1799–1929, retailers

various printed marks applied to wares made
elsewhere to order, the various addresses are
a guide to dating:

W.P. & G. Phillips	Oxford St. *c.* 1858–97
W.P. & G. Phillips	New Bond St. *c.* 1859–89
Phillips & Co.	Mount St. *c.* 1897–1906
Phillips Ltd.	Bond St. *c.* 1908–1929

Phillips, Anthony *Wapping, London*

1981, studio-potter, earthenware

Phillips, Charles *see* Royal Potteries

Phillips, Edward *Shelton, Staffs.*

1855–62, earthenware & bone-china

EDWARD PHILLIPS   bone-china not as
SHELTON   yet identified
STAFFORDSHIRE   printed

Phillips, Edward & George *Longport, Staffs.*

PHILLIPS   1822–34, earthenware
LONGPORT   E. & G.P.   E. & G. PHILLIPS
            LONGPORT

printed name or initials in a variety of marks

Phillips, George *Longport, Staffs.*

PHILLIPS   1834–48, earthenware
impressed or printed name with
or without Staffs. knot.
'LONGPORT' also added at times

Phillips & Co. J.   *Newton Abbot, Devon*
1868–87, earthenware
ΦIΛEΩ II7I7ON   printed or impressed

Phillips & Maling *Sunderland, Tyne & Wear*
Phillips & Maling are thought to have been
running the North Hylton pottery from *c.* 1780–
about 1815, prior to the transfer of the
pottery to Ouseburn, Newcastle, but there
is no record of a partnership and no marked
wares are known

Phillips, J.   *Sunderland, Tyne & Wear*
c. 1807–65, Sunderland or Garrison Pottery
(already owner of North Hylton Pottery)
earthenware, with printed or lustre
decoration
Various impressed marks include: J. PHILLIPS,
J. PHILLIPS/SUNDERLAND/POTTERY (*c.* 1807–12)
PHILLIPS & CO. (*c.* 1813–19), DIXON, AUSTIN & CO.
(*c.* 1820–26), DIXON, AUSTIN, PHILLIPS & CO.,
DIXON, AUSTIN & CO. (1827–40), DIXON,
PHILLIPS & CO. (1840–65)

Phillips, Peter & Julie   *Trottiscliffe, Kent, & France*
studio-potters in
stoneware

Phillips & Son., Thomas   *Burslem, Staffs.*
c. 1845–6, earthenware
T. PHILLIPS & SON/BURSLEM   printed or impressed

Physick & Cooper   *Hanley, Staffs.*
   P. & C.   1899–1900, earthenware
  (over crown) printed

Pierce, Aphra J.   *see* Della Robbia

Pierce & Co., W.   *Benthall, Shrops.*
     c. 1800–18, earthenware

 W. PIERCE & CO.

Pilkington Tile & Pottery Co.   *nr. Manchester, Lancs.*
    P   *c.* 1897–1937; 1948–57, ornamental
         earthenware
 incised mark on wares from *c.* 1897–1904
 printed trade-mark *c.* 1904–5, then
 impressed until 1914

 factory mark, VIII for
 1908

 c. 1914–38   'ROYAL LANCASTRIAN'

marks of notable designers:

Lewis F. Day Walter Crane C. E. Cundall R. Joyce

Jessie Jones G. M. Forsyth Gladys Rodgers W. Mycock

Pinder, Thomas   *Burslem, Staffs.*

PINDER BURSLEM   1849–51, earthenware
printed or impressed

Pinder, Bourne & Co.   *Burslem, Staffs.*

               1862–82, earthenware (owned
P.B. & CO.   by Doulton from 1878).
PINDER, BOURNE   printed in a variety of
& CO.   marks. Year marks at times
               applied e.g. 12.80 = Dec. 1880

Pinder, Bourne & Hope   *Burslem, Staffs.*

P.B. & H.   *c.* 1851–62, earthenware
PINDER, BOURNE   initials or full name
& HOPE   printed in various marks

Pinxton Works   *Pinxton, Derbys.*

c. 1796–1813, porcelains.
John Coke & William Billingsley
c. 1796–1799
John Coke, *c.* 1799–1806
John Cutts, *c.* 1806–1813
Pinxton porcelain is rarely marked, only
cursive 'P' as above, or 'Pinxton' in full
are generally accepted; marks previously
quoted are now doubtful

Pirie, Ian   *Stonehaven, Kincardins.*

studio-potter, working in
stone-ware & porcelain

Pitcairns Ltd.   *Tunstall, Staffs.*

1895–1901, earthenware

printed

P.J.   *see* Ramsbury
H.

Plant, Benjamin   *Longton, Staffs.*

1775–1815, earthenware & stoneware.
now thought to be a working potter who
sometimes signed his work, not a master-potter

rare incised mark on a
pair of lions

Plant Bros.   *Burslem & Longton, Staffs.*

1889–1907, bone-china
'B' in mark = Burslem,
1889–98
'L' = Longton, 1899–1906

Plant, Enoch   *Burslem, Staffs.*

1898–1905, earthenware
printed or impressed but
similar crowns are a common
form of mark

Plant & Co., J. *Stoke, Staffs.*

1893–1900, earthenware

STOKE POTTERY   printed

Plant & Co., R.H. *Longton, Staffs.*

c. 1881–98, bone-china

printed

Plant & Sons, R. *Longton, Staffs.*

P. & S.   1895–1901, earthenware
L   printed in cartouche

Plant Ltd., R.H. & S.L. *Longton, Staffs.*

1898– , bone-china
wide range of printed marks
with 'R.H. & S.L.P.', monogram,
full-name or 'TUSCAN CHINA',
trade-mark from *c.* 1898.
Taken over by Wedgwood Group
in 1966, renamed ROYAL TUSCAN in 1989

Plant, Thomas *Lane End, Staffs.*

1825–50, earthenware figures

Pleydell-Bouverie, Katharine *Coleshill, Wilts.*

b. 1895–*d.* 1985, studio-potter

286

potting at Coleshill, Wilts, 1924–46
moving to Warminster, Wilts, 1946–

incised or stamped

Plymouth Porcelain Works   *Plymouth, Devon*

1768–70, hard-paste porcelain
sign for tin, in underglaze-blue,
red or gold
impressed repairer's mark, also to
be seen on some Bow, Worcester
& Bristol porcelain, probably
the work of John Toulouse.
Production transferred to Bristol in 1770

Plymouth Pottery Co. Ld.   *Plymouth, Devon*
P.P.COY.L.   1856–63, earthenware
STONE CHINA   printed under Royal Arms

p m   *see* Meanley, P.

Podmore China Co.   *Hanley, Staffs.*
1921–41, bone-china
P.C.C.   monogram printed in frame under
crown, with PODMORE CHINA

Podmore, Walker & Co.   *Tunstall, Staffs.*
P.W. & CO.   1834–59, earthenware
initials used in a variety of printed marks.
'P.W.& W.' printed from *c.* 1856, acknowledging
Enoch Wedgwood as a partner

Pointon & Co. Ltd.   *Hanley, Staffs.*
1883–1916, earthenware &
POINTONS   bone-china
STOKE-ON-TRENT
printed with Royal Arms
POINTON or POINTONS impressed

Pollex, John   *Plymouth, Devon*
1971–, studio-potter, earthenware

Pollard, William   *Swansea & Carmarthen, Wales*
c. 1829–32, talented flower-painter.
Pollard's work whilst at the Swansea factory
is unmarked, but his independent decorating
at Carmarthen has 'Pollard, Carmarthen' painted

Poole, J.E.   *Burslem, Staffs.*
POOLE   1796–early 19th. C.
impressed   earthenware

Poole Pottery Ltd.   *Poole, Dorset*
1873–1921, art pottery & tiles
CARTER & CO.   CARTER POOLE
impressed or incised   (date)
Supplier of 'blanks' to William De Morgan.
Becomes: CARTER, STABLER & ADAMS, 1921–63
when title POOLE POTTERY LTD. was adopted.
'LTD.' added in 1929.
1971, new group comprises Poole Pottery Ltd.,
Carter & Co. and Pilkington Tiles, under

Thomas Tilling, who in turn were taken over
1983 by BTR (British Tyre & Rubber Co.)

POOLE
ENGLAND

impressed
or
printed 1950–

1961–

Poole, Richard   *Hanley, Staffs.*

R. POOLE   1790–5, earthenware
impressed

Poole, Thomas   *Longton, Staffs.*

1880–1952 bone-china
c. 1925 retitled: Thomas Poole
(Longton) Ltd.

impressed or printed crown, common to others

printed, 1912–
Trade-name: 'ROYAL STAFFORD'
used from *c.* 1912
1948, merged with Gladstone
China Ltd. and from 1952

until at least 1990, known as ROYAL STAFFORD
CHINA

Poole & Unwin   *Longton, Staffs.*

P. & U.   1871–6, earthenware &
printed or impressed   stoneware

Port Dundas Pottery Co.Ltd.   *Glasgow, Scotland*
                    c. 1840–1925, stoneware under
James Miller & Co. (formerly Cochran & Couper)

PORT DUNDAS   PORT DUNDAS
GLASGOW POTTERY   GLASGOW
                        POTTERY COY.
impressed or painted

Portland Pottery Ltd.   *Cobridge, Staffs.*

1946–53, earthenware
'P.P.C.' monogram trade-mark
of 1946–
PORTLAND POTTERY
printed in a variety of
marks, often including name of pattern.
Acquired by Lawley Group 1948, taken over by S. Pearson
& Son in 1952, renamed Allied English Potteries in 1964,
merging with Doulton & Co. in 1972, now Royal Doulton,
since 1984

Portmeiron Potteries Ltd.   *Stoke, Staffs.*

                  1962–present, earthenware,
PORTMEIRON   stone-ware & porcelain
POTTERY   trade-name:
STOKE-ON-TRENT   PORTMEIRON
MADE IN ENGLAND
Became a public company in 1988, and acquired
Crown Winsor property & equipment in 1990

Portovase   *see* Buchan & Co. Ltd., A.W.

Possill Pottery Co.   *see* Nautilus Pottery Co.

Poulson Bros. Ltd.   *see* Ferrybridge Pottery

Pountney & Co.Ltd.   *Bristol, Glos.*

               1849– earthenware

P. & CO.   POUNTNEY & CO.

initials or name in a variety of printed marks.
'Ltd.' added from 1889. Purchased Cauldon
Potteries Ltd. in 1958 and from 1962 known
as Cauldon Bristol Potteries Ltd.

                                 BRISTOL
                         REINFORCED VITRITE
                               ENGLAND

   printed, 1954–   1958–

Pountney & Allies   *Bristol, Glos.*

               c. 1816–35, earthenware

P.   P. & A.   P.A.   P.A.
                           B.P.   BRISTOL POTTERY

printed, impressed or painted in marks

                      impressed mark

Pountney & Goldney   *Bristol, Glos.*

               1836–49, earthenware

BRISTOL POTTERY   & above impressed mark

   impressed   with 'POUTNEY & GOLDNEY'

Powell, Alfred & Louise   *London*

               c. 1904–39, pottery painters
               working for Wedgwoods from

c. 1904 and later making and painting
their own wares in Bloomsbury

painted mark of   painted mark of
Alfred (*d.* 1960)   Louise
                                   (late 1940's)

Powell, John   *London*

POWELL   *c.* 1810–30, decorator &
91, WIMPOLE ST.   retailer
painted

Powell, William   *Bristol, Glos.*

                          c. 1830–1906, stoneware

                          BRISTOL TEMPLE
                          GATE POTTERY

Powell & Bishop   *Hanley, Staffs.*

P. & B.   *c.* 1866–78, earthenware & bone-china

            BEST   POWELL & BISHOP
        P. & B.

initials or name in a variety of impressed
or printed designs

        'Caduceus' registered as trade-
                          mark in 1876, but continued
                          in use by Powell, Bishop &
                          Stonier until 1891

Powell, Bishop & Stonier   *Hanley, Staffs.*

1878–91, earthenware & bone-china.

'P.B. & S.'

printed or impressed in a
variety of marks.
'Chinaman' mark registered in 1880
and continued by Bishop & Stonier
who added 'BISTO'

P.P.   *see* Pearl Pottery Co. Ltd.
Pendley Pottery
Phillips, P.

P.P.Co.Ltd.   *see* Pearl Pottery Co.Ltd.

P.P.Coy.L.   *see* Plymouth Pottery Co.Ltd.

P.R. monogram   *see* Rogers, Phil

Pratt & Co.Ltd.F.R.   *Fenton, Staffs.*

c. 1818– earthenware, best known

F. & R.P.   for multi-coloured transfer-prints.

printed *c.* 1818–40   F. & R.P. & CO.

printed, *c.* 1840–

other various printed marks include full-name.
Taken over *c.* 1925 by Cauldon Potteries Ltd.
who used name of Pratt with their own.
1958 Cauldon Potteries Ltd. taken over by
Pountney of Bristol

Pratt & Co., John   *Fenton, Staffs.*

c. 1851–78, earthenware & probably
bone-china

J.P. & CO.(L)   printed in a variety of
marks, sometimes with name of pattern
'LTD.' added from 1872

Pratt, Hassall & Gerrard   *Fenton, Staffs.*
P.H.G. P.H. & G.   1822–34, earthenware
printed in a variety of marks

Pratt & Simpson   *Fenton, Staffs.*
        P. & S.   1873–83, earthenware
        printed

Pratt, William   *Lane Delph, Staffs.*
        PRATT   *c.* 1780–99, earthenware
on moulded wares

Price Bros   *Burslem, Staffs.*

                    1896–1903, earthenware
                    This mark was continued by
                    Price Bros. (Burslem) Ltd.
                    to *c.* 1910

Price Bros. (Burslem) Ltd.   *Burslem, Staffs.*
                    1903–1961, earthenware
above mark continued to *c.* 1910
Later printed marks include full-name
sometimes with trade-names: 'PALM ATHLO'
'ATHLO WARE' or 'MATTONA WARE'

Price & Kensington Potteries Ltd.   *Longport, Staffs.*
                    1962– at least 1990, earthenware
        PRICE/BROS.   1962–3, 'PRICE/KENSINGTON' 1963–
printed in laurel wreath

Primavesi & Son, F.   *Cardiff & Swansea, Wales*
                          c. 1850–1915, ceramic retailers
F.PRIMAVESI & SON.   '& SON' from c. 1860.
     CARDIFF   printed in a variety
   of marks, some with Royal Arms

Princess Anne   *see* Shore & Coggins

Procter & Co. Ltd., George   *Longton Staffs.*
     G.P. & CO.   1892–1940, earthenware & bone-china
          L   G.P. & CO.
   initials printed in a variety of marks
   trade-name: 'GLADSTONE CHINA' from c. 1924

Procter, John   *Longton, Staffs.*
     J.P.   1846–47, bone-china
      L   printed or impressed

Procter & Co., J.H.   *Longton, Staffs.*
   WARRANTED   1856–c. 84, earthenware
        P   printed or impressed under crown

P.S.   *see* Starkey, P.

P.S. monogram   *see* Smith, Peter
                         Stoodley, P.

P. & S.   *see* Pratt & Simpson

P. & S.   *see* Plant & Sons, R.
     L

P. & U.   *see* Poole & Unwin

Purbeck Pottery Ltd.   *Bournemouth, Dorset*
   1965– , stoneware

Purbeck
Pottery
England

all printed

Purves, Charles & Thomas   *see* Elgin Pottery

P.W. & Co. or P.W. & W.   *see* Podmore, Walker & Co.

Q

Queen Anne   *see* Shore & Coggins

Queen's China   *see* Ford & Sons
                              Rosina China Co. Ltd.
                              Warrilow, G.

Queen's Ware   *see* Skinner & Walker
                              Smith & Co., William

Quick, Kenneth   *St. Ives, Cornwall*

1945–*d.* 1963, studio-potter
with Bernard Leach from 1945–*c.* 55,
at Tregenna Hill, 1955–60, back
to Leach 1960–63, and to Japan 1963

R

R.   *see* Ridgway, Job

R   *see* Coates, Russell

R. (in sunburst)   *see* Rathbone, Samuel & John

Radford, E.   *see* Wood Ltd., H.J.

Radford Handcraft Pottery   *Burslem, Staffs.*
    G. RADFORD   1933–48, earthenware
     BURSLEM   printed signature

Radford (Ltd.) Samuel   *Longton & Fenton, Staffs.*

                      1878–1957, bone-china
                      moved to Fenton *c.* 1885
                      various printed 'S.R.' monograms
                      used to *c.* 1938.
                      printed mark *c.* 1880–
  RADFORDS CROWN CHINA, printed *c.* 1938–

Radfordian: trade-name of above entry

Rainbow Pottery Co.   *Fenton, Staffs.*
                      1931–41, earthenware
  RAINBOW POTTERY
      FENTON   printed or impresed
  MADE IN ENGLAND

Rainforth & Co.   *Leeds, Yorks.*
                    1792–1800, earthenware
  RAINFORTH & CO.   RAINFORTH & C.
        printed or impressed

R.A.K. & Co.   *see* Kidson, under Geddes & Son, J.

Ramsbury   *Ramsbury, Wilts.*

1945, earthenware & stoneware
Peter Holdsworth

printed or impressed

Randall, Thomas M.   *Madeley, Shrops.*

c. 1825–40, decorator of English
& Sèvres porcelain; with factory
at Madeley for production of
soft-paste porcelain
painted mark

Ratcliffe, William   *Hanley, Staffs.*

R
HACKWOOD

c. 1831–40, earthenware
printed or impressed

Ratcliffe & Co.   *Longton, Staffs.*

1891–1914, earthenware

printed

Rathbone, Harold Steward   *see* Della Robbia

Rathbone, Smith & Co.   *Tunstall, Staffs.*
R.S. & CO.   1883–97, earthenware
printed in a variety of marks

Rathbone & Co., T.   *Tunstall, Staffs.*

T.R. & CO.   1898–1923, earthenware
TUNSTALL

printed in a variety of
marks

printed from *c.* 1919

Rathbone & Co., Thomas   *Portobello, Scotland*
    T.R. & CO.   *c.* 1810–45, earthenware
    T.RATHBONE
      P   printed or impressed

Ray, George   *Lane End, Staffs.*
                1832–65, probably only modeller
    G. RAY   inscribed on bust
    LANE END

R.B.   *see* Robinson Bros.

R.B.D.   *see* Barrett-Danes, Ruth

R.B. & S.   *see* Leeds

R. & C.   *see* Read & Clementson

R.C. & A.   *see* Read, Clementson & Anderson

R.C. & Co.   *see* Cochran & Co.R., under Geddes & Son, John

R.C.R. monogram   *see* Collier, S. & E.

R. & D. with lion   *see* Redfern & Drakeford

R.E. stylized monogram   *see* Everett, Raymond

Read & Clementson   *Shelton, Staffs.*
    R. & C.   1833–5, earthenware
  printed in a variety of backstamps

Read, Clementson & Anderson   *Shelton, Staffs.*
    R.C. & A.   *c.* 1836, earthenware
  printed in a variety of marks

Redfern & Drakeford Ltd.   *Longton, Staffs.*

1892–1933, bone-china

printed or impressed mark
c. 1892–1909, trade-name:
'BALMORAL CHINA' added from
c. 1909

Reed, James & John (son)   *Mexborough, Yorks.*
    REED   *c.* 1839–49, earthenware
  impressed   factory renamed MEXBRO POTTERY
  under son, John Reed, from *c.* 1849–1873

Reed & Taylor   *see* Ferrybridge Pottery

Reeves, James   *Fenton, Staffs.*
              1870–1948, earthenware
    J.R.   J.R.   J. REEVES
  printed or impressed   F

Regal Pottery Co.Ltd.   *Cobridge, Staffs.*
              1925–31, earthenware

REGAL WARE/MADE IN ENGLAND   (under crown)

Regal Ware   *see* Regal Pottery Co. Ltd.
                      Richardson, A.G.
                      Richardsons (Cobridge) Ltd.

Regency China Ltd.   *Longton, Staffs.*

1953– at least 1990, bone-china

Reid & Co.   *Longton, Staffs.*

1914–46, bone-china
under direction of T.C. Wild & Co.
renamed ROSLYN CHINA in 1946.
printed mark of *c.* 1914

1964, merged with Lawley Group
under original name of Thomas Wild
& Sons Ltd., becoming Allied
English Potteries, now Royal Doulton

R.F. & S.   *see* Floyd & Sons, R.

R.G.   *see* Garner, Robert

R.G.S. or **R.G.S. & Co.**   *see* Scrivener & Co., R.G.

R.H. or **R.H. & S.**   *see* Hammersley, Ralph

R.H. & Co.   *see* Hall & Co., Ralph

R/Hackwood   *see* Ratcliffe, William

Rhodes & Proctor   *Burslem, Staffs.*
      R. & P.   1883–5, earthenware
   printed in a variety of marks

R.H.P. & Co.   *see* Plant & Co., R.H.

R.H. & Sons   *see* Hammersley & Sons, R.
                         Heron & Son, R.

Rich, Mary   *nr. Truro, Cornwall*

                        1962, studio-potter, in stoneware,
                        porcelain only since 1983

Richards, Christine-Ann   *London*
                        1975–, studio-potter in porcelain
   CAR   car   marks

Richards, Frances E.   *London*
                        1922–31, studio-potter

                        incised mark with date

Richardson, Albert G.   *Cobridge, Staffs.*
      A.G.R.   *c.* 1920–21, earthenware
   initials in printed mark, with trade-name:
   REGAL WARE

Richardson & Co.Ltd, A.G.   *Tunstall & Cobridge, Staffs.*
                     1915–1974, earthenware
      CROWN   Moved to Cobridge in 1934.
      DUCAL   Acquired by Enoch Wedgwood (Tunstall)
      WARE   Ltd. in 1974 and WEDGWOOD GROUP
      ENGLAND   from 1980, as Unicorn Pottery
  A.G.R. & CO. LTD.   printed marks
    trade-names: CROWN DUCAL, OLD HALL, IVORY WARE

Richardson, George   *Wrotham, Kent*
        G.R.   *c.* 1642–77, slip-trailed wares
  initials in slip, with decoration

Richardsons (Cobridge) Ltd.   *Cobridge, Staffs.*
    REGAL WARE   1921–25, earthenware
    R(C) LTD
  (printed with crown within wreath)

Ridgway & Abington   *Hanley, Staffs.*
              c. 1837–60, earthenware, Parian
              & probably bone-china
E.RIDGWAY & ABINGTON usually impressed on
     HANLEY   moulded jugs with the
               publishing date

Ridgway, Job   *Hanley, Staffs.*
    R.   J.R.   *c.* 1802–8, earthenware
  rather uncertain printed marks which may
  relate to Job Ridgway

Ridgway & Sons, Job   *Hanley, Staffs.*
  RIDGWAY & SONS   *c.* 1808–14, earthenware
  impressed or printed in various marks

Ridgway & Co., John   *Hanley, Staffs.*

                      c. 1830–55, earthenware,
                      stoneware & bone-china

     J.R.   JOHN RIDGWAY   JHN.RIDGWAY

name or initials printed in a variety of
marks from *c.* 1830–41, frequently with
Royal Arms
Same names & initials from *c.* 1841 with
the addition of '& CO', often with name
of pattern

Ridgway, John & William   *Hanley, Staffs.*

                      1814–*c.* 1830, earthenware &
                      bone-china

     J.W.R.   J. & W.R.   J. & W. RIDGWAY

impressed or printed marks in a variety of
styles usually including name of pattern

   'vase & anchor' mark, impressed,
applied in relief or printed
and continued in use by William
Ridgway

Ridgway, Bates & Co., John.   *Hanley, Staffs.*

                      1856–58, earthenware, Parian &
    J.R.B. & CO.   bone-china

printed in various backstamps with name of pattern

    J. RIDGWAY
    BATES & CO.   impressed

Ridgway, Morley, Wear & Co.   *Hanley, Staffs.*

                      c. 1836–42, earthenware

R.M.W. & CO.   RIDGWAY, MORLEY
                              WEAR & CO.
printed initials or names in a variety
of marks, usually with name of pattern

Ridgway & Morley   *Hanley, Staffs.*
       R. & M.   1842–44, earthenware
RIDGWAY & MORLEY   initials or name
   printed in a variety of marks

          printed *c.* 1842–44

Ridgway Potteries Ltd.   *Stoke, Staffs.*
                              1955– , earthenware & bone-
         china
                              Ridgway owned by Lawleys Ltd.
                              from 1948, then S. Pearson &
                              Son (1952), Allied English
                              Potteries, 1964, now Royal
                              Doulton.

printed marks in use in 1972
'RIDGWAY' trade-name in use in 1990

Ridgway & Robey   *Hanley, Staffs.*
                       c. 1837–40, rare porcelain figures

RIDGWAY & ROBEY   printed with full
    HANLEY   publishing date

Ridgway, Sparks & Ridgway   *Hanley, Staffs.*
    R.S.R.   1873–9, earthenware
printed in a variety of marks, often
with name of pattern or within
Staffordshire knot

Ridgway, Son & Co.,William   *Hanley, Staffs.*
  W. RIDGWAY   *c.* 1830–45, earthenware,
    W.R.   stoneware & bone-china
printed or impressed, *c.* 1830–34
    W. RIDGWAY & CO.   W.R. & CO.
name or initials printed in a variety
of marks, *c.* 1834–45. '& SON' from *c.* 1838

Ridgways or Ridgways (Bedford Works) Ltd.   *Hanley, Staffs.*

        1879–
        trade-mark from 1880
        'Stoke on Trent' added later
  RIDGWAYS   J. & W.R.   W.R.
printed in a variety of marks from *c.* 1891
RIDGWAYS (BEDFORD WORKS) LTD   from 1916–
By 1948 Ridgway (Bedford Works) Ltd. had
been acquired by Allied English Potteries, but
traded under own name until 1955, when renamed
Ridgway Potteries Ltd. Since 1972 have been
part of Royal Doulton Group

Rie, Lucie (*b.* 1902)   *Austria & London*
studio-potter, working in earthenware,
stoneware & porcelain

moved to London in 1938 and worked
with Hans Coper from 1947–58

          impressed monogram mark

Rigby & Stevenson   *Hanley, Staffs.*
      R. & S.   1894–1954, earthenware
printed in a variety of marks

Riley, John & Richard   *Burslem, Staffs.*
      J. & R.RILEY   1802–28, earthenware &
                                     rarely marked bone-china
painted, printed or impressed name in
various forms of mark
'RILEY'S on strap enclosing Semi-China

Ring & Co., Joseph   *Bristol, Avon*
      RING & CO.   *c.* 1785–1812, earthenware
      impressed   From 1793, Ring & Carter

Rivers & Co.,William   *Hanley, Staffs.*
      RIVERS   *c.* 1816–1820, earthenware &
      impressed   possibly bone-china

R.K.   *see* King, Ruth

Riddle & Co., James   *Longton, Staffs.*
      RIDDLE & BRYAN   *c.* 1835–40, earthenware
          LONGTON   & bone-china
      printed mark

R.L. & Co. monogram   *see* Lowe, Ratcliffe & Co.

R. & L.   *see* Robinson & Leadbeater

R.M.   *see* Malkin, Ralph

R. & M.   *see* Ridgway & Morley
                      Roper & Meredith

R.M.A.   *see* Richard M. Astbury

R.M.& S.   *see* Malkin & Sons, R.

R.M.W. & Co.   *see* Ridgway, Morley, Wear & Co.

R. & N.   *see* Rowley & Newton Ltd.

Roberts, David   *Huddersfield, Yorks.*
                             studio-potter, specializing in
                             raku ware

Robinson Brothers   *Castleford, Yorks.*
         R.B.   1887–1902, stoneware
     printed or impressed in a variety of marks

Robinson & Son, John   *Castleford, Yorks.*
        J.R. & S.   c. 1902–33, stoneware
        impressed
Robinson, Joseph   *Burslem, Staffs.*
     J. ROBINSON   J.R.   1876–98, earthenware
      BURSLEM   B   printed or impressed

Robinson & Leadbeater   *Stoke, Staffs.*

(R & L)   *c.* 1860–1924, Parian & bone-
china. 'LTD.' added from
c. 1905
trade-name: Royal Ivory Porcelain

Robinson & Son   *Longton, Staffs.*
R. & S.   *c.* 1881–1903, bone-china
L   printed or impressed initials
in a variety of marks, or in Staffs.
knot with date of 1850

Robinson, W.H.   *Longton, Staffs.*
W.H.ROBINSON   1901–3, bone-china
LONGTON   trade-name:
BALTIMORE CHINA   BALTIMORE CHINA

Robinson & Wood   *Hanley, Staffs.*
R. & W.   1832–6, earthenware
printed in a variety of marks

Robinson, Wood & Brownfield   *Cobridge, Staffs.*
R.W. & B.   1838–41, earthenware
printed in a variety of backstamps

Robison, James W.   *Huddersfield, Yorks.*
     studio-potter, specializing
Jim Robison   in large forms for outdoor
     decoration, etc. Active in 1989

Rochford, Bryan   *Cheshunt, Herts.*
     1960– , studio-potter

Rockingham Works   *nr. Swinton, Yorks.*
                          c. 1745–1842, earthenware
                          c. 1825–42, porcelain also

	BINGLEY
c. 1778–87	impressed

Brameld & Co., 1806–42	BRAMELD	
	impressed	
c. 1826–30	ROCKINGHAM	ROCKINGHAM
	WORKS,	BRAMELD
	BRAMELD	
c. 1830–42	ROYAL	
	ROCKINGHAM	
	WORKS	
	BRAMELD	

'griffin-mark', *c.* 1826–30
from crest of Earl Fitzwilliam,
Marquis of Rockingham

from *c.* 1830–42
'Royal' added to title
of factory
mark in red *c.* 1826–30, puce 1830–42
'Manufacturer to the King' added to mark
in 1830–37 (William IV)

Baguley, Isaac   1842–55, decorator at
  Rockingham of various porcelains
Baguley, Alfred   1855–65 at Rockingham
  and at Mexborough, *c.* 1865–91

BAGULEY	ROCKINGHAM WORKS
ROCKINGHAM	BAGULEY
WORKS	MEXBRO

Rock Pottery   *see* Reed, James & John

Roddy & Co., E.   *Burslem, Staffs.*
STAFFORDSHIRE   1925–8, earthenware
RODDY
WARE
ENGLAND   printed

Roeginga Pottery   *Rainham, Kent*
1938–9, earthenware

incised marks
Oscar & Grace Davies, née Barnsley
re-opened 1948–*c.* 56 by Alfred Wilson Ltd.
taken over in *c.* 1956 by E.J. Baker as
Rainham Pottery Ltd.

Rogers, John & George   *Longport, Staffs.*
ROGERS   *c.* 1784–1814, earthenware &
impressed   unidentified porcelain

Rogers & Son, John   *Longport, Staffs.*
c. 1814–21, earthenware &
unidentified porcelain
ROGERS   J.R.S.   ROGERS & SON
impressed marks

Rogers, Phil   *Rhayader, Powys*
c. 1989– , studio-potter, stoneware

Roper & Meredith   *Longton, Staffs.*
R. & M.   1913–24, earthenware
LONGTON   printed in circle under crown

Rope, Ellen Mary   *see* Della Robbia

Rosina China Co. Ltd.   *Longton, Staffs.*

1941– , bone-china.
merged with Elizabethan Fine
Bone China Ltd., 1987, but
traded independently until 1988.
1989, new company known as
Crownford China Co. Ltd. with
trade-names: QUEEN'S & ELIZABETHAN

Roslyn China   *Longton, Staffs.*

1946–64, bone-china.
Reid & Co. renamed Roslyn China
in 1946 and renamed Royal Albert
Ltd. in 1971, when part of Allied
English Potteries; now
Royal Doulton Ltd.

Rose, John   *see* Coalport Porcelain Works

Roseate Porcelain   *see* Birks, Rawlins & Co.Ltd.

Roth & Co., John R.   *U.S.A.*
name of American firm, seen on some
Ridgway exports, *c.* 1930–56.
     JONROTH   J.H.R. & CO. monogram
             printed

Rowley & Newton Ltd.   *Longton, Staffs.*
    R. & N.   1895–1901, earthenware &
      or   bone-china
lion with R. & N. beneath

Royal Albert   *see* Doulton
                        Wild & Sons Ltd.

Royal Albion China Co.   *Longton, Staffs.*
                        c. 1921–48, bone-china, trade-name:
ROYAL ALBION CHINA included in printed marks, with
crown or outline of England and Wales. Printed mark
from *c.* 1930: crown, Made in England/'BONE CHINA' &
capital 'M'.

Royal Aller Vale & Watcombe Pottery Co.   *Torquay, Devon*
                        c. 1901–62
                        (previously Aller Vale Art Pottery)
ROYAL ALLER VALE   DEVON MOTTO
                                                    WARE
          ROYAL   printed or impressed
          TORQUAY   from *c.* 1901
          POTTERY

          ROYAL   stamped in black
          WATCOMBE   *c.* 1935–1962
          TORQUAY
          ENGLAND

Royal Alma   *see* Thomas Cone Ltd.

Royal Bourbon Ware   *see* Pearl Pottery Co.Ltd.
                                      New Pearl Pottery Co.Ltd.

Royal Bradwell Art Ware   *see* Wood & Son (Longport) Ltd.,A.

Royal Essex Art Pottery   *see* Bingham, Edward

Royal Grafton   *see* Jones & Sons Ltd., A.B.

Royal Harvey   *see* Gibson & Sons Ltd.

Royal Leighton   *see* Leighton Pottery Ltd.

Royal Mayfair   *see* Chapmans Longton Ltd.

Royal Park trade-name of Healacraft China
1980 Ltd., under receivership 1990

Royal Patent Ironstone   *see* Turner, Goddard & Co.

Royal Potteries   *Weston-super-Mare, Som.*

PHILLIPS W.S.MARE	1847–1870, earthenware & tiles
PHILLIPS (crown) WESTON-S-MARE	Phillips & Sons, Charles garden ornaments & tiles impressed marks
JOHN MATTHEWS ROYAL POTTERY WESTON-SUPER-MARE	1871–1888 Matthews, John, making garden statuary, vessels & tiles
CONWAY. G. WARNE POTTERIES WESTON-SUPER-MARE impressed	1888–1923, making ornamental pottery, bricks & tiles
ROYAL POTTERIES WESTON-SUPER-MARE	impressed

New WESTON-SUPER-MARE POTTERY, TILE &
Brick Co. Ltd. completed *c*. 1900 (closed
1914–18)

Royal Semi Porcelain   *see* Clarke & Co., E.

Royal Stafford   *see* Poole, Thomas

Royal Stafford China   *Longton, Staffs.*
                    1952–88, bone china
variety of printed marks including
'ROYAL STAFFORD', trade-name: MERLIN WARE.
In receivers hands 1985, then various owners
and taken over by County Potteries (Fenton)
in Janury 1988. In co-operation with German firm, 1991

Royal Staffordshire Pottery   *see* Wilkinson Ltd., A.J.

Royal Standard   *see* Chapmans (Longton) Ltd.

Royal Stanley   *see* Colclough & Co.
                 Stanley Pottery Ltd.

Royal Stuart   *see* Stevenson, Spencer & Co. Ltd.

Royal Swan   *see* Booths & Colclough Ltd.

Royal Torquay Pottery   *see* Royal Aller Vale & Watcombe Pottery

Royal Tudor Ware   *see* Barker Bros.Ltd.

Royal Tunstall   *see* Wedgwood & Co.Ltd.

Royal Westminster *see* Anchor Porcelain Co.

Royal Wessex *see* Churchill

Royal Winton *see* Grimwades Ltd.

Royal York *see* Salisbury Crown China Co.

Royall & Lansan *see* Lancaster & Sons Ltd.

R.P. monogram *see* Rochford, Bryan

R. & P. *see* Rhodes & Proctor

R.S. *see* Silverman R.
Stevenson, Ralph

R.S. monogram *see* Radford Ltd., S.

R. & S. *see* Rigby & Stevenson

R. & S. *see* Robinson & Sons
L
R.S. & Co. *see* Rathbone, Smith & Co.

R.S.R. *see* Ridgway, Sparks & Ridgway

R.S. & S. *see* Stevenson & Son, R.

R.S.W. or **R.S. & W.** *see* Stevenson, R. & Williams

R.S.W. *see* Rye Pottery
RYE

R. & T.   *see* Reed & Taylor under Ferrybridge

Rubay Art Ware   *see* Rubian Art Pottery

Rubian Art   *see* Grimwades Ltd.

Rubian Art Pottery Ltd.   *Fenton, Staffs.*
      L.S. & G.   1906–33, earthenware
   impressed or printed, 1906–30.
   RUBAY ART WARE   impressed or printed, *c.* 1926–33
   Under Grimwades Ltd. from 1913

Ruscoe, William   *Stoke, Staffs.*

WR

      *c.*1920–*d.* 1990, earthenware
      figures. To Exeter in 1944.
   incised or painted monogram from *c.* 1920
   full year-date added to monogram from *c.* 1925
   Wm.Ruscoe or William Ruscoe signature in
   full from *c.* 1925

Ruskin Pottery   *see* Taylor W. Howson

Russell, Gertrude   *see* Della Robbia

R.V.W.   *see* Wildblood, Richard Vernon

R. & W.   *see* Robinson & Wood

R.W.&B.   *see* Robinson, Wood & Brownfield

R.W.D.   *see* Duckworth, Ruth

R.W.F.   *see* Wells, R.F.

Rye Pottery   *Rye, Sussex*

    1869– mark of *c.* 1900
pottery (including tin-glaze)
c. 1869–1920
(Sussex Rustic Ware)
's.a.w.' Sussex Art Ware
c. 1920–39
J.C. Cole & W.V.
Cole, 1947–
various marks including
name 'RYE'
Walter V. Cole, 1957–

RYE

S

S   *see* Caughley
        Shorthose, John
        Spode, Josiah
        Skipwith, M. & E.
        Wells, Reginald

S. Bros.   *see* Stubbs Bros.

S. & Co.   *see* Isleworth
          Sowter & Co.

S. Ltd.   *see* Swinnertons Ltd.

S. & Sons.   *see* Southwick Pottery

S.A. & Co.   *see* Alcock & Co., Samuel

Sadler & Sons Ltd., James   *Burslem, Staffs.*
                    1899– , earthenware

ENGLAND
J.S.S.B.   impressed, 1899–*c.* 1937

SADLER
BURSLEM   impressed or printed, 1937–
ENGLAND

                    printed, *c.* 1947–

Sadler & Green   *Liverpool, Lancs.*
  Sadler, John & Green, Guy, 1756–99
  printers only their work seen on tiles,
  creamware, Longton Hall, Worcester, etc.

sailing ship   *see* Adderleys Ltd.

St. Anthony's Pottery   *see* Sewell, J.

St. Marychurch   *see* Watcombe Pottery Co.

St. Peter's Pottery   *see* Fell & Co.,T.

Salazar, Fiona   *London*
  NAME IN FULL   *c.* 1982, studio-potter,
                    earthenware

Salisbury China   *see* Salisbury Crown China Co.

Salisbury Crown China Co.   *Longton, Staffs.*

1927–61, bone-china
printed mark of *c.* 1952–
trade-names: Salisbury, Royal
York
1961 purchased by Royal Stafford
China & renamed Salisbury China
Co., 1973, merged with the Alfred Clough Group

Salon China   *see* Salt & Nixon

Salopian   *see* Caughley Works

Salopian Art Pottery Co.   *Benthall, Shrops.*
    SALOPIAN   1882–*c.* 1912, earthenware
    impressed

Salt, Ralph   *Hanley, Staffs.*
       SALT   *c.* 1820–46, earthenware figures
    impressed on moulded scroll

Salt Bros.   *Tunstall, Staffs.*
    SALT BROS   1897–1904, earthenware
    TUNSTALL
    ENGLAND   printed or impressed, other
    printed mark includes 'BROWNHILLS POTTERY'
    and full-name

Salt & Nixon   *Longton, Staffs.*
      S. & N.   1901–34, bone-china
        L   various printed marks with initials
    or trade-name: SALON CHINA

Samford Ware   *see* Ford & Co., Samuel

Samuel, Audrey   *London*

1949– , studio-potter

A·S

incised or painted

Sandland Ware   *see* Lancaster & Sandland Ltd.

Sandlands & Colley Ltd.   *Hanley, Staffs.*

SANDLANDS & COLLEY

c. 1907–1910, earthenware & bone-china

& 's.c.' monogram under crown, printed

Sant & Vodrey   *Cobridge, Staffs.*

s. & v.   1887–93, earthenware
COBRIDGE   printed or impressed

Saracen Pottery Co.   *see* Bayley, Murray & Co.

Saunders, Samuel E.   *Isle of Wight*

1930–40, studio-pottery
same monogram used at various
Isle of Wight addresses

Savoy China   *see* Birks, Rawlins & Co. Ltd.

S.B.   *see* Bayer, Svend

S.B. monogram in wings   *see* Stubbs Bros.

S. & B.   *see* Sefton & Brown

S. & B.   *see* Smith & Binnall
   T

S.B. & S.   *see* Bridgwood & Son, Sampson

S.C.   *see* Clive, Stephen

S. & C.   *see* Shore & Coggins

S.C.Co.   *see* Star China Co.
                      Clive, Stephen

S.C.H.   *see* Shore, Coggins & Holt
   L

Schloessingk, Micky   *Gower, Wales*
                              studio-potter in salt-glazed stoneware
                              c. 1989–

Scotia Pottery   *see* Bodley & Co., E.F.

Scott, Anthony   *Sunderland, Tyne & Wear*
                      1788–96, earthenware. Southwick Pottery

            A. SCOTT & CO.   SCOTT, SOUTHWICK
                              c. 1800–29
      ANTHONY SCOTT & SONS   S. & SONS.

            A. SCOTT & SONS.   SCOTT & SONS
            SCOTT & SONS   SOUTHWICK
                              1829–38
            SCOTT BROTHERS   SCOTT BROTHERS
                 & CO.   SCOTT BROS   S.B. & CO.
                              1838–54

        A. SCOTT   SCOTT
         c. 1854–72   1882–97
    A SCOTT & SON   S. & S.   SCOTT
              c. 1872–82 , impressed or printed

Scott Brothers   *Portobello, Scotland*
                       1825–c. 1840, stoneware
              SCOTT   SCOTT
          impressed marks   P.B.
    'P.B.' probably for Portobello, but when
    with a number could be 'pattern-book'

Scott, David   *Mountsorrel, Leics.*
        D.S.   c. 1984– , studio-potter,
                          working in red earthenware

Scrivener & Co. R.G.   *Hanley, Staffs.*
        R.G.S.   c. 1870–83, earthenware
    R.G.S.& CO.   & bone-china
    printed or impressed in a variety of marks

S.E.   *see* Elkin, Samuel

S. & E.   *see* Swift & Elkin

Sefton & Brown   *Ferrybridge, Yorks.*
    S. & B.   S. & B.   1897–1919, earthenware
              F.B.
    printed or impressed in a variety of marks

Selman, J. & W.   *Tunstall, Staffs.*
        SELMAN   c. 1864–5, earthenware figures
    rare impressed mark

Senolith   *see* Buchan & Co., A.W.

S.E.S. monogram   *see* Saunders, Samuel E.

Sewell, J.   *Newcastle upon Tyne, Tyne & Wear*
   St. Anthony's Pottery 1780–1908
   various owners:
   1780–86 King & Co., James
   1787–95 Chatto & Griffith
   1795–1800 Huntley, William
   1800–04 Foster & Cutter
   1804–28 Sewell, Joseph
   1828–52 Sewell & Donkin
   1852–78 Sewell & Co.
   (1878–82 pottery closed)
   1882–86 Lloyd, William
   1886–92 pottery closed)
   1892–1908 Patterson, Thomas, & finally closed
   marks: ST. ANTHONY   impressed 1780–1820
                  SEWELL   SEWELL   1804–28
            ST. ANTHONY S
         SEWELL & DONKIN   1828–52
            SEWELL & CO.   1852–78

         PATTERSON   1892–1908

S.F. monogram   *see* Minton (Felix Summerley)

S. & F.   *see* Smith & Ford

S.F. & Co.   *see* Fielding & Co., S.

S. & G.   *see* Isleworth & Shore, J.

S. & G./Isleworth   *see* Isleworth

S.H.   *see* Hancock & Sons, S.
S.H. & S.   *see* Stevenson & Hancock
S.H. & Sons   *see* Stevenson & Hancock
S.H. monogram   *see* Stevenson & Hancock

Shaw, Anthony   *Tunstall & Burslem, Staffs.*
  ANTHONY SHAW   1851–*c*. 1900, earthenware

A. SHAW	A.SHAW	SHAW
	BURSLEM	BURSLEM

  a variety of printed or impressed marks,
  often including Royal Arms & name of pattern.
  Moved from Tunstall to Burslem *c*. 1860
  '& Son' from *c*. 1882–*c*. 98
  '& Co.' from *c*. 1898–1900

Shaw & Copestake Ltd.   *Longton, Staffs.*
  SYLVAC WARE 1894–1989, earthenware
  various printed or impressed marks include
  name of SylvaC, 'LTD.' from 1936
  Purchased by Thomas Lawrence (Longton) Ltd.
  in 1938. Trade-name: FALCON WARE
  1964, Shaw & Copestake & Thomas Lawrence merge
  1982 leased to Longton Ceramics, who failed
  in 1984. SylvaC & Falcon wares produced under
  Crown Winsor. 1989 company closed, property
  & equipment to Portmeiron

Shaw & Sons Ltd., G.   *Rotherham, Yorks.*
  G.B. & S.   1887–1948, earthenware
  printed in a variety of marks

Shaw & Sons (Longton) Ltd, John   *Longton, Staffs.*

c. 1931–63, earthenware &
bone-china
trade-name: BURLINGTON
early mark, J.S.S. monogram
with Burlington Art Pottery

printed mark *c.* 1949–

Shaw, Ralph   *Cobridge, Staffs.*
   early 18th C. slip-decorated earthenware
   'Made by Ralph Shaw,
  October 31, Cobridge gate'
   rare inscription dated 1740 or '46

Shaw & Sons   *Tunstall, Staffs.*
     s. & s.   1892–1910, earthenware
      s.   impressed or printed

Shelley   *see* Shelley Potteries Ltd.
           Wileman & Co.

Shelley Potteries Ltd.   *Longton, Staffs.*

1925–65, bone-china
1965, renamed SHELLEY CHINA LTD.
now part of Royal Doulton Ltd.

Shepherd & Co., Alfred   *Longton, Staffs.*
  A.SHEPHERD & CO.   1864–*c.* 70, bone-china
  printed with 'EAGLE WORKS.LONGTON'
     A.S. & CO.   impressed

Sherwin & Cotton   *Hanley, Staffs.*

1877–1930, tiles

SHERWIN & COTTON
impressed or incised

impressed

Shirley, Cecil John   *see* Della Robbia

Shirley & Co., Thomas   *Greenock, Scotland*
T.S. & COY.   *c.* 1840–57, earthenware
T.S. & C.   impressed marks

Shore & Co.   *see* Isleworth

Shore & Coggins   *Longton, Staffs.*

1911–64, bone-china
trade-names: BELL CHINA,
QUEEN ANNE, PRINCESS ANNE

printed *c.* 1913
1918, purchased by T.C. WILD & SONS
1930, Ltd.Co.; 1964 Taken over by Lawley
now part of Royal Doulton Ltd.

Shore, Coggins & Holt   *Longton, Staffs.*
S.C.H.   1905–10, bone china
L   printed mark under crown

Shore, J.   *Isleworth, London*
SHORE & CO.   *c.* 1760–1825, earthenware
S. & CO.   S. & G.   SHORE & GOULDING

S. & G.   impressed marks
ISLEWORTH

Note: S. & G. seen on Wedgwood-type wares are
more likely to have been made by Schiller
& Gerbing, Bodenbach, Bohemia, after 1829

Shore & Co., J.   *Longton, Staffs.*
J.S. & CO.   *c.* 1887–1905, bone-china
printed in a variety of marks

Shorter & Son, Ltd.   *Stoke, Staffs.*

1905–64, earthenware
purchased by Crown Devon
(S. Fielding & Co.Ltd.)
Fielding closed in 1982.
Trade-names in marks:
BATAVIA WARE, SUNRAY POTTERY,
CROWN DEVON

printed *c.* 1940–

Shorthose & Co.   *Hanley, Staffs.*
c. 1817– , earthenware &
SHORTHOSE & CO.   bone-china
printed on piece with copy of Worcester
crescent mark, which probably dates from
the earlier period of Shorthose & Heath

Shorthose, John   *Hanley, Staffs.*
S   1807–23, earthenware &
probably porcelain
SHORTHOSE   impressed marks

Shorthose & Heath   *Hanley, Staffs.*
   SHORTHOSE &   *c.* 1795–1815, earthenware
   HEATH   impressed or printed

S.I. monogram   *see* Leach, Janet

Sibley Pottery Ltd.   *Wareham, Dorset*
                          1922–62, earthenware &
   Sibley   stoneware
   rare incised mark *c.* 1922–28
   Sibley Ware   impressed with
   HANDMADE   sketch of pottery
ENGLAND STONEWARE   1946–53

Silchester Ware   *see* Collier, S. & E.

Silverman, Ray   *Hornchurch, Essex*
                          1962– , studio-potter in
porcelain & stoneware

Simpson, John   *probably Burslem, Staffs.*
   I.S.   *c.* 1710–15, slip-trailed wares
   initials slip-trailed in decoration

Simpson, Ralph   *probably Burslem, Staffs.*
                          c. 1651–*c.* 1724, slip-trailed
                          earthenware
   RALPH SIMPSON   name in slip as part of decoration

Simpson, William   *Tunstall, Staffs.*
                          Late 18th–early 19th C.
   WILLIAM SIMPSON   slip-trailed earthenware

Simpsons (Potters) Ltd.   *Cobridge, Staffs.*

1944– active in 1990, earthenware
Full-name printed in marks including
trade-names: AMBASSADOR WARE (*c.* 1944–),
SOLIAN WARE (*c.* 1944), LOH YUEH MEI KUEI,
(*c.* 1951), VOGUE (*c.* 1954), CHINASTYLE (*c.* 1957),
MARLBOROUGH OLD ENGLISH IRONSTONE (*c.* 1959)

S.J.   *see* Johnson Ltd.,Samuel
S.J.B.
S.J.Ltd.

S. & J.B.   *see* Burton, Samuel & John

Skinner & Co., George   *Stockton-on-Tees, Cleveland*

G.S. & CO.   *c.* 1855–70,
earthenware
printed in a variety of marks, sometimes
with name of pattern & impressed marks
of previous occupiers William Smith & Co.

Skinner & Walker   *Stockton-on-Tees, Cleveland*

S. & W.   *c.* 1870–80,
QUEEN'S WARE   earthenware
STOCKTON

S. & W'S   QUEEN'S WARE
PEARL WARE   STOCKTON
printed or impressed marks

Skipwith, Michael & Elizabeth   *Totnes, S. Devon*

1957– (Michael alone, 1981–)
(Lotus Pottery) studio-potters

S.K.W.   *see* Wardell, S.

S.L.   *see* Longbottom, Samuel

S. & L.   *see* Stanley & Lambert

Slack & Brownlow   *Tonbridge, Kent*
   TONBRIDGE WARE   *c.* 1928–34, earthenware

TONBRIDGE	printed or impressed with
CASTLE WARE	sketch of castle

S.M.   *see* Malkin, Samuel

S.M. & Co.   *see* (Samuel) Moore & Co.

Smith & Co., Ambrose   *Burslem, Staffs.*
   A.S. & CO.   *c.* 1784–6, earthenware
  impressed or printed

Smith, Annie   *see* Della Robbia

Smith & Binnall   *Tunstall, Staffs.*
                  1897–1900, earthenware

                  printed mark

Smith & Ford   *Burslem, Staffs.*
                    1895–8,
  printed   earthenware

Smith, Frank   *Rye, Sussex*

1962– , studio-potter
working in stoneware

Smith, George F.   *Stockton-on-Tees, Cleveland*

G.F.S. & CO.   *c.* 1855–60,
                     earthenware
G.F.S.   printed or impressed

Smith, James   *Stoke, Staffs.*

1898–1924, bone-
china &
earthenware

printed or   JAMES SMITH
impressed 1922–   printed

printed mark,
c. 1898–1922

Smith, Peter   *Penzance, Cornwall*

Bojewyan Pottery
1975– , studio-potter
in earthenware

Smith, Sampson   *Longton, Staffs.*

                     1851–1960, earthenware & bone-china
SAMPSON SMITH   figures
    1851   'LTD.' from 1918
  LONGTON

's.s.' monograms used on most 20th C.
printed marks, with trade-names:
'WETLEY' or 'OLD ROYAL CHINA'
1959, purchased by Alfred Clough Ltd.
1960, closed

Smith & Co.,Thomas   *London*
   T.SMITH & CO.   1879–93, stoneware
   OLD KENT RD.
      LONDON   incised or impressed

Smith, Theophilus   *Tunstall, Staffs.*
    T. SMITH   1790–*c.* 97, earthenware
  impressed

Smith (Junr) & Co., William   *Stockton-on-Tees, Cleveland*
  W.S.JNR. & CO.   *c.* 1845–84, earthenware
  W.S.JR.&CO.
  printed or impressed, 1845–55
      W.S.   printed or impressed
   STOCKTON   *c.* 1870–84

Smith & Co., William   *Stockton-on-Tees, Cleveland*
            c. 1825–55, earthenware
  W.S. & CO.   W.S. & CO.   printed or
  STAFFORD   impressed in a variety
  POTTERY   of marks

  W.S. & CO'S.   W.S.& CO'S
  WEDGEWOOD   QUEEN'S WARE
                   STOCKTON
Note: spelling of WEDGEWOOD from 1848
             (no second 'E' in early pottery).

Smith Ltd.,W.T.H.   *Longport, Staffs.*

W.T.H.SMITH LTD.   1898–1905,
LONGPORT   earthenware
printed around globe under crown

Sneyd, Thomas   *Hanley, Staffs.*

T. SNEYD   1846–7, earthenware
HANLEY   impressed mark

Sneyd & Hill   *Hanley, Staffs.*

SNEYD & HILL   *c.* 1845, earthenware
HANLEY
STAFFORDSHIRE
POTTERIES   printed mark

S. & N.   *see* Salt & Nixon
  L

S. & Co.   *see* Sowter & Co.

Soho Pottery Ltd.   *Tunstall & Cobridge, Staffs.*

1901–44, earthenware
1901–6, Tunstall
1906–44, Cobridge

trade-names with Soho
early mark   Pottery Ltd: SOLIAN WARE,
AMBASSADOR WARE, QUEENS GREEN, HOMESTEAD
WARE & CHANTICLEER
SIMPSONS (POTTERS) LTD. of Cobridge continue
to use many of the Soho Pottery Ltd. trade-names
plus MARLBOROUGH, IRONSTONE &
CHINASTYLE, after take-over in *c.* 1906

Solly, John   *Rye, Sussex*

1953, studio-potter, earthenware
& stoneware

impressed

PEASMARSH   moved from Maidstone in
JOHN   1986
SOLLY
RYE.E.SX.

Soon   *see* Wells, Reginald

Southcliffe & Co.Ltd.   *see* Creigau Pottery

South Wales Pottery   *Llanelly, Wales*
c. 1839–58, earthenware

CHAMBERS   S. WALES
LLANELLY   POTTERY
                       W. CHAMBERS
Chambers & Co.   printed or impressed, c. 1839–54

SOUTH WALES   S.W.P.   printed or
POTTERY   impressed
Coombs & Holland, c. 1854–58

Southwick Pottery   *see* Scott, Anthony

Sowter & Co., Robert   *Mexborough, Yorks.*
1800–1808, earthenware

SOWTER'S & CO.
MEXBRO   S. & CO.
rare impressed

Sparks, George   *see* Worcester

Spode, Josiah (*d.* 1797)   *Stoke, Staffs.*

Spode	*c.* 1770– , earthenware,
impressed	stoneware & porcelain
c. 1800–20	Copeland & Garrett from
	1833–47

'SPODE' in underglaze-blue, 1810–23

'StokeChina', rare impressed mark, *c.* 1796–1800

'SPODE' or 'Spode', with pattern number, painted in red from *c.* 1799–1833

      'Spode'   in underglaze blue

                         c. 1790–1805

printed in various underglaze colours, *c.* 1805–33

 impressed, *c.* 1822–33

printed marks from *c.* 1822–33

      rare 1806–8   1826–33

marks of Copeland & Garrett period 1833–47

COPELAND	COPELAND & GARRETT	impressed
& GARRETT	circular mark, enclosing 'LATE SPODE'	
1833–47	1833–40	

'COPELAND & GARRETT' impressed around 'NEW FAYENCE'
1833–47

**COPELAND
& GARRETT**

impressed mark from *c.* 1839

printed marks of 1833–47

printed 1838–47

COPELAND 1847–

impressed 1847–54   1860–80

337

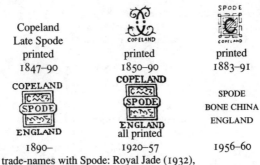

Copeland
Late Spode
printed
1847–90

printed
1850–90

printed
1883–91

COPELAND
SPODE
ENGLAND

1890–

COPELAND
SPODE
ENGLAND
all printed

1920–57

SPODE
BONE CHINA
ENGLAND

1956–60

trade-names with Spode: Royal Jade (1932),
ONYX (1932), Velamour (1932–4), Flemish Green
(1949–65), Fortuna (1955–60)
1974, acquired by Worcester Royal Porcelain
Co. Ltd., merging into Royal Worcester Spode Ltd.
in 1976
1988, Derby International Ltd. purchased
Royal Worcester Spode, but from Dec. 1988
Spode Ltd. & Royal Worcester Ltd. operate
separately under the American company
now retitled The Porcelain & Fine China
Companies Ltd.

Springburn   *see* Campbellfield Pottery Co.

S.R. monogram   *see* Colclough & Co.
                                    Radford Ltd.,Samuel

S.S. monogram   *see* Smith Ltd., Sampson

S. & S.   *see* Southwick Pottery
                        Sutherland & Sons, Daniel

S. & S.   *see* Shaw & Sons
  S

S.T.   *see* Taylor, Sutton

Stabler, Harold & Phoebe   *Dorset & London*
                              First half of 20th C. designers
                              & potters. Producing figures and groups
                              in Hammersmith, London, *c.* 1910
   Harold Stabler (*d.* 1945) was a partner in
   Carter, Stabler & Adams; Poole from 1921
   acting as artistic consultant
       STABLER
     HAMMERSMITH   HAROLD STABLER
       LONDON
     impressed   moulded
   Phoebe Stabler (*d.* 1955) was designing
   figures for Doulton by 1913, also
   modelled for the Poole Pottery, Ashstead
   Potters and Worcester. Mark, impressed
   PHOEBE STABLER

stag, prancing   *see* Wade & Son Ltd.,George

Standard China   *see* Chapmans (Longton) Ltd.

Standige, Gary   *Aylesford, Kent*
                              c. 1974, studio potter in
                              stoneware & porcelain

Stanley Bone China   *see* Amison & Co. Ltd., Charles

Stanley & Lambert   *Longton, Staffs.*
   S. & L.   *c.* 1850–54, earthenware
 printed in a variety of marks

Stanley Pottery Ltd.   *Longton, Staffs.*

      1928–31, earthenware &
      bone-china
      marks of former owners,
      Colclough & Co. were
      continued

Stanyer, A.   *Burslem, Staffs.*
   A.S.   A.S. *c.* 1916–41, earthenware
   B   ENG.
   ENG.   B.   impressed marks

Star China Co.   *Longton, Staffs.*
    S.C.CO.   *c.* 1899–1919, bone-china
 printed with star & crown and from *c.* 1904
 the trade-name 'PARAGON CHINA' was included.
 After various take-overs this company
 was renamed ROYAL ALBERT under Doulton
 Group in 1989

Star Pottery   *Glasgow, Scotland*

      1880–1907, stoneware &
      majolica
      impressed or printed

Starkey, Peter *Whitchurch, Heref.*

1973–, studio-potter,
salt-glazed stoneware

Staffordshire knot, in triangle *see* Sherwin & Cotton

Steel, Daniel *Burslem, Staffs.*

STEEL 1790–1824, earthenware &
stoneware

STEEL BURSLEM impressed marks

Steele & Wood *Stoke, Staffs.*

1875–1892, tiles

printed or impressed

Steelite International since 1989 a
factory at Meir Park Stoke, supplying
biscuit bone-china to Burslem

Sterling Pottery Ltd. *Fenton, Staffs.*

1947–53, earthenware
from *c.* 1950, marks include
'RIDGWAY', who were owned
by Lawleys Ltd. from
1948

Stevenson, Andrew   *Cobridge, Staffs.*
    STEVENSON   *c.* 1816–30, earthenware

    A. STEVENSON   impressed

         A. STEVENSON WARRANTED STAFFORDSHIRE
impressed in circular form containing
crown

          impressed

Stevenson, Ralph   *Cobridge, Staffs.*
    R. STEVENSON   1810–32, earthenware
    R.S.
    STEVENSON   all impressed
    (crown)
    STAFFORDSHIRE

Stevenson & Son, Ralph   *Cobridge, Staffs.*
              c. 1832–35, earthenware &
  R. STEVENSON & SONS   possibly bone-china
    printed in a variety of marks on earthenware
    but bone-china as yet unidentified

Stevenson, Alcock & Williams   *Cobridge, Staffs.*
    STEVENSON   *c.* 1820–35, earthenware &
    ALCOCK &   probably bone-china
    WILLIAMS   printed

Stevenson & Hancock   *see* Derby

Stevenson, Sharp & Co.   *see* Derby

Stevenson, Spencer & Co.Ltd.   *Longton, Staffs.*

printed, *c.* 1948–

c. 1948–60, earthenware & bone-china
various other printed marks
include trade-names: ROYAL
STUART or WILLOW

Stevenson, William   *Hanley, Staffs.*

W. STEVENSON
HANLEY
impressed

c. 1802– , earthenware &
stoneware

Stevenson & Williams   *Cobridge, Staffs.*

R.S.W.
R.S. & W.
c. 1825

printed or impressed with initials or
full name of marks often with title
of pattern on earthenware

Stiff, James   *Lambeth, London*

J.STIFF
J.STIFF & SONS

c. 1840–1913, stoneware
impressed marks with the

addition of '& SONS' from *c.* 1863
Taken over by Doulton in 1913

Stoke Pottery (with crown)   *see* Grimwades

Stoodley, Peter   *Lymington, Hants.*

1952–, studio-potter, stoneware

Stritch, John   *Limerick, Ireland*

Made by
John Stritch.
Limerick, 4th June, 1761

c. 1760– , tin-glazed earthenware
(delftware)
inscription

Stringer, Harry Horlock   *Barnes, London*

1953– , stoneware & porcelain
at present, previously earthenware

monogram of 'Taggs Yard'
address of pottery

impressed

Stubbs Bros.   *Fenton, Staffs.*

1899–1904, bone-china

printed

Stubbs, Joseph   *Burslem, Staffs.*

STUBBS   *c.* 1822–35, earthenware

JOSEPH STUBBS   impressed or printed
LONGPORT

Stubbs & Kent   *Burslem, Staffs.*

c. 1828–30, earthenware

impressed or printed

Studio Szeiler   *Hanley, Staffs.*

c. 1951–*c.* 1989, earthenware

printed or impressed

Sudlow & Sons Ltd., R.   *Burslem, Staffs.*
1893– , earthenware
full-name marks impressed or printed from
c. 1920. Part of Howard Pottery Co.Ltd.
from 1965, taken over by Coloroll Ceramics,
1990

Summerbank Pottery Ltd.   *Tunstall, Staffs.*
SUMMERBANK   1952– at least 1991, earthenware
name changed to SUMMERBANK POTTERY (1970) Ltd.
(name of modeller)   COOPERCRAFT
SUMMERBANK POTTERY   MADE IN
STAFFORDSHIRE   ENGLAND
ENGLAND

Summerly, Felix (Henry Cole)   *see* Minton

Sunderland or 'Garrison' Pottery,   *see* Phillips, J.

Sunfield Pottery   *Stourbridge, W.Midlands*
1937– , earthenware & stoneware

impressed or printed

Sutcliffe & Co. Ltd., C.P.   *Manchester, Lancs.*
*c.*1885–1801, tiles

printed or impressed

345

Sutherland China   *see* Hudson, William
                         Hudson & Middleton Ltd.

Sutherland & Sons, Daniel   *Longton, Staffs.*
         S. & S.   *c.* 1863–77, Parian & earthenware
    impressed or printed

S. & V.   *see* Sant & Vodrey

S.W.   *see* Walton, S.

S. & W.   *see* Skinner & Walker

Swain, Helen   *Waltham Forest, London*
                         1945– , studio-potter,
    $H/S\ 85$ was with Royal Doulton, Lambeth

Swansea Pottery   *Swansea, Wales*
                         c. 1783–1870, earthenware &
      SWANSEA   porcelain
    impressed
    CAMBRIAN POTTERY   CAMBRIA

                    CAMBRIAN.

    impressed or printed, *c.* 1783–1810
      DILLWYN & CO.   D. & CO.   DILLWYN & CO.
    impressed or printed, *c.* 1811–17   SWANSEA

          BEVINGTON & CO.   T. & J. BEVINGTON
                    impressed, *c.* 1817–25
    BEVINGTON & CO., T. & J.   *c.* 1817–21
        BEVINGTON, T.J.   1821–1825

DILLWYN   D   DILLWYN
SWANSEA
impressed or printed, *c.* 1824–50

CYMRO
STONE CHINA
impressed
c. 1847–50

printed, 1847–50
Evans, David & Glasson
c. 1850–62
impressed or printed

D.J.EVANS & CO.   EVANS & CO.
printed in a variety of marks, often
including title of pattern, *c.* 1862–70

marks on porcelain, 1814–22

      SWANSEA

Swansea

impressed, 1814–22 printed or written
DILLWYN & CO.   DILWYN & CO.
impressed, 1814–17   SWANSEA

BEVINGTON & CO.   impressed *c.* 1820

Swift & Elkin   *Longton, Staffs.*
      S. & E.   1840–45, earthenware
printed in a variety of marks, usually
with title of pattern

Swinnertons Ltd.   *Hanley, Staffs.*
                          1906–59, earthenware

   SWINNERTONS   printed, *c*. 1906–17
      HANLEY
                     'LTD.' added from 1911,
various printed marks with either full-name,
'S.LTD.' or trade-name of VITRION,
ROYAL WESSEX, or HAMPTON IVORY.
1959, taken over by Lawley Group;
1964, part of Allied English Potteries;
1973, in Royal Doulton Group

S.W.P.   *see* South Wales Pottery

Sx   *see* Caughley

Sykes, Steven   *Richmond, Surrey*
     Steven Sykes   1948–55, studio-potter
written signature

SylvaC   *see* Shaw & Copestake,Ltd.

Sylvan Pottery Ltd.   *Hanley, Staffs.*

                          1946 – at least 1990, but
probably decorating only,
trade-name SylvaC, first
used by Shaw & Copestake, *c*. 1894

T

Tams, John   *Longton, Staffs.*

	c. 1875–at least 1990,
J.TAMS	earthenware
J.T.	name or initials printed in
	a variety of marks, often with
J.T.	title of pattern, 1875–90.
monogram	with 'CROWN POTTERY', wreath & crown.

'& SONS' added in 1903, 'LTD.' from 1912,
becoming John Tams PLC in 1988. Various
trade-names: Nankin Ware (1913–), Elephant
Brand (*c.* 1952–), Top-of-the World (*c.* 1955–),
TAMS REGENT (*c.* 1958), Chinine (*c.* 1960–).
1989, took over Finney & Sons Ltd., A.T.
and today produce wares with their trade-
name, DUCHESS BONE CHINA, together with
own, JOHN TAMS

Tams & Lowe   *Longton, Staffs.*

| T. & L. | 1865–74, earthenware |

printed in a variety of marks, often
including name of pattern

Tantallow Ceramics   *Berwick, Scotland*

TANTALLOW	1962–, earthenware
CERAMICS	
NORTH BERWICK	

T.A. & S.G.   *see* Green, T.A. & S.

Taylor & Co., T.   *Newcastle upon Tyne, Tyne & Wear*
                                    c. 1821–27, earthenware at the

	Tyne Pottery.
TAYLOR & CO.	printed. Further owners:
	Wood, Joseph *c.* 1827–27
	Patterson, Thomas, 1827–29
	Codling & Co. 1833–*c.* 37
	Patterson & Co. *c.* 1837

Taylor, George   *Hanley, Staffs.*
c. 1784–1811, earthenware &
GEO. TAYLOR   stoneware
G.TAYLOR   impressed or incised

Taylor & Kent   *Longton, Staffs.*
T. & K.   1876–1983, bone-china
L   printed or impressed in a
variety of marks, often with
name of pattern
Company purchased in 1947, renamed
ELIZABETHAN FINE BONE CHINA LTD. in 1983.
Merged in 1987 with The Rosina China Co. Ltd.
and since 1989 have been The Crownford China
Co. Ltd. Trade-names: Queen's China &
Elizabethan. Crownford purchased by
Arthur Wood & Son Ltd. 1993

Taylor, Nicholas   *Denholme, Yorks.*
mark of   1893–1909, earthenware
incised signature

Taylor, Sutton   *Aberford, Leeds*
studio-potter, earthenware
and lustrewares, working in 1989

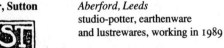

Taylor, Tunnicliffe & Co.   *Hanley & Longton, Staffs.*
      T.T.   1868– , earthenware & bone-china
      T.T.&CO.   now owned by Bullers Ltd. at
                          Longton
  c. 1868–80, printed in a variety of marks

                  printed, *c.* 1875–98

Taylor, William Howson (*d.* 1935)   *Smethwick, nr. Birmingham*
                        1898–1935, earthenware
                        painted or incised, *c.* 1898–

                        impressed, *c.* 1904–15

    RUSKIN   RUSKIN POTTERY   RUSKIN
    ENGLAND

                      impressed, *c.* 1904–
    RUSKIN   W. HOWSON TAYLOR
  MADE IN ENGLAND   RUSKIN
                        ENGLAND
                      printed or impressed,
                      c. 1920

T.B.   *see* Bevington, Thomas

T. & B.   *see* Tomkinson & Billington

T.B. & Co.   *see* Booth & Co., Thomas

T.B.G. or **T. & B.G.**   *see* Godwin, T. & B.

T.B.H. monogram   *see* Bell-Hughes, Terry

T.B. & S.   *see* Boote, Ltd., T. & R.
               Booth & Son, T.

T.C. monogram   *see* Cone Ltd.,T.

T.C. or **T.C.**   *see* Cone Ltd.,T.
 L   **Longton**

T. & C.F.   *see* Ford, T. & C.

T.C.W. or as monogram   *see* Wild & Sons Ltd.,T.C.

Temple Gate Pottery   *see* Powell, William

T.F.   *see* Ford, Thomas
           Fuchs, T.

T.F. & Co.   *see* Fell & Co., Thomas
               Forester & Co.,T.
               Furnival & Co.,T.

T.F. & Sons, monogram   *see* Furnival & Sons.,T.

T.G.   *see* Godwin, Thomas
           Green, Thomas

T.G.B.   *see* Booth, Thomas G.

T.G. & F.B.   *see* Booth, T.G. & F.

T.G.G. & Co. Ltd.   *see* Green & Co.,T.G.

T.H. in shield   *see* Bell-Hughes, Terry

Thomas & Co.,Uriah   *Hanley, Staffs.*
                   1888–1905, earthenware &
                   majolica
                   printed or impressed
                   over 'Hanley' or 'Hanley England'

Thompson, Joseph   *nr. Ashby de la Zouch, Leics.*
                   c. 1818–56, earthenware,
                   stoneware & *terra-cotta*

J.THOMPSON	J.THOMPSON	
impressed	HARTSTONE	printed
	NEAR	
	ASHBY DE LA ZOUCH	
From 1856:	THOMPSON BROTHERS	

Thomson, E.G.   *see* Wedgwood & Sons Ltd., J.

Thomson, John   *Glasgow, Scotland*
                   1826–88, black & brown earthenware
From 1865 until 1888: John Thomson & Sons.

STONE	JOHN THOMSON	THOMSON
WARE	(anchor)	
J.T.	GRANITE	
(in shield)	impressed, 1826–65	

Later marks from 1865–88:
     J.T.
     STONE
     WARE
(in ornamental frame)

Thorley China Ltd.   *Longton, Staffs.*
THORLEY CHINA   *c.* 1940–70, bone-china
      LTD.
(printed under crown)

Thorpe, Owen   *Churchstoke, Powys*
                                    Studio-potter, in stoneware
                                    or full signature

T.H. & P.   *see* Turner, Hassall & Peake

T.I.   *see* Ifield, Thomas

T.I. & Co.   *see* Ingleby & Co.,Thomas

T.I. & J.E.   *see* Emberton, T.I. & J.

Till & Sons, Thomas   *Burslem, Staffs.*
                                    c. 1850–1928, earthenware

                            TILL   TILL & SONS
                            '& SONS' added *c.* 1861

printed *c.* 1861– , later marks with full-name
include a globe from *c.* 1800; 'England' from
c. 1891 and 'TILLSON WARE' from *c.* 1922

Tittensor, Charles   *Shelton, Staffs.*
      TITTENSOR   *c.* 1815–23, earthenware
mark impressed on figures & printed on
other wares

Tittensor, Jacob   *Stoke, Staffs.*
   Jacob Tittensor   1780–95, earthenware
  signature, very rare mark

T. & L.   *see* Tams & Lowe

T.L.K. or **T. & K.**   *see* Taylor & Kent Ltd.
        L

T.M. monogram with lion   *see* Morris, Thomas

T.M.R.   *see* Randall, Thomas

T.N. & Co.   *see* Nicholson, Thomas

T.O. monogram   *see* Thorpe, O.

Toft   *see* Minton

Toft, Ralph, James & Thomas   *Hanley, Staffs.*
                              c. 1670–1710, slip-trailed earthenwares
  Ralph Toft (*b.* 1638) James Toft (*b.* 1673)
  Thomas Toft (*d.* 1689). Names written in
  slip with decoration

Tollow, Vera   *Goudhurst, Kent*
    TOLLOW   1954– , studio-potter
  name written in full

Tomkinson & Billington   *Longton, Staffs.*
    T. & B.   *c.* 1868–70, earthenware &
  printed in a   bone-china
  variety of marks

Tomlinson & Co.   *see* Ferrybridge

Tonbridge Ware   *see* Slack & Brownlow

Tooth & Co.   *nr Burton-on-Trent, Derbys.*

TOOTH & AULT	1883–87, earthenware
TOOTH & CO.	1887–1933

trade-mark of Bretby Art
Pottery, 1884–
printed or impressed
'ENGLAND' added in 1891

initials of Henry Tooth
c. 1883–1900

CLANTA		CLANTA
c. 1914–		WARE

Tooth, Henry   *see* Linthorpe Pottery

Torquay Pottery Co.   *see* Torquay Terra-Cotta Co. Ltd.

Torquay Terra-Cotta Co. Ltd.   *Torquay, Devon*

TORQUAY	TORQUAY	impressed or
	TERRA-COTTA CO.	printed, 1875–90
	LIMITED	

printed or impressed
1883– *c.* 1905

HELE CROSS	stamped mark of
POTTERY	1905–1918
TORQUAY	

Closed from *c.* 1904–1908, and re-opened
as TORQUAY POTTERY CO., making *terra-cotta* wares until *c.* 1940

Townsend, D.   *see* Iden Pottery

Townsend, George.   *Longton, Staffs.*
   G. TOWNSEND   1850–65, earthenware &
printed with   bone-china
Royal Arms & name of pattern in a
variety of marks

T.P.L.   *see* Ledgar, Thomas P.

T. & R.B.   *see* Boote Ltd.,T. & R.

T. & R.Co.   *see* Rathbone & Co.,Thomas
                          Rathbone & Co.,T.

  trees, copse, impressed   *see* Wood, R. or J.

Trentham Art Ware   *see* DEVONSHIRE POTTERIES LTD.

Trentham Bone China Ltd.   *Longton, Staffs.*
                           1952–7, bone-china
                           trade-names: TRENTHAM &
                           ROYAL CROWN POTTERY

Trey, Marianne de   *Totnes, Devon*
                         1947– , studio-pottery in
                         porcelain & stoneware

                         incised or
                         painted

357

tridents, crossed   *see* Swansea Pottery

T.R.& P.   *see* Tundley, Rhodes & Proctor

T.S. & Co.   *see* Clyde Pottery Co.

T.T. or **T.T. & Co.**   *see* Taylor, Tunnicliffe & Co. Ltd.

T. & T.   *see* Turner & Tomkinson

T.U. & Co. monogram   *see* Thomas & Co.,Uriah

Tundley, Rhodes & Proctor   *Burslem, Staffs.*
     T.R.&P.   1873–83, earthenware
  printed in a variety of marks, often
  including name of pattern

Tunnicliffe Michael   *Tunstall, Staffs.*

                   1828–41, bone-china &
                   proably earthenware

                   moulded in relief

Tunnicliffe & Pascoe   *see* Ashby Potters' Guild

Turner & Abbott   *Longton, Staffs.*
  TURNER & ABBOTT   1781–92, earthenware &
     impressed   stoneware

Turner & Co.   *see* Turner, John

Turner, Goddard & Co.   *Tunstall, Staffs.*

TURNER, GODDARD & CO.	1867–74, earthenware

printed in a variety of marks. Trade-name:
ROYAL PATENT IRONSTONE

Turner & Sons, G.W.   *Tunstall, Staffs.*

TURNERS	1873–95, earthenware & china
G.W.T.& SONS	G.W.T.S.
impressed	G.W.T.& S.
	G.T.& S.

initials printed in a variety of marks,
sometimes with Royal Arms, 'England' added *c.* 1891

Turner, John   (*d.* 1787)   *Lane End, Staffs.*

TURNER	1762–1806, earthenware
I.TURNER	from 1803
TURNER & ABBOTT	impressed names
1781–2	printed or impressed after
	Turner was made potter to
	the Prince of Wales in 1784.
	TURNER & CO.
	impressed

TURNER.

TURNER/MIST SOLE AGENT   impressed

Turner's Patent   painted mark on
ironstone-type ware
1800–05

sons, William & John II continued the business after the death
of their father in 1787; with Glover & Simpson, 1803–4
& W. Turner, Glover & Simpson, 1804–6
John Turner I was with the New Hall Co. 1781–2

Turner, Hassall & Peake   *Stoke, Staffs.*
   TURNER, HASSALL   *c.* 1863–71, earthenware,
      & PEAKE   Parian & bone-china
      T.H.P.   printed or impressed in a
  variety of marks, often with name of pattern

Turner, Thomas   *see* Caughley Works

Turner & Tomkinson   *Tunstall, Staffs.*
    TURNER &   1860–72, earthenware
   TOMKINSON   names or initials printed
      T.T.   in a variety of marks

Turner & Wood   *Stoke, Staffs.*
   TURNER & WOOD   *c.* 1878–88, earthenware,
      STOKE   Parian & bone-china
  impressed
Turners   *see* Turner & Sons, G.W.

Turner's Patent   *see* Turner, John

Tuscan   *see* Decoro Pottery
            Plant Ltd., R.H. & S.L.

T.W. & Co.   *see* Wild & Co.,Thomas C.
            Wood & Co.,Thomas

Twemlow, John   *Shelton, Staffs.*
     J.T.   1795–7, earthenware & stoneware
  impressed

Twigg, Joseph   (*d.* 1843)   *nr. Swinton, Yorks.*
               c. 1809–73 at Newhill Pottery, earthenware

also at Kilnhurst Pottery 1839–84

J.T.
TWIGG   Joseph Twigg   *c.* 1820–39
impressed
TWIGG
NEWHILL   Joseph Twigg & sons, Newhill
impressed   *c.* 1834–60
TWIGG's mark common to both potteries
c. 1840–84

T Y stylized monogram   *see* Stringer, H.H.

Tyne Main Pottery   *see* Davies & Co.

Tyne Pottery   *see* Taylor & Co.

U

U.C.& N.   *see* Clark, Uriah (Dicker Pottery)

U.H.P.Co.   *see* Upper Hanley Pottery Co.

U.H. & W.   *see* Unwin, Holmes & Worthington

U.M.& T.   *see* Unwin, Mountford & Taylor

Universal Pottery (Longton) Ltd.   *Longton, Staffs.*

1949–62, earthenware
other printed marks include
'UNIVERSAL WARE', around
chequered panels

Unwin & Co., Joseph   *Longton, Staffs.*
     UNWIN   1877–1926, earthenware
  moulded in relief   '& CO.' added from 1891

Unwin, Mountford & Taylor   *Hanley, Staffs.*
     U.M. & T.   *c.* 1864, earthenware
  initials printed in a variety of marks,
  sometimes with name of pattern

Unwin, Holmes & Worthington   *Hanley, Staffs.*
     U.H. & W.   *c.* 1865–8, earthenware
  printed in a variety of marks, often
  with name in full & name of pattern

Upchurch Pottery   *Rainham, Kent*
     UPCHURCH   1913–61, earthenware

     UPCHURCH   1945–61 impressed marks
       SEEBY   including name of agent
                   from 1945

Upper Hanley Pottery Co.   *Hanley & Cobridge, Staffs.*
     U.H.P.CO.   1895–1910, earthenware
     ENGLAND   moved from Hanley to Cobridge,
                  1902. 'LTD.' added from *c.* 1900
  impressed or printed marks, sometimes
  with name in full

U.T. & Co. monogram   *see* Thomas & Co., Uriah

V

Vale   *see* Colclough China Ltd.
          Colclough, H.J.

Vedgwood a seemingly deliberate wrong spelling of WEDGWOOD,
    used by William Smith & Co. of Stockton-on-Tees on creamware,
    with impressed mark

Venables & Baines   *Burslem, Staffs.*
    VENABLES &   *c.* 1851–3, earthenware
    BAINES
    printed or impressed

Venables & Co., John   *Burslem, Staffs.*
    J.VENABLES   *c.* 1853–5, earthenware
    & CO.   printed or impressed

Vergette, Nicholas   *London*
                                1946–58, studio-potter

V. N.V

                        painted or incised

Vernon & Son, James   *Burslem, Staffs.*
        J.V.   1860–80, earthenware
        printed
        J.V. & S.   J.V.junr.
        printed from *c.* 1875, when '& Son' was
        added to a variety of marks

Victoria   *see* Cartwright & Edwards

Victoria Porcelain (Fenton) Ltd.   *Fenton, Staffs.*

1949–57, earthenware

printed mark, other marks all
include full-name

Victoria & Trentham Potteries Ltd.   *Fenton, Staffs.*

c. 1957-60, earthenware & bone-china
above printed mark continued with the
addition of 'TRENTHAM'

Viking Pottery Co.   *Cobridge, Staffs.*

c. 1936–63, earthenware &
bone-china
printed, other marks include
full details

Vitrilain   *see* Wedgwood & Co.Ltd.

Vitro Hotel Ware   *see* Grimwade Ltd.

Vodrey's Pottery   *Dublin, Ireland*

VODREY DUBLIN   1872–*c.* 85, earthenware
    POTTERY
impressed, not to be confused with the
American Vodrey Pottery Co., *c.* 1896.

Vulcan Ware   *see* Elektra Porcelain Co.Ltd.

Vyse, Charles (*d.* 1968)   *Chelsea, London*

1919–*c.* 1963, earthenware & stoneware

C.V. C.V.	Charles Vyse
CHELSEA	
impressed or	written signature
incised	including year

painted	VYSE C. VYSE
C. VYSE	incised or painted over
CHELSEA	year, on stoneware

| C. VYSE | impressed or incised, |
| CHELSEA | no year date after 1946 |

W

W   *see* Walley, Edward
            Wallwork, Alan
            Wardle & Co.Ltd.
            Wheeldon, J.
            Winkley, D.
            Winterburn, M.
            Wood, Enoch
            Worcester

W, in triangle   *see* Dunn, Constance

W. Bros.   *see* Wild Bros.

W. & Co.   *see* Whittaker & Co.

W. & Co.   *see* Wade & Co.
  B

W. & Sons   *see* Williamson & Sons, H.M.

W. & A.   *see* Wardle & Ash
                    Wild & Adams

W.A.A. or **W.A.A. & Co**.   *see* Adderley & Co., W.A.

W.A. & Co.   *see* Adams & Sons (Potters) Ltd., W.

Wade & Co.   *Burslem, Staffs.*
      WADE'S   1887–1927, earthenware
      W. & CO.   name or initials printed
        B   in a variety of marks

Wade & Son Ltd., George   *Burslem, Staffs.*
      WADE   1922–1989, earthenware
      Figures

c. 1936

    printed   *c.* 1947–
'WADE CERAMICS' from 1989, owned by
Beaufort Industries

Wade, Heath & Co. Ltd.   *Burslem, Staffs.*
                  1927– , earthenware
                  WADEHEATH
                  ORCADIA   & various
                  WARE   printed or
                             impressed marks
                             including 'WADE'

c. 1927–   *c.* 1934–

Wade (Ireland) Ltd.   *Portadown, N.Ireland*
                          1953– porcelain, industrial &
                          artware. Tablewares from
                          Jan. 1989. Seagoe Ceramics 1991–
WADE (ULSTER) LTD.   impressed,
PORCELAIN   1953–

MADE IN IRELAND
impressed or printed,
1953–

Wagstaff & Brunt   *Longton, Staffs.*
WAGSTAFF & BRUNT   1879–1927, earthenware
LONGTON   & bone-china

W. & B.   name or initials printed in
LONGTON   a variety of marks

Wain & Sons Ltd., H.A.   *Longton, Staffs.*

Melba Ware   1946– , earthenware
                             From *c.* 1985 retitled
                             MELBA-WAIN, active in
                             1990

printed, 1951–

Waine & Co. Ltd., Charles   *Longton, Staffs.*
C.W.LTD   1891–1919, bone-china
printed under crown, or 'C.W.' monogram

367

'LTD.' from 1913, & trade-name: VENETIA CHINA

Walford, J.F.   *Redhill, Surrey &*

                         Crowborough, Sussex
                         studio-potter, 1948–

Walker & Son   *Rotherham, Yorks.*
                         c. 1772– , earthenware
WALKER   Joined by William Hawley by 1777.
                         1794, owned by R. & W. Stanley
                         & others until *c.* 1800

Walker & Carter   *Longton & Stoke, Staffs.*
   W. & C.   1866–89, earthenware
   printed in a variety of marks, often
   with name of pattern

Walker, Cassandia Annie   *see* Della Robbia

Walker, Thomas   *Tunstall, Staffs.*
   T.WALKER   1845–51, earthenware
                         various printed backstamps
   THOS. WALKER   including name

Walker, William   *London*
                         c. 1795–*c.* 1800, retailer
   WALKER MINORIES   impressed on earthenware
                         made to order

Wallace & Co. J.   *Newcastle upon Tyne, Tyne and Wear*
                         1838–1893, earthenware
                         Newcastle Pottery

WALLACE & CO. printed together with
various backstamps with pattern names.

T. Wallace & Son,
1838–40
James Wallace & Co.
1840–58
Wallace & Co.
1858–93
when factory closed

Walley, Edward *Cobridge, Staffs.*

1845–56, earthenware & porcelain
including Parian

EDWARD WALLEY
COBRIDGE
STAFFORDSHIRE

printed under Royal
Arms

IRONSTONE
CHINA

W

E. WALLEY

printed in a
variety of backstamps

impressed

Walley, John *Burslem, Staffs.*

J.WALLEY

1850–67, earthenware

J. WALLEY'S
WARE

printed or impressed

This name is common to other potters

Wallwork, Alan *Lyme Regis, Dorset*

1957– , studio-potter, in stoneware
& porcelain

Walter, Josie   *Bonsall, Derbys.*

studio-potter

Walters, Helen   *London*

1945– , studio-potter, now
Helen Swain

1945–53   Painted or incised

Walton Pottery Co. Ltd.   *see* Gordon, William

Walton, John   *Burslem, Staffs.*

c. 1806–*c.* 1835, earthenware figures
mark impressed on moulded
scroll on reverse of figures
or groups

Walton, J.H.   *Longton, Staffs.*

1912–21, bone-china
printed or impressed
in a variety of marks

Walton, Sarah   *Polegate, Sussex*

1972– , studio-potter in stoneware,
porcelain & outdoor sculptures

Warburton, John   *Cobridge, Staffs.*

WARBURTON impressed   *c,* 1802–25, earthenware

Warburton, John   *Newcastle upon Tyne, Tyne & Wear*
                              c. 1745– *c.* 1892, earthenware
   J. WARBURTON   included in rare transfer-prints
   N. ON TYNE
Isaac Warburton from *c.* 1795, and then Ellen
Warburton until closure in 1817. Later
re-opened and worked by various owners
making unidentified wares until *c.* 1892

Warburton, Peter (*d.*1813)   *Shelton, Staffs.*
                              c. 1802– , potter & printer
                              at New Hall from *c.* 1810, when he
                              patented his method of bat-printing
                              in gold and various metals
'Warburton's Patent' painted under crown

Warburton, Peter & Francis   *Cobridge, Staffs.*
   P.&F.   *c.* 1795–1802, earthenware
   WARBURTON   P. & F.W.
                          impressed marks

Ward, John   *Newport, Dyfed*
                              1970– , studio-potter

Wardell, Sasha   *Chethams, Beds. & France*
                              studio-potter in bone-china
                              1982–

Wardle & Ash   *Shelton, Staffs.*
   W. & A.   1859–65, earthenware & Parian
impressed or names in full

Wardle & Co. *Hanley, Staffs.*

      1871–1935, earthenware, majolica

   WARDLE   and Parian

impressed 1871–

printed, 1885–90   printed *c.* 1890–1935

Became Wardle Art Pottery in 1910, and
from 1935 part of Cauldon Potteries Ltd.,
who in 1958 were purchased by Pountney
of Bristol

Wardle & Co., John *Mexborough, Yorks.*

JOHN WARDLE & CO.   1866–68, earthenware

        similar mark from 1864–66

NEAR ROTHERHAM   with 'WILKINSON & WARDLE'.

DENABY POTTERY   printed

Warne, Conway Gould *see* Royal Potteries

Warrilow & Sons, Ltd., George *Longton, Staffs,*

    G.W.   *c.* 1887–1940, bone-china

printed in a variety of marks

   G.W. & S.   printed after *c.* 1892, when

   G.W. & SONS   'SONS' was added. 'LTD.'

        added from *c.* 1928.

From 1941 became the ROSINA CHINA CO. LTD.
using trade-names: ROSINA, or QUEEN'S

Washington Pottery Ltd.   *Shelton, Staffs.*

1946– , earthenware, operating
in 1991 as WASHINGTON POTTERY
(STAFFORDSHIRE) LTD.

Watcombe Pottery Co.   *St Mary Church, Devon*

1867–1901, earthenware, *terra-cotta*

WATCOMBE
TORQUAY

impressed, 1867–

transfer-printed & impressed
mark *c.* 1875–95, during Francis
Evans period. Many impressed
or printed marks including
WATCOMBE TORQUAY, some with date
e.g. 1190 = Nov. 1890
impressed, *c.* 1890

  ST MARYCHURCH   *c.* 1898–1905
  ENGLAND

Wathen, James B.   *Fenton, Staffs.*

J.B.W.

1864–9, earthenware

J.B.W.
F

initial printed in a variety
of marks

Wathen & Lichfield   *Fenton, Staffs.*

1862–4, earthenware

W. & L.	printed in a variety of marks
FENTON	

Watson Potteries, Henry   *Wattisfield, Suffolk*
c. 1808, earthenware & stoneware
WATTISFIELD WARE   impressed, c. 1947–

printed or impressed
1948–

Watson's Pottery   *Prestonpans, Scotland*
WATSON   c. 1750–1840, earthenware
early impressed mark
WATSON & CO.   printed, c. 1800–40.

Watson, Dorothy   *Rolvenden, Kent*

1921–, studio-potter
impressed or printed for
Bridge Pottery

Wayte & Ridge   *Longton, Staffs.*
as yet no   c. 1864–65, Parian & bone-china
marks have   Suggested only Parian ware
been recorded   made & other wares sold as
agents

W.B.   *see* Brownfield, William

W. & B.   *see* Wagstaff & Brunt
Wedgwood & Sons Ltd., J.,
Wood & Baggaley
Wood & Bowers

W. & B.   *see* Wood & Brownfield

W. & B. Ltd.   *see* Wood & Barker

W.B./H   *see* Bennett (Hanley) Ltd.,W.

W.B.K.   *see* Kent (Porcelains) Ltd.,W.

W.B. & S   *see* Brownfield, William
W.B. & Son
W.B. & Sons

W. & C.   *see* Walker & Carter
                 Wood & Challinor
                 Wood & Clarke

W. & C. monogram   *see* Wileman & Co.

W.C. & Co.   *see* Wood, Challinor & Co.

W.C.S. monogram   *see* Casson, Sheila

W.E.   *see* Emberton, William

Weatherby & Sons Ltd.   *Hanley, Staffs.*
                       1891– , earthenware
  J.H.W. & SONS   printed in a variety of marks
                       from *c.* 1891
  FALCON WARE   trade-name adopted *c.* 1925
  Weatherby Ware   printed *c.* 1936–

Wedgewood   *see* Smith & Co.,William

Wedg-Wood   *see* Wood, John Wedge

Wedgwood   *see* Podmore, Walker & Co.
                          Wedgwood & Sons Ltd., Josiah
                          Wedgwood & Co., Ralph

Wedgwood & Bentley   *see* Wedgwood & Sons Ltd., J.

Wedgwood & Co.   *see* Ferrybridge Pottery
                                  Podmore, Walker & Co.
                                  Wedgwood & Co. Ltd.
                                  Wedgwood & Co., Ralph

Wedgwood & Co. Ltd.   *Tunstall, Staffs.*
                                        1860– , earthenware
WEDGWOOD & CO.   impressed from *c.* 1860

                                        printed mark from
                                        c. 1862, after registration
                                        of trade-mark
                                        'LTD.' added from 1900

WEDGWOOD & CO.   impressed, 1900–
          LTD.

Prior to 1860 this firm was Podmore, Walker
& Enoch Wedgwood and re-named Enoch Wedgwood
(Tunstall) Ltd. in 1965. Various printed marks
include full-title sometimes with trade-names:
IMPERIAL PORCELAIN (*c.* 1906–), WACOLWARE
(*c.* 1951), EVERWARE (*c.* 1956), ROYAL TUNSTALL
(*c.* 1957–), VITRILAIN (1962–)
Taken over by Wedgwood Group, 1980, renamed
Unicorn Pottery, brand name: 'Bull in a China Shop'

Wedgwood & Co. Ltd., H.F. *Longton, Staffs.*

	c. 1941–59, earthenware & bone-
H.F.W. & CO. LTD.	china
	initials or trade-name included
ISLINGTON	in a variety of printed marks

Wedgwood & Sons Ltd., Josiah *Burslem,*
Etruria & Barlaston

1759–, earthenware, stoneware, Parian & bone-china

very rare incised initials or   'J.W.'

signature, *c.* 1760   wedgwood WEDGWOOD

rare, *c.* 1759–69

c. 1759   WEDGWOOD

Wedgwood & Bentley   WEDGWOOD
partnership, 1769–80   & BENTLEY
concerned only with
the manufacture of   WEDGWOOD
ornamental neo-classical   & BENTLEY
wares   ETRURIA

impressed on cameos, etc.   W. & B.
impressed or raised mark

c. 1780–98   Wedgwood

rare impressed mark   WEDGWOOD & SONS
c. 1790
printed on bone-china   WEDGWOOD
c. 1812–34   red, blue or gold

rare printed mark on stone china, *c.* 1827–61	WEDGWOOD'S STONE CHINA
impressed mark *c.* 1840–5	WEDGWOOD ETRURIA
impressed on 'pearlware' *c.* 1840–68	PEARL
as above, post–1868	P

From 1860 the Wedgwood factory in addition to their usual name-mark, adopted a system of date-marking consisting of three letters side by side: the first indicates the month, the second a potter's mark and the third the year of manufacture. As from 1907 the first letter, which had hitherto denoted the month of manufacture, was replaced by a number indicating the cycle of year marks in use; previously there was no indication whether the piece was made in the first, second, or third cycle.

This system was further changed in 1930 when the cycle number was replaced by the chronological number of the month, e.g.: January = 1, February = 2, etc., and the initial which had previously indicated the year was now replaced by the last two years of the actual date of manufacture.

Examples: Month	Potter	Year	
Y	O	R	May, 1863
L	O	E	July, 1902
Cycle	Potter	Year	
3	O	N	1911
4	O	A	1924

Month	Potter	Year	
3	O	32	March, 1932
11	O	48	November, 1948

Monthly marks indicated by the first letter from
1860–1864:

January	J	April	A	July	V	October	O
February	F	May	Y	August	W	November	N
March	M	June	T	September	S	December	D

1865–1907:

January	J	April	A	July	L	October	O
February	F	May	M	August	W	November	N
March	R	June	T	September	S	December	D

First cycle of year marks:

O	1860	R	1863	U	1866	X	1869
P	1861	S	1864	V	1867	Y	1870
Q	1862	T	1865	W	1868	Z	1871

Second cycle of year marks:

A	1872	H	1879	O	1886	V	1893
B	1873	I	1880	P	1887	W	1894
C	1874	J	1881	Q	1888	X	1895
D	1875	K	1882	R	1889	Y	1896
E	1876	L	1883	S	1890	Z	1897
F	1877	M	1884	T	1891		
G	1878	N	1885	U	1892		

Note: 'ENGLAND' added to mark from 1891

Third cycle of year marks:

A	1898	H	1905	O	1912	V	1919
B	1899	I	1906	P	1913	W	1920
C	1900	J	1907	Q	1914	X	1921
D	1901	K	1908	R	1915	Y	1922
E	1902	L	1909	S	1916	Z	1923
F	1903	M	1910	T	1917		
G	1904	N	1911	U	1918		

Fourth cycle of year marks:

A	1924	C	1926	E	1928
B	1925	D	1927	F	1929

the last two years of the date then appear in full.

'Portland Vase' mark printed
on bone-china from *c.* 1878
occasionally seen impressed
on earthenware, *c.* 1891–1900
Note: 'ENGLAND' added
afer 1891 'MADE IN
ENGLAND' from about 1910
'*Bone China*' added *c.* 1920

printed on creamwares
from *c.* 1940

Lessore, Emile, decorator
c. 1858–76

Thomson, E. G.,   E.G. Thomson
decorator, *c.* 1870
Barnard, Harry, decorator
c. 1900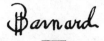

marks on red stonewares,
probably Wedgwood
second-half of
18th century   impressed

1986, taken over by Waterford Glass Group P.L.C.
1989, renamed Waterford Wedgwood; by 1990
Wedgwood Group comprised eighteen companies
including: William Adams & Sons (Potters)
Ltd., Mason's Ironstone China Ltd., Susie
Cooper Ltd., R.H. & S.L. Plant Ltd., Coalport
China Ltd., Franciscan Tableware Inc.,
Crown Staffordshire China Co.Ltd., Johnson
Bros. (Hanley) Ltd., J.& G. Meakin Ltd.,
W.R. Midwinter Ltd., Enoch Wedgwood (Tunstall)
Ltd., Josiah Wedgwood & Sons, Ltd., Furnivals
(Staffordshire) Ltd., New Chelsea China Co.Ltd.,
Winsor Bishop & Co.Ltd., Gered Antiques Ltd.,
Precision Studios Ltd., The Goldsmiths
and Silversmiths Assn, London.
From Dec. 1990 Wedgwood was operating
independently from Waterford Glass

Wedgwood, Ralph   *Ferrybridge, Yorks.*
                         1798– , earthenwares
Wedgwood & Co.   WEDGWOOD & CO.
impressed marks used by the partners
Tomlinson, Foster, Wedgwood & Co., but

probably used earlier by Ralph
Wedgwood at Burslem between *c*. 1790–6

Welch, Robin   *Eye, Suffolk*
    R W   1960– , studio-potter
    (date)   in stoneware
various marks including full name,
some with last two numerals of year

Wellhouse Pottery   *Brixham, Devon*

                    1982– , earthenware

                    stamped mark of 1986

Wellington China   *see* Cope & Co.Ltd., J.H.

Wellington Pottery   *see* Williamson, John

Wellington Pottery Ltd.   *Hanley, Staffs.*

                    1899–1901, earthenware

                    printed or impressed

Wells, Reginald   *Wrotham, Kent, Chelsea, London*
                         & Storrington, Sussex
    R.F.WELLS   *c*. 1909–51, studio-potter
incised or painted at Wrotham on early wares
    COLDRUM   COLDRUM   COLDRUM
    c. 1909–   WROTHAM   CHELSEA

R. Wells was working in Chelsea from
c. 1910–24 & at Storrington *c.* 1925–51

                   incised, *c.* 1910–

SOON   impressed or incised in Sussex

Wemyss Ware   *see* Heron & Son., R.

Wenford Bridge Pottery   *see* Cardew, M. & S.

West Highland Pottery Co. Ltd.   *Dunoon, Scotland*

                   1961, earthenware
trade-names: FLOW WARE,
ARGYLL, COWAL, printed

West Surrey Ceramic Co. Ltd.   *Hindhead, Surrey*
1956–, earthenware & stoneware

Surrey Ceramics England   **KP ENGLAND**

printed or impressed
'K P' for Kingswood Pottery

Westminster Pottery Ltd.   *Hanley, Staffs.*
1948–56, earthenware

printed

CASTLECLIFFE WARE:
trade-mark from 1952

Wetley China *see* Smith, Sampson

W.E.W. *see* Withinshaw, W.E.

W.F. or **W.F.B.** *see* Fifield, William

W.F. & Co. *see* Whittingham, Ford & Co.

W.F.H. *see* Holland, W.F.

W.F. & R. *see* Whittingham, Ford & Riley

W.H. *see* Hackwood, W.
             Hudson, W.

W. & H. *see* Hulme & Sons, Henry
                Wildblood & Heath
                Worthington & Harrop

W. & H. *see* Hulme & Sons, Henry
  B   Wood & Hulme

W. & H. monogram *see* Hawley, Webberley & Co.

W. H. & Co. *see* Whittaker, Heath & Co.

384

W.H.G.   *see* Goss Ltd., William Henry

Wheeldon, John   *Bolehill, Derby*

         c. 1975, studio-potter in
porcelain and black stoneware

Whieldon Ware   *see* Winkle & Co. Ltd., F.

White, Mary   *W.Germany since 1980*

         1962– , studio-potter, porcelain
and stoneware

White, William J.   *Fulham, London*

     w.w.   *c.* 1750–*c.* 1850, stoneware
     (date)
     incised   W.J.WHITE   W.WHITE
                          (date)
   (this pottery was on the site of John
Dwight's 17th-Century works)

W.H.L.   *see* Lockitt, William H.
   H

Whittaker & Co.   *Hanley, Staffs.*
     w. & co.   1886–92, earthenware
   printed in a variety of marks, often
with name of pattern

Whittaker, Heath & Co.   *Hanley, Staffs.*
     w.h. & co.   1892–8, earthenware
   printed in a variety of marks

Whittingham, Ford & Co. *Burslem, Staffs.*
    W.F. & CO.   1868–73, earthenware
    printed in a variety of marks, often
    including name of pattern

Whittingham, Ford & Riley *Burslem, Staffs.*
    W.F. & R.   1876–82, earthenware
    printed in a variety of marks, often
    including name of pattern

W.H. & S.   *see* Hackwood & Sons, W.
    or   Wildblood, Heath & Sons Ltd.
W.H. & S.
   L

Whyman, Caroline *London*

                c. 1973– , studio-potter
                porcelain

Wigornia   *see* Worcester

Wild & Adams Ltd. *Longton, Staffs.*
    W. & A.   1909–27, earthenware
    or full name   'LTD' added 1923
    printed or impressed
    Trade-name: ROYAL CROWN WARE

Wild Bros *Longton, Staffs.*
    J.S.W   *c.* 1904–27, bone-china
    initials printed in a variety of marks
    'W. BROS.' printed as above. 'J.S.W.' monogram
    printed under crown, *c.* 1922–7

Wild & Sons Ltd., Thomas C. *Longton, Staffs.*
T.W. & CO.   *c.* 1896–1970, bone-china
printed or impressed, *c.* 1896–1904 or
'T.C.W.' under crown

printed, *c.* 1905–7

printed, *c.* 1927–

trade-names: ROYAL ALBERT
CROWN CHINA (1905–35), ROYAL
ALBERT BONE CHINA (1935–)

Renamed T.C. WILD & SONS in 1917, & THOMAS
C. WILD & SONS in 1922; 'LTD.' added in 1932,
merged with Lawley Group in 1964 and renamed
ROYAL ALBERT LTD. in 1971; now part of
ROYAL DOULTON

Wildblood, Heath & Sons Ltd. *Longton, Staffs.*
c. 1887–1927, bone-china
'& SONS LTD.' in 1899
trade-name: CLIFTON CHINA

printed, 1899–

printed, 1908–

Wildblood & Ledgar *Longton, Staffs.*
     W. & L.   1896–1900, earthenware
   printed in a variety of marks

Wildblood, Richard Vernon *Longton, Staffs.*
                       c. 1886–8, bone-china

      printed

Wileman, James & Charles *Fenton, Staffs.*
     J. & C.W.   1864–8, bone-china & earthenware
     J.F. & C.W.   initials printed in a variety
                      of marks
     C.J.W.   printed, *c.* 1868
     J.W. & CO.   printed, *c.* 1864–8

Wileman, James F. *Fenton, Staffs.*
                       1870–72, earthenware & bone-
     J.F.W.   china
     J.F.WILEMAN   printed in a variety of
   marks, often with name of pattern

Wileman & Co. *Fenton, Staffs.*
                       c. 1872–1925, earthenware &
      bone-china
                       printed, *c.* 1892–

Renamed SHELLEYS in 1925, & SHELLEYS
CHINA LTD. in 1965; taken over in 1966 &
now part of Royal Doulton Ltd., with SHELLEY

still in use as trade-name

Wilkins, Elizabeth   *see* Della Robbia

Wilkinson Ltd., Arthur J.   *Burslem, Staffs.*
1885–1964, earthenware & stoneware. 'LTD.'
added from 1896. Many various printed
marks including either full-name or trade-
name: ROYAL SEMI-PORCELAIN (*c.* 1891–),
ROYAL IRONSTONE CHINA (*c.* 1896–), ROYAL
STAFFORDSHIRE POTTERY (*c.* 1907–), CLARICE
CLIFF (*c.* 1930–), HONEYGLAZE (*c.* 1947–)

Taken over by W. R. Midwinter Ltd. in 1965,
merging in 1968 with J. & G. Meakin and
Newport Pottery as English Tableware Group,
who were taken over by Wedgwood Group in 1970

Wilkinson & Wardle   *Mexborough, Yorks.*
1864–68, earthenware

WILKINSON & WARDLE
DENABY POTTERIES   printed or impressed
                          with knot, 1864–6

      W.W.
DENABY POTTERIES

JOHN WARDLE & CO.   John Wardle & Co.
NEAR ROTHERHAM   from 1866–8
DENABY POTTERY

Williams, William   *see* Della Robbia

Williamson & Sons, H.M.   *Longton, Staffs.*
c. 1879–1941, bone-china

printed, *c.* 1903–

printed, *c.* 1908

various other printed marks with 'H.M.W.'
or 'W. & Sons'. Later marks with trade-name,
HEATHCOTE CHINA, from *c.* 1912

Williamson, John   *Glasgow, Scotland*
                                       c. 1840–94, *terra-cotta* pots
         WELLINGTON   early impressed or printed
         POTTERY   mark pre–1840, under Adam Cubie

         WILLIAMSON   impressed or printed,
         WELLINGTON   *c.* 1840–94
         POTTERY

Willow   *see* Stevenson, Spencer & Co. Ltd.

Willow Art China   *see* Hewitt & Leadbeater

Wilson & Sons, David   *Hanley, Staffs.*
         WILSON   *c.* 1801–17, earthenware & bone-china
         impressed

Wilson & Co., Isaac   *Middlesbrough, Yorks.*

I.W. & CO.   1852–87, earthenware
impressed
I.W. & CO.   I.W. & CO.
MIDDLESBROUGH   MIDDLESBRO'
printed in a variety of backstamps
with named patterns including:
Devon, Rhine, Hop Pickers & Caprera,
sometimes with impressed initials 'I.W.& CO.'

Wilson & Sons, J.   *Fenton, Staffs.*

                        bone-china, *c.* 1898–1926
                        printed
                        Wilson & Co., *c.* 1898–1900
                        J. Wilson & Sons, *c.* 1900–26

Wilson, Robert   *Hanley, Staffs.*
WILSON   1795–1801, earthenware
impressed

Wilson & Proudman   *Ashby-de-la-Zouch, Leics.*
                        1835–42, earthenware & stoneware.
WILSON &   impressed
PROUDMAN

Wiltshaw & Robinson Ltd.   *Stoke, Staffs.*
                                c. 1890–1957, earthenware & bone-china

                                Trade-names from *c.* 1890:
                                CARLTON WARE & CARLTON CHINA

                                Renamed Carlton Ware Ltd., 1958.
1989, name, pattern books & moulds purchased
by new company & CARLTON WARE being made in 1990

Windsor   *see* Co-operative Wholesale Society Ltd.

winged shilling coin   *see* Winkle & Wood

Winkle & Co. F.   *Stoke, Staffs.*

F.W. & CO.	1890–1931, earthenware
ENGLAND	printed or impressed, 1890–1910.
	'LTD.' added from 1911–
F. WINKLE & CO.	printed in a variety of marks

printed, 1890–1925

misleading printed or impressed
mark used by Winkle & Co., 1908–25.
The wares of the well-known
18th century potter, who was in
partnership with Josiah Wedgwood from 1754–59,
were not marked
Taken over in 1931 by Ridgways (Bedford Works)
Ltd., who are now part of Royal Doulton

Winkle & Wood   *Hanley, Staffs.*

1885–90, earthenware

printed

Winkley, David   *Taunton, Som*

c. 1963, studio-potter in stoneware
& porcelain

Winterburn, Mollie   *Ystrad Meurig, Dyfed*
                                    studio-potter

Winterton Pottery (Longton) Ltd.   *Longton, Staffs.*
WINTERTON   1927–54, earthenware
(crown)
WARE   printed, *c.* 1927–41

Bluestone   printed, *c.* 1939–41
Ware

                    Acquired by Coloroll Ceramics, *c.* 1946/7

Winton   *see* Grimwade Ltd.

Withinshaw, W.E.   *Burslem, Staffs.*
W.E.W.   *c.* 1873–8, earthenware &
W.E.WITHINSHAW   bone-china
printed or impressed in a variety
of marks

W.J. monogram   *see* Walford, J.F.

W.& J.B.   *see* Butterfield, W. & J.

W. & J.H.   *see* Harding, W.J.

W.K. & Co.   *see* Kirkby & Co., William

W.L.L. in triangle   *see* Lowe, William

W. & L.   *see* Wathen & Lichfield
                     Wildblood & Ledgar

W.M.   *see* Moorcroft, William

W.N.   *see* Newland, William

W.N.E. (Compass points)   *see* Green & Clay

Wolfe & Co.   *see* Wolfe, Thomas

Wolfe, Thomas   *Liverpool, Lancs. & Stoke.*
                     1783–96, earthenware
          WOLFE   rare impressed mark
     From *c.* 1796–1800, producing a hybrid hard-
     paste porcelain at Liverpool in partnership
     with Miles Mason, & John Luckock (or Lucock)
  WOLFE & HAMILTON   rare impressed mark on
          STOKE   porcelain made at Stoke in
     the *c.* 1800–09 partnership with son-in-law,
     Robert Hamilton.
          WOLFE   impressed mark on earthenwares made
     by Wolfe at Stoke until he died in 1818.
     Various porcelains were also probably made but
     as yet are unidentified

Wondrausch, Mary   *Guildford, Surrey*
     studio-potter, earthenware, potting in 1989

Wood, Arthur   *Longport, Staffs.*
>   A.W.   1904–28, earthenware
>   L   impressed or printed sometimes with
>   'ENGLAND'

Wood & Son (Longport) Ltd., Arthur   *Longport, Staffs.*
>   1928– operating in 1991.
>   ARTHUR WOOD   full-name printed in a variety
>   of marks. Trade-name: ROYAL BRADWELL
>   included on some marks from *c.* 1945;
>   'ROYAL BRADWELL/Art Ware', from *c.* 1954

Wood & Baggaley   *Burslem, Staffs.*
>   W. & B.   1870–80, earthenware
>   initials printed in a variety of marks,
>   often including name of pattern

Wood & Barker, Ltd.   *Burslem, Staffs.*
>   W. & B. LTD.   1897–1903, earthenware
>   printed with decorative frame including
>   name of pattern

Wood & Bowers   *Burslem, Staffs.*
>   W. & B.   1839, earthenware
>   printed in a variety of marks, including
>   name of pattern, but these initials are
>   common to other potters

Wood & Brownfield   *Cobridge, Staffs.*
>   W. & B.   c. 1838–50, earthenware
>   impressed or printed in a variety of marks
>   sometimes including name of pattern
>   W. & B./PEARL WHITE/COBRIDGE   impressed

Wood & Challinor   *Tunstall, Staffs.*
   W. & C.   1828–43, earthenware
  printed in a variety of marks, often with
  name of pattern

Wood, Challinor & Co.   *Tunstall, Staffs.*
   W.C. & CO. *c.* 1860–64, earthenware
  printed in a variety of marks, often with
  name of pattern

Wood & Clarke   *Burslem, Staffs.*
       c. 1871–2, earthenware

       printed with name of pattern

  W. & C.

Wood, Enoch   *Burslem, Staffs.*
       c. 1784–*c.* 1790, earthenware
  WOOD   E. WOOD   E.W.   W.
      all impressed
 ENOCH WOOD   E. WOOD   ENOCH WOOD
  SCULPSIT   SCULPSIT
 impressed, moulded or incised marks

Wood & Caldwell   *Burslem, Staffs.*
 WOOD & CALDWELL *c.* 1790–1818, earthenware
  impressed

Wood & Sons, Enoch   *Burslem, Staffs.*
       1818–1846, earthenware

ENOCH WOOD
& SONS
BURSLEM
STAFFORDSHIRE
mostly impressed on wares
made for export to the U.S.A.

E.W. & S.   E.WOOD & SONS   E. & E. & W.

E. & E.WOOD   E. & E.WOOD   all printed in
BURSLEM   a variety of styles

Wood Ltd., H.J. *Burslem, Staffs.*

1884– , earthenware
early printed mark

Bursley-Ware   E. Radford
Charlotte Rhead   England
England   Handpainted
c. 1930–   *c.* 1935–

Trade names: CHINESE ROSE,   INDIAN TREE
c. 1960–   *c.* 1962–
printed

Wood, Emily M. *see* Della Robbia

Wood & Hawthorne *Cobridge, Staffs.*
WOOD &   1882–7, earthenware
HAWTHORNE
ENGLAND   printed with Royal Arms &
often name of pattern

Wood & Hulme   *Burslem, Staffs.*
    W. & H.   1882–1905, earthenware
    B.   printed or impressed

Wood, Isaiah   *Burslem, Staffs.*
    ISA WOOD   *c.* 1710–15, earthenware
    1712   very rare incised mark

Wood & Co., J.B.   *Longton, Staffs.*
                      1897–1926, earthenware

                      printed or impressed
                      1910–26

Wood, J.H.   *see* Iden Pottery

Wood, John Wedge   *Burslem & Tunstall, Staffs.*
    W.W.   1841–60, earthenware
    impressed
'WEDGWOOD', name printed in a variety of
marks, but no connection with the firm
of Josiah Wedgwood

Wood, Nigel   *Winchester, Hants.*
                      1973– , studio-potter in porcelain,
    MEON   stoneware & *terra-cotta*. Author
                      of books on ceramic subjects,
                      including 'Iron in the Fire'

Wood & Pigott   *Tunstall, Staffs.*
                      1869–71, earthenware

W. & P.   printed in a variety of marks,
                   often with name of pattern

Wood, Ralph   *Burslem, Staffs.*
                  c. 1748–*c.* 1830, earthenware figures,
                  etc.
including the work of:
Ralph Wood (Snr.) 1715–72
John Wood (son) 1746–97
Ralph Wood II (son) 1748–95
Ralph Wood III 1775–1801
John Wood II, 1778–1848

R. WOOD   Ra WOOD   Ra WOOD
      Ralph Wood   BURSLEM
incised or impressed *c.* 1770–1801

   rare impressed rebus mark
                       of trees (wood) *c.* 1780–95.
                       Unmarked Wood-type figures are
                       now thought to be the work of
John Wood, *c.* 1785–90, not Ralph Wood, his
brother

Wood & Co., Thomas   *Burslem, Staffs.*
T.W. & CO.   1885–96, earthenware
printed or impressed

Wood & Sons, Thomas   *Burslem, Staffs.*
T.W. & S.   1896–7, earthenware
printed in a variety of marks, often with
name of pattern

Wood & Sons Ltd.   *Burslem, Staffs.*
                  1865–, earthenware

very wide range of printed marks, all
including full-name of pottery, often
including trade-name, such as Ivory Ware,
Handcraft Ware, Paris Ware, Beryl, etc.
'SON' included up to *c.* 1907, 'SONS' from
c. 1907 and 'LTD.' from *c.* 1910

Wood, Son & Co.   *Cobridge, Staffs.*
                              1869–79, earthenware
WOOD, SON & CO.   printed under Royal Arms

Wood & Co., W.   *Burslem, Staffs.*
     W.W. & CO.   1873–1932, earthenware
printed or impressed in a variety of marks
from *c.* 1873. Same initials in Staffordshire
knot from *c.* 1880–1915, with crown added
above from 1915–1932

Woods Ware   *see* Wood & Sons, Ltd.

Woods, Richard   *Malvern, Worcs.*
     R. WOODS   *c.* 1850–, retailer
printed on wares made to order

Woodward & Co.   *see* Cardigan Potteries

Woodward Ltd., James   *Burton-on-Trent, Derbys.*
                    1859–88, *terra-cotta* & majolica

                    printed or impressed

Wooldridge & Walley   *Burslem, Staffs.*

       W. & W.   1898–1901, earthenware

         B   printed in a variety of marks,

                        often including name of pattern

Wooliscroft, George   *Tunstall, Staffs.*

   G. WOOLISCROFT   1851–64, printed or impressed with

        or   name of pattern, etc.

   G. WOOLISCROFT

Woolley, Richard   *Longton, Staffs.*

     WOOLLEY   1809–1811, earthenware &

  rare impressed   stoneware

Worcester Porcelains   *Worcester, Worcs.*

1751 (Lund & Miller's Bristol factory

est. 1748, taken over in 1752)

soft-paste porcelain (soapstone)

workmen's marks

in underglaze blue

'open' crescent on painted

wares, 1755–83

Royal Worcester Ltd. acquired Spode in 1974.

1976, Royal Worcester Spode Ltd. Purchased in 1988

by company now known as The Porcelain & Fine China Co. Ltd.

'WIGORNIA' rare relief moulded mark
on one recorded cream-boat. 1751–5.
'Wigornia is the Latinized name for Worcester.

crescent-mark with
crossed-hatched lines
on printed wares   in underglaze blue

any crescents in gilt or enamel colour
probably indicate outside decorator or
reproduction
on painted and printed
wares

painted in blue

marks on wares decorated
with 'Japan patterns'
c. 1760–75

in blue

'fretted square' mark
usually on heavily decorated
wares with scale-blue ground
c. 1755–75 (frequently seen
on reproductions)

in blue

Worcester imitation of Meissen
crossed-swords mark
c. 1760–70

in blue

printed numerals disguised as Chinese
characters, numbers 1–9, until the 1969
excavations at Worcester factory site were
thought to be marks of Caughley (Salop)

'Flight' period, 1783–92
'small crescent', 1783–92

mark in blue, 1783–92

mark in blue 1788–92

'Flight & Barr' period
1792–1804

F. & B.

'Barr', *c.* 1792–1804

incised

'Barr Flight & Barr' period
1804–13

BFB
impressed

Barr, Flight & Barr
Worcester
Flight & Barr
Coventry Street
London
Manufacturers to their
Majesties and
Royal Family

BARR, FLIGHT
& BARR
ROYAL PORCELAIN
WORKS
WORCESTER
LONDON HOUSE
NO. I
COVENTRY STREET

'Flight, Barr & Barr' period
1813–40

impressed

(factory taken over by Chamberlains, 1840–51)

Kerr & Binns *c.* 1851–62

Kerr & Binns, '54' = 1854
mark on outstanding
examples, including decorator's
initials (bottom left)

standard mark, printed or
impressed, *c.* 1852–62
Note: crown added
in 1862

'Worcester Royal Porcelain Company Ltd.'
(Royal Worcester) 1862–present

standard mark, 1862–present
early version, with 'C'
in centre replacing crescent
in Kerr & Binn's version
numbers below = last 2 years
of date

From 1867 a letter indicating the year of
manufacture was printed under the factory mark
according to the following table:

A	1867	G	1872	M	1877	T	1882	Y	1887
B	1868	H	1873	N	1878	U	1883	Z	1888
C	1869	I	1874	P	1879	V	1884	O	1889
D	1870	K	1875	R	1880	W	1885		
E	1871	L	1876	S	1881	X	1886		

'a' in Old English script in 1890; date letter
omitted in 1891.
'Royal Worcester England' written around mark
from 1891, after which, dots, stars and other
letters and forms were added to the mark each
year as listed below until 1963 when the year in
full is added.

1892, dot to left of crown, 1893 dot either side of
crown; dots were then added to either side of
crown until 1915, thus:

1894	3 dots	1900	9 dots	1906	15 dots	1912	21 dots
1895	4 dots	1901	10 dots	1907	16 dots	1913	22 dots
1896	5 dots	1902	11 dots	1908	17 dots	1914	23 dots
1897	6 dots	1903	12 dots	1909	18 dots	1915	24 dots
1898	7 dots	1904	13 dots	1910	19 dots		
1899	8 dots	1905	14 dots	1911	20 dots		

In 1916 the dots alongside the crown were
replaced by a star under the mark, dots were then
added to either side of this star until 1927:

1916 1 star
1917 star & 1 dot
1918 star & 2 dots
1919 star & 3 dots
1920 star & 4 dots
1921 star & 5 dots

1922 star & 6 dots
1923 star & 7 dots
1924 star & 8 dots
1925 star & 9 dots
1926 star & 10 dots
1927 star & 11 dots

then as follows:

1928 ▭

1929 ◇

1930 ÷

1931 ◯◯

1932 ◯◯◯

1933 ◯◯◯ •

further dots were then added to three interlaced
circles as follows:

1934 circles & 2 dots
1935 circles & 3 dots
1936 circles & 4 dots
1937 circles & 5 dots

1938 circles & 6 dots
1939 circles & 7 dots
1940 circles & 8 dots
1941 circles & 9 dots

from 1941 to 1948 inclusive there were no changes in
the year-mark

1949 V
1950 W
1951 W and 1 dot
1952 W and 2 dots

1953 W and 3 dots
1954 W and 4 dots
1955 W and 5 dots

1956 R in place of W
     with 6 dots
1957 R and 7 dots
1958 R and 8 dots
1959 R and 9 dots

1960 R and 10 dots
1961 R and 11 dots
1962 R and 12 dots
1963 R and 13 dots

From 1963 all new patterns have the year in full.

(*By courtesy of the Worcester Royal Porcelain Co. Ltd.*)

Hancock, Robert, *b.* 1730, *d.* 1817
engraver of transfer-prints
c. 1756–65

RI . Worcester

initials of Hancock
and rebus of Richard
Holdship on prints

(Hancock associated with
Turner of Caughley in
1776)

Chamberlain, *c.* 1786–1851
decorators from *c.* 1786–*c.* 1790, then
manufacturers of soft-paste porcelain
c. 1790–1814

*Chamberlains
Worcs No 276*

in red

written or printed
c. 1816–40
(under crown)

*Chamberlain's
Worcester,
& 155
New Bond Street
London,
Royal Porcelain
Manufactory*

c. 1814–16

*Chamberlain's
Worcester,
& 63 Piccadilly,
London*

written or printed

incised, *c.* 1815–22

CHAMBERLAINS
ROYAL PORCELAIN
WORCESTER

printed mark under
crown, *c.* 1840–51
('& Co.' from this
date)

CHAMBERLAIN & CO.
WORCESTER
155 New Bond St.
& No. 1
COVENTRY ST.
LONDON

written or printed
c. 1840–50

CHAMBERLAIN & CO.
WORCESTER

impressed or printed
c. 1847–50

CHAMBERLAINS

printed *c.* 1850–52

(then Kerr & Binns, p. 404)

Doe and Rogers,
c. 1820–35
porcelain decorators

Doe & Rogers
Worcester

Grainger, Wood & Co.
c. 1805–11, porcelain
rare mark

Grainger Wood & Co.
Worcester, Warranted

Grainger, Lee & Co.
c. 1814–*c.* 37
porcelain

Grainger, Lee & Co.
Worcester
painted

c. 1820–30 painted   New China Works
                                      Worcester

c. 1812–30 painted   Royal China Works
                                      Worcester

Grainger, George   GEO. GRAINGER
c. 1839–1902   CHINA WORKS
porcelain   WORCESTER
painted or printed mark
c. 1839–60
'& Co.' added c. 1850   G. GRAINGER & CO.
                                      WORCESTER

's.p.' for 'Semi-   G.G. & CO.   S.P.
Porcelain', c.   S.P.   G.G.W.
1850–   impressed or printed
initials included in   G.W.
printed marks, 1850–60
1850–89   G. & CO.W.

printed mark on copies   GRAINGER & CO.
of 'Dr. Wall' period wares   WORCESTER
c. 1860–80
printed or impressed
c. 1870–89

c. 1889–1902 ('England'
added in 1891)

letters added under mark to indicate year of
manufacture from 1891–1902:

A	1891	D	1894	G	1897	J	1900
B	1892	E	1895	H	1898	K	1901
C	1893	F	1896	I	1899	L	1902

George Grainger & Co. was taken over by
Worcester Royal Porcelain Co. Ltd. in 1889 and
closed down in 1902.

Hadley & Sons, James
porcelain and earthenware
1896–1905
signature on work

incised or impressed

modelled by Hadley for
Worcester Royal Porcelain Co.
c. 1875–94
printed or impressed
1896–97
1897–1902,
impressed

FINE ART
HADLEY'S
TERRA-COTTA

printed mark 1897–1902
(centre ribbon omitted
from 1900)

printed mark, 1902–5

Locke & Co., porcelain
1895–1915

LOCKE & CO.
WORCESTER

'globe-mark', *c.* 1895–1904
'Ltd.' added in *c.* 1900

Sparks, George, *c.*   Sparks Worcester
1836–54, decorator of   written mark
Worcester and Coalport porcelain

Wornell, Gary   *Aldeburgh, Suffolk*

                    1976– , studio-potter in porcelain
                    & *terra-cotta*

Worthington & Green   *Shelton, Staffs.*
   WORTHINGTON   1844–64, earthenware,
        &   Parian & bone-china.
     GREEN   impressed mark

Worthington & Harrop   *Hanley, Staffs.*
   w. & h.   1856–73, earthenware & Parian.
   printed in a variety of marks, often
   with name of pattern

W. & P.   *see* Wood & Pigott

W. R. or **W.R. & Co.**   *see* Ridgway, Son & Co., W.

W.R. monogram   *see* Roscoe, William

W. & R.   *see* Wiltshaw & Robinson

W. R. & Co.   *see* Ridgway & Co., William

Wren, Rosemary   *Strathpeffer, Ross & Cromarty IV*

c. 1945– , studio-potter
stoneware birds, animals, etc.
(*see also* Peter Crotty)

W.R.F.   *see* Wells, Reginald F.

W.R.S. & Co.   *see* Ridgway Son & Co., William

W.S. & Co.   *see* Smith & Co., William

W. & S.E.   *see* Edge, William & Samuel

W.S.Junr. & Co.   *see* Smith (Junr.) & Co.,W.

W. & Sons.   *see* Williamson & Sons, H.M.

W.T. monogram   *see* Watcombe Pottery Co.

Wulstan Pottery Co.Ltd.   *Hanley, Staffs.*

c. 1940–58, earthenware

printed

W.V. monogram   *see* Rye Pottery (Walter V.Cole)
C.

W.W.   *see*   White, William J.
                   Wilkinson & Wardle
                   Wood, John Wedge

W. & W.   *see* Wooldridge & Walley
   B

W. W. & Co.   *see* Wood & Co.,W.

W. Z.   *see* Zillwood, W.

Y

Yale & Barker   *Longton, Staffs.*

	1841–57, earthenware & bone-china
Y. & B.	from 1846–54.
	Yale & Barker, 1841–42
SEMI-CHINA	Yale, Barker & Barker, 1843–46
WARRANTED	Yale, Barker & Hall, 1846–52
Y. & B.	Barker & Hall, 1853–57
	initials printed in a
Y.B. & H.	variety of marks

Yates, John   *Hanley, Staffs.*

J.Y.	*c.* 1784–1835, earthenware, stoneware
	and bone-china from *c.* 1820.
YATES	printed or impressed in a variety
	of marks

Yates, William   *Leeds, Yorks.*

| YATES | *c.* 1840–76, retailer only |
| LEEDS | name printed or painted |

Y. & B. or **Y.B. & H.**   *see* Yale & Barker

Y.M. stylized monogram   *see* Young, M.

Ynysmedw Pottery   *Swansea, Wales*
> Y.M.P.   *c.* 1850–70, earthenware &
>   stoneware
> Y.P.   impressed

Young, Joanna & Andrew   *Lower Gresham, Norfolk*
>   1975, studio-potters
> A & J YOUNG GRESHAM

Young, Monica   *Richmond, Yorks.*
>   1974– , studio-potter, stoneware

Z

Zanobia Ware   *see* Elektra Porcelain Co. Ltd.

Zillwood, W.   *Amesbury, Wilts.*
> W.Z.   late 18th-19th Cs.
> incised

APPENDIX A

Patent Office Registration Mark

From 1842 until 1883 many manufacturers' wares are marked with the following 'diamond-mark', which is an indication that the design was registered with the British Patent Office; ceramics and glass are Classes IV and III, as indicated in the topmost section of the mark, and gave copyright protection for a period of three years (see Appendix B and Preface, page ix).

The date of the 'diamond mark' only indicates the time of registration, but a popular form of decoration was often produced for far longer than the three years. Printed marks usually refer to the applied pattern, whereas impressed or moulded applied versions are more likely to relate to the form of the ware.

When checking date to determine the name of the manufacturer it will sometimes be the case that the design was registered by retailers, wholesalers or even foreign manufacturers.

'Diamond-marks' impressed into bone-china can often be more accurately read when held before a strong artificial light.

Example of ceramic
design registered on
23rd May 1842

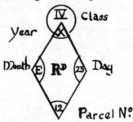

Index to letters for each year and month from 1842 to 1867:

Years

1842	X	1849	S	1856	L	1863	G
1843	H	1850	V	1857	K	1864	N
1844	C	1851	P	1858	B	1965	W
1845	A	1852	D	1859	M	1866	Q
1846	I	1853	Y	1860	Z	1867	T
1847	F	1954	J	1861	R		
1848	U	1855	E	1862	O		

Months

January	C	July	I	
February	G	August	R	For September 1857
March	W	September	D	query letter R used
April	H	October	B	from 1st-19th Sept.
May	E	November	K	For December 1860
June	M	December	A	query letter K used.

Index to letters for each year and month from 1868 to 1883:

Example of ceramic design,
registered on 6th January 1868

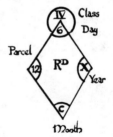

416

Years

1868	X	1872	I	1876	V	1880	J
1869	H	1873	F	1877	P	1881	E
1870	C	1874	U	1878	D	1882	L
1871	A	1875	S	1879	Y	1883	K

Months

Jan.	C	April	H	July	I	Oct.	B
Feb.	G	May	E	Aug.	R	Nov.	K
Mar.	W	June	M	Sept.	D	Dec.	A

For Registration marks brought in with W for the year, see below:
From 1st to 6th March, 1878, the following Registration Mark was issued:

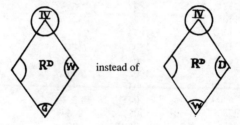

instead of

From 1884 this method of dating registrations ceased and the designs were numbered consecutively in the following manner: 'Rd. 12345' or 'Rd. No. 12345'. The following table gives a guide up until 1990 to the range of numbers used within a year:

Registered in January		Registered in January	
1	1884	630190	1914
19754	1885	644935	1915
40480	1886	653521	1916
64520	1887	658988	1917
90483	1888	662872	1918
116648	1889	666128	1919
141273	1890	673750	1920
163767	1891	680147	1921
185713	1892	687144	1922
205240	1893	694999	1923
224720	1894	702671	1924
246975	1895	710165	1925
268392	1896	718057	1926
291241	1897	726330	1927
311658	1898	734370	1928
331707	1899	742725	1929
351202	1900	751160	1930
368154	1901	760583	1931
385180	1902	769670	1932
403200	1903	779292	1933
424400	1904	789019	1934
447800	1905	799097	1935
471860	1906	808794	1936
493900	1907	817293	1937
518640	1908	825231	1938
535170	1909	832610	1939
552000	1910	837520	1940
574817	1911	838590	1941
594195	1912	839230	1942
612431	1913	839980	1943

Registered in January		Registered in January	
841040	1944	934515	1968
842670	1945	939875	1969
845550	1946	944932	1970
849730	1947	950046	1971
853260	1948	955342	1972
856999	1949	960708	1973
860854	1950	965185	1974
863970	1951	969249	1975
866280	1952	973838	1976
869300	1953	978426	1977
872531	1954	982815	1978
876067	1955	987910	1979
879282	1956	993012	1980
882949	1957	998302	1981
887079	1958	1004456	1982
891665	1959	1010583	1983
895000	1960	1017131	1984
899914	1961	1024174	1985
904638	1962	1031358	1986
909364	1963	1039055	1987
914536	1964	1047478	1988
919607	1965	1056076	1989
924510	1966	2003698	1990
929335	1967		

The numbering sequence stopped with 1061406 in August 1989 and the new sequence for designs filed after August 1st 1989 started with 2.000.000.

Following the Patents, Designs and Trade Marks Act of 1883, in which year the well-known 'diamond' mark ceased and the registration mark changed to the letters 'Rd' or 'Rd No', followed by the numeral, the period of protection was extended from three years to five. In 1907, a further Patents and Designs Act extended the protection given to registered designs for another five years at the Comptroller's discretion.

At the time of writing, 1991, the design registration records until 1910 are in the Public Records Office, Ruskin Avenue, Kew, Richmond, Surrey, TW9 4DU. The records from then to the present are housed at the Design Registry Room 1124A, State House, High Holborn, London, WC1, but enquiries should first be made to the Patent Office (Designs Registry) 25, Southampton Buildings, London, WC2A 1AY (tel: 071-405 8721).

APPENDIX B

Index of Names and Dates of Manufacturers, Retailers, Wholesalers and others who registered designs from 1842 to 1883

(See Appendix A, page 415, and Preface, page ix)

Date	Parcel No.	Patent No.	Factory, Retailer Wholesaler, etc	Place
1842				
Sept 22	1	1694	James Dixon & Sons	Sheffield
Nov 2	1	2152	Joseph Wolstenholme	Sheffield
3	1	2163	idem	Sheffield
26	3	2503–4	Henry Hunt	London
Dec 2	3	2599–00	Joseph Clementson	Shelton
30	2	3346	James Edwards	Burslem
1843				
Jan 24	2	4296–7	John Ridgway & Co.	Shelton
Feb 3	4	4462	T. Woodfield	London
21	1	5266–70	Samuel Alcock & Co.	Burslem
Mar 21	5	5993–4	Josiah Wedgwood & Sons	Etruria
31	6	6266	Samuel Alcock & Co.	Burslem
May 2	4	6978	Josiah Wedgwood & Sons	Etruria
5	1	7037	W. S. Kennedy	Burslem
11	2	7074	idem	Burslem
13	4	7122	Jones & Walley	Cobridge
June 14	5	7503–5	Samuel Alcock & Co.	Burslem
Aug 30	8	9678–80	James Edwards	Burslem
Oct 6	2	10370	idem	Burslem
Nov 10	3	11292	Minton & Co.	Stoke
28	5	11690	Thos. Dimmock & Co.	Shelton
Dec 14	10	12331	G. F. Bowers & Co.	Tunstall

APPENDIX B

Date	Parcel No.	Patent No.	Factory, Retailer Wholesaler, etc	Place
1844				
Feb 15	9	16264–5	Samuel Alcock & Co.	Burslem
20	4	16374–5	idem	Burslem
Mar 1	6	16687	Hamilton & Moore	Longton
5	3	16831	Mellor, Venables & Co.	Burslem
7	4	16871	J. & T. Lockett	Lane End
Apr 3	3	17566–72	Thos. Edwards	Burslem
11	4	17714	Hilditch & Hopwood	Lane End
May 7	4	18207	Thos. Dimmock & Co.	Shelton
June 29	3	19182	idem	Shelton
July 20	5	19977–9	John Ridgway & Co.	Shelton
30	2	20332–4	Herbert Minton & Co.	Stoke
Aug 15	3	20779	King, Knight & Elkin	Stoke
21	7	21069–73	Herbert Minton & Co.	Stoke
Sept 9	7	21450	Cyples, Barlow & Cyples	Lane End
19	4	21700–1	Jn. Ridgeway & Co.	Shelton
21	2	21715	Henry Hunt	London
30	7	21960	Charles Meigh	Hanley
Oct 14	4	22158	Copeland & Garrett	Stoke
17	3	22192	Clementson, Young & Jameson	Shelton
30	4	22394–6	Herbert Minton & Co.	Stoke
Nov 6	4	22424	idem	Stoke
11	5	22490	James Edwards	Burslem
13	4	22499–500	John Ridgway & Co.	Shelton
22	4	22834	Thos. Dimmock & Co.	Shelton
26	3	22883	Ray & Wynne	Longton
Dec 2	3	22919–20	Copeland & Garrett	Stoke
7	4	23207–10	Thos. Edwards	Burslem
16	6	23593	Willm. Ridgway, Son & Co.	Hanley
24	2	23843	John Meir & Son	Tunstall
1845				
Jan 11	6	24846	George Phillips	Longport

APPENDIX B

Date	Parcel No.	Patent No.	Factory, Retailer Wholesaler, etc	Place
15	2	24996	Clementson, Young & Jameson	Shelton
21	6	25199	T. J. & J. Mayer	Longport
27	5	25273	John Rose & Co.	Coalport
Feb 26	5	26532–3	W. S. Kennedy	Burslem
27	3	26543	George Phillips	Longport
Mar 5	1	26608	Copeland & Garrett	Stoke
6	5	26617	Herbert Minton & Co.	Stoke
17	10	26939	idem	Stoke
20	1	26949	idem	Stoke
31	4	27034	Thos. Pearce	London
Apr 10	1	27202	idem	London
25	2	27350	Copeland & Garrett	Stoke
26	1	27352	George Pearce	London
26	3	27354	T. & R. Boote, Walley & Jones	Burslem, Cobridge and Hanley
30	2	27383	Jacob Furnival & Co.	Cobridge
May 8	2	27451	Herbert Minton & Co.	Stoke
10	3	27482	Walley & T. & R. Boote	Cobridge and Burslem
31	1	27800	Francis Morley	Shelton
June 19	1	28150	George Phillips	Longport
26	3	28296	Minton & Co.	Stoke
July 5	1	28668–71	George Phillips	Longport
5	2	28672	Enoch Wood	Burslem
26	1	29173	William Adams & Sons	Stoke
Aug 28	3	29993	Joseph Clementson	Shelton
Sept 4	3	30161–3	Copeland & Garrett	Stoke
11	2	30286	Thos. Phillips & Son	Burslem
19	1	30383	Minton & Co.	Stoke
Oct 6	1	30543–4	H. Minton & Co.	Stoke
21	1	30699	Copeland & Garrett	Stoke

APPENDIX B

Date	Parcel No.	Patent No.	Factory, Retailer Wholesaler, etc	Place
22	2	30701	Clementson & Young	Shelton
Nov 15	2	31128	Bayley & Ball	Longton
22	2	31329	Minton & Co.	Stoke
Dec 4	4	31670–3	John Ridgway	Shelton
27	2	32553	James Edwards	Burslem
29	2	32555	Joseph Clementson	Shelton
30	3	32601	Furnival & Clark	Hanley
1846				
Jan 7	2	32698	Joseph Clementson	Shelton
24	2	33319	Jacob Furnival & Co.	Cobridge
Feb 26	5	34031	T. J. & J. Mayer	Longport
Mar 2	4	34108	Minton & Co.	Stoke
11	2	34281–5	W. S. Kennedy	Burslem
Apr 7	1	34564–66	idem	Burslem
17	3	34684	Copeland & Garrett	Stoke
May 21	3	35030–1	H. Minton & Co.	Stoke
26	2	35116–7	idem	Stoke
June 6	1	35219	W. Chamberlain & Co.	Worcester
26	2	35777	H. Minton & Co.	Stoke
30	3	35795	John Goodwin	Longton
July 11	1	36047	J. K. Knight	Longton
16	1	36167	Ridgway, Son & Co.	Hanley
17	1	36263	John Ridgway & Co.	Shelton
21	1	36278	F. Morley & Co.	Shelton
Aug 1	2	36447–8	Josiah Wedgwood & Sons	Etruria
3	1	36450	idem	Etruria
3	2	36451–2	H. Minton & Co.	Stoke
Sept 3	2	37170	G. Phillips	Longport
3	3	37171–2	F. Morley & Co.	Shelton
14	4	37254	Copeland & Garrett	Stoke
26	2	37419–21	John Ridgway & Co.	Shelton
29	3	37586	T. J. & J. Mayer	Longport
Oct 26	1	37806	F. Morley & Co.	Shelton
26	5	37864	J. Edwards	Burslem

Date	Parcel No.	Patent No.	Factory, Retailer Wholesaler, etc	Place
Nov 3	1	37935	Ridgway & Abington	Hanley
5	2	37986	G. Phillips	Longport
12	3	38068	C. Meigh	Hanley
16	2	38113	H. Minton & Co.	Stoke
21	2	38291–2	Thos. Furnival & Co.	Hanley
Dec 3	4	38606	Ridgway & Abington	Hanley
4	2	38610	H. Minton & Co.	Stoke
10	3	38786	Joseph Clementson	Shelton
14	3	39480	James Edwards	Burslem
14	4	39481	Minton & Co.	Stoke
16	1	39519	John Goodwin	Longton
17	2	39544–5	Copeland & Garrett	Stoke
26	5	39614	Henry Hunt	London
29	2	39703	Edward Challinor	Tunstall
31	3	39746	Josiah Wedgwood & Sons	Etruria
1847				
Jan 9	4	40104–5	John Ridgway & Co.	Shelton
9	7	40110	Copeland & Garrett	Stoke
Feb 2	7	41213	T. & R. Boote	Burslem
8	5	41266–7	T. J. & J. Mayer	Longton
15	4	41459–60	Copeland & Garrett	Stoke
Mar 17	3	42044	John Wedge Wood	Tunstall
17	6	42047–8	John Ridgway & Co.	Shelton
22	2	42233	Bailey & Ball	Longton
23	7	42279	Herbert Minton & Co.	Stoke
30	1	42363	James Edwards	Burslem
Apr 3	6	42435	Samuel Alcock & Co.	Burslem
27	1	42804	idem	Burslem
May 12	4	43154	Copeland & Garrett	Stoke
14	1	43170–1	Herbert Minton & Co.	Stoke
June 11	4	43536	James Edwards	Burslem
11	6	43557	Joseph Alexander	Norwich
21	5	43728	John Rose & Co.	Coalport
25	2	43780	James Edwards	Burslem

APPENDIX B

Date	Parcel No.	Patent No.	Factory, Retailer Wholesaler, etc	Place
July 5	5	43916–7	Mellor, Venables & Co.	Burslem
15	1	44014–5	idem	Burslem
16	5	44036–9	James Edwards	Burslem
27	3	44398	T. J. & J. Mayer	Longport
Aug 3	3	44872	John Rose & Co.	Coalport
16	2	45088	James Edwards	Burslem
17	2	45091–2	W. T. Copeland	Stoke
19	3	45175	H. Minton & Co.	Stoke
26	2	45367	James Edwards	Burslem
Sept 9	3	45730	William Taylor Copeland	Stoke
16	3	45822	idem	Stoke
25	5	45992	John Wedge Wood	Tunstall
Oct 1	4	46130	Thos. Peake	Tunstall
2	5	46192–4	John Ridgway & Co.	Shelton
4	3	46232	H. Minton & Co.	Stoke
8	4	46265	John Wedge Wood	Tunstall
13	1	46299	W. T. Copeland	Stoke
23	2	46516–8	H. Minton & Co.	Stoke
27	1	46529	John Ridgway & Co.	Shelton
Nov 11	4	46886	H. Minton & Co.	Stoke
23	4	47183	J. Wedgwood & Co.	Etruria
Dec 1	2	47417–20	John Rose & Co.	Coalport
10	3	47562–3	Minton & Co. & John Bell	Stoke
15	4	48130	Minton & Co.	Stoke
1848				
Jan 1	4	48540–2	Barker & Till	Burslem
6	4	48717	Geo. Grainger	Worcester
18	2	49040	W. T. Copeland	Stoke
Feb 11	3	49780–1	H. Minton & Co.	Stoke
29	12	50473	Minton & Co.	Stoke
Mar 4	4	50549	Minton & Co.	Stoke
7	1	50635–6	Ridgway & Abington	Hanley
14	2	50798	W. T. Copeland	Stoke
15	2	50803	idem	Stoke

426

APPENDIX B

Date	Parcel No.	Patent No.	Factory, Retailer Wholesaler, etc	Place
20	7	50994	Wood & Brownfield	Cobridge
27	8	51185–91	J. & S. Alcock Jnr.	Cobridge
Apr 15	4	51542	John Ridgway & Co.	Shelton
17	6	51599	Frederick Harrison	London
22	3	51661	Josiah Wedgwood & Sons	Etruria
27	4	51763	idem	Etruria
28	5	51768	Giovanni Franchi	London
May 30	3	52162	Thos. Peake	Tunstall
June 20	4	52402	G. F. Bowers & Co.	Tunstall
30	2	52529	W. T. Copeland	Stoke
30	3	52530	Ridgway & Abington	Hanley
Aug 10	3	53782	Geo. Grainger	Worcester
16	8	53876	Thos. Pinder	Burslem
23	2	54018	John Wedge Wood	Tunstall
26	2	54067	John Meir & Son	Tunstall
Sept 15	3	54438	W. T. Copeland	Stoke
18	4	54487	Charles Meigh	Hanley
25	4	54578–9	Giovanni Franchi	London
30	7	54662	John Ridgway & Co.	Shelton
Oct 17	3	54901	T. & R. Boote	Burslem
Nov 4	2	55174	W. T. Copeland	Stoke
13	4	55337	idem	Stoke
21	5	55456–7	Minton & Co.	Stoke
27	2	55766	John Ridgway & Co.	Shelton
Dec 16	3	56631–3	James Edwards	Burslem
28	2	56845	John Ridgway	Shelton
1849				
Jan 3	2	56978	William Adams & Sons	Stoke
20	2	57506–8	W. Davenport & Co.	Longport
Feb 2	4	58069	Mellor, Venables & Co.	Burslem
16	5	58461	Minton & Co.	Stoke
16	11	58474	Ridgway & Abington	Hanley
26	2	58578	John Rose & Co.	Coalport
Mar 13	2	58874	Joseph Clementson	Shelton

Date	Parcel No.	Patent No.	Factory, Retailer Wholesaler, etc	Place
26	5	59232	Minton & Co.	Stoke
27	2	59245	Cope & Edwards	Longton
31	2	59286	John Ridgway & Co.	Shelton
Apr 2	5	59308	Podmore, Walker & Co.	Tunstall
10	4	59400	W. T. Copeland	Stoke
16	6	59571	C. J. Mason	Longton
May 24	1	60081	Mr. Wedge Wood	Tunstall
June 7	3	60265	T. J. & J. Mayer	Longport
July 16	2	61347	Ridgway & Abington	Hanley
Aug 11	4	61865	W. T. Copeland	Stoke
15	2	61986	H. Minton & Co.	Stoke
17	2	62003	W. T. Copeland	Stoke
27	5	62316	Mellor, Venables & Co.	Burslem
Sept 14	6	62498	F. & R. Pratt & Co.	Fenton
28	6	62690–4	J. Ridgway	Shelton
Oct 10	2	62883	idem	Shelton
12	4	62914	Minton & Co.	Stoke
26	5	63267	J. Hollinshead	Shelton
Nov 8	6	63490	John Cliff Quince	London
9	4	63523	W. T. Copeland	Stoke
17	2	63718	Minton & Co.	Stoke
22	2	64319	W. T. Copeland	Stoke
30	5	64627	John Rose & Co.	Coalport
Dec 6	3	64739	W. T. Copeland	Stoke
15	4	64982	T. J. & J. Mayer	Longport
1850				
Jan 3	1	65884	W. Davenport & Co.	Longport
14	4	66266–7	J. Ridgway	Shelton
26	6	66862	G. Grainger	Worcester
Feb 13	1	67398	idem	Worcester
13	3	67413	J. & M. P. Bell & Co.	Glasgow
27	4	67783	G. Grainger	Worcester
Mar 9	3	67987	W. T. Copeland	Stoke
30	9	68489	John Rose & Co.	Coalport

Date	Parcel No.	Patent No.	Factory, Retailer Wholesaler, etc	Place
Apr 4	4	68623	T. J. & J. Mayer	Longport
8	1	68720	J. Clementson	Shelton
13	7	68797	Minton & Co.	Stoke
18	11	68959	John Rose & Co.	Coalport
24	3	69142	William Pierce	London
25	3	69149	Minton & Co.	Stoke
June 4	1	69679	J. & M. P. Bell & Co.	Glasgow
5	3	69685	Barker & Son	Burslem
21	4	69884	E. Walley	Cobridge
July 2	2	70088	T. J. & J. Mayer	Longport
16	5	70364	C. & W. K. Harvey	Longton
Sept 9	5	71843	Thomas Till	Burslem
16	8	71952	J. & M. P. Bell & Co.	Glasgow
16	9	71953–4	J. Ridgway	Shelton
19	2	71989	W. T. Copeland	Stoke
21	1	72057	Mellor, Venables & Co.	Burslem
Oct 9	2	72395–6	Minton & Co.	Stoke
17	6	72544	W. T. Copeland	Stoke
Nov 4	4	73327	J. Wedgwood & Sons	Etruria
20	7	73693	F. Morley & Co.	Shelton
22	3	73719	John Rose & Co.	Coalport
Dec 5	3	74138	F. Morley & Co.	Shelton
19	5	74785	John Rose & Co.	Coalport
19	6	74786	T. J. & J. Mayer	Longport
20	6	75148	W. T. Copeland	Stoke
1851				
Jan 20	4	75883–4	James Green	London
Feb 10	9	76664	William Brownfield	Cobridge
Mar 17	13	77481–91	J. Ridgway & Co.	Shelton
31	4	77986	J. & M. P. Bell & Co.	Glasgow
Apr 9	2	78268	Thos. Till & Son	Burslem
11	4	78309–10	J. & M. P. Bell & Co.	Glasgow
11	6	78312	W. S. Kennedy	Burslem
14	7	78398–401	J. & M. P. Bell & Co.	Glasgow

Date	Parcel No.	Patent No.	Factory, Retailer Wholesaler, etc	Place
26	3	78634	E. Walley	Cobridge
May 30	4	79085	W. T. Copeland	Stoke
June 7	4	79164	J. Ridgway & Co.	Shelton
11	2	79183	W. T. Copeland	Stoke
11	3	79184	Ralph Scragg	Hanley
19	5	79300	W. T. Copeland	Stoke
July 10	3	79588	R. Britton & Co.	Leeds
14	3	79684	W. T. Copeland	Stoke
21	7	79750–3	T. & R. Boote	Burslem
24	2	79782	Thos. Till & Son	Burslem
26	3	79802	C. Collinson & Co.	Burslem
Aug 16	2	80184	Ridgway & Abington	Hanley
Sept 2	4	80365	T. J. & J. Mayer	Longport
19	3	80629–30	T. & R. Boote	Burslem
29	4	80815–16	James Edwards	Burslem
30	3	80826	idem	Burslem
Oct 1	1	80827	W. T. Copeland	Stoke
7	3	80887	Chamberlain & Co.	Worcester
10	4	80910–1	W. Brownfield	Cobridge
10	6	80913	T. & R. Boote	Burslem
14	4	80980	Thos. Till & Son	Burslem
16	4	80989	W. Brownfield	Cobridge
17	3	80997	George Bowden Sander	London
21	3	81057	Wm. Ridgway	Shelton
Nov 1	5	81225–6	Geo. B. Sander	London
10	4	81492	Ralph Scragg	Hanley
12	6	81510–12	Minton & Co.	Stoke
13	2	81518	Charles Meigh & Son	Hanley
14	4	81558	Geo. B. Sander	London
Dec 2	2	81815	T. J. & J. Mayer	Burslem
4	3	81843–4	Minton & Co.	Stoke
5	5	81864	John Ridgway & Co.	Shelton
8	8	81960	W. T. Copeland	Stoke
15	6	82052	Geo. B. Sander	London

APPENDIX B

Date	Parcel No.	Patent No.	Factory, Retailer Wholesaler, etc	Place
1852				
Jan 27	1	83342	W. & G. Harding	Burslem
Feb 17	1	83826	Venables & Baines	Burslem
Mar 4	2	84133–4	Wm. Brownfield	Cobridge
13	3	84239	Wm. Ridgway	Shelton
22	7	84385	Ralph Scragg	Hanley
24	3	84406	James Edwards	Burslem
24	4	84407	Minton & Co.	Stoke
25	1	84410	John Milner	Cobridge
26	3	84471	J. & M. P. Bell & Co.	Glasgow
Apr 1	1	84541	Thos. Till & Son	Burslem
8	4	84615	idem	Burslem
21	4	84837	George Ray	Longton
May 5	5	85001–2	J. M. Blashfield	London
6	5	85008	Geo. Bowden Sander	London
7	2	85010–3	J. M. Blashfield	London
14	5	85081	W. T. Copeland	Stoke
18	1	85102	Minton & Co.	Stoke
June 1	2	85224–5	J. M. Blashfield	London
5	5	85248	Minton & Co.	Stoke
14	4	85354	W. T. Copeland	Stoke
21	2	85404	J. & T. Lockett	Longton
July 5	3	85619	J. Pankhurst & Co.	Hanley
23	3	85803–4	Minton & Co.	Stoke
Aug 4	3	86070–1	W. T. Copeland	Stoke
13	5	86126	Thos. Till & Son	Burslem
25	4	86318	Chas. Meigh & Son	Hanley
25	5	86319	Geo. Bowden Sander	London
Sept 3	7	86473	Minton & Co.	Stoke
15	5	86649	Thos. Till & Son	Burslem
16	1	86657	Minton & Co.	Stoke
24	1	86815	idem	Stoke
27	3	86857	Warburton & Britton	Leeds
Oct 1	6	86931	W. T. Copeland	Stoke
7	5	87040	Ralph Scragg	Hanley

APPENDIX B

Date	Parcel No.	Patent No.	Factory, Retailer Wholesaler, etc	Place
23	4	87219	Davenports & Co.	Longport
25	2	87228	Wm. Brownfield	Cobridge
30	3	87464	Marple, Turner & Co.	Hanley
Nov 4	5	87541	John Holland	Tunstall
11	3	87633	Minton & Co.	Stoke
22	3	87883	J. Pankhurst & J. Dimmock	Hanley
25	4	88037	Keys & Mountford	Stoke
Dec 16	4	88350	John Rose & Co.	Coalport
27	1	88693	Warburton & Britton	Leeds
1853				
Jan 3	3	88808–9	W. T. Copeland	Stoke
12	6	88978	Thos. Goodfellow	Tunstall
14	3	88987	Davenports & Co.	Longport
18	2	89050	idem	Longport
Feb 4	9	89469	J. Pankhurst & J. Dimmock	Hanley
10	2	89626	Geo. Wooliscroft	Tunstall
11	6	89646	Thos. Worthington & J. Green	Shelton
12	3	89661–3	Minton & Co.	Stoke
17	4	89722–3	W. S. Kennedy & Co.	Burslem
26	5	89958	W. T. Copeland	Stoke
Mar 10	2	90253	J. & M. P. Bell & Co.	Glasgow
17	5	90360	J. W. Pankhurst & Co.	Hanley
19	2	90372	Minton & Co.	Stoke
Apr 4	6	90610	John Rose & Co.	Coalport
23	2	90876	Wm. Adams & Sons	Stoke
May 7	5	91121–4	John Alcock	Cobridge
June 7	3	91329	Geo. Wood & Co.	Shelton
14	2	91405–6	Livesley, Powell & Co.	Hanley
22	3	91469	Pankhurst & Dimmock	Hanley
24	3	91487	Geo. Wooliscroft	Tunstall
24	11	91512–3	Ridgway & Co.	Shelton

APPENDIX B

Date	Parcel No.	Patent No.	Factory, Retailer Wholesaler, etc	Place
July 18	4	91737 ⸱	John Edwards	Longton
20	2	91749–50	J. H. Baddeley	Shelton
Aug 8	1	92001	Anthony Shaw	Tunstall
10	2	92018	Holland & Green	Longton
Sept 3	2	92340	T. & R. Boote	Burslem
6	3	92364	F. Morley & Co.	Shelton
21	2	92631–2	James Edwards	Burslem
Oct 5	2	92768–70	Venables, Mann & Co.	Burslem
10	3	92859	Barrow & Co.	Fenton
11	5	92864	Ralph Scragg	Hanley
12	3	92867	James Edwards	Burslem
12	4	92868–9	Livesley, Powell & Co.	Hanley
19	4	92952	Minton & Co.	Stoke
22	1	93008–9	T. J. & J. Mayer	Longport
Nov 24	2	93438–9	Thos. Till & Son	Burslem
26	2	93452	W. T. Copeland	Stoke
30	5	93483	Wm. Adams & Sons	Stoke
Dec 6	4	93536	J. Alcock	Cobridge
24	3	93706–7	Samuel Moore & Co.	Sunderlnd
24	4	93708	J. Alcock	Cobridge
1854				
Jan 10	4	94326	W. & G. Harding	Burslem
13	1	94343–4	Deaville & Baddeley	Hanley
14	3	94632	Samuel Moore & Co.	Sunderlnd
21	3	94727	J. & M. P. Bell & Co.	Glasgow
30	4	94815	Samuel Alcock & Co.	Burslem
Feb 23	3	95163	W. T. Copeland	Stoke
Mar 11	4	95275	Samuel Alcock & Co.	Burslem
20	1	95388	Thos. Till & Son	Burslem
22	2	95397	James Edwards & Son	Longport
24	3	95420	Minton & Co.	Stoke
27	3	95448	Geo. Baguley	Hanley
27	6	95451	J. Deaville	Hanley
31	1	95469	Holland & Green	Longton

Date	Parcel No.	Patent No.	Factory, Retailer Wholesaler, etc	Place
Apr 1	4	95510	Wm. Brownfield	Cobridge
4	3	95523	Woollard & Hattersley	Cambdge
5	3	95542	Ralph Scragg	Hanley
6	3	95553	Samuel Alcock & Co.	Burslem
10	3	95575	J. Deaville	Hanley
10	4	95576	Samuel Alcock & Co.	Burslem
11	5	95587-8	Pearson, Farrall & Meakin	Shelton
15	1	95611	Geo. Baguley	Hanley
21	3	95646	Warburton & Britton	Leeds
May 4	3	95733	John Ridgway & Co.	Shelton
8	3	95751	Wm. Brownfield	Cobridge
June 3	2	96003	Thos. Till & Son	Burslem
9	2	96039	Chas. Meigh & Son	Hanley
21	5	96085-6	T. & R. Boote	Burslem
July 18	2	96296	idem	Burslem
18	4	96298	Alcock & Co.	Burslem
Sept 5	3	96773	Samuel Alcock & Co.	Burslem
12	2	96826	W. T. Copeland	Stoke
Oct 2	3	96980	Wm. Brownfield	Cobridge
6	4	97141	Davenports & Co.	Longport
9	4	97160	T. J. & J. Mayer	Longport
31	2	97508	Geo. Ray	Longton
Nov 10	5	97659	John Ridgway & Co.	Shelton
Dec 27	3	98640	Samuel Alcock & Co.	Burslem
27	4	98641	Pankhurst & Dimmock	Hanley
29	1	98648	F. & R. Pratt & Co.	Fenton
1855				
Jan 4	2	98696	Worthington & Green	Shelton
6	4	98786	Samuel Alcock & Co.	Burslem
15	2	99042	Pinder, Bourne & Hope	Burslem
15	4	99051	Brougham & Mayer	Tunstall
19	3	99086	Pankhurst & Dimmock	Hanley
30	1	99188	John Edwards	Longton

APPENDIX B

Date	Parcel No.	Patent No.	Factory, Retailer Wholesaler, etc	Place
Feb 3	4	99231	J. & M. P. Bell & Co.	Glasgow
5	7	99282	Coomb(e)s & Holland	Llanelly
7	2	99310	John Alcock	Cobridge
17	3	99394	Pratt & Co.	Fenton
26	3	99488	Lockett, Baguley & Cooper	Shelton
28	4	99528	J. Ridgway & Co.	Shelton
Mar 1	5	99538–40	Minton & Co.	Stoke
5	3	99579	Elsmore & Forster	Tunstall
13	4	99653	Warburton & Britton	Leeds
17	1	99679	Wm. Baker	Fenton
Apr 7	7	99814	W. T. Copeland	Stoke
17	4	99876	Stephen Hughes & Son	Burslem
26	1	99972–4	Wm. Brownfield	Cobridge
28	7	100008	Venables, Mann & Co.	Burslem
May 10	5	100094	Beech, Hancock & Co.	Burslem
14	3	100116	Minton & Co.	Stoke
June 7	4	100246–7	John Alcock	Cobridge
11	3	100299	Saml. Alcock & Co.	Burslem
July 4	5	100624	J. Thompson	Staffs.
24	1	100816	Chas. Meigh & Son	Hanley
Aug 6	1	101019	James Dudson	Shelton
8	5	101026	J. Edwards & Son	Longport
11	1	101082	Geo. Grainger & Co.	Worcester
20	3	101127	Thos. Ford	Shelton
27	2	101229–31	Barrow & Co.	Fenton
Sept 27	4	101623–4	Saml. Bevington & Son	Shelton
Oct 3	2	101681	Geo. Mayor & Co.	London
3	3	101682	Minton & Co.	Stoke
17	8	101932	John Williamson	Glasgow
25	3	102325	D. Chetwynd	Cobridge
29	6	102355	G. W. Reade	Burslem
Nov 1	3	102415	Josiah Wedgwood & Sons	Etruria
22	4	102744	J. & M. P. Bell & Co.	Glasgow
28	3	102785	Wm. Brownfield	Cobridge

435

APPENDIX B

Date	Parcel No.	Patent No.	Factory, Retailer Wholesaler, etc	Place
1856				
Jan 5	3	103103	J. Edwards	Longton
15	4	103404	James Pankhurst & Co.	Hanley
23	3	103506	J. Roberts	Kent (Upnor)
23	4	103507	Minton & Co.	Stoke
31	4	103616	Josiah Wedgwood & Sons	Etruria
Mar 11	1	104078	Davenports & Co.	Longport
12	3	104090	Pratt & Co.	Fenton
Apr 7	2	104313–16	A. Shaw	Tunstall
7	3	104317	J. & M. P. Bell & Co.	Glasgow
18	2	104392	Wm. Beech	Burslem
18	3	104393	Ralph Scragg	Hanley
18	6	104396	E. Walley	Cobridge
18	7	104397	Ridgway & Abington	Hanley
30	3	104602–3	Wm. Brownfield	Cobridge
May 8	2	104694	Minton & Co.	Stoke
22	1	104762	idem	Stoke
June 13	3	105059	Chas. Meigh & Son	Hanley
28	3	105223	Worthington & Green	Hanley
30	7	105258	J. Clementson	Shelton
July 28	3	105492	E. Challinor	Tunstall
30	5	105702	J. Edwards & Son	Longport
Aug 12	2	105871	F. & R. Pratt & Co.	Fenton
19	5	105926	idem	Fenton
22	4	105955–9	T. & R. Boote	Burslem
Sept 1	3	106161	W. T. Copeland	Stoke
Oct 2	3	106477	H. Baggaley	Hanley
16	2	106671–2	Minton & Co.	Stoke
22	3	106770	W. T. Copeland	Stoke
Nov 7	6	106950	F. & R. Pratt & Co.	Fenton
14	9	107038	Davenports & Co.	Longport
27	3	107708	idem	Longport
27	6	107714	Wm. Brownfield	Cobridge
29	1	107783–5	E. Walley	Cobridge

APPENDIX B

Date	Parcel No.	Patent No.	Factory, Retailer Wholesaler, etc	Place
Dec 11	4	107955	W. T. Copeland	Stoke
18	2	108052	Mayer & Elliott	Longport
23	4	108105	idem	Longport
1857				
Jan 15	5	108605	F. & R. Pratt & Co.	Fenton
26	7	108785	J. Edwards	Longport
Feb 4	5	108854–5	John Meir & Son	Tunstall
9	4	108930	Minton & Co.	Stoke
17	3	109063	idem	Stoke
23	9	109180	Podmore, Walker & Co.	Hanley
Mar 20	4	109427	John Alcock	Cobridge
Apr 16	1	109738	John Alcock	Cobridge
29	1	109810	W. T. Copeland	Stoke
June 5	3	110096–7	Wm. Brownfield	Cobridge
19	1	110160	W. T. Copeland	Stoke
19	2	110161	Wilkinson & Rickhuss	Hanley
25	1	110247	J. & M. P. Bell & Co.	Glasgow
July 30	2	110780	Ridgway, Bates & Co.	Shelton
Aug 4	5	110806	Taylor, Pears & Co.	Fenton
11	3	110862	Kerr & Binns	Worcester
Sept 7	2	111105	W. T. Copeland	Stoke
Oct 3	3	111495–6	Doulton & Watts	London
5	5	111515–6	idem	London
14	1	111585	Ridgway & Abington	Hanley
17	1	111642	Mayer Bros. & Elliott	Longport
17	2	111643–4	T. & R. Boote	Burslem
22	1	111677	Pratt & Co.	Fenton
Nov 3	3	111831–2	Maw & Co.	Broseley
28	2	112263	Kerr & Binns	Worcester
Dec 4	4	112350	Minton & Co.	Stoke
9	2	112354	Wm. Brownfield	Cobridge

Date	Parcel No.	Patent No.	Factory, Retailer Wholesaler, etc	Place
1858				
Jan 29	3	112875	Cockson & Harding	Hanley
29	4	112876	E. & W. Walley	Cobridge
Mar 25	2	113290	Kerr & Binns	Worcester
Apr 9	2	113387	idem	Worcester
17	4	113456	Ridgway & Abington	Hanley
22	5	113565	T. & R. Boote	Burslem
30	5	113631	Minton & Co.	Stoke
May 6	4	113668	J. Edwards	Longton
25	4	113864	A. Shaw	Burslem
31	1	113900	Holland & Green	Longton
31	4	113903	Wm. Adams	Tunstall
June 2	1	113905–6	Wm. Brownfield	Cobridge
23	6	114048	Samuel Alcock & Co.	Burslem
July 13	2	114214	Mayer & Elliott	Longport
29	4	114532	Samuel Alcock & Co.	Burslem
Aug 24	2	114763	Wm. Brownfield	Cobridge
Sept 3	2	115120	Sharpe Bros. & Co.	Swadlncte
6	5	115197	James Edwards	Longport
10	3	115217	John Edwards	Longton
10	6	115343	Bridgwood & Clarke	Burslem
Oct 5	2	115901	Minton & Co.	Stoke
5	3	115902	Wm. Brownfield	Cobridge
7	1	115953	Ridgway & Abington	Hanley
18	3	116176	Minton & Co.	Stoke
29	2	116468	B. Green	Fenton
Nov 3	8	116585	James Stiff	London
5	5	116607	Wm. Savage	Winchstr
11	2	116737	E. & W. Walley	Cobridge
Dec 8	11	117336–8	T. & R. Boote	Burslem
8	12	117339	J. Clementson	Hanley
17	6	117443	W. T. Copeland	Stoke
23	2	117516	J. Clementson	Hanley
23	9	117530	W. T. Copeland	Stoke
27	4	117559	J. Clementson	Hanley

APPENDIX B

Date	Parcel No.	Patent No.	Factory, Retailer Wholesaler, etc	Place
1859				
Jan 25	4	118119	W. T. Copeland	Stoke
Feb 2	3	118294	T. & R. Boote	Burslem
3	2	118303–4	Davenports & Co.	Longport
8	6	118415	Leveson Hill (Excrs. of)	Stoke
Mar 19	1	118827	Alsop, Downes, Spilsbury & Co.	London
21	7	118891	T. & R. Boote	Burslem
29	7	119137	idem	Burslem
May 7	1	119721–2	E. & W. Walley	Cobridge
10	2	119760	Samuel Alcock & Co.	Burslem
20	1	119968	Wm. Brownfield	Cobridge
26	1	120096	Lockett, Baguley & Cooper	Hanley
July 2	2	120560	W. T. Copeland	Stoke
Aug 6	7	121140	F. & R. Pratt & Co.	Fenton
27	6	121724	Samuel Alcock & Co.	Burslem
Sept 1	3	121833	James Edwards & Son	Longport
Oct 12	4	122959	Wm. Adams	Tunstall
14	4	123116	W. T. Copeland	Stoke
25	1	123389–91	Minton & Co.	Stoke
28	1	123604	Davenports & Co.	Longport
Nov 2	3	123738–40	Elsmore & Forster	Tunstall
5	4	123816	Wm. Brownfield	Cobridge
17	4	124140–3	Minton & Co.	Stoke
23	4	124274	idem	Stoke
Dec 10	5	124653	Josiah Wedgwood & Sons	Etruria
14	2	124716	E. & W. Walley	Cobridge
15	3	124725	Minton & Co.	Stoke
1860				
Jan 10	4	125365	W. T. Copeland	Stoke
23	7	125863	Mayer & Elliott	Longport
Feb 14	9	126446–7	W. T. Copeland	Stoke

APPENDIX B

Date	Parcel No.	Patent No.	Factory, Retailer Wholesaler, etc	Place
Mar 1	2	126950	Bates, Brown-Westhead & Moore	Hanley
27	1	127513	idem	Hanley
Apr 5	1	127766	Geo. Grainger & Co.	Worcester
12	4	127965	Minton & Co.	Stoke
May 2	2	128476	John Meir & Son	Tunstall
19	9	129129	Lockett, Baguley & Cooper	Hanley
30	10	129578	Edward Corn	Burslem
June 6	4	129680–2	Wm. Brownfield	Cobridge
22	2	130106	Minton & Co.	Stoke
28	2	130135	Minton & Co.	Stoke
Aug 21	2	131943	John Wedge Wood	Tunstall
Sept 24	3	133411	Minton & Co.	Stoke
29	7	133788	idem	Stoke
Oct 13	5	134204	B. Green	Fenton
18	4	134519–20	Bates, Brown-Westhead & Moore	Hanley
19	4	134555–7	J. Clementson	Shelton
19	5	134558–9	Holland & Green	Longton
29	3	134936	Minton & Co.	Stoke
29	9	134968	Wm. Brownfield	Cobridge
Nov 23	9	136032	T. & R. Boote	Burslem
Dec 3	3	136285–6	Bates, Brown-Westhead & Moore	Hanley
12	3	136643	Bates & Co.	Hanley
1861				
Jan 8	6	137217	T. & R. Boote	Burslem
21	7	137529	Wedgwood & Co.	Tunstall
Feb 15	3	138356	J. Furnival & Co.	Cobridge
27	5	138535	James Edwards & Son	Longport
Mar 7	7	138861–2	Turner & Tomkinson	Tunstall
19	3	139053	W. T. Copeland	Stoke
19	4	139054–5	W. H. Kerr & Co.	Worcester

APPENDIX B

Date	Parcel No.	Patent No.	Factory, Retailer Wholesaler, etc	Place
Apr 5	3	139360	Pinder, Bourne & Hope	Burslem
6	1	139369–72	Minton, Hollins & Co.	Stoke
12	3	139714–5	Davenports & Co.	Longport
18	5	139881	T. & R. Boote	Burslem
20	6	139945	F. & R. Pratt	Fenton
25	2	140200	James Dudson	Hanley
May 3	8	140367	W. T. Copeland	Stoke
6	3	140478	The Hill Pottery Co.	Burslem
6	5	140480–1	The Old Hall Earthenware Co.	Hanley
9	3	140578–9	Bates, Brown–Westhead & Moore	Hanley
13	7	140679	Minton & Co.	Stoke
14	2	140683	W. H. Kerr & Co.	Worcester
25	2	141055	idem	Worcester
31	3	141114	Cork, Edge & Malkin	Burslem
June 4	1	141214	Bates, Brown–Westhead & Moore	Hanley
7	5	141288	The Hill Pottery Co.	Burslem
11	2	141326–7	W. T. Copeland	Stoke
13	6	141369	Minton & Co.	Stoke
July 4	2	141715	Lockett & Cooper	Hanley
5	2	141727	Beech & Hancock	Tunstall
6	2	141732	Wm. Brownfield	Cobridge
18	4	141869–70	Josiah Wedgwood & Sons	Etruria
Aug 19	7	142755	T. & R. Boote	Burslem
22	7	142847	Wedgwood & Co.	Tunstall
23	2	142850	G. W. Reade	Cobridge
Sept 6	6	143313	Wm. Brownfield	Cobridge
12	6	143400	J. & J. Peake	Newcastle
17	2	143702	W. T. Copeland	Stoke
18	7	143769	Wm. Beech	Burslem
26	7	144179	John Cliff & Co.	London
Oct 10	5	144757	W. H. Kerr & Co.	Worcester
11	3	144767	Mountford & Scarratt	Fenton

APPENDIX B

Date	Parcel No.	Patent No.	Factory, Retailer Wholesaler, etc	Place
15	3	144896	Leveson Hill (Excrs of)	Stoke
18	3	145157	W. T. Copeland	Stoke
24	5	145499	Hulse, Nixon & Adderley	Longton
28	7	145686–7	Bates, Brown–Westhead & Moore	Hanley
Nov 15	3	146352–4	J. Clementson	Hanley
29	5	146924	Josiah Wedgwood & Sons	Etruria
Dec 4	7	147309–10	Wm. Brownfield	Cobridge
5	5	147322	Till, Bullock & Smith	Hanley
20	7	147820	Lockett & Cooper	Hanley
20	9	147823	Wedgwood & Co.	Tunstall
1862				
Jan 11	5	148517	Wm. Brownfield	Cobridge
25	3	148870	idem	Cobridge
Feb 1	4	149090	Elliot Bros.	Longport
10	6	149290	W. H. Kerr & Co.	Worcester
10	8	149292	Minton & Co.	Stoke
27	4	149673–4	James Dudson	Hanley
Mar 1	6	149716	T. & R. Boote	Burslem
13	6	149938	W. T. Copeland	Stoke
13	7	149939	Wm. Adams	Tunstall
14	8	149955	J. Knight	Fenton
14	9	149956	Wedgwood & Co.	Tunstall
14	10	149957–8	Wm. Brownfield	Cobridge
21	6	150100	Thompson Bros.	Burton-on-Trent
22	9	150152	T. & R. Boote	Burslem
27	1	150241	J. & M. P. Bell & Co.	Glasgow
28	5	150301–3	idem	Glasgow
29	3	150322	Minton & Co.	Stoke
Apr 1	5	150377	Josiah Wedgwood & Sons	Etruria
4	2	150455	Minton & Co.	Stoke
4	5	150458	J. & T. Furnival	Cobridge

Date	Parcel No.	Patent No.	Factory, Retailer Wholesaler, etc	Place
7	12	150515	Geo. Grainger & Co.	Worcester
9	3	150538	The Old Hall Earthenware Co. (Ltd.)	Hanley
17	5	151029–30	Thompson Bros.	Burton
24	2	151141	Turner & Tomkinson	Tunstall
May 1	7	151351	Eardley & Hammersley	Tunstall
3	3	151378	G. L. Ashworth Bros.	Hanley
5	5	151456	John Cliff	London
9	9	151568–9	Brown–Westhead, Moore & Co.	Hanley
14	3	151672–3	Geo. Jones & Co.	Stoke
27	3	151995	E. Challinor	Tunstall
29	5	152013	J. Furnival & Co.	Cobridge
June 24	5	152709	T. C. Brown–Westhead, Moore & Co.	Hanley
July 2	4	152859	Minton & Co.	Stoke
4	8	152963	J. Clementson	Hanley
12	4	153112	idem	Hanley
14	2	153127	Beech & Hancock	Tunstall
19	6	153366	J. Clementson	Hanley
31	3	153476	Jones & Ellis	Longton
31	4	153477	Minton & Co.	Stoke
Aug 16	5	153821	Richard Edwards	Longport
16	7	153823	J. H. Baddeley	Hanley
18	4	153827	Hulse, Nixon & Adderley	Longton
19	4	153844	G. L. Ashworth & Bros.	Hanley
25	3	154143–4	E. F. Bodley & Co.	Burslem
30	3	154220	Thos. Fell & Co.	Newcastle upon Tyne
30	4	154221	T. & R. Boote	Burslem
Sept 6	2	154401	Malkin, Walker & Hulse	Longton
11	3	154678	Minton & Co.	Stoke
12	2	154693	Thos. Cooper	Longton

Date	Parcel No.	Patent No.	Factory, Retailer Wholesaler, etc	Place
17	6	154812	Hope & Carter	Burslem
22	7	155103	Minton & Co.	Stoke
26	1	155220–2	Hope & Carter	Burslem
Oct 1	7	155263–4	Thos. Fell & Co.	Newcastle upon Tyne
9	3	155550	Hill Pottery	Burslem
15	2	156190	Turner & Tomkinson	Tunstall
23	8	156715–7	Wm. Baker & Co.	Fenton
Nov 11	3	157274	E. F. Bodley & Co.	Burslem
19	5	157547	Geo. Wooliscroft	Tunstall
28	4	157907	Minton & Co.	Stoke
Dec 3	5	158052–3	T. C. Brown–Westhead Moore & Co.	Hanley
5	2	158091	Wm. Brownfield	Cobridge
9	5	158221	Thomas Cooper	Hanley
17	5	158480	The Old Hall Earthenware Co. (Ltd.)	Hanley
18	3	158498	Geo. Jones	Stoke
1863				
Jan 12	6	159083	Davenport, Banks & Co.	Etruria
16	2	159123	Minton & Co.	Stoke
16	8	159153	Liddle, Elliot & Sons	Longport
29	1	159551	Josiah Wedgwood & Sons	Etruria
30	3	159573	T. & R. Boote	Burslem
Feb 2	3	159613	Minton & Co.	Stoke
17	4	159972	T. & R. Boote	Burslem
24	5	160110	James Stiff & Sons	London
Mar 6	2	160319	G. L. Ashworth & Bros.	Hanley
13	2	160456	Hope & Carter	Burslem
13	3	160457	Wilkinson & Sons	Hanley
20	8	160752	Worthington & Green	Hanley
20	9	160753–4	John Pratt & Co.	Fenton
21	2	160759	Beech & Hancock	Tunstall

Date	Parcel No.	Patent No.	Factory, Retailer Wholesaler, etc	Place
21	4	160761	Hulse, Nixon & Adderley	Longton
21	5	160762	James Edwards & Son	Burslem
23	2	160791–2	Bodley & Harrold	Burslem
Apr 11	1	161404	J. Macintyre	Burslem
23	4	161852	T. C. Brown–Westhead Moore & Co.	Hanley
25	1	161861	Beech & Hancock	Tunstall
30	3	162021	Wilkinson & Son	Hanley
May 4	6	162122	Harding & Cotterill	Burton-on-Trent
11	3	162261–2	E. Pearson	Cobridge
12	1	162267	Bodley & Harrold	Burslem
15	10	162304	Harding & Cotterill	Burton-on-Trent
22	4	162618–9	W. T. Copeland	Stoke
26	9	162765	T. C. Brown–Westhead, Moore & Co.	Hanley
·June 4	5	162976	The Old Hall Earthenware Co. (Ltd.)	Hanley
8	15	163188	Minton & Co.	Stoke
8	16	163189	Wm. Brownfield	Cobridge
July 14	2	164213	Turner & Tomkinson	Tunstall
15	3	164221	H. Venables	Hanley
20	3	164353	Wm. Brownfield	Cobridge
24	3	164468–9	W. T. Copeland	Stoke
28	6	164635	Minton & Co.	Stoke
Aug 11	3	165045–⅂	Turner & Tomkinson	Tunstall
12	4	165171	Hancock, Whittingham & Co.	Burslem
21	1	165317	J. Clementson	Hanley
28	5	165448	H. Venables	Hanley
Sept 7	6	165720	T. & R. Boote	Burslem
28	4	166439	H. Venables	Hanley
28	6	166441–2	James Edwards & Son	Longport

APPENDIX B

Date	Parcel No.	Patent No.	Factory, Retailer Wholesaler, etc	Place
Oct 2	5	166625	H. Venables	Hanley
6	5	166775	Thompson Bros.	Burton
14	7	167289	Wm. Brownfield	Cobridge
15	2	167299	F. Brewer & Son	Longton
17	1	167374	T. & R. Boote	Burslem
22	5	167536	Eardley & Hammersley	Tunstall
24	5	167560	Josiah Wedgwood & Sons	Etruria
26	7	167594–5	The Old Hall Earthenware Co. (Ltd.)	Hanley
28	8	167715	George Jones & Co.	Stoke
31	3	167761–3	Edmund T. Wood	Tunstall
Nov 3	5	168132	John Meir & Son	Tunstall
4	7	168188	T. & R. Boote	Burslem
6	1	168234–5	Geo. Jones & Co.	Stoke
16	10	168765	Wm. Kirkham	Stoke
26	12	169553	Wm. Brownfield	Cobridge
27	3	169561	Bodley & Harrold	Burslem
Dec 2	5	169774	J. W. Pankhurst	Hanley
2	6	169775	T. & R. Boote	Burslem
18	4	170294	F. & R. Pratt & Co.	Fenton
23	2	170418	Wm. Brownfield	Cobridge
30	1	170590	T. C. Brown–Westhead Moore & Co.	Hanley
1864				
Jan 5	2	170759	Wm. Brownfield	Cobridge
11	5	170883	Malkin, Walker & Hulse	Longton
Feb 2	5	171421	Josiah Wedgwood & Sons	Etruria
5	5	171520	Hope & Carter	Burslem
6	3	171536	Thos. Goode & Co.	London
13	6	171673	W. T. Copeland	Stoke
22	7	171970	Cork, Edge & Malkin	Burslem
25	6	172060	Liddle, Elliot & Son	Longport
29	6	172183	J. & D. Hampson	Longton
Mar 3	4	172212	Geo. L. Ashworth & Bros.	Hanley

APPENDIX B

Date	Parcel No.	Patent No.	Factory, Retailer Wholesaler, etc	Place
12	5	172559	Cork, Edge & Malkin	Burslem
18	1	172648	T. C. Brown–Westhead, Moore & Co.	Hanley
22	3	172815–6	Minton & Co.	Stoke
23	4	172876	Burgess & Leigh	Burslem
Apr 9	4	173200	Josiah Wedgwood & Sons	Etruria
15	4	173659	Geo. Jones	Stoke
18	5	173671	Minton & Co.	Stoke
21	4	173785	T. C. Brown–Westhead Moore & Co.	Hanley
21	8	173799	Liddle, Elliot & Son	Longport
23	11	173996	Geo. L. Ashworth & Bros.	Hanley
26	3	174112	Bodley & Harrold	Burslem
27	4	174138	Hope & Carter	Burslem
29	2	174168	Wm. Brownfield	Cobridge
May 9	3	174424	R. T. Boughton & Co.	Burslem
10	5	174455–8	Geo. Jones & Co.	Stoke
11	3	174475	R. H. Grove	Barlaston
18	5	174795	Geo. Ray	Longton
21	1	174817	J. & D. Hampson	Longton
June 9	7	175330	Minton & Co.	Stoke
16	3	175500	Hope & Carter	Burslem
30	4	175927	Wm. Brownfield	Cobridge
30	10	175935	The Worcester Royal Porcelain Co. Ltd.	Worcester
July 2	3	175959	Wood & Sale	Hanley
9	5	176164	Pinder, Bourne & Co.	Burslem
11	8	176235–6	idem	Burslem
18	6	176597	Bodley & Harrold	Burslem
18	7	176598	Evans & Booth	Burslem
19	4	176701	Hope & Carter	Burslem
19	8	176706	Wood & Sale	Hanley
28	4	176916	Holland & Green	Longton
Aug 10	2	177455	James Fellows	W/hmptn
20	10	177912	Geo. Jones & Co.	Stoke

447

Date	Parcel No.	Patent No.	Factory, Retailer Wholesaler, etc	Place
26	5	178037	T. C. Brown–Westhead Moore & Co.	Hanley
Sept 6	5	178264	W. T. Copeland	Stoke
10	1	178410	Minton & Co.	Stoke
12	2	178433	idem	Stoke
14	4	178521	Bodley & Harrold	Burslem
16	6	178597–8	Geo. L. Ashworth & Bros.	Hanley
19	1	178680–1	Josiah Wedgwood & Sons	Etruria
21	1	178693–4	Minton & Co.	Stoke
22	6	178823–7	Josiah Wedgwood & Sons	Etruria
Oct 4	2	179445	Geo. Jones & Co.	Stoke
12	4	179656	Wm. Brownfield	Cobridge
27	4	180444	Evans & Booth	Burslem
28	2	180449	The Worcester Royal Porcelain Co. Ltd.	Worcester
28	4	180453	Bodley & Harrold	Burslem
28	9	180483	Minton & Co.	Stoke
29	2	180486	Chas. Collinson & Co.	Burslem
31	3	180569	Cork, Edge & Malkin	Burslem
Nov 1	7	180695	W. T. Copeland	Stoke
4	3	180713	Livesley, Powell & Co.	Hanley
10	2	181214–5	Elsmore & Forster	Tunstall
10	3	181296	Hope & Carter	Burslem
10	10	181286	Geo. Jones & Co.	Stoke
24	5	181722	T. C. Brown–Westhead Moore & Co.	Hanley
29	1	181843	Hope & Carter	Burslem
Dec 9	1	182203	Wm. Kirkham	Stoke
10	8	182249	Hope & Carter	Burslem
31	6	182699	Geo. Jones & Co.	Stoke
1865				
Jan 6	3	182806	Hope & Carter	Burslem
6	4	182807	Minton & Co.	Stoke
14	4	183331	Geo. Jones & Co.	Stoke

APPENDIX B

Date	Parcel No.	Patent No.	Factory, Retailer Wholesaler, etc	Place
Feb 1	1	183650–2	Minton & Co.	Stoke
2	4	183706–7	Geo. L. Ashworth & Bros.	Hanley
13	7	183940	F. & R. Pratt & Co.	Fenton
14	4	183945	Liddle, Elliot & Son	Longport
27	4	184220	Livesley, Powell & Co.	Hanley
Mar 31	3	185473	Hope & Carter	Burslem
Apr 1	4	185520	Wm. Brownfield	Cobridge
3	4	185613	Minton & Co.	Stoke
22	5	186266	Thos. Till & Sons	Burslem
22	7	186273	James Edwards & Son	Burslem
26	5	186325	idem	Burslem
28	4	186349	Hope & Carter	Burslem
28	7	186354	Henry Alcock & Co.	Cobridge
29	3	186361	The Worcester Royal Porcelain Co. (Ltd.)	Worcester
May 2	8	186477	Livesley, Powell & Co.	Hanley
15	2	186841	J. T. Hudden	Longton
17	2	186901	Minton & Co.	Stoke
June 6	6	187358–9	J. T. Hudden	Longton
9	4	187403	The Worcester Royal Porcelain Co. (Ltd.)	Worcester
13	5	187533	idem	Worcester
14	6	187574	The Hill Pottery Co. Ltd.	Burslem
15	2	187576	J. T. Hudden	Longton
16	1	187583	Evans & Booth	Burslem
17	5	187633	The Worcester Royal Porcelain Co. (Ltd.)	Worcester
29	2	187847–8	Ed. F. Bodley & Co.	Burslem
30	4	187861	The Hill Pottery Co. Ltd.	Burslem
July 3	7	187972	T. C. Brown–Westhead, Moore & Co.	Hanley
12	3	188167	James Edwards & Son	Burslem
Aug 21	6	189155	J. Furnival & Co.	Cobridge
23	5	189283	Josiah Wedgwood & Sons	Etruria
Sept 11	4	189700	R. T. Boughton & Co.	Burslem

Date	Parcel No.	Patent No.	Factory, Retailer Wholesaler, etc	Place
11	5	189701	Thos. Cooper (Excrs of)	Hanley
14	2	189718	T. C. Brown–Westhead, Moore & Co.	Hanley
18	6	189782	Liddle, Elliot & Son	Longport
28	4	190200	Minton & Co.	Stoke
30	4	190656	S. Barker & Son	Swinton
Oct 13	8	190903	T. C. Brown–Westhead, Moore & Co.	Hanley
24	4	191292	Edward Johns	Staffs.
30	4	191407–8	Wm. Brownfield	Cobridge
Nov 10	4	192236	Pinder Bourne & Co. & Anthony Shaw	Burslem
23	10	192793	The Old Hall Earthenware Co. Ltd.	Hanley
29	8	192963	James Edwards & Son	Burslem
Dec 2	3	193061	The Worcester Royal Porcelain Co. (Ltd.)	Worcester
23	3	193844	James Dudson	Hanley
1866				
Jan 2	4	194063	Pratt & Co.	Fenton
3	6	194194	J. T. Close & Co.	Stoke
13	2	194450	Ed. F. Bodley & Co.	Burslem
17	4	194537	Burgess & Leigh	Burslem
24	1	194696	Minton & Co.	Stoke
31	5	194840	James Edwards & Son	Burslem
Feb 2	7	194949	W. T. Copeland	Stoke
Mar 2	2	195644	Ford, Challinor & Co.	Tunstall
10	1	195841	The Old Hall Earthenware Co. (Ltd.)	Hanley
Apr 14	6	196551	Walker & Carter	Longton
14	7	196552–4	Geo. L. Ashworth & Bros.	Hanley
16	8	196619	The Old Hall Earthenware Co. (Ltd.)	Hanley
18	4	196651	James Edwards & Son	Burslem

APPENDIX B

	Date	Parcel No.	Patent No.	Factory, Retailer Wholesaler, etc	Place
	20	7	196672–3	Wm. Brownfield	Cobridge
May 1		4	196987–8	J. Furnival & Co.	Cobridge
	25	1	197705–6	Hope & Carter	Burslem
June 4		4	197857	James Broadhurst	Longton
	12	1	198135–7	John Edwards	Fenton
	21	4	198383–4	Pinder, Bourne & Co.	Burslem
	30	4	198589	Thos. Minshall	Stoke
July 19		5	199186	J. T. Hudden	Longton
	25	3	199295	Geo. Jones	Stoke
Aug 17		3	200006	Morgan, Wood & Co.	Burslem
	29	4	200324	Ed. F. Bodley & Co.	Burslem
Sept 6		4	200599	F. & R. Pratt & Co.	Fenton
	13	9	201040	T. & C. Ford	Hanley
	15	8	201089	Geo. L. Ashworth & Bros.	Hanley
	20	8	201495	Anthony Keeling	Tunstall
Oct 8		3	202103–5	Minton & Co.	Stoke
	13	3	202493	Thos. Furnival	Cobridge
Nov 3		6	203173	Minton & Co.	Stoke
	12	3	203538	W. T. Copeland	Stoke
	14	8	203817	T. C. Brown–Westhead, Moore & Co.	Hanley
	15	4	203912	Geo. Grainger & Co.	Worcester
Dec 13		4	204764	Liddle, Elliot & Son	Longport
	14	8	204794	Samuel Barker & Son	Swinton
	15	5	204863	T. C. Brown–Westhead, Moore & Co.	Hanley
	19	5	205088	John Meir & Son	Tunstall
	24	2	205201	J. T. Hudden	Longton
1867					
Jan 8		5	205372	James Edwards & Son	Burslem
	17	3	205596	Ed. F. Bodley & Co.	Burslem
	23	2	205759	The Worcester Royal Porcelain Co. (Ltd.)	Worcester
Feb 9		1	206033	Ed. F. Bodley & Co.	Burslem

Date	Parcel No.	Patent No.	Factory, Retailer Wholesaler, etc	Place
23	5	206275	Worthington & Harrop	Hanley
Mar 2	7	206422	Josiah Wedgwood & Sons	Etruria
4	4	206497	T. C. Brown–Westhead, Moore & Co.	Hanley
5	6	206517	Powell & Bishop	Hanley
6	4	206522	The Old Hall Earthenware Co. (Ltd.)	Hanley
9	3	206564	John Edwards	Fenton
11	2	206662	Josiah Wedgwood & Sons	Etruria
14	1	206718	Davenport Banks & Co.	Etruria
15	7	206762–6	Wm. Brownfield	Cobridge
18	5	206867–8	Cockson & Chetwynd & Co.	Cobridge
19	5	206881	James Edwards & Son	Burslem
20	2	206887	Josiah Wedgwood & Sons	Etruria
21	10	206971	James Edwards & Son	Burslem
25	3	206994	Josiah Wedgwood & Sons	Etruria
26	4	207024–5	Minton & Co.	Stoke
Apr 3	5	207163	idem	Stoke
4	2	207165	Josiah Wedgwood & Sons	Etruria
4	9	207201	Elsmore & Forster	Tunstall
17	1	207564	Chas. Hobson	Burslem
23	3	207616	Adams, Scrivener & Co.	Longton
24	2	207636	W. T. Copeland	Stoke
May 6	3	207938	J. & M. P. Bell & Co.	Glasgow
7	4	207977	John Meir & Son	Tunstall
8	6	208002	T. C. Brown–Westhead Moore & Co.	Hanley
18	7	208394	Wm. McAdam	Glasgow
22	6	208434–5	Clementson Bros.	Hanley
June 6	3	208750	Josiah Wedgwood & Sons	Etruria
11	6	208819	Clementson Bros.	Hanley
11	7	208820	Cockson, Chetwynd & Co.	Cobridge
13	3	208891	W. & J. A. Bailey	Alloa
21	4	209057	Wm. Brownfield	Cobridge

APPENDIX B

Date	Parcel No.	Patent No.	Factory, Retailer Wholesaler, etc	Place
21	8	209062	E. & D. Chetwynd	Hanley
24	4	209087	idem	Hanley
July 1	7	209290	Joseph Ball	Longton
4	5	209362	E. J. Ridgway	Hanley
8	3	209431	Geo. L. Ashworth & Bros.	Hanley
12	5	209530	Geo. Jones	Stoke
15	2	209556	Josiah Wedgwood & Sons	Etruria
17	2	209601	E. & D. Chetwynd	Hanley
25	3	209726	Hope & Carter	Burslem
Aug 28	10	210598	The Worcester Royal Porcelain Co. Ltd.	Worcester
Sept 16	7	211275	Thos. Goode & Co.	London
17	3	211290	Wedgwood & Co.	Tunstall
21	1	211536	Geo. L. Ashworth & Bros.	Hanley
25	9	211873–4	Powell & Bishop	Hanley
Oct 2	1	211995	Minton & Co.	Stoke
3	5	212054	Thompson Bros.	Burton-on-Trent
3	6	212055	Minton & Co.	Stoke
7	4	212078	idem	Stoke
10	1	212194	Thos. Booth.	Hanley
24	5	212765	Ford, Challinor & Co.	Tunstall
26	1	212881	W. T. Copeland & Sons	Stoke
28	4	212956	idem	Stoke
29	3	212964	Josiah Wedgwood & Sons	Etruria
30	3	212974	J. T. Hudden	Longton
31	7	213065	Powell & Bishop	Hanley
Nov 6	7	213430	W. & J. A. Bailey	Alloa
7	4	213436	James Edwards & Son	Burslem
18	9	214000	Ford, Challinor & Co.	Tunstall
Dec 3	3	214618	W. T. Copeland & Sons	Stoke
12	6	214981	F. & R. Pratt & Co.	Fenton
20	3	215085	Josiah Wedgwood & Sons	Etruria
27	1	215314	J. & J. B. Bebbington	Hanley

APPENDIX B

Date	Parcel No.	Patent No.	Factory, Retailer Wholesaler, etc	Place
1868				
Jan 3	1	215481	Minton & Co.	Stoke
7	8	215636	Thompson Bros.	Burton-on-Trent
7	11	215642	Cockson, Chetwynd & Co.	Cobridge
8	5	215674	T. & R. Boote	Burslem
9	7	215698	Taylor, Tunnicliffe & Co.	Hanley
10	2	215705	Cork, Edge & Malkin	Burslem
11	2	215725	Wm. Brownfield	Cobridge
13	2	215735	Geo. L. Ashworth & Bros.	Hanley
16	13	215879	The Old Hall Earthenware Co. (Ltd.)	Hanley
25	3	216186	Hope & Carter	Burslem
30	6	216333	J. Furnival & Co.	Cobridge
31	8	216347	Josiah Wedgwood & Sons	Etruria
31	14	216363	T. & R. Boote	Burslem
Feb 5	4	216451	Adams, Scrivener & Co.	Longton
5	8	216470	E. Hodgkinson	Hanley
10	8	216676–8	Minton & Co.	Stoke
12	1	216699	Josiah Wedgwood & Sons	Etruria
14	10	216821	John Mortlock	London
18	1	216895	Josiah Wedgwood & Sons	Etruria
18	2	216896–7	T. C. Brown–Westhead, Moore & Co.	Hanley
20	9	216988	Minton & Co.	Stoke
25	6	217070	John Rose & Co.	Coalport
27	5	217100	Alcock & Diggory	Burslem
28	7	217112	W. & J. A. Bailey	Alloa
Mar 5	12	217208	Thos. Goode & Co.	London
5	15	217212	Minton & Co.	Stoke
25	7	217615	W. T. Copeland & Sons	Stoke
25	8	217616–7	The Worcester Royal Porcelain Co. (Ltd.)	Worcester
26	3	217630	Walker & Carter	Longton
Apr 1	6	217727	Minton & Co.	Stoke

APPENDIX B

Date	Parcel No.	Patent No.	Factory, Retailer Wholesaler, etc	Place
6	6	217938–9	Pinder, Bourne & Co.	Burslem
16	7	218139	Geo. L. Ashworth & Bros.	Hanley
21	6	218285	Beech & Hancock	Tunstall
23	8	218387	R. Hammersley	Tunstall
28	7	218466	T. G. Green	Burton-on-Trent
May 13	1	218664	Adams, Scrivener & Co.	Longton
14	2	218764	Hope & Carter	Burslem
14	6	218773	Philip Brookes	Fenton
26	5	218951	T. C. Brown–Westhead Moore & Co.	Hanley
26	6	218952	Pinder, Bourne & Co.	Burslem
28	3	218967	Holdcroft & Wood	Tunstall
28	5	218969–71	Minton & Co.	Stoke
28	7	218973	J. & T. Bevington	Hanley
30	4	219042	T. & R. Boote	Burslem
June 8	4	219174	Burgess & Leigh	Burslem
12	5	219316–7	Wm. Brownfield	Cobridge
16	4	219344	W. P. & G. Phillips	London
22	5	219484	Minton & Co.	Stoke
July 10	3	219756	Josiah Wedgwood & Sons	Etruria
16	3	219833	Hackney & Co.	Longton
20	2	219942–3	Hope & Carter	Burslem
24	4	219997	W. T. Copeland & Sons	Stoke
30	6	220183	Adams, Scrivener & Co.	Longton
Aug 1	5	220236–7	T. & R. Boote	Burslem
13	1	220772	Josiah Wedgwood & Sons	Etruria
15	8	220821–4	James Edwards & Son	Burslem
17	2	220828	Ed. F. Bodley & Co.	Burslem
21	2	220906	Ralph Malkin	Fenton
31	7	221124	T. & R. Boote	Burslem
Sept 1	1	221125–6	James Wardle	Hanley
4	6	221203–4	Gelson Bros.	Hanley
5	3	221214	T. C. Brown–Westhead, Moore & Co.	Hanley

455

Date	Parcel No.	Patent No.	Factory, Retailer Wholesaler, etc	Place
5	6	221217–9	McBirney & Armstrong	Belleek
9	4	221311	Hope & Carter	Burslem
9	5	221312	F. Jones & Co.	Longton
9	6	221313	Wedgwood & Co.	Tunstall
9	9	221316	J. & T. Bevington	Hanley
12	3	221521–2	Minton & Co.	Stoke
14	4	221548	Thos. Booth & Co.	Burslem
17	4	221688	T. C. Sambrook & Co.	Burslem
21	4	221814–7	George Ash	Hanley
25	4	221881–2	Minton & Co.	Stoke
25	13	222083–4	T. C. Brown–Westhead, Moore & Co.	Hanley
Oct 8	7	222460	Minton & Co.	Stoke
9	2	222476	J. Holdcroft	Stoke
9	3	222477	Hope & Carter	Burslem
9	5	222482–4	Davenports & Co.	Longport
14	8	222736	Geo. Jones	Stoke
17	4	223063	Minton & Co.	Stoke
21	8	223308	W. P. & G. Phillips	London
22	1	223309	McBirney & Armstrong	Belleek
22	5	223314–5	James Edwards & Son	Burslem
Nov 3	5	223817–8	Minton & Co.	Stoke
3	6	223819	T. C. Brown–Westhead, Moore & Co.	Hanley
6	13	224090	Powell & Bishop	Hanley
9	5	224172	Josiah Wedgwood & Sons	Etruria
16	3	224382	Knapper & Blackhurst	Tunstall
17	1	224389	Moore Bros.	Cobridge
21	5	224539	Minton & Co.	Stoke
24	5	224645	T. C. Brown–Westhead Moore & Co.	Hanley
25	4	224724	Cork, Edge & Malkin	Burslem
Dec 1	4	224953	T. C. Brown–Westhead, Moore & Co.	Hanley

Date		Parcel No.	Patent No.	Factory, Retailer Wholesaler, etc	Place
	3	5	225073–4	The Worcester Royal Porcelain Co. (Ltd.)	Worcester
	11	5	225410	Ed. T. Bodley & Co.	Burslem
	12	4	225425	Wm. Brownfield	Cobridge
	14	7	225441	Cockson, Chetwynd & Co.	Cobridge
	23	5	225734	Minton & Co.	Stoke
	23	6	225735	The Worcester Royal Porcelain Co. (Ltd.)	Worcester
	31	6	225993	Geo. L. Ashworth & Bros.	Hanley
	31	7	225994	R. Hammersley	Tunstall
1869					
Jan	1	8	226051	Geo. Jones	Stoke
	4	4	226098	Minton & Co.	Stoke
	7	6	226131	Thos. Goode & Co.	London
	21	6	226527–8	Minton & Co.	Stoke
	22	5	226570	Gelson Bros.	Hanley
	22	13	226581	T. C. Brown–Westhead, Moore & Co.	Hanley
	25	3	226625	Worthington & Son	Hanley
	28	5	226738	Minton & Co.	Stoke
	28	10	226747–8	George Ash	Hanley
Feb	1	7	226910	T. C. Brown–Westhead, Moore & Co.	Hanley
	2	4	226928	Geo. Yearsley	Longton
	9	5	227219	Minton & Co.	Stoke
	11	10	227277	Geo. Jones	Stoke
	15	1	227307	Thos. Booth & Co.	Burslem
	19	2	227345	Josiah Wedgwood & Sons	Etruria
	22	6	227403	idem	Etruria
	22	11	227409	McBirney & Armstrong	Belleek
	22	13	227411	Pinder, Bourne & Co.	Burslem
	27	5	227518	Josiah Wedgwood & Sons	Etruria
Mar	1	8	227556–8	Worthington & Son	Hanley
	3	8	227619	Thos. Till & Sons	Burslem

APPENDIX B

Date	Parcel No.	Patent No.	Factory, Retailer Wholesaler, etc	Place
6	8	227668	F. Primavesi	Cardiff
8	6	227696	F. & R. Pratt & Co.	Fenton
9	1	227743–4	Geo. Jones	Stoke
9	3	227746	idem	Stoke
10	10	227823	F. Primavesi	Cardiff
24	1	228141	J. F. Wileman	Fenton
Apr 1	1	228290	Wood & Pigott	Tunstall
2	6	228377	Wm. Brownfield	Cobridge
2	7	228378	Minton & Co.	Stoke
6	3	228430	Baker & Chetwynd	Burslem
7	2	228455	Minton & Co.	Stoke
7	4	228457	The Worcester Royal Porcelain Co. (Ltd.)	Worcester
12	4	228572	Taylor, Tunnicliffe & Co.	Hanley
12	5	228573	Liddle, Elliot & Son	Longport
20	5	228764	idem	Longport
28	13	228937	J. & T. Bevington	Hanley
May 11	1	229319	Adams, Scrivener & Co.	Longton
13	16	229405	James Edwards & Son	Burslem
21	1	229523	Worthington & Son	Hanley
26	4	229627	Thos. Booth	Hanley
27	8	229642–4	Davenport & Co.	Longport
June 3	6	229837	McBirney & Armstrong	Belleek
8	7	229959	W. P. & G. Phillips & Pearce	London
19	5	230183–4	Wm. Brownfield	Cobridge
25	4	230429	James Edwards & Son	Burslem
26	9	230455	Minton & Co.	Stoke
July 3	9	230707–8	Josiah Wedgwood & Sons	Etruria
6	3	230739	John Meir & Son	Tunstall
19	8	231101	James Wardle	Hanley
20	2	231124	Josiah Wedgwood & Sons	Etruria
21	6	231153–4	George Ash	Hanley
23	6	231215	Minton & Co.	Stoke
24	4	231222	W. T. Copeland & Sons	Stoke

APPENDIX B

Date	Parcel No.	Patent No.	Factory, Retailer Wholesaler, etc	Place
26	4	231241	Leveson Hill (Excrs of)	Stoke
27	4	231256	J. T. Hudden	Longton
Aug 2	6	231504	W. T. Copeland	Stoke
3	5	231602	John Edwards	Fenton
4	4	231613	Tomkinson Bros. & Co.	Hanley
11	13	231812	W. P. & G. Phillips & Pearce	London
19	6	232307	W. T. Copeland & Sons	Stoke
26	6	232474	idem	Stoke
31	6	232586–7	John Pratt & Co.	Lane Delph
31	12	232598	W. T. Copeland & Sons	Stoke
Sept 4	3	232822	Minton & Co.	Stoke
8	5	232878	W. T. Copeland & Sons	Stoke
8	6	232879	Pinder, Bourne & Co.	Burslem
9	3	232890	John Pratt & Co.	Lane Delph
10	4	232903	Minton & Co.	Stoke
21	7	233411	Gelson Bros.	Hanley
22	10	233527	W. & J. A. Bailey	Alloa
30	8	233864–6	T. C. Brown–Westhead Moore & Co.	Hanley
Oct 1	3	233923–4	Minton & Co.	Stoke
4	6	234016	idem	Stoke
14	3	234465	McBirney & Armstrong	Belleek
15	6	234486	Geo. Jones	Stoke
23	4	235012	idem	Stoke
26	2	235158	James Ellis & Son	Hanley
27	5	235168	McBirney & Armstrong	Belleek
29	3	235399–400	Minton & Co.	Stoke
29	4	235401–2	Powell & Bishop	Hanley
Nov 2	12	235589	Ed. Clarke	Tunstall
3	12	235691	T. C. Brown–Westhead, Moore & Co.	Hanley

Date	Parcel No.	Patent No.	Factory, Retailer Wholesaler, etc	Place
8	1	235827–9	McBirney & Armstrong	Belleek
8	2	235830	T. C. Brown–Westhead, Moore & Co.	Hanley
9	11	235966	Tams & Lowe	Longton
10	3	235974	Wm. Brownfield	Cobridge
13	5	236184–5	McBirney & Armstrong	Belleek
15	8	236203–7	Liddle, Elliot & Son	Longport
18	5	236435	Alcock & Diggory	Burslem
19	12	236478	The Worcester Royal Porcelain Co. (Ltd.)	Worcester
20	8	236533	Thos. Goode & Co.	London
20	9	236534	John Mortlock	London
23	1	236585	McBirney & Armstrong	Belleek
24	4	236628	Minton & Co.	Stoke
26	3	236653	idem	Stoke
Dec 1	3	236756	Geo. Jones	Stoke
3	9	236829	Wm. Brownfield	Cobridge
17	7	237224	Minton & Co.	Stoke
18	2	237229	Powell & Bishop	Hanley
18	3	237230	McBirney & Armstrong	Belleek
20	8	237358	George Ash	Hanley
22	7	237500	Geo. Jones	Stoke
24	1	237552	Gelson Bros.	Hanley
28	2	237565	John Pratt & Co.	Lane Delph
31	2	237644	Minton & Co.	Stoke
1870				
Jan 1	5	237691	T. C. Brown–Westhead, Moore & Co.	Hanley
3	4	237742	Geo. Jones	Stoke
7	9	237899	Pellatt & Co.	London
15	12	238147–8	Liddle, Elliot & Son	Longport
27	8	238388	Chas. Hobson	Burslem
29	3	238436	Minton & Co.	Stoke

APPENDIX B

Date	Parcel No.	Patent No.	Factory, Retailer Wholesaler, etc	Place
Feb 1	6	238527–8	T. C. Brown–Westhead, Moore & Co.	Hanley
3	13	238595–6	idem	Hanley
4	7	238603	Powell & Bishop	Hanley
7	5	238627	Wiltshaw, Wood & Co.	Burslem
7	6	238628	W. & J. A. Bailey	Alloa
9	2	238663	Josiah Wedgwood & Sons	Etruria
10	8	238688	Minton & Co	Stoke
11	12	238761–2	W. P. & G. Phillips & Pearce	London
15	6	238898–9	T. C. Brown–Westhead Moore & Co.	Hanley
25	2	239139	Minton & Co.	Stoke
28	6	239239	idem	Stoke
Mar 2	4	239304	idem	Stoke
7	6	239422	Chas. Hobson	Burslem
8	1	239424–6	Geo. Jones	Stoke
10	1	239474	idem	Stoke
10	9	239510	Powell & Bishop	Hanley
11	8	239528	Leveson Hill (Excrs of)	Stoke
14	4	239548	T. C. Brown–Westhead, Moore & Co.	Hanley
15	6	239585	Thos. Till & Sons	Burslem
16	2	239590–1	Minton & Co.	Stoke
17	4	239610–1	McBirney & Armstrong	Belleek
17	7	239622	The Worcester Royal Porcelain Co. (Ltd.)	Worcester
17	9	239628	J. Mortlock	London
18	6	239642	Minton & Co.	Stoke
23	9	239793–4	J. Blackshaw & Co.	Stoke
25	4	239968	Hope & Carter	Burslem
25	5	239969–70	Minton & Co.	Stoke
26	1	240000–1	idem	Stoke
26	2	240002	Worthington & Son	Hanley

APPENDIX B

Date	Parcel No.	Patent No.	Factory, Retailer Wholesaler, etc	Place
28	9	240079	The Old Hall Earthenware Co. Ltd.	Hanley
Apr 7	9	240383	Cork, Edge & Malkin	Burslem
7	10	240384–5	Baker & Co.	Fenton
7	11	240386	Harvey Adams & Co.	Longton
9	1	240458	Minton & Co.	Stoke
11	3	240493	The Worcester Royal Porcelain Co. Ltd.	Worcester
13	4	240516	Thos. Goode & Co.	London
14	7	240570	Minton & Co.	Stoke
May 5	1	241231	James Oldham & Co.	Hanley
6	5	241264–5	McBirney & Armstrong	Belleek
10	4	241367–8	George Ash	Hanley
13	8	241474	T. C. Brown–Westhead, Moore & Co.	Hanley
17	7	241544	idem	Hanley
18	6	241567–8	Bates, Elliott & Co.	Longport
21	6	241649	The Old Hall Earthenware Co. Ltd.	Hanley
21	12	241666	James Edwards & Son	Burslem
25	7	241754	idem	Burslem
26	5	241960	Minton & Co.	Stoke
30	15	242077	Geo. Jones	Stoke
June 3	8	242154	F. & R. Pratt & Co.	Fenton
7	15	242233	Hope & Carter	Burslem
7	16	242234	Thos. Booth	Hanley
9	3	242391	T. C. Brown–Westhead, Moore & Co.	Hanley
10	1	242392–4	Wm. Brownfield	Cobridge
11	3	242439	James Edwards & Son	Burslem
17	7	242503–8	Minton, Hollins & Co.	Stoke
22	1	242634–5	Harvey Adams & Co.	Longton
22	3	242637–8	Minton, Hollins & Co.	Stoke
22	4	242639	The Worcester Royal Porcelain Co. Ltd.	Worcester

APPENDIX B

Date	Parcel No.	Patent No.	Factory, Retailer Wholesaler, etc	Place
27	1	242715	Geo. Jones	Stoke
July 5	5	242859	Baker & Co.	Fenton
8	7	243049–50	James Wardle	Hanley
13	8	243176	James Edwards & Son	Burslem
14	9	243197–9	Minton, Hollins & Co.	Stoke
14	10	243200	The Worcester Royal Porcelain Co. Ltd.	Worcester
15	1	243207	W. T. Copeland & Sons	Stoke
16	2	243235	James Wardle	Hanley
19	6	243352	F. & R. Pratt & Co.	Fenton
20	5	243368	Thos. Booth	Hanley
21	1	243378	idem	Hanley
22	1	243385	Cork, Edge & Malkin	Burslem
27	1	243480	Beech, Unwin & Co.	Longton
Aug 1	2	243555	R. G. Scrivener & Co.	Hanley
4	4	243646	James Wardle	Hanley
4	5	243647–8	J. Broadhurst	Longton
9	2	243807	Wm. Brownfield	Cobridge
22	4	244137–8	T. & R. Boote	Burslem
23	6	244173	Geo. Jones	Stoke
25	5	244223	T. & R. Boote	Burslem
Sept 7	7	244703	Bailey & Cooke	Hanley
10	9	244741	Minton & Co.	Stoke
16	5	244961	idem	Stoke
19	2	244976	Wm. Brownfield	Cobridge
27	4	245227	Elsmore, Forster & Co.	Tunstall
27	6	245229	W. P. & G. Phillips & D. Pearce	London
28	11	245265	Gelson Bros.	Hanley
Oct 4	7	245463	Joseph Holdcroft	Longton
4	8	245464	Minton & Co.	Stoke
6	4	245604	idem	Stoke
6	5	245605	James Broadhurst	Longton
7	3	245620	Minton & Co.	Stoke
8	9	245668	Powell & Bishop	Hanley

Date	Parcel No.	Patent No.	Factory, Retailer Wholesaler, etc	Place
19	2	245985–6	Geo. Jones	Stoke
22	2	246149	Wm. Brownfield	Cobridge
25	6	246181	T. C. Brown–Westhead, Moore & Co.	Hanley
Nov 4	9	246927	idem	Hanley
9	8	247047	John Meir & Son	Tunstall
9	9	247048	Pellatt & Co.	London
10	5	247071–3	Minton & Co.	Stoke
10	10	247079–80	Wm. Brownfield	Cobridge
12	3	247248	McBirney & Armstrong	Belleek
12	8	247255	Minton, Hollins & Co.	Stoke
22	3	247944	Geo. Jones	Stoke
24	3	248041	Minton & Co.	Stoke
24	8	248049	Bates, Elliott & Co.	Longport
25	1	248051	Minton & Co.	Stoke
25	2	248052	Turner, Goddard & Co.	Tunstall
26	9	248114–6	T. & R. Boote	Burslem
Dec 1	7	248242	Wm. Brownfield	Cobridge
2	11	248294	T. C. Brown–Westhead, Moore & Co.	Hanley
5	4	248309–15	Minton, Hollins & Co.	Stoke
16	5	248869	Bates, Elliott & Co.	Longport
17	11	248899	idem	Longport
19	9	248953	Harvey, Adams & Co.	Longton
27	4	249104	James Edwards & Son	Burslem
1871				
Jan 2	2	249235	Gelson Bros.	Hanley
6	3	249331	Minton & Co.	Stoke
7	8	249356	Bates, Elliott & Co.	Longport
9	4	249388–93	McBirney & Armstrong	Belleek
10	7	249439	Geo. Jones	Stoke
11	4	249464	J. Mortlock	London
12	7	249479	McBirney & Armstrong	Belleek
12	12	249490	Soane & Smith	London

APPENDIX B

Date	Parcel No.	Patent No.	Factory, Retailer Wholesaler, etc	Place
24	4	249811	idem	London
26	8	249903–6	Minton, Hollins & Co.	Stoke
27	9	249927	The Worcester Royal Porcelain Co. Ltd.	Worcester
30	2	249972	Gelson Bros.	Hanley
Feb 2	3	250020	James Edwards & Son	Burslem
6	5	250168–71	McBirney & Armstrong	Belleek
8	9	250231	James Macintyre & Co.	Burslem
11	9	250291	T. C. Brown–Westhead, Moore & Co.	Hanley
13	6	250366	Edge, Malkin & Co.	Burslem
13	7	250367	Worthington & Son	Hanley
13	9	250369	Powell & Bishop	Hanley
13	10	250370	Ed. F. Bodley & Co.	Burslem
15	7	250416–8	Powell & Bishop	Hanley
17	7	250440–1	Thos. Peake	Tunstall
20	2	250478–9	Elsmore & Forster	Tunstall
28	8	250657	The Watcombe Terra Cotta Clay Co. Ltd.	Devon
Mar 9	4	250865	J. & T. Bevington	Hanley
14	4	250954	John Pratt & Co.	Lane Delph
15	10	251013	Bates, Elliott & Co.	Longport
27	1	251246	Wm. Brownfield & Son	Cobridge
29	1	251329	Thos. Furnival & Son	Cobridge
Apr 4	4	251453	McBirney & Armstrong	Belleek
22	4	251966	John Pratt & Co.	Stoke
24	4	251988	Josiah Wedgwood & Sons	Etruria
26	12	252068	Minton, Hollins & Co.	Stoke
27	7	252093–4	Wood & Clarke	Burslem
27	8	252095–7	W. P. & G. Phillips & Pearce	London
28	1	252128	Wood & Clarke	Burslem
29	6	252156	idem	Burslem
29	7	252157	James Edwards & Son	Burslem

465

APPENDIX B

Date	Parcel No.	Patent No.	Factory, Retailer Wholesaler, etc	Place
May 1	9	252171–3	T. C. Brown–Westhead, Moore & Co.	Hanley
2	3	252176	Ambrose Bevington	Hanley
2	4	252177–80	Wm. Brownfield & Son	Cobridge
3	4	252188	John Jackson & Co.	Rother'm
6	1	252258	W. P. & G. Phillips & Pearce	London
9	9	252387	Liddle, Elliott & Co.	Longport
11	13	252487	Powell & Bishop	Hanley
13	6	252503	Elsmore & Forster	Tunstall
22	9	252709	McBirney & Armstrong	Belleek
24	10	252756	John Meir & Son	Tunstall
June 2	4	253017	T. C. Brown–Westhead, Moore & Co.	Hanley
7	7	253069	Grove & Stark	Longton
16	9	253335	John Twigg	Rother'm
17	3	253339–40	Minton & Co.	Stoke
19	9	253378–9	Pinder, Bourne & Co.	Burslem
22	1	253472	Thos. Till & Sons	Burslem
23	9	253571	Bates, Elliott & Co.	Longport
July 4	8	253796–8	W. T. Copeland	Stoke
14	6	254013	Taylor, Tunnicliffe & Co.	Hanley
15	2	254030	Thos. Booth	Hanley
19	2	254074	Ambrose Bevington	Hanley
22	8	254130–3	Haviland & Co.	London and Limoges
25	12	254239	Bates, Elliott & Co.	Longport
29	6	254344	Hope & Carter	Burslem
Aug 2	3	254429	Robinson & Leadbeater	Stoke
9	7	254757	Bates, Elliott & Co.	Longport
18	10	254899	Pratt & Co.	Fenton
28	5	255267	James Wardle	Hanley
29	2	255274	Geo. Jones	Stoke
30	4	255320	Thos. Barlow	Longton

466

APPENDIX B

Date	Parcel No.	Patent No.	Factory, Retailer Wholesaler, etc	Place
31	9	255333	J. H. & J. Davis	Hanley
Sept 15	7	255821	J. Bevington & Co.	Hanley
15	10	255825	Thos. Barlow	Longton
19	2	255849	Minton & Co.	Stoke
25	8	256079	T. C. Brown–Westhead, Moore & Co.	Hanley
28	5	256215	Thos. Booth & Co.	Tunstall
Oct 4	7	256357–60	Minton & Co.	Stoke
4	9	256362	Pinder, Bourne & Co.	Burslem
6	6	256427–9	Moore & Son	Longton
9	8	256538	E. J. Ridgway & Son	Hanley
10	3	256582	J. T. Hudden	Longton
10	6	256586	T. C. Brown–Westhead, Moore & Co.	Hanley
11	4	256598	McBirney & Armstrong	Belleek
14	6	256687	Thos. Booth & Co.	Tunstall
14	7	256688	Josiah Wedgwood & Sons	Etruria
14	8	256689	McBirney & Armstrong	Belleek
18	4	256853	Moore & Son	Longton
19	6	256907	W. T. Copeland & Sons	Stoke
24	3	257126	Robert Cooke	Hanley
31	5	257258	Minton & Co.	Stoke
31	6	257259	Edge, Hill & Palmer	Longton
Nov 3	4	257364–5	R. G. Scrivener & Co.	Hanley
3	5	257366	J. F. Wileman	Fenton
15	4	257728	John Thomson & Sons	Glasgow
23	6	257944–6	Thos. Ford	Hanley
Dec 1	6	258095	Geo. Jones	Stoke
15	5	258773	Robinson & Leadbeater	Stoke
16	7	258816	McBirney & Armstrong	Belleek
22	6	258949	F. & R. Pratt	Fenton
23	3	258956–7	Geo. Jones	Stoke
29	10	259053	T. C. Brown–Westhead, Moore & Co.	Hanley

APPENDIX B

Date	Parcel No.	Patent No.	Factory, Retailer Wholesaler, etc	Place
1872				
Jan 1	5	259076	Moore & Son	Longton
1	6	259077	Edge Malkin & Co.	Burslem
5	3	259264	McBirney & Armstrong	Belleek
6	1	259271	Minton & Co.	Stoke
18	6	259801	The Worcester Royal Porcelain Co. Ltd.	Worcester
20	6	259854	Geo. Jones	Stoke
30	7	260081	W. T. Copeland & Sons	Stoke
Feb 2	2	260187	Moore & Son	Longton
2	11	260240–1	Turner & Tomkinson	Tunstall
3	4	260255–6	Geo. Jones	Stoke
7	3	260297	Ambrose Bevington	Hanley
15	3	260463	Powell & Bishop	Hanley
16	6	260503	McBirney & Armstrong	Belleek
16	7	260504–6	Geo. Jones	Stoke
19	6	260565	Wm. H. Goss	Stoke
20	4	260578	The Worcester Royal Porcelain Co. Ltd.	Worcester
22	3	260640	Minton & Co.	Stoke
Mar 4	3	260868	Geo. Jones	Stoke
4	4	260869–70	Minton & Co.	Stoke
4	6	260872	Minton, Hollins & Co.	Stoke
7	7	260992–3	Harvey, Adams & Co.	Longton
7	10	260998	Bates, Elliott & Co.	Burslem
8	5	261006–8	Minton, Hollins & Co.	Stoke
9	1	261016	McBirney & Armstrong	Belleek
13	8	261120	Minton, Hollins & Co.	Stoke
16	6	261190	Minton & Co.	Stoke
18	6	261207	idem	Stoke
20	10	261325	The Worcester Royal Porcelain Co. Ltd.	Worcester
21	14	261379	R. M. Taylor	Fenton
22	5	261391	J. Holdcroft	Longton

Date	Parcel No.	Patent No.	Factory, Retailer Wholesaler, etc	Place
22	8	261394	T. C. Brown–Westhead, Moore & Co.	Hanley
26	3	261453–4	Robinson & Leadbeater	Stoke
26	6	261458	Phillips & Pearce	London
Apr 5	4	261638	Wedgwood & Co.	Tunstall
5	5	261639	Minton & Co.	Stoke
6	1	261646–7	J. Holdcroft	Longton
9	6	261724	T. C. Brown–Westhead, Moore & Co.	Hanley
10	11	261749	Thos. Furnival & Son	Cobridge
17	13	261976	E. J. Ridgway & Son	Hanley
19	5	262013	Minton, Hollins & Co.	Stoke
24	5	262203	John Pratt & Co. Ltd.	Lane Delph
27	9	262354	Moore & Son	Longton
May 2	9	262425–6	Harvey Adams & Co.	Longton
2	11	262428–9	Thos. Furnival & Son	Cobridge
3	9	262471–2	Minton & Co.	Stoke
3	11	262474	Bates, Elliott & Co.	Burslem
6	3	262483–5	Moore & Son	Longton
6	8	262493	Bates, Elliott & Co.	Burslem
6	9	262494–5	Minton, Hollins & Co.	Stoke
10	1	262651	Moore & Son	Longton
11	4	262672	Thos. Booth & Sons	Hanley
27	1	262951	Geo. Jones	Stoke
27	3	262953	Minton, Hollins & Co.	Stoke
29	2	262990	Geo. Jones	Stoke
29	5	262993–4	Geo. Grainger & Co.	Worcester
30	1	262999– 3000	Minton & Co.	Stoke
June 3	6	263106	The Watcombe Terra Cotta Clay Co. Ltd.	Devon
5	3	263134	Hope & Carter	Burslem
6	6	263162	Wm. Brownfield & Son	Cobridge
7	4	263191	Minton, Hollins & Co.	Stoke

APPENDIX B

Date	Parcel No.	Patent No.	Factory, Retailer Wholesaler, etc	Place
11	5	263315	Josiah Wedgwood & Sons	Etruria
11	12	263348	W. T. Copeland & Sons	Stoke
18	3	263496-7	Geo. L. Ashworth & Bros.	Hanley
18	4	263498-9	Minton, Hollins & Co.	Stoke
21	7	263541-2	idem	Stoke
22	5	263561	Minton & Co.	Stoke
22	8	263565	Wm. Brownfield & Son	Cobridge
27	1	263771	T. C. Brown–Westhead, Moore & Co.	Hanley
July 2	2	263883-4	Robinson & Leadbeater	Stoke
2	3	263885	Josiah Wedgwood & Sons	Etruria
13	5	264081	Gelson Bros.	Hanley
15	4	264194	Robinson & Leadbeater	Stoke
16	5	264206-7	Minton, Hollins & Co.	Stoke
19	5	264299-303	R. M. Taylor	Fenton
20	3	264306-7	Geo. Jones	Stoke
24	2	264490	W. & T. Adams	Tunstall
29	7	264613	J. Dimmock & Co.	Hanley
31	3	264636-7	Minton & Co.	Stoke
Aug 2	1	264685-6	E. J. Ridgway & Son	Stoke
14	4	265105	T. Booth & Co.	Tunstall
16	1	265167-8	Wm. Brownfield & Sons	Cobridge
19	4	265254	W. E. Cartlidge	Hanley
19	5	265255	W. & J. A. Bailey	Alloa
Sept 2	3	265666	McBirney & Armstrong	Belleek
2	8	265687	Bates, Elliott & Co.	Burslem
12	6	265969	Minton, Hollins & Co.	Stoke
25	9	266628-31	Minton, Hollins & Co.	Stoke
26	2	266633	F. Jones	Longton
26	5	266636	W. E. Cartlidge	Hanley
Oct 7	7	266959	T. C. Brown–Westhead, Moore & Co.	Hanley
11	5	267060-4	Josiah Wedgwood & Sons	Etruria
12	10	267103-4	Bates, Elliott & Co.	Burslem

APPENDIX B

Date	Parcel No.	Patent No.	Factory, Retailer Wholesaler, etc	Place
14	4	267112	Minton, Hollins & Co.	Stoke
17	8	267265	Josiah Wedgwood & Sons	Etruria
18	5	267317–9	Geo. Jones	Stoke
30	2	267523	J. F. Wileman	Fenton
30	5	267527	The Brownhills Pottery	Tunstall
30	9	267534	Maw & Co.	Broseley
Nov 2	6	267588–91	The Worcester Royal Porcelain Co. Ltd.	Worcester
4	3	267618	Geo. Grainger & Co.	Worcester
11	2	267806	W. E. Cartlidge	Hanley
12	4	267839	Minton & Co.	Stoke
14	13	267893–5	Wm. Brownfield & Son	Cobridge
14	14	267896	Moore Bros.	Longton
18	3	267972	Holland & Green	Longton
30	8	268309	Belfield & Co.	Preston-pans
Dec 2	5	268322	T. C. Brown–Westhead, Moore & Co.	Hanley
4	3	268388	John Pratt & Co. Ltd.	Lane Delph
10	2	268724–5	Minton & Co.	Stoke
11	8	268748–9	The Old Hall Earthenware Co. Ltd.	Hanley
14	5	268806–7	Wm. Brownfield & Son	Cobridge
24	1	269197	Cockson & Chetwynd	Cobridge
27	4	269269	John Adams (Excrs of)	Longton
27	5	269270	R. G. Scrivener & Co.	Hanley
27	8	269275	John Meir & Son	Tunstall
1873				
Jan 10	1	269585	Geo. Jones	Stoke
13	4	269621	W. T. Copeland & Sons	Stoke
14	8	269686	J. Defries	London
15	2	269690	Worthington & Son	Hanley

APPENDIX B

Date	Parcel No.	Patent No.	Factory, Retailer Wholesaler, etc	Place
29	1	269993–70001	Minton, Hollins & Co.	Stoke
29	2	270002–4	Moore Bros.	Longton
Feb 1	1	270042–50	Minton, Hollins & Co.	Stoke
10	2	270298	W. & J. A. Bailey	Alloa
12	4	270354	Bates, Elliott & Co.	Burslem
15	1	270385	Minton & Co.	Stoke
19	14	270600–1	J. & T. Bevington	Hanley
25	6	270700	Geo. Jones	Stoke
27	4	270751	Thos. Till & Sons	Burslem
27	8	270755	Minton, Hollins & Co.	Stoke
Mar 6	1	271031–2	Minton & Co.	Stoke
6	9	271057	The Brownhills Pottery Co.	Tunstall
26	6	271561–2	Geo. Jones	Stoke
Apr 3	6	271851	Minton & Co.	Stoke
15	4	272091	Taylor, Tunnicliffe & Co.	Hanley
19	2	272206	Minton & Co.	Stoke
23	6	272293	Gelson Bros.	Hanley
28	5	272364–5	Powell & Bishop	Hanley
29	3	272384–5	Geo. Jones	Stoke
May 3	2	272637	Thos. Till & Sons	Burslem
3	7	272642–6	Wm. Brownfield & Son	Cobridge
3	8	272647–8	Minton & Co.	Stoke
6	2	272662	idem	Stoke
12	8	272835	T. C. Brown-Westhead, Moore & Co.	Hanley
14	7	272896–7	Moore Bros.	Longton
16	6	272983	Minton, Hollins & Co.	Stoke
17	4	272988–90	John L. Johnson & Co.	Longton
22	5	273089	Worthington & Son	Hanley
26	7	273158–9	Moore Bros.	Longton
26	8	273160	Soane & Smith	London
29	4	273246	Worthington & Son	Hanley
29	8	273251	Thos. Ford	Hanley

APPENDIX B

Date	Parcel No.	Patent No.	Factory, Retailer Wholesaler, etc	Place
30	15	273376	T. C. Brown–Westhead, Moore & Co.	Hanley
June 11	4	273662–3	Bates, Elliott & Co.	Burslem
17	3	273736–7	Taylor, Tunnicliffe & Co.	Hanley
19	3	273804	Pinder & Bourne & Co.	Burslem
28	4	274047	Thos. Goode & Co.	London
30	3	274054–5	Minton, Hollins & Co.	Stoke
July 3	9	274162	Minton, Hollins & Co.	Stoke
4	7	274183	T. C. Brown–Westhead, Moore & Co.	Hanley
28	2	274663	Chas. Hobson	Burslem
28	8	274701	John Meir & Sons	Tunstall
29	3	274704	McBirney & Armstrong	Belleek
31	1	274725–6	Mintons	Stoke
Aug 5	2	274804	Baker & Chetwynd	Burslem
14	10	275050	T. C. Brown–Westhead, Moore & Co.	Hanley
25	1	275514–5	Geo. Jones	Stoke
27	1	275600	The Worcester Royal Porcelain Co. Ltd.	Worcester
30	2	275661	T. C. Brown–Westhead, Moore & Co.	Hanley
Sept 2	8	275755	Edge, Malkin & Co.	Burslem
4	3	275816	Mintons	Stoke
10	7	275994	Powell & Bishop	Hanley
15	3	276151	T. C. Brown–Westhead, Moore & Co.	Hanley
16	4	276159	idem	Hanley
17	8	276213	The Worcester Royal Porcelain Co. Ltd.	Worcester
19	4	276338	T. C. Brown-Westhead, Moore & Co.	Hanley
25	8	276517	Harvey, Adams & Co.	Longton
25	10	276522	Jane Beech	Burslem
29	2	276566	Wm. Brownfield & Son	Cobridge

APPENDIX B

Date	Parcel No.	Patent No.	Factory, Retailer Wholesaler, etc	Place
Oct 4	3	276796–8	Moore Bros.	Longton
4	4	276799	Heath & Blackhurst	Burslem
6	6	276816–7	T. C. Brown–Westhead, Moore & Co.	Hanley
11	6	277136	Mintons	Stoke
13	3	277148–9	Geo. Jones	Stoke
22	6	277385	Mintons	Stoke
Nov 3	3	277844	Hope & Carter	Burslem
3	4	277845–7	Geo. Jones	Stoke
6	6	277969	Wedgwood & Co.	Tunstall
10	7	278169	T. C. Brown-Westhead, Moore & Co.	Hanley
12	3	278185	Worthington & Son	Hanley
Dec 2	6	278769–70	Taylor, Tunnicliffe & Co.	Hanley
4	6	278821	The Old Hall Earthenware Co. Ltd.	Hanley
5	1	278822	Harvey, Adams & Co.	Longton
5	8	278867	Wm. Brownfield & Son	Cobridge
10	12	279180	Geo. Jones & Sons	Stoke
27	7	279437	idem	Stoke
1874				
Jan 1	3	279476–7	Bates, Elliott & Co.	Burslem
10	15	279655–6	Davenports & Co.	London (and Longport)
20	3	279938	Powell & Bishop	Hanley
21	7	279964	W. T. Copeland & Sons	Stoke
23	5	280010	John Meir & Son	Tunstall
30	4	280153–6	Haviland & Co.	Limoges and London
Feb 9	4	280343	The Worcester Royal Porcelain Co. Ltd.	Worcester
9	5	280344	Bodley & Co.	Burslem

474

Date	Parcel No.	Patent No.	Factory, Retailer Wholesaler, etc	Place
11	2	280350	Thos. Booth & Sons	Hanley
14	9	280492	Worthington & Son	Hanley
19	1	280609	Geo. Jones & Sons	Stoke
25	6	280785	Robinson & Leadbeater	Stoke
25	7	280786	Geo. Jones & Sons	Stoke
26	7	280802–4	Minton, Hollins & Co.	Stoke
Mar 2	1	280853	McBirney & Armstrong	Belleek
3	4	280907	Geo. Jones & Sons	Stoke
4	3	280919	Mintons	Stoke
4	8	280925	The Worcester Royal Porcelain Co. Ltd.	Worcester
13	6	281106	J. Dimmock & Co.	Hanley
14	2	281129	Mintons	Stoke
17	5	281190	Powell & Bishop	Hanley
21	5	281301	idem	Hanley
24	4	281319	Mintons	Stoke
27	2	281404	Worthington & Son	Hanley
28	3	281429–30	Geo. Jones & Sons	Stoke
30	1	281437	Worthington & Son	Hanley
Apr 7	4	281639	The Worcester Royal Porcelain Co. Ltd.	Worcester
14	4	281776	A. Bevington	Hanley
15	7	281822	Mintons	Stoke
20	7	281871–80	Minton, Hollins & Co.	Stoke
21	8	281899	Geo. Jones & Sons	Stoke
22	1	281902	Wm. Brownfield & Son	Cobridge
23	8	281954	T. C. Brown–Westhead, Moore & Co.	Hanley
25	2	281984	Geo. Jones & Sons	Stoke
29	7	282088	Ridgway, Sparks & Ridgway	Hanley
29	9	282091	T. Furnival & Son	Cobridge
30	2	282098	Thos. Booth & Sons	Hanley
May 5	3	282134	Bates, Elliott & Co.	Burslem
9	3	282218–9	Geo. Jones & Sons	Stoke

APPENDIX B

Date	Parcel No.	Patent No.	Factory, Retailer Wholesaler, etc	Place
11	2	282249–51	Moore Bros.	Longton
11	3	282252	J. Thomson & Sons	Glasgow
11	4	282253	Holland & Green	Longton
20	11	282497	Bates, Elliott & Co.	Burslem
21	5	282526	Mintons	Stoke
22	8	282555	idem	Stoke
23	4	282567–8	Geo. Jones & Sons	Stoke
June 1	7	282662	The Worcester Royal Porcelain Co. Ltd.	Worcester
6	2	282799–802	Wm. Brownfield & Son	Cobridge
6	5	282806	Chas. Ford	Hanley
16	6	282982	Cockson & Chetwynd	Cobridge
17	7	283041	Edge, Malkin & Co.	Burslem
18	1	283050	Mintons	Stoke
23	3	283201	Williamson & Son	Longton
23	7	283208	The Worcester Royal Porcelain Co. Ltd.	Worcester
25	5	283266–8	Thos. Ford	Hanley
26	4	283275	Pinder, Bourne & Co.	Burslem
July 10	2	283547	Mintons	Stoke
13	6	283570–1	T. C. Brown–Westhead, Moore & Co.	Hanley
27	1	283980	Hulse & Adderley	Longton
30	5	284053	Minton, Hollins & Co.	Stoke
Aug 1	8	284131–5	Mintons	Stoke
1	9	284136	Cockson & Chetwynd	Cobridge
6	7	284204	T. C. Brown–Westhead, Moore & Co.	Hanley
8	2	284254–5	Wm. Brownfield & Son	Cobridge
15	4	284417	Bates, Elliott & Co.	Burlsem
22	6	284562	J. T. Hudden	Longton
28	4	284699–700	Geo. Jones & Sons	Stoke
31	6	284779	T. J. & J. Emberton	Tunstall

APPENDIX B

Date	Parcel No.	Patent No.	Factory, Retailer Wholesaler, etc	Place
Sept 1	3	284791	Thos. Till & Sons	Burslem
3	11	284883	Geo. Adler	Saxony and London
3	12	284884–5	Cockson & Chetwynd	Cobridge
4	3	284897	Mintons	Stoke
5	4	284916–7	The Worcester Royal Porcelain Co. Ltd.	Worcester
5	7	284920	Furnival & Son	Cobridge
7	3	284936–7	Thos. Booth & Sons	Hanley
10	3	285013	Wm. Brownfield & Son	Cobridge
12	1	285181	Mintons	Stoke
15	2	285281	Geo. Jones & Sons	Stoke
16	7	285304	M. Bucholz	London
17	4	285322	R. Britton & Sons	Leeds
30	4	285776	Wm. Brownfield & Son	Cobridge
Oct 2	5	285826–8	Geo. Grainger & Co.	Worcester
3	4	285841–4	Moore Bros.	Longton
6	3	286000	Mintons	Stoke
6	4	286001	Grove & Stark	Longton
10	4	286134	Mintons	Stoke
12	2	286171	Powell & Bishop	Hanley
17	8	286359–60	Bates, Elliott & Co.	Burslem
21	8	286424	Geo. Jones & Sons	Stoke
24	3	286504–5	Robinson & Leadbeater	Stoke
27	1	286530	George Ash	Hanley
28	9	286563	Pinder, Bourne & Co.	Burslem
Nov 2	3	286715	James Edwards & Son	Burslem
3	4	286720–2	W. & E. Corn	Burslem
6	3	286759	Wm. Brownfield & Son	Cobridge
7	4	286774–80	Thos. Ford	Hanley
10	3	286794	Geo. Jones & Sons	Stoke
12	3	286931	Mintons	Stoke
12	12	286942	Bates, Elliott & Co.	Burslem
20	12	287317	F. & R. Pratt & Co.	Fenton

Date	Parcel No.	Patent No.	Factory, Retailer Wholesaler, etc	Place
25	7	287438–9	Minton, Hollins & Co.	Stoke
Dec 1	5	287598	W. T. Copeland & Sons	Stoke
4	6	287638	Thos. Barlow	Longton
5	4	287676	Holmes & Plant	Burslem
7	8	287694–7	T. C. Brown–Westhead, Moore & Co.	Hanley
8	2	287699	Geo. Jones & Sons	Stoke
10	4	287731	Pinder, Bourne & Co.	Burslem
10	11	287752–6	The Worcester Royal Porcelain Co. Ltd.	Worcester
12	3	287776	Geo. Jones & Sons	Stoke
12	5	287785	Port Dundas Pottery Co.	Port Dundas
18	6	287982	Geo. Jones & Sons	Stoke
18	7	287983	Ambrose Bevington	Hanley
18	9	287985	Geo. Grainger & Co.	Worcester
18	11	287990–7	Minton, Hollins & Co.	Stoke
1875				
Jan 2	4	288241–2	T. C. Brown–Westhead, Moore & Co.	Hanley
6	3	288276–8	Minton, Hollins & Co.	Stoke
12	3	288366	The Worcester Royal Porcelain Co. Ltd.	Worcester
16	9	288502	The Brownhills Pottery Co.	Tunstall
18	8	288521	T. C. Brown–Westhead, Moore & Co.	Hanley
20	3	288552	Robinson & Leadbeater	Stoke
20	4	288553–6	Wm. Brownfield & Son	Cobridge
21	2	288682	Geo. Jones & Sons	Stoke
23	9	288755–8	T. C. Brown–Westhead, Moore & Co.	Hanley
28	5	288830	Mintons	Stoke
29	1	288861–2	Worthington & Son	Hanley
Feb 3	7	288972	Chas. Ford	Hanley

APPENDIX B

Date	Parcel No.	Patent No.	Factory, Retailer Wholesaler, etc	Place
5	5	289076	T. & R. Boote	Burslem
6	2	289083	Moore Bros.	Longton
9	1	289172	Pinder, Bourne & Co.	Burslem
9	2	289173	Geo. Jones & Sons	Stoke
12	6	289280	J. Maddock & Sons	Burslem
15	2	289310	Moore Bros.	Longton
17	7	289334	Mintons	Stoke
23	5	289503	J. Maddock & Sons	Burslem
23	6	289504	Geo. Jones & Sons	Stoke
23	8	289507–8	George Ash	Hanley
24	3	289535	Stephen Clive	Tunstall
Mar 5	2	289769	Wm. Brownfield & Son	Cobridge
12	5	289874–6	Geo. Jones & Sons	Stoke
24	13	290153	Minton, Hollins & Co.	Stoke
24	14	290154–5	T. C. Brown–Westhead, Moore & Co.	Hanley
30	1	290186	Thos. Booth & Sons	Hanley
31	5	290209–10	Wm. Brownfield & Son	Cobridge
Apr 3	7	290259	J. Dimmock & Co.	Hanley
3	9	290261–2	E. F. Bodley & Son	Burslem
7	3	290352	Mintons	Stoke
9	6	290393–4	Wm. Brownfield & Son	Cobridge
10	7	290407–8	Powell & Bishop	Hanley
15	5	290500	R. Malkin	Fenton
17	1	290738	Pinder, Bourne & Co.	Burslem
20	1	290787	J. Dimmock & Co.	Hanley
20	2	290788	Mintons	Stoke
21	5	290812	Stephen Clive	Tunstall
22	3	290841–2	W. P. & G. Phillips	London
22	4	290843–6	Minton, Hollins & Co.	Stoke
May 3	8	290998	Soane & Smith	London
7	7	291109	Geo. Jones & Sons	Stoke
7	8	291110	Burgess & Leigh	Burslem
11	6	291229	Thos. Goode & Co.	London
20	1	291440	Bates, Elliott & Co.	Burslem

APPENDIX B

Date	Parcel No.	Patent No.	Factory, Retailer Wholesaler, etc	Place
20	3	291444	J. Dimmock & Co.	Hanley
22	1	291458	Holland & Green	Longton
26	6	291518–20	T. C. Brown–Westhead, Moore & Co.	Hanley
28	10	291556	Campbellfield Pottery Co.	Glasgow
28	12	291558	J. Mortlock	London
31	8	291568	Geo. Jones & Sons	Stoke
31	18	291611	Ridgway, Sparks & Ridgway	Hanley
June 2	9	291749–51	Minton, Hollins & Co.	Stoke
5	7	291870–1	W. P. & G. Phillips	London
7	3	291882	W. & T. Adams	Tunstall
8	4	291911	The Worcester Royal Porcelain Co. (Ltd.)	Worcester
10	6	292005	Wm. Brownfield & Son	Cobridge
12	5	292034	Chas. Stevenson	Greenock
12	6	292035	Maddock & Gater	Burslem
12	10	292042	Thos. Furnival & Son	Stoke
15	5	292080	Josiah Wedgwood & Sons	Etruria
19	6	292184	Thos. Till & Sons	Burslem
26	2	292367–70	Geo. Jones & Sons	Stoke
July 5	1	292542	Wm. Brownfield & Son	Cobridge
7	8	292579–80	Moore Bros.	Longton
8	5	292620	idem	Longton
20	4	292985	E. J. D. Bodley	Burslem
23	10	293035	T. C. Brown–Westhead, Moore & Co.	Hanley
27	5	293114	F. W. Grove & J. Stark	Longton
28	7	293129	Minton, Hollins & Co.	Stoke
Aug 19	7	293748	F. W. Grove & J. Stark	Longton
28	6	294038–9	W. P. & G. Phillips	London
Sept 2	3	294147	T. Elsmore & Son	Tunstall
13	2	294434–5	Geo. Jones & Sons	Stoke
14	9	294514	Minton, Hollins & Co.	Stoke
18	2	294571–2	Geo. Jones & Sons	Stoke

Date	Parcel No.	Patent No.	Factory, Retailer Wholesaler, etc	Place
21	1	294595	R. Cochran & Co.	Glasgow
24	2	294657	H. Aynsley & Co.	Longton
25	3	294662	F. W. Grove & J. Stark	Longton
28	6	294768–9	T. C. Brown–Westhead, Moore & Co.	Hanley
30	4	294825–7	John Edwards	Fenton
Oct 2	6	294906	Josiah Wedgwood & Sons	Etruria
6	4	294936	R. Cooke	Hanley
11	4	295001	Powell & Bishop	Hanley
11	10	295014–5	The Brownhills Pottery Co.	Tunstall
16	8	295131	Burgess, Leigh & Co.	Burslem
28	3	295443	Minton, Hollins & Co.	Stoke
30	9	295473–4	W. P. & G. Phillips	London
Nov 5	3	295551–3	Geo. Jones & Sons	Stoke
8	4	295792–8	Minton, Hollins & Co.	Stoke
8	8	295803	W. T. Copeland & Sons	Stoke
12	1	295908	Geo. Jones & Sons	Stoke
12	2	295909	Burgess, Leigh & Co.	Burslem
13	8	295933	The Worcester Royal Porcelain Co. Ltd.	Worcester
Dec 1	2	296475	Wm. Brownfield & Son	Cobridge
1	9	296508	Gelson Bros.	Hanley
3	4	296531	Geo. Jones & Sons	Stoke
6	8	296644	John Meir & Son	Tunstall
10	3	296770	Mintons	Stoke
11	5	296813	F. W. Grove & J. Stark	Longton
11	8	296818	Soane & Smith	London
13	8	296834–49	Minton, Hollins & Co.	Stoke
15	2	296939–40	Mintons China Works	Stoke
15	3	296941–5	Mintons	Stoke
24	4	297217–8	Chas. Ford	Hanley
24	6	297221	Bates, Walker & Co.	Burslem
29	5	297245	Edge, Malkin & Co.	Burslem
29	6	297246–7	T. C. Brown–Westhead, Moore & Co.	Hanley

Date	Parcel No.	Patent No.	Factory, Retailer Wholesaler, etc	Place
30	2	297250	Mintons	Stoke
30	8	297276	Mintons, Hollins & Co.	Stoke
1876				
Jan 4	4	297343	Mintons	Stoke
6	2	297471	Moore Bros.	Longton
11	7	297587	E. J. D. Bodley	Burslem
21	13	297791	Bale & Co.	Etruria
22	6	297809–11	Geo. Jones & Sons	Stoke
22	8	297813	Chas. Ford	Hanley
24	1	297817	Mintons	Stoke
24	4	297845	J. Friedrich	London
24	6	297863–4	Bates, Walker & Co.	Burslem
26	2	297977	Edge, Malkin & Co.	Burslem
26	3	297978	Powell & Bishop	Hanley
28	8	298018	James Edwards & Son	Burslem
29	3	298027–9	Wm. Brownfield & Son	Cobridge
Feb 1	2	298049	idem	Cobridge
2	7	298063	Josiah Wedgwood & Sons	Etruria
2	12	298069	Ridgway, Sparks & Ridgway	Hanley
3	5	298077	Powell & Bishop	Hanley
4	6	298103	Mintons	Stoke
4	12	298141–2	The Worcester Royal Porcelain Co. Ltd.	Worcester
8	9	298235	Bates, Walker & Co.	Burslem
19	5	298458	Geo. Jones & Sons	Stoke
21	4	298473	The Worcester Royal Porcelain Co. Ltd.	Worcester
22	3	298480–3	Minton, Hollins & Co.	Stoke
29	9	298693	J. Dimmock & Co.	Hanley
Mar 2	8	298821–4	T. Gelson & Co.	Hanley
2	11	298832	The Brownhills Pottery Co.	Tunstall
10	8	299076–8	Minton, Hollins & Co.	Stoke

APPENDIX B

Date	Parcel No.	Patent No.	Factory, Retailer Wholesaler, etc	Place
14	5	299177	T. C. Brown–Westhead, Moore & Co.	Hanley
17	5	299236	Mintons	Stoke
18	3	299246	Robinson & Chapman	Longton
23	8	299366	E. J. D. Bodley	Burslem
24	7	299380	Bates, Walker & Co.	Burslem
28	8	299474	W. E. Withinshaw	Burslem
30	4	299497–9	Geo. Jones & Sons	Stoke
Apr 8	6	299773	Bates, Walker & Co.	Burslem
11	4	299819	Thos. Gelson & Co.	Hanley
12	4	299830	Powell & Bishop	Hanley
12	11	299852	J. Dimmock & Co.	Hanley
21	7	300020	Minton, Hollins & Co.	Stoke
21	10	300037–8	Furnival & Son	Cobridge
22	5	300105	The Worcester Royal Porcelain Co. Ltd.	Worcester
27	3	300260	Mintons	Stoke
May 8	7	300421–3	T. C. Brown–Westhead, Moore & Co.	Hanley
10	3	300463	Geo. Jones & Sons	Stoke
11	9	300491	F. & R. Pratt & Co.	Fenton
16	7	300603–4	Mintons	Stoke
22	3	300682	Moore Bros.	Longton
22	4	300683–5	Josiah Wedgwood & Sons	Etruria
23	7	300734–7	Haviland & Co.	Limoges and London
24	3	300746	Mintons	Stoke
25	6	300779	Moore Bros.	Longton
29	8	300809–10	Geo. Jones & Sons	Stoke
June 3	2	301030	Mintons	Stoke
3	5	301035–7	E. J. D. Bodley	Burslem
7	1	301087	Thos. Gelson & Co.	Hanley
8	4	301099	Mintons	Stoke
9	6	301164	W. T. Copeland & Sons	Stoke

APPENDIX B

Date	Parcel No.	Patent No.	Factory, Retailer Wholesaler, etc	Place
15	1	301254	Henry Meir & Son	Tunstall
15	9	301267–9	Minton, Hollins & Co.	Stoke
19	2	301302	Josiah Wedgwood & Sons	Etruria
19	9	301310	J. Holdcroft	Longton
21	4	301330	Mintons	Stoke
22	4	301342	Thos. Gelson & Co.	Hanley
23	5	301402	Mintons	Stoke
26	6	301443–4	Minton, Hollins & Co.	Stoke
28	8	301543	J. Aynsley	Longton
July 1	3	301589–90	Mintons	Stoke
1	4	301591	John Tams	Longton
3	2	301596	Ford & Challinor	Tunstall
5	1	301619	Thos. Till & Sons	Burslem
5	7	301641	W. T. Copeland & Sons	Stoke
10	3	301877	Thos. Gelson & Co.	Hanley
12	2	301926	E. J. D. Bodley	Burslem
18	3	301984	Soane & Smith	London
26	3	302125	Geo. Jones & Sons	Stoke
28	10	302178	Thos. Gelson & Co.	Hanley
28	11	302179	Powell & Bishop	Hanley
31	8	302220	G. Grainger & Co.	Worcester
Aug 8	1	302384	Robinson & Chapman	Longton
25	8	302901	F. & R. Pratt & Co.	Fenton
Sept 5	5	303289–90	Bates & Walker & Co.	Burslem
6	9	303308	Pinder & Bourne & Co.	Burslem
6	10	303309	Wm. Brownfield & Sons	Cobridge
9	8	303455	Worthington & Son	Hanley
9	9	303456–7	T. C. Brown–Westhead, Moore & Co.	Hanley
11	1	303459	E. J. D. Bodley	Burslem
12	6	303522–3	Geo. Jones & Sons	Stoke
18	10	303677	G. L. Ashworth & Bros.	Hanley
20	3	303731–2	Hollinshead & Kirkham	Burslem
22	3	303757	Powell & Bishop	Hanley
26	5	303853	Hope & Carter	Burslem

APPENDIX B

Date	Parcel No.	Patent No.	Factory, Retailer Wholesaler, etc	Place
26	10	303918	T. C. Brown–Westhead, Moore & Co.	Hanley
28	2	303926–7	Moore Bros.	Longton
28	10	303942	Hope & Carter	Burslem
Oct 7	2	304128	Wm. Harrop	Hanley
7	3	304129–31	Wm. Brownfield & Sons	Cobridge
7	4	304132–3	Josiah Wedgwood & Sons	Etruria
7	6	304144–5	Wm. Adams	Tunstall
9	1	304149–50	Geo. Jones & Sons	Stoke
12	8	304321	Ambrose Bevington	Hanley
17	4	304376	T. C. Brown–Westhead, Moore & Co.	Hanley
17	9	304383	Wardle & Co.	Hanley
19	3	304428	Burgess, Leigh & Co.	Burslem
20	2	304454–66	Mintons	Stoke
21	3	304473	Edge, Malkin & Co.	Burslem
23	2	304489	Mintons	Stoke
31	2	304910–4	Wm. Brownfield & Sons	Cobridge
Nov 1	2	304926	Moore Bros.	Longton
7	3	305065	Robert Jones	Hanley
8	3	305080	Geo. Jones & Sons	Stoke
8	9	305090	Wm. Brownfield & Sons	Cobridge
9	10	305150	Belfield & Co.	Preston-pans
11	9	305173	Moore Bros.	Longton
13	3	305181	Mintons	Stoke
14	2	305189	Josiah Wedgwood & Sons	Etruria
14	8	305195	Clementson Bros.	Hanley
17	3	305222	Banks & Thorley	Hanley
18	3	305233	Minton, Hollins & Co.	Stoke
18	7	305264	Minton, Hollins & Co.	Stoke
18	9	305266	The Worcester Royal Porcelain Co. Ltd.	Worcester
23	5	305312	Wm. Adams	Tunstall
24	15	305461–2	Thos. Furnival & Sons	Cobridge

APPENDIX B

Date	Parcel No.	Patent No.	Factory, Retailer Wholesaler, etc	Place
28	2	305510	W. Hudson & Son	Longton
29	11	305568	Thos. Furnival & Sons	Cobridge
Dec 5	2	305684	Wedgwood & Co.	Tunstall
11	2	305829	John Tams	Longton
12	11	305885	The Campbell Brick & Tile Co.	Stoke
14	1	305934	Harvey Adams & Co.	Longton
14	11	305973	J. Dimmock & Co.	Hanley
18	9	306100	James Beech	Longton
20	7	306184	J. & T. Bevington	Hanley
21	2	306202	F. W. Grove & J. Stark	Longton
23	5	306282	Chas. Ford	Hanley
27	15	306341	The Campbell Brick & Tile Co.	Stoke
28	6	306367	Harvey Adams & Co.	Longton
1877				
Jan 4	10	306564	The Campbellfield Pottery Co.	Glasgow
17	5	306953	The Worcester Royal Porcelain Co. Ltd.	Worcester
20	2	307028	F. W. Grove & J. Stark	Longton
24	10	307213	Wm. Brownfield & Sons	Cobridge
25	6	307236	Wood & Co.	Burslem
25	7	307237–9	Geo. Jones & Sons	Stoke
26	3	307258	Mintons	Stoke
26	4	307259	Powell & Bishop	Hanley
Feb 1	6	307432	James Edwards & Son	Burslem
2	7	307495–7	The Worcester Royal Porcelain Co. Ltd.	Worcester
3	4	307506–7	Minton, Hollins & Co.	Stoke
5	2	307525–7	McBirney & Armstrong	Belleek
7	3	307551	Holland & Green	Longton
7	7	307570–2	Wm. Brownfield & Sons	Cobridge
9	7	307603	Robinson & Co.	Longton

APPENDIX B

Date	Parcel No.	Patent No.	Factory, Retailer Wholesaler, etc	Place
9	11	307613	T. C. Brown–Westhead, Moore & Co.	Hanley
12	3	307646	James Beech	Longton
14	16	307782	The Worcester Royal Porcelain Co. Ltd.	Worcester
15	10	307794	Minton, Hollins & Co.	Stoke
16	9	307866	John Rose & Co.	Coalport
19	2	307877	Wm. Brownfield & Sons	Cobridge
20	8	307892	G. Grainger & Co.	Worcester
21	6	307906	Mintons	Stoke
21	9	307909	W. T. Copeland & Sons	Stoke
24	3	307983	Thos. Hughes	Burslem
27	2	308010	Mintons	Stoke
Mar 1	4	308116–21	Hallam, Johnson & Co.	Longton
8	14	308329	W. T. Copeland & Sons	Stoke
10	7	308357	Geo. Jones & Sons	Stoke
14	9	308493	The Campbell Brick & Tile Co.	Stoke
20	3	308650–2	Clementson Bros.	Hanley
20	8	308662	J. Dimmock & Co.	Hanley
22	14	308718	E. J. D. Bodley	Burslem
24	1	308781–2	Powell & Bishop	Hanley
31	7	308916	E. F. Bodley & Co.	Burslem
Apr 3	1	308918	Powell & Bishop	Hanley
4	5	308932	J. Mortlock	London
5	2	308934	Ford, Challinor & Co.	Tunstall
12	11	309233	J. Dimmock & Co.	Hanley
23	4	309617	John Tams	Longton
26	2	309680	J. & T. Bevington	Hanley
26	7	309696	The Worcester Royal Porcelain Co. Ltd.	Worcester
27	10	309746	John Rose & Co.	Coalport
May 2	2	309818–21	Geo. Jones & Sons	Stoke
4	13	309917	The Old Hall Earthenware Co. Ltd.	Hanley

APPENDIX B

Date	Parcel No.	Patent No.	Factory, Retailer Wholesaler, etc	Place
5	4	309922	Josiah Wedgwood & Sons	Etruria
12	7	310034	Thos. Furnival & Sons	Cobridge
16	5	310175	Wm. Brownfield & Sons	Cobridge
18	6	310267	Josiah Wedgwood & Sons	Etruria
22	5	310359–61	Wm. Brownfield & Sons	Cobridge
24	8	310448	T. C. Brown–Westhead, Moore & Co.	Hanley
30	13	310556	T. Furnival & Sons	Cobridge
June 1	2	310599	J. & R. Hammersley	Hanley
5	6	310670	E. J. D. Bodley	Burslem
7	1	310709	idem	Burslem
7	2	310710	Joseph Holdcroft	Longton
8	7	310761–4	Minton, Hollins & Co.	Stoke
9	3	310775–6	Baker & Co.	Fenton
13	2	310909	idem	Fenton
15	7	310972	Ridgway, Sparks & Ridgway	Hanley
19	4	311031	Ford & Challinor	Tunstall
19	6	311033	Murray & Co.	Glasgow
22	3	311141	Walker & Carter	Stoke
22	13	311181–6	Steele & Wood	Stoke
22	14	311187	E. F. Bodley & Co.	Burslem
26	11	311366	T. Furnival & Sons	Cobridge
28	9	311423	idem	Cobridge
29	10	311448–9	Sherwin & Cotton	Hanley
July 2	3	311523	W. T. Copeland & Sons	Stoke
6	2	311626	Mintons	Stoke
7	4	311684	Ridge, Meigh & Co.	Longton
9	2	311711	Minton, Hollins & Co.	Stoke
14	2	311883–4	John Tams	Longton
17	9	312019–21	James Edwards & Son	Burslem
20	7	312062–4	Haviland & Co.	London and Limoges
20	15	312113	Taylor, Tunnicliffe & Co.	Hanley

Date	Parcel No.	Patent No.	Factory, Retailer Wholesaler, etc	Place
23	2	312125	John Edwards	Fenton
25	5	312187	Ford, Challinor & Co.	Tunstall
26	6	312311–4	Minton, Hollins & Co.	Stoke
31	1	312421	McBirney & Armstrong	Belleek
31	2	312422	Minton & Hollins & Co.	Stoke
Aug 1	4	312434	Holmes, Stonier & Hollinshead	Hanley
3	14	312521	The Campbell Brick & Tile Co.	Stoke
13	5	312909	Haviland & Co.	London and Limoges
15	7	313009	The Campbell Brick & Tile Co.	Stoke
17	11	313080	Ridgway, Sparks & Ridgway	Stoke
18	6	313099–101	Minton, Hollins & Co.	Stoke
18	7	313102	Furnival & Son	Cobridge
23	6	313280	W. Hudson & Son	Longton
25	2	313324	Wm. Wood & Co.	Burslem
25	3	313325–9	Minton, Hollins & Co.	Stoke
28	9	313381	T. C. Brown–Westhead, Moore & Co.	Hanley
Sept 11	3	314046	G. W. Turner & Sons	Tunstall
19	5	314292	Minton, Hollins & Co.	Stoke
20	3	314385	Josiah Wedgwood & Sons	Etruria
22	7	314470–1	Mintons	Stoke
22	13	314480	Minton, Hollins & Co.	Stoke
25	5	314548	Mintons	Stoke
28	9	314675	J. Holdcroft	Longton
Oct 2	7	314890	Bates, Walker & Co.	Burslem
3	2	314896	Robinson & Leadbeater	Stoke
4	4	314906–7	J. & T. Bevington	Hanley
10	3	315102	John Edwards	Fenton

APPENDIX B

Date	Parcel No.	Patent No.	Factory, Retailer Wholesaler, etc	Place
10	5	315104–5	Wm. Brownfield & Sons	Cobridge
15	2	315271–2	Geo. Jones & Sons	Stoke
16	6	315400–1	Powell & Bishop	Hanley
19	8	315473	Minton, Hollins & Co.	Stoke
19	13	315479	T. C. Brown–Westhead, Moore & Co.	Hanley
24	10	315565	F. W. Grove & J. Stark	Longton
24	14	315574	F. & R. Pratt & Co.	Fenton
30	7	315684	Wedgwood & Co.	Tunstall
31	6	315765	Geo. Jones & Sons	Stoke
Nov 5	4	315918	Powell & Bishop	Hanley
6	11	315954–6	Wm. Brownfield & Sons	Cobridge
7	1	316087–9	E. J. D. Bodley	Burslem
7	2	316090	Mintons	Stoke
7	10	316101	Pinder, Bourne & Co.	Burslem
9	8	316122	Taylor, Tunnicliffe & Co.	Hanley
15	12	316309	T. C. Brown–Westhead, Moore & Co.	Hanley
20	9	316502	James Edwards & Sons	Burslem
21	8	316526	Davenports & Co.	Longport
22	1	316542–3	The Old Hall Earthenware Co. Ltd.	Hanley
22	13	316560	B. & S. Hancock	Stoke
24	7	316605	J. Dimmock & Co.	Hanley
29	3	316723	J. Holdcroft	Longton
Dec 1	5	316763	J. Holdcroft	Longton
1	6	316764	Oakes, Clare & Chadwick	Burslem
5	2	316842	E. J. D. Bodley	Burslem
6	4	316863	Mintons	Stoke
7	14	316912	J. Unwin	Longton
14	1	317112	J. Dimmock & Co.	Hanley
15	10	317203	The Worcester Royal Porcelain Co. Ltd.	Worcester
21	6	317404	Mintons	Stoke

APPENDIX B

Date	Parcel No.	Patent No.	Factory, Retailer Wholesaler, etc	Place
21	10	317410	T. Furnival & Sons	Cobridge
22	5	317427–8	Wm. Brownfield & Sons	Cobridge
29	6	317494	T. C. Brown–Westhead, Moore & Co.	Hanley
1878				
Jan 3	4	317537–9	Minton, Hollins & Co.	Stoke
9	4	317692–4	The Brownhills Pottery Co.	Tunstall
10	12	317733	J. Mortlock & Co.	London
14	1	317756	J. Maddock & Sons	Burslem
14	2	317757	Cotton & Rigby	Burslem
14	3	317758	Wm. Adams	Tunstall
14	6	317763	Minton, Hollins & Co.	Stoke
15	5	317780	Josiah Wedgwood & Sons	Etruria
18	5	317826	Taylor, Tunnicliffe & Co.	Hanley
22	6	317940	J. Dimmock & Co.	Hanley
24	6	318041	W. T. Copeland & Sons	Stoke
25	9	318107–8	Wm. Brownfield & Sons	Cobridge
28	11	318141	T. C. Brown–Westhead, Moore & Co.	Hanley
30	3	318158–9	Geo. Jones	Stoke
30	15	318189–90	The Brownhills Pottery Co.	Tunstall
31	1	318210	B. & S. Hancock	Stoke
Feb 1	4	318239	Geo. Jones & Sons	Stoke
1	11	318265–6	Minton, Hollins & Co.	Stoke
1	16	318275–9	The Derby Crown Porcelain Co. Ltd.	Derby
5	5	318397	The Campbell Brick & Tile Co.	Stoke
9	6	318469	J. Dimmock & Co.	Hanley
11	5	318543–4	T. C. Brown–Westhead, Moore & Co.	Hanley
12	5	318556–63	Derby Crown Porcelain Co. Ltd.	Derby
20	6	318800	Minton, Hollins & Co.	Stoke

APPENDIX B

Date	Parcel No.	Patent No.	Factory, Retailer Wholesaler, etc	Place
20	7	318801	The Worcester Royal Porcelain Co. Ltd.	Worcester
21	10	318821	W. E. Cartlidge	Burslem
22	8	318843	The Campbell Brick & Tile Co.	Stoke
28	3	319041	Dunn, Bennett & Co.	Hanley
Mar 5	2	319190	F. W. Grove & J. Stark	Longton
6	5	319201	Minton, Hollins & Co.	Stoke
7	4	319219	John Edwards	Fenton
9	1	319278-9	The Brownhills Pottery Co.	Tunstall
9	8	319293	Moore Bros.	Longton
9	11	319296	Powell & Bishop	Hanley
11	1	319310-1	Taylor, Tunnicliffe & Co.	Hanley
13	1	319370	Mintons	Stoke
13	7	319387	J. & T. Bevington	Hanley
13	10	319394	W. T. Copeland & Sons	Stoke
15	10	319507	John Rose & Co.	Coalport
23	8	319634-6	Derby Crown Porcelain Co. Ltd.	Derby
25	9	319679	F. J. Emery	Burslem
27	6	319725-6	G. W. Turner & Sons	Tunstall
27	15	319867-72	Minton, Hollins & Co.	Stoke
Apr 2	6	320030	Belfield & Co.	Preston-pans
10	4	320281	Mintons	Stoke
13	9	320373	McBirney & Armstrong	Belleek
17	4	320482	Mintons	Stoke
17	14	320568-9	Ridgway, Sparks & Ridgway	Stoke
20	2	320606	Thos. Furnival & Sons	Cobridge
20	6	320616	The Worcester Royal Porcelain Co. Ltd.	Worcester
24	2	320669	Wm. Brownfield & Sons	Cobridge
27	12	320793	McBirney & Armstrong	Belleek
30	7	320874-5	Josiah Wedgwood & Sons	Etruria

APPENDIX B

Date	Parcel No.	Patent No.	Factory, Retailer Wholesaler, etc	Place
May 3	2	321028	Josiah Wedgwood & Sons	Etruria
3	9	321163	Robinson & Leadbeater	Stoke
8	9	321231–2	Bates & Bennett	Cobridge
14	6	321361	Elsmore & Son	Tunstall
17	12	321575	J. Dimmock & Co.	Hanley
20	9	321632–4	Derby Crown Porcelain Co. Ltd.	Derby
21	11	321693	Banks & Thorley	Hanley
23	3	321704	Josiah Wedgwood & Sons	Etruria
23	4	321705	Moore Bros.	Longton
24	2	321726	Josiah Wedgwood & Sons	Etruria
27	20	322007	E. J. D. Bodley	Burslem
29	9	322039	Minton, Hollins & Co.	Stoke
June 1	5	322130	J. Mortlock & Co.	London
4	9	322168	F. Furnival & Sons	Cobridge
5	14	322223–4	W. T. Copeland & Sons	Stoke
7	1	322309	Geo. Jones & Sons	Stoke
8	8	322390	Wm. Wood & Co.	Burslem
12	10	322471	Harvey Adams & Co.	Longton
13	2	322476	John Tams	Longton
13	3	322477	McBirney & Armstrong	Belleek
19	7	322597–8	E. F. Bodley & Co.	Burslem
21	8	322662	Allen & Green	Fenton
27	7	322931–2	Josiah Wedgwood & Sons	Etruria
29	1	322948	Wood, Son & Co.	Cobridge
July 1	1	322971	Burgess & Leigh	Burslem
3	2	323132	Mintons	Stoke
6	7	323315–20	Joseph Cliff & Sons	Leeds
8	6	323396	Josiah Wedgwood & Sons	Etruria
9	8	323434	Mintons	Stoke
9	9	323435	Josiah Wedgwood & Sons	Etruria
9	10	323436	J. Dimmock & Co.	Hanley
10	14	323508	Bates & Bennett	Cobridge
11	1	323521	Soane & Smith	London
11	11	323596	W. & J. A. Bailey	Alloa

APPENDIX B

Date	Parcel No.	Patent No.	Factory, Retailer Wholesaler, etc	Place
12	4	323604	Josiah Wedgwood & Sons	Etruria
12	13	323626	Samuel Lear	Hanley
12	15	323628	T. C. Brown–Westhead, Moore & Co.	Hanley
15	1	323650–1	Pratt & Simpson	Fenton
17	9	323774–5	Wm. Adams	Tunstall
18	2	323778	Ambrose Bevington	Hanley
20	1	323847	J. Bevington	Hanley
20	6	323893	John Meir & Son	Tunstall
20	11	323910–1	E. J. D. Bodley	Burslem
26	3	324177	Josiah Wedgwood & Sons	Etruria
30	2	324324	idem	Etruria
30	6	324336	Powell, Bishop & Stonier	Hanley
30	12	324347	E. Clarke	Longport
31	8	324383	Mintons	Stoke
31	13	324388	James Edwards & Son	Burslem
Aug 6	3	324576	Moore Bros.	Longton
7	3	324730	Thos. Hughes	Burslem
9	10	324848	Derby Crown Porcelain Co. Ltd.	Derby
9	12	324870–2	Craven, Dunnill & Co. Ltd.	Jackfield
14	4	325029–34	S. H. Sharp	Leeds
16	9	325094	The Campbell Brick & Tile Co.	Stoke
23	1	325278	Moore Bros.	Longton
23	7	325319	J. Dimmock & Co.	Hanley
Sept 3	12	325612	G. & L. Wohlauer	Dresden
5	3	325716	Moore Bros.	Longton
9	5	325992–4	Wm. Brownfield & Sons	Cobridge
10	2	326006	Josiah Wedgwood & Sons	Etruria
12	6	326146	J. Bevington	Hanley
13	5	326155	G. L. Ashworth & Bros.	Hanley

Date	Parcel No.	Patent No.	Factory, Retailer Wholesaler, etc	Place
13	16	326198	The Worcester Royal Porcelain Co. Ltd.	Worcester
20	19	326482	R. Wotherspoon & Co.	Glasgow
24	3	326785	T. Bevington	Hanley
28	5	326970-1	Minton, Hollins & Co.	Stoke
30	1	327000	Mintons	Stoke
Oct 2	2	327035	Mintons	Stoke
3	8	327110	J. T. Hudden	Longton
4	8	327227	F. & R. Pratt & Co.	Fenton
5	4	327235	Jones Bros. & Co.	W/hmptn
5	13	327271	The Worcester Royal Porcelain Co. Ltd.	Worcester
8	6	327359	Moore Bros.	Longton
8	7	327360	Bates, Gildea & Walker	Burslem
9	9	327392	Josiah Wedgwood	Etruria
11	8	327556	Minton, Hollins & Co.	Stoke
14	8	327625-6	W. T. Copeland & Sons	Stoke
23	1	328018	The Brownhills Pottery Co.	Tunstall
23	11	328144-5	Pinder & Bourne & Co.	Burslem
24	1	328146	T. Furnival & Sons	Cobridge
24	2	328147	J. Dimmock & Co.	Hanley
24	13	328274	The Worcester Royal Porcelain Co. Ltd.	Worcester
26	4	328320	Wm. Brownfield & Sons	Cobridge
30	3	328436-7	Minton, Hollins & Co.	Stoke
30	5	328439-40	Mintons	Stoke
Nov 1	3	328620	J. Bevington	Hanley
4	1	328699	Edge, Malkin & Co.	Burslem
5	11	328774	H. Burgess	Burslem
5	17	328790-2	E. J. D. Bodley	Burslem
6	3	328795	Samuel Lear	Hanley
13	13	329075	John Rose & Co.	Coalport
15	1	329108	Craven, Dunnill & Co. Ltd.	Jackfield
15	11	329147	F. & R. Pratt & Co.	Fenton
16	5	329157	J. Dimmock & Co.	Hanley

Date	Parcel No.	Patent No.	Factory, Retailer Wholesaler, etc	Place
20	13	329378	Cliff & Tomlin	Leeds
23	2	329456	E. & C. Challinor	Fenton
26	14	329673	T. & R. Boote	Burslem
27	9	329709	J. McIntyre & Co.	Burslem
29	14	329782–3	W. & E. Corn	Burslem
Dec 2	7	329901	T. C. Brown–Westhead, Moore & Co.	Hanley
2	8	329902	J. F. Meakin	London
3	9	329922	J. McIntyre & Co.	Burslem
4	2	329939	Wm. Brownfield & Sons	Cobridge
6	3	330061	Mintons	Stoke
7	2	330097	A. Shaw	Burslem
19	8	330485	Thos. Hughes	Burslem
27	13	330677	T. & R. Boote	Burslem
28	4	330687	J. Gaskell, Son & Co.	Burslem
1879				
Jan 7	7	330920	W. T. Copeland & Sons	Stoke
8	11	330965–6	Minton, Hollins & Co.	Stoke
9	8	330997–8	Wm. Brownfield & Sons	Cobridge
14	5	331152	The New Wharf Pottery Co.	Burslem
14	6	331153	The Campbell Brick & Tile Co.	Stoke
16	3	331228	B. & S. Hancock	Stoke
16	13	331342	F. & R. Pratt & Co.	Fenton
20	15	331418–9	Derby Crown Porcelain Co. Ltd.	Derby
22	4	331458	Dunn, Bennett & Co.	Hanley
28	11	331597	W. T. Copeland & Sons	Stoke
29	2	331600	T. Furnival & Sons	Cobridge
29	3	331601	T. Bevington	Hanley
29	15	331677	E. J. D. Bodley	Burslem
Feb 1	13	331775	Clementson Bros.	Hanley
3	1	331777	Josiah Wedgwood & Sons	Etruria

Date	Parcel No.	Patent No.	Factory, Retailer Wholesaler, etc	Place
5	7	331892–3	Mintons	Stoke
8	1	332030	Mintons	Stoke
14	4	332251	T. Furnival & Sons	Cobridge
15	2	332266	The Campbell Brick & Tile Co.	Stoke
17	6	332296	McBirney & Armstrong	Belleek
24	2	332606	W. P. Jervis	Stoke
24	3	332607–9	W. & T. Adams	Tunstall
25	4	332642	Mintons	Stoke
28	1	332823	E. Chetwynd	Stoke
28	7	332831	Clementson Bros.	Hanley
Mar 1	1	332837	T. Furnival & Sons	Cobridge
4	4	332938	F. W. Grove & J. Stark	Longton
6	10	333047	Powell, Bishop & Stonier	Hanley
12	4	333210	Edge, Malkin & Co.	Burslem
12	12	333235–6	W. T. Copeland & Sons	Stoke
13	1	333241–4	Wm. Davenport & Co.	Longport
13	14	333301	Clementson Bros.	Hanley
14	9	333319	E. Clarke	Longport
17	2	333368	Powell, Bishop & Stonier	Hanley
18	1	333431	Josiah Wedgwood & Sons	Etruria
19	2	333485	J. Hawthorn	Cobridge
26	17	333751–2	The Worcester Royal Porcelain Co. Ltd.	Worcester
28	6	333801	Clementson Bros.	Hanley
29	4	333813	Beck, Blair & Co.	Longton
Apr 3	9	334030	T. C. Brown–Westhead, Moore & Co.	Hanley
4	12	334052–3	Pinder, Bourne & Co.	Burslem
9	5	334137	H. Alcock & Co.	Cobridge
10	12	334200	T. C. Brown–Westhead, Moore & Co.	Hanley
12	1	334206	The Worcester Royal Porcelain Co. Ltd.	Worcester

APPENDIX B

Date	Parcel No.	Patent No.	Factory, Retailer Wholesaler, etc	Place
15	6	334241–2	T. C. Brown–Westhead, Moore & Co.	Hanley
23	8	334508	T. C. Brown–Westhead, Moore & Co.	Hanley
24	3	334531	Josiah Wedgwood & Sons	Etruria
May 2	5	334803	A. Bevington	Hanley
5	1	334860–1	T. Furnival & Sons	Cobridge
5	6	334897	Bates, Gildea & Walker	Burslem
6	7	334923–5	Sampson Bridgwood & Son	Longton
7	11	334978	The Worcester Royal Porcelain Co. Ltd.	Worcester
9	15	335057	idem	Worcester
13	4	335148–51	Pinder & Bourne & Co.	Burslem
13	8	335167–8	Clementson Bros.	Hanley
14	9	335182	T. C. Brown–Westhead, Moore & Co.	Hanley
14	13	335187–8	E. J. D. Bodley	Burslem
19	1	335308–9	Wm. Brownfield & Sons	Cobridge
21	5	335496	Harvey Adams & Co.	Longton
23	2	335551–2	Sampson Bridgwood & Son	Longton
23	14	335608	Harvey Adams & Co.	Longton
29	2	335715	John Tams	Longton
29	12	335739–40	Pinder, Bourne & Co.	Burslem
30	3	335744	McBirney & Armstrong	Belleek
30	10	335791	J. Dimmock & Co.	Hanley
30	12	335793	F. W. Grove & J. Stark	Longton
31	4	335805	Minton, Hollins & Co.	Stoke
June 10	4	336030	T. Furnival & Sons	Cobridge
11	8	336075	Thos. Till & Sons	Burslem
13	13	336132	T. C. Brown–Westhead, Moore & Co.	Hanley
18	4	336185	F. W. Grove & J. Stark	Longton
24	11	336415	Josiah Wedgwood & Sons	Etruria
25	1	336417	Clementson Bros.	Hanley

APPENDIX B

Date	Parcel No.	Patent No.	Factory, Retailer Wholesaler, etc	Place
26	13	336471–4	Haviland & Co.	Limoges and London
27	11	336496	Shorter & Boulton	Stoke
30	12	336586–7	Birks Bros. & Seddon	Cobridge
July 2	2	336676	Josiah Wedgwood & Sons	Etruria
7	2	336917	J. F. Wileman	Fenton
8	1	336930	Mintons	Stoke
8	16	336967–8	T. C. Brown–Westhead, Moore & Co.	Hanley
9	12	337058	idem	Hanley
10	2	337060	T. Bevington	Hanley
10	3	337061	Moore Bros.	Longton
16	4	337157–8	A. Bevington & Co.	Hanley
16	14	337177	T. C. Brown–Westhead, Moore & Co.	Hanley
25	4	337497	Mintons	Stoke
26	6	337536	Minton, Hollins & Co.	Stoke
31	2	337660	Mintons	Stoke
Aug 2	2	337814	H. M. Williamson & Sons	Longton
5	12	337945–7	J. Mortlock & Co.	London
6	6	337958	Wardle & Co.	Hanley
13	2	338135	F. W. Grove & J. Stark	Longton
22	4	338559	McBirney & Armstrong	Belleek
27	13	338872	Bates, Gildea & Walker	Burslem
Sept 4	6	339193	T. C. Brown–Westhead, Moore & Co.	Hanley
10	13	339373	idem	Hanley
17	4	339685–6	Wm. Brownfield & Sons	Cobridge
18	10	339979	T. C. Brown–Westhead, Moore & Co.	Hanley
26	4	340431	J. T. Hudden	Longton
29	3	340569	Edge, Malkin & Co.	Burslem
Oct 9	6	341137	Bates, Gildea & Walker	Burslem

499

APPENDIX B

Date	Parcel No.	Patent No.	Factory, Retailer Wholesaler, etc	Place
10	2	341151	T. C. Brown–Westhead, Moore & Co.	Hanley
11	5	341229–30	E. J. D. Bodley	Burslem
15	1	341347	Mintons	Stoke
16	5	341466	J. Roth	London
16	16	341500	Minton, Hollins & Co.	Stoke
17	2	341502	G. L. Ashworth & Bros.	Hanley
18	3	341629	Josiah Wedgwood & Sons	Etruria
23	12	341864	C. Pillivuyt & Co.	London
24	4	341882–3	The Campbell Brick & Tile Co.	Stoke
27	9	341997	E. F. Bodley & Co.	Burslem
29	5	342098	Mintons	Stoke
29	7	342100	Clementson Bros.	Hanley
29	15	342152	F. D. Bradley	Longton
30	4	342158	Mintons	Stoke
Nov 3	12	342396	Minton, Hollins & Co.	Stoke
3	14	342398	Tundley, Rhodes & Procter	Burslem
6	2	342461	Josiah Wedgwood & Sons	Etruria
6	3	342462–3	Moore Bros.	Longton
6	4	342464–72	Burmantofts (Wilcock & Co.)	Leeds
12	11	342769	The Worcester Royal Porcelain Co. Ltd.	Worcester
15	12	342921	C. Ford	Hanley
15	16	342925–7	W. T. Copeland & Sons	Stoke
17	2	342929	Powell, Bishop & Stonier	Hanley
19	5	343017	idem	Hanley
20	4	343070–1	Elsmore & Son	Tunstall
21	6	343148	Mintons	Stoke
21	14	343166	Soane & Smith	London
22	7	343219	The Worcester Royal Porcelain Co. Ltd.	Worcester
28	5	343530	Wm. Brownfield & Sons	Cobridge

APPENDIX B

Date	Parcel No.	Patent No.	Factory, Retailer Wholesaler, etc	Place
28	6	343531	A. Bevington & Co.	Hanley
29	3	343585	Mintons	Stoke
29	4	343586	T. C. Brown–Westhead, Moore & Co.	Hanley
Dec 1	2	343618	J. Holdcroft	Longton
2	4	343652–3	T. C. Brown–Westhead, Moore & Co.	Hanley
2	5	343654	Elsmore & Son	Tunstall
2	17	343716	J. Aynsley & Sons	Longton
6	2	343815–6	T. & R. Boote	Burslem
10	14	344077	Clementson Bros.	Hanley
11	4	344082–4	Moore Bros.	Longton
17	11	344387	Ridgways	Stoke
19	1	344452	Clementson Bros.	Hanley
19	3	344454	Burmantofts (Wilcock & Co.)	Leeds
20	5	344478	Josiah Wedgwood & Sons	Etruria
22	2	344503	Mintons	Stoke
24	2	344568	Sherwin & Cotton	Hanley
1880				
Jan 3	1	344838	Sherwin & Cotton	Hanley
7	3	344961–2	T. Bevington	Hanley
7	4	344963	T. & R. Boote	Burslem
7	5	344964–9	Soane & Smith	London
7	8	344972	Minton, Hollins & Co.	Stoke
8	9	344997	The Old Hall Earthenware Co. Ltd.	Hanley
9	3	345003	Sherwin & Cotton	Hanley
9	12	345045	T. G. Allen	London
13	1	345131	T. C. Brown–Westhead, Moore & Co.	Hanley
14	11	345184–5	The Worcester Royal Porcelain Co. Ltd.	Worcester
16	8	345288	S. Fielding & Co.	Stoke

APPENDIX B

Date	Parcel No.	Patent No.	Factory, Retailer Wholesaler, etc	Place
16	14	345299	Brockwell & Son	London
21	7	345469–71	Pinder, Bourne & Co.	Burslem
22	2	345481	Mintons	Stoke
22	8	345493–4	Minton, Hollins & Co.	Stoke
23	5	345511	Mintons	Stoke
26	11	345719	Wm. Brownfield & Sons	Cobridge
27	13	345798	Wardle & Co.	Hanley
28	3	345801	T. C. Brown–Westhead, Moore & Co.	Hanley
28	4	345802	J. Aynsley & Sons	Longton
28	12	345833	Powell, Bishop & Stonier	Hanley
29	9	345860–1	E. J. D. Bodley	Burslem
30	2	345864	Taylor, Tunnicliffe & Co.	Hanley
Feb 3	11	345952	Powell, Bishop & Stonier	Hanley
9	18	346202	Whittingham, Ford & Riley	Burslem
10	4	346208–10	Mintons	Stoke
11	10	346344	T. Bevington	Hanley
12	4	346360	W. A. Adderley	Longton
12	7	346363	Wm. Brownfield & Sons	Cobridge
14	14	346467	Bates, Gildea & Walker	Burslem
18	12	346594	The Derby Crown Porcelain Co. Ltd.	Derby
24	2	346832	Mintons	Stoke
24	11	346870	Wm. Harrop & Co.	Hanley
25	18	346920	Clementson Bros.	Hanley
25	23	346945	Sherwin & Cotton	Hanley
26	6	346952–3	Minton, Hollins & Co.	Stoke
26	7	346954	Moore Bros.	Longton
Mar 3	6	347138	J. Holdcroft	Longton
4	8	347203	Soane & Smith	London
8	4	347344	T. Furnival & Sons	Cobridge
8	10	347360	W. Harrop & Co.	Hanley
12	4	347476	W. A. Adderley	Longton
16	3	347599	J. F. Wileman & Co.	Fenton
16	11	347645	Sherwin & Cotton	Hanley

Date	Parcel No.	Patent No.	Factory, Retailer Wholesaler, etc	Place
16	12	347646–7	J. Macintyre & Co.	Burslem
17	6	347660	Josiah Wedgwood & Sons	Etruria
18	3	347690–6	Moore Bros.	Longton
22	4	347838	Powell, Bishop & Stonier	Hanley
23	4	347872	Taylor, Tunnicliffe & Co.	Hanley
25	6	348018	Mintons	Stoke
30	4	348110	Sherwin & Cotton	Hanley
31	3	348114	Thos. Peake	Tunstall
Apr 12	6	348606–8	Bates, Gildea & Walker	Burslem
15	11	348761	Ridgways	Stoke
19	11	348911–3	The Worcester Royal Porcelain Co. Ltd.	Worcester
22	11	349025–6	Sherwin & Cotton	Hanley
22	5	349027	W. H. Grindley & Co.	Tunstall
26	1	349221	T. Furnival & Sons	Cobridge
27	11	349239–41	Moore Bros.	Longton
27	13	349318–23	The Worcester Royal Porcelain Co. Ltd.	Worcester
29	4	349340–1	Mintons	Stoke
30	6	349380	T. Furnival & Sons	Cobridge
May 3	3	349438–43	Wm. Brownfield & Sons	Cobridge
5	13	349528	S. Fielding & Co.	Stoke
10	6	349693	Powell, Bishop & Stonier	Hanley
11	15	349791	Soane & Smith	London
13	8	349852–3	Mintons	Stoke
13	15	349869	Minton, Hollins & Co.	Stoke
14	26	349939	Bates, Gildea & Walker	Burslem
25	4	350098	Wm. Brownfield & Sons	Cobridge
26	6	350142	Mintons	Stoke
June 1	4	350251	Mintons	Stoke
2	3	350353	Sherwin & Cotton	Hanley
7	6	350476	J. Dimmock & Co.	Hanley
8	1	350477	Geo. Jones & Sons	Stoke
10	3	350554	Sherwin & Cotton	Hanley
10	4	350555	E. J. D. Bodley	Burslem

APPENDIX B

Date	Parcel No.	Patent No.	Factory, Retailer Wholesaler, etc	Place
10	12	350613	J. Dimmock & Co.	Hanley
11	3	350616	Josiah Wedgwood & Sons	Etruria
14	12	350842	J. Roth	London
15	4	350848	Buckley, Wood & Co.	Burslem
16	3	350972	Wedgwood & Co.	Tunstall
17	4	351025	Samuel Lear	Hanley
17	15	351058	Ridgways	Stoke
17	16	351059	J. Macintyre & Co.	Burslem
17	20	351063	The Crystal Porcelain Co.	Hanley
17	21	351064	J. Dimmock & Co.	Hanley
19	11	351186	Josiah Wedgwood & Sons	Etruria
19	15	351190	J. Roth	London
22	1	351259	W. H. Grindley & Co.	Tunstall
26	13	351496–7	The Worcester Royal Porcelain Co. Ltd.	Worcester
July 5	11	351866	Westwood & Moore	Brierley Hill
7	4	351909	Sherwin & Cotton	Hanley
7	5	351910	Mintons	Stoke
7	15	351928	F. J. Emery	Burslem
12	4	352094	Mintons	Stoke
13	12	352138	Thos. Barlow	Longton
15	3	352192	Dunn, Bennett & Co.	Hanley
15	4	352193	F. W. Grove & J. Stark	Longton
16	9	352224	Sherwin & Cotton	Hanley
16	10	352225	Moore Bros.	Longton
16	19	352278	S. Fielding & Co.	Stoke
28	2	352872	The Brownhills Pottery Co.	Tunstall
31	8	353079	The Old Hall Earthenware Co. Ltd.	Hanley
Aug 4	3	353108	Pinder, Bourne & Co.	Burslem
11	14	353543	Clementson Bros.	Hanley
14	12	353713–4	Wm. Davenport & Co.	Longport
17	6	353746	Sherwin & Cotton	Hanley
18	3	353818	Josiah Wedgwood & Sons	Etruria

APPENDIX B

Date	Parcel No.	Patent No.	Factory, Retailer Wholesaler, etc	Place
21	2	354026	Sherwin & Cotton	Hanley
21	10	354081	W. A. Adderley	Longton
23	5	354092	Jackson & Gosling	Longton
23	6	354093–4	T. C. Brown–Westhead, Moore & Co.	Hanley
24	10	354154	E. J. D. Bodley	Burslem
Sept 3	3	354639	T. C. Brown–Westhead, Moore & Co.	Hanley
4	7	354766–7	J. Beech & Son	Longton
11	3	355091–100	Wm. Brownfield & Sons	Cobridge
14	6	355169	Mintons	Stoke
15	6	355231	G. L. Ashworth & Bros.	Hanley
15	12	355255–7	Minton, Hollins & Co.	Stoke
23	3	355575	Ambrose Wood	Hanley
25	6	355651–4	Minton, Hollins & Co.	Stoke
27	5	355745–6	John Marshall & Co.	Bo'ness, Scotland
29	3	355947–8	The Brownhills Pottery Co.	Tunstall
30	4	355987	The Worcester Royal Porcelain Co. Ltd.	Worcester
Oct 1	3	356014	Wade & Colclough	Burslem
6	4	356163	Josiah Wedgwood & Sons	Etruria
12	4	356514	Mintons	Stoke
13	5	356532	Josiah Wedgwood & Sons	Etruria
20	10	356970	Burgess & Leigh	Burslem
21	13	357033–5	The Worcester Royal Porcelain Co. Ltd.	Worcester
22	4	357039	E. F. Bodley & Son	Burslem
22	12	357088	J. Aynsley & Sons	Longton
26	13	357298–9	Minton, Hollins & Co.	Stoke
27	5	357305	Taylor, Tunnicliffe & Co.	Hanley
27	20	357429	J. Tams	Longton
27	21	357430	G. Woolliscroft & Son	Etruria
28	2	357466	Sherwin & Cotton	Hanley

Date	Parcel No.	Patent No.	Factory, Retailer Wholesaler, etc	Place
30	6	357560	Jones & Hopkinson	Hanley
Nov 2	2	357609	W. H. Grindley & Co.	Tunstall
4	4	357656–7	W. & T. Adams	Tunstall
4	15	357724–5	Minton, Hollins & Co.	Stoke
9	4	357954	Josiah Wedgwood & Sons	Etruria
10	2	358062–3	Wilcock & Co. (Burmantofts)	Leeds
10	13	358141	Bednall & Heath	Hanley
18	3	358466	S. Radford	Longton
18	14	358500	Mintons	Stoke
19	15	358552	The Crown Derby Porcelain Co. Ltd.	Derby
24	4	358747	F. W. Grove & J. Stark	Longton
24	5	358748	Bates, Gildea & Walker	Burslem
Dec 6	2	359292	Powell, Bishop & Stonier	Hanley
7	10	359321–6	Pinder, Bourne & Co.	Burslem
8	5	359342–3	Wittmann & Roth	London
15	15	359668–71	Wm. Brownfield & Sons	Cobridge
18	2	359784	Bates, Gildea & Walker	Burslem
24	8	359997	T. C. Brown–Westhead, Moore & Co.	Hanley
29	7	360042–4	Doulton & Co.	Lambeth
31	1	360100	The Old Hall Earthenware Co. Ltd.	Hanley
31	4	360103–5	Sherwin & Cotton	Hanley
1881				
Jan 5	7	360326	J. Roth	London
6	2	360331	B. & S. Hancock	Stoke
6	8	360355	F. D. Bradley	Longton
7	13	360484	Sherwin & Cotton	Hanley
12	5	360633	idem	Hanley
14	10	360747	The Worcester Royal Porcelain Co. Ltd.	Worcester
14	18	360799	E. J. D. Bodley	Burslem

Date	Parcel No.	Patent No.	Factory, Retailer Wholesaler, etc	Place
15	4	360806–7	Holmes, Stonier & Hollinshead	Hanley
20	3	360900	Mintons	Stoke
21	11	360954	W. & T. Adams	Tunstall
26	4	361116–7	Minton, Hollins & Co.	Stoke
27	15	361151	The Worcester Royal Porcelain Co. Ltd.	Worcester
28	3	361170	G. Woolliscroft & Son	Hanley
Feb 8	5	361537	F. W. Grove & J. Stark	Longton
8	6	361538–41	Wm. Brownfield & Sons	Cobridge
11	10	361668	F. J. Emery	Burslem
15	6	361748	W. A. Adderley	Longton
16	3	361784	F. D. Bradley	Longton
17	2	361813	Murray & Co.	Glasgow
18	3	361868	S. Radford	Longton
19	15	361927	S. S. Bold	Hanley
21	4	361937	Taylor, Waine & Bates	Longton
24	8	362086	Wm. Harrop & Co.	Hanley
25	14	362166	J. Macintyre & Co.	Burslem
28	9	362242	E. J. D. Bodley	Burslem
Mar 3	5	362423	J. Dimmock & Co.	Hanley
7	11	362545	J. Aynsley & Sons	Longton
8	3	362548	F. W. Grove & J. Stark	Longton
14	1	362815	E. J. D. Bodley	Burslem
17	9	362992	Shorter & Boulton	Stoke
19	4	363026–7	Mintons	Stoke
23	4	363157	Mintons	Stoke
24	2	363206–7	T. S. Pinder	Burslem
24	3	363208	W. A. Adderley	Longton
29	6	363421	T. A. Simpson	Hanley
31	2	363461	J. T. Hudden	Longton
Apr 7	2	363720	Sherwin & Cotton	Hanley
7	9	363732	The Old Hall Earthenware Co. Ltd.	Hanley
8	2	363738	W. Harrop & Co.	Hanley

APPENDIX B

Date	Parcel No.	Patent No.	Factory, Retailer Wholesaler, etc	Place
8	3	363739	Wedgwood & Co.	Tunstall
8	14	363785	The Worcester Royal Porcelain Co. Ltd.	Worcester
9	5	363793	R. H. Plant & Co.	Longton
11	1	363800	A. Bevington & Co.	Hanley
12	4	363849–50	Mintons	Stoke
14	10	363975	Mintons	Stoke
16	17	364110	J. Marshall & Co.	Bo'ness, Scotland
19	3	364116	Sherwin & Cotton	Hanley
19	5	364118	T. & R. Boote	Burslem
21	4	364172	Sherwin & Cotton	Hanley
21	5	364173–4	E. J. D. Bodley	Burslem
23	7	364238	J. F. Wileman	Fenton
28	12	364488	W. T. Copeland & Sons	Stoke
30	3	364528	Trubshaw, Hand & Co.	Longton
30	4	364529	Josiah Wedgwood & Sons	Etruria
May 3	4	364604	Wm. Wood & Co.	Burslem
3	5	364605	Sherwin & Cotton	Hanley
4	2	364624	idem	Hanley
4	3	364625–7	Wm. Brownfield & Sons	Cobridge
5	2	364648	W. & T. Adams	Tunstall
6	4	364736	R. H. Plant & Co.	Longton
11	3	364941	J. Tams	Longton
13	2	365005	Mintons	Stoke
16	2	365066	Josiah Wedgwood & Sons	Etruria
17	9	365134–5	J. Mortlock & Co.	London
20	11	365206	W. A. Adderley	Longton
21	3	365211	Powell, Bishop & Stonier	Hanley
24	5	365391	G. L. Ashworth & Bros.	Hanley
24	6	365392–3	Mintons	Stoke
24	7	365394	F. J. Emery	Burslem
25	3	365424	Powell, Bishop & Stonier	Hanley
25	9	365442–4	The Worcester Royal Porcelain Co. Ltd.	Worcester

Date	Parcel No.	Patent No.	Factory, Retailer Wholesaler, etc	Place
25	10	365445–6	Josiah Wedgwood & Sons	Etruria
26	7	365461	G. Woolliscroft & Son	Hanley
30	1	365539	T. Furnival & Sons	Cobridge
30	2	365540	The Decorative Art Tile Co.	Hanley
June 1	3	365730	Mintons	Stoke
1	13	365793	J. Mortlock & Co.	London
3	4	365827	S. P. Ledward	Cobridge
4	3	365852	T. Furnival & Sons	Cobridge
4	4	365853	The Decorative Art Tile Co.	Hanley
7	3	365875	E. F. Bodley & Son	Burslem
7	4	365876–7	The Decorative Art Tile Co.	Hanley
7	17	365914–6	The Worcester Royal Porcelain Co. Ltd.	Worcester
8	6	365955	The Crystal Porcelain Co.	Hanley
13	1	366015	S. Lear	Hanley
16	8	366078–9	S. Fielding & Co.	Stoke
18	1	366093	Jackson & Gosling	Longton
21	13	366220–2	Birks Bros. & Seddon	Cobridge
21	20	366246	Gildea & Walker	Burslem
July 2	1	366634	McBirney & Armstrong	Belleek
2	5	366643	T. Furnival & Sons	Cobridge
6	7	366809	Josiah Wedgwood & Sons	Etruria
9	10	366922–3	Wardle & Co.	Hanley
14	6	367133–4	T. C. Brown–Westhead, Moore & Co.	Hanley
15	5	367150	Wm. Corbitt & Co.	Rthrham
16	3	367213	Trubshaw, Hand & Co.	Longton
18	4	367249	G. Hall	Worcester
19	2	367259	The Dalehall Brick & Tile Co.	Burslem
25	2	367418	J. H. Davis	Hanley
28	3	367516	McBirney & Armstrong	Belleek

APPENDIX B

Date	Parcel No.	Patent No.	Factory, Retailer Wholesaler, etc	Place
28	4	367517	A. Wood	Hanley
28	14	367538	Ridgways	Stoke
29	2	367542–3	Sherwin & Cotton	Hanley
29	3	367544	Whittmann & Roth	London
30	3	367549	Sampson Bridgwood & Son	Longton
30	4	367550	Sherwin & Cotton	Hanley
30	5	367551	Mintons	Stoke
30	15	367590	W. T. Copeland & Sons	Stoke
Aug 2	1	367608	E. J. D. Bodley	Burslem
5	12	367892–3	Pinder, Bourne & Co.	Burslem
10	13	368044	The Old Hall Earthenware Co. Ltd.	Hanley
20	11	368686	The Worcester Royal Porcelain Co. Ltd.	Worcester
23	3	368802	F. W. Grove & J. Stark	Longton
24	11	368942	T. & R. Boote	Burslem
27	3	369202	S. Lear	Hanley
27	9	369215–8	Gildea & Walker	Burslem
29	7	369248	W. & T. Adams	Tunstall
Sept 2	4	369389	Dale, Page & Goodwin	Longton
3	11	369526	T. A. Simpson	Hanley
6	1	369538	The Derby Crown Porcelain Co. Ltd.	Derby
7	10	369654	Adams & Sleigh	Burslem
9	11	369731	The Worcester Royal Porcelain Co. Ltd.	Worcester
10	12	369778–81	J. Roth	London
16	10	370093	Geo. Jones & Sons	Stoke
22	9	370400	Bold & Michelson	Hanley
23	21	370470–2	Minton, Hollins & Co.	Stoke
27	9	370611	Pinder, Bourne & Co.	Burslem
28	4	370620	E. J. D. Bodley	Burslem
28	13	370633	Gildea & Walker	Burslem
29	3	370636	Geo. Jones & Sons	Stoke
30	3	370702–3	Davenports Ltd.	Longport

APPENDIX B

Date	Parcel No.	Patent No.	Factory, Retailer Wholesaler, etc	Place
30	15	370725–8	Mintons	Stoke
Oct 4	6	370885	Wm. Brownfield & Sons	Cobridge
6	5	370998	J. & R. Boote	Burslem
6	7	371000	The Campbell Brick & Tile Co.	Stoke
7	27	371098	Mintons	Stoke
8	3	371102	Adams & Sleigh	Burslem
11	16	371247	The Worcester Royal Porcelain Co. Ltd.	Worcester
12	14	371330–1	Mintons	Stoke
13	3	371337	Adderley & Lawson	Longton
13	5	371339	T. & R. Boote	Burslem
20	1	371866	Thos. Begley	Burslem
20	2	371867	Robinson & Chapman	Longton
22	1	371959	Mintons	Stoke
26	8	372138	Mintons	Stoke
26	16	372171	T. C. Brown-Westhead, Moore & Co.	Hanley
27	1	372185	Robinson & Chapman	Longton
29	3	372347	T. & R. Boote	Burslem
29	4	372348	Wm. Brownfield & Sons	Cobridge
29	11	372376	Wardle & Co.	Hanley
29	14	372379	Minton, Hollins & Co.	Stoke
31	11	372464	T. A. Simpson	Hanley
Nov 2	1	372489–90	T. C. Brown-Westhead, Moore & Co.	Hanley
3	12	372613	The Worcester Royal Porcelain Co. Ltd.	Worcester
4	24	372727	idem	Worcester
8	1	372918	T. & R. Boote	Burslem
9	6	372979	F. W. Grove & J. Stark	Longton
9	7	372980–2	E. J. D. Bodley	Burslem
10	2	372995	Brough & Blackhurst	Longton
19	3	373541	Sampson Bridgwood & Son	Longton

Date		Parcel No.	Patent No.	Factory, Retailer Wholesaler, etc	Place
	19	12	373573	The Worcester Royal Porcelain Co. Ltd.	Worcester
	21	1	373575	J. Bevington	Hanley
	22	9	373615	J. Tams	Longton
	22	17	373647	Ambrose Wood	Hanley
	23	13	373707	Shorter & Boulton	Stoke
	25	1	373821	Adams & Sleigh	Burslem
	25	15	373860	J. Roth	London
	29	10	374058	The Worcester Royal Porcelain Co. Ltd.	Worcester
Dec	2	16	374229	J. Roth	London
	5	11	374376	John Rose & Co.	Coalport
	8	9	374498	Adderley & Lawson	Longton
	9	2	374516	E. J. D. Bodley	Burslem
	10	7	374579	T. C. Brown–Westhead, Moore & Co.	Hanley
	12	12	374628	John Fell	Longton
	16	3	374782	Mintons	Stoke
	20	9	374948	Bednall & Heath	Hanley
	21	3	374955	F. Grosvenor	Glasgow
	21	9	374987	The Worcester Royal Porcelain Co. Ltd.	Worcester
	24	5	375054	J. Broadhurst	Fenton
1882					
Jan	3	6	375415	Holmes, Plant & Maydew	Burslem
	4	2	375426–7	W. T. Copeland & Sons	Stoke
	4	7	375439	J. Roth	London
	4	9	375444	F. & R. Pratt & Co.	Fenton
	7	2	375494	W. H. Grindley & Co.	Tunstall
	7	11	375580	Ridgways	Hanley
	10	5	375599	S. Lear	Hanley
	11	1	375709–12	Minton, Hollins & Co.	Stoke
	13	4	375815–6	The Decorative Art Tile Co.	Hanley

APPENDIX B

Date	Parcel No.	Patent No.	Factory, Retailer Wholesaler, etc	Place
18	10	376032	Robinson & Son	Longton
26	5	376425	J. T. Hudden	Longton
26	16	376443	S. Fielding & Co.	Stoke
27	8	376461	Craven, Dunnill & Co. Ltd.	Jackfield
30	2	376528	Hollinshead & Kirkham	Tunstall
30	3	376529	F. W. Grove & J. Stark	Longton
Feb 1	1	376580	Edge, Malkin & Co.	Burslem
3	4	376672–3	T. C. Brown–Westhead, Moore & Co.	Hanley
4	10	376754	Minton, Hollins & Co.	Stoke
6	4	376764–6	The Campbell Tile Co.	Stoke
7	2	376798	Wm. Mills	Hanley
8	7	376839	Wardle & Co.	Hanley
15	4	377048	F. W. Grove & J. Stark	Longton
16	6	377135–7	Mintons	Stoke
18	5	377273	J. F. Wileman & Co.	Fenton
23	17	377488–9	Minton, Hollins & Co.	Stoke
24	3	377492	Taylor, Tunnicliffe & Co.	Hanley
Mar 1	11	377779	The Worcester Royal Porcelain Co. Ltd.	Worcester
1	12	377780	Minton, Hollins & Co.	Stoke
7	7	378051	idem	Stoke
13	3	378252	J. T. Hudden	Longton
15	3	378337	Powell, Bishop & Stonier	Hanley
15	4	378338	Murray & Co.	Glasgow
20	5	378643	W. A. Adderley	Longton
23	2	378739	W. & T. Adams	Tunstall
23	15	378823	T. A. Simpson	Hanley
27	3	378937	D. Chapman	Longton
27	10	378959	Shorter & Boulton	Stoke
28	12	378988	Ambrose Wood	Hanley
28	16	378993–4	A. Bevington & Co.	Hanley
30	13	379076	John Rose & Co.	Coalport
30	17	379080	S. Fielding & Co.	Stoke
31	3	379088	A. Bevington & Co.	Hanley

APPENDIX B

Date	Parcel No.	Patent No.	Factory, Retailer Wholesaler, etc	Place
Apr 4	2	379212–3	Wm. Brownfield & Sons	Cobridge
11	6	379434	Geo. Jones & Sons	Stoke
11	7	379435–6	Minton, Hollins & Co.	Stoke
21	7	379767	Sampson Bridgwood & Son	Longton
27	14	380072	The New Wharf Pottery Co.	Burslem
May 2	5	380194	G. L. Ashworth & Bros.	Hanley
3	1	380199	S. Radford	Longton
5	2	380401	Wood, Hines & Winkle	Hanley
6	5	380418	Powell, Bishop & Stonier	Hanley
6	6	380419–20	Whittaker, Edge & Co.	Hanley
8	18	380549–50	Davenports Ltd.	Longport
9	3	380553–4	H. Alcock & Co.	Cobridge
9	4	380555	Whittaker, Edge & Co.	Hanley
9	7	380558	Wm. Brownfield & Sons	Cobridge
9	11	380564	Minton, Hollins & Co.	Stoke
10	4	380571–2	John Edwards	Fenton
10	14	380676	S. Fielding & Co.	Stoke
13	6	380789	Geo. Jones & Sons	Stoke
17	2	380869–70	E. J. Bodley	Burslem
24	4	381376	Minton, Hollins & Co.	Stoke
24	21	381434	Doulton & Co.	Burslem
25	11	381480	W. A. Adderley	Longton
27	3	381568	Samuel Lear	Hanley
30	5	381611	W. H. Grindley & Co.	Tunstall
June 5	6	381805	Mintons	Stoke
5	7	381806	Wood, Hines & Winkle	Hanley
9	3	381964	Hall & Read	Burslem
9	4	381965–6	W. A. Adderley	Longton
13	11	382126	A. Shaw & Son	Burslem
13	14	382130–1	Wardle & Co.	Hanley
21	4	382406	Wm. Lowe	Longton
21	5	382407–8	Sampson Bridgwood & Son	Longton
21	11	382472	The Old Hall Earthenware & Co. Ltd	Hanley

APPENDIX B

Date	Parcel No.	Patent No.	Factory, Retailer Wholesaler, etc	Place
23	1	382593–4	Josiah Wedgwood & Sons	Etruria
23	5	382598	Burgess & Leigh	Burslem
28	2	382721	The Derby Crown Porcelain Co.	Derby
July 1	8	382829	Taylor, Tunnicliffe & Co.	Hanley
3	2	382842	Mintons	Stoke
3	3	382843	E. J. D. Bodley	Burslem
4	3	382859	Wright & Rigby	Hanley
6	4	383020–1	Wm. Brownfield & Sons	Cobridge
14	3	383436–7	Geo. Jones & Sons	Stoke
14	10	383468	Wardle & Co.	Hanley
14	14	383482	Beech & Tellwright	Cobridge
17	8	383549	Wood & Son	Burslem
19	7	383641	Wardle & Co.	Hanley
20	1	383694–6	John Edwards	Fenton
22	8	383802	Geo. Jones & Sons	Stoke
25	3	383855	F. Grosvenor	Glasgow
25	9	383869–71	The Brownhills Pottery Co. Ltd.	Tunstall
26	4	383893	Adderley & Lawson	Longton
28	3	384078	Hawley & Co.	Longton
31	2	384160–1	Sampson Bridgwood & Son	Longton
31	9	384171–2	Mintons	Stoke
Aug 5	4	384353–4	Wm. Brownfield & Sons	Cobridge
10	5	384464	Wright & Rigby	Hanley
21	2	385106	John Tams	Longton
21	8	385129	Adams & Bromley	Hanley
25	2	385411	Mintons	Stoke
26	4	385490	Wm. Wood & Co.	Burslem
28	2	385527	Belfield & Co.	Preston-pans
28	9	385544	Mintons	Stoke
29	12	385623	Wm. Brownfield & Sons	Cobridge
30	14	385693	The Worcester Royal Porcelain Co. Ltd.	Worcester

APPENDIX B

Date	Parcel No.	Patent No.	Factory, Retailer Wholesaler, etc	Place
31	3	385701	A. Bevington & Co.	Hanley
Sept 6	2	385954	Hawley & Co.	Longton
8	5	386085–6	Mintons	Stoke
9	3	386126	Taylor, Tunnicliffe & Co.	Hanley
11	4	386178	Adams & Bromley	Hanley
16	2	386388–9	Hulme & Massey	Longton
19	2	386542	W. H. Grindley & Co.	Tunstall
28	4	387147–8	T. C. Brown–Westhead, Moore & Co.	Hanley
28	22	387229	Bridgett & Bates	Longton
29	2	387231–2	The Brownhills Pottery Co.	Tunstall
Oct 6	2	387598–603	Mintons	Stoke
9	3	387771	W. T. Copeland & Sons	Stoke
9	4	387772	Dean, Capper & Dean	Hanley
11	3	387958–60	Sampson Bridgwood & Son	Longton
11	4	387961	Wood & Son	Burslem
12	17	388200	T. Furnival & Sons	Cobridge
16	4	388296	Wood & Son	Burslem
19	4	388395	Lowe, Ratcliffe & Co.	Longton
31	2	389136	Wm. Lowe	Longton
Nov 1	14	389201	Stonier, Hollinshead & Oliver	Hanley
4	19	389390	The Worcester Royal Porcelain Co. Ltd.	Worcester
8	2	389554	Mintons	Stoke
10	10	389793	Ridgways	Stoke
10	12	389795–7	Pratt & Simpson	Fenton
11	2	389801	Powell, Bishop & Stonier	Hanley
13	1	389893	Edge, Malkin & Co.	Burslem
13	2	389894	Sampson Bridgwood & Son	Longton
14	3	389911–2	Ed. Steel	Hanley
15	7	390004–5	S. Fielding & Co.	Stoke
16	3	390023	Taylor, Tunnicliffe & Co.	Hanley
21	4	390255	J. Holdcroft	Longton

Date	Parcel No.	Patent No.	Factory, Retailer Wholesaler, etc	Place
21	8	390264	Gildea & Walker	Burslem
22	11	390285	S. Fielding & Co.	Stoke
24	19	390588	Minton, Hollins & Co.	Stoke
27	3	390617	H. Alcock & Co.	Cobridge
27	4	390618	The Derby Crown Porcelain Co. Ltd.	Derby
27	5	390619	J. F. Wileman & Co.	Fenton
Dec 2	8	390976	Minton, Hollins & Co.	Stoke
4	7	390985	A. Bevington & Co.	Hanley
6	2	391068–9	T. C. Brown–Westhead, Moore & Co.	Hanley
13	1	391361–2	Mintons	Stoke
13		391363–4	Josiah Wedgwood	Etruria
14	6	391409	S. Lear	Hanley
15	3	391460	The Old Hall Earthenware Co. Ltd.	Hanley
18	9	391596	J. Lockett & Co.	Longton
19	3	391620	H. Kennedy	Glasgow
21	4	391768	E. J. D. Bodley	Burslem
21	5	391769	Wood, Hines & Winkle	Hanley
22	2	391818	F. W. Grove & J. Stark	Longton
22	14	391846	Lorenz Hutschenreuther	Bavaria
23	4	391855	J. F. Wileman	Fenton
23	12	391917	The New Wharf Pottery Co.	Burslem
23	14	391922–7	The Worcester Royal Porcelain Co.	Worcester
27	1	391929	The New Wharf Pottery Co.	Burslem
1883				
Jan 2	2	392166	The Derby Crown Porcelain Co. Ltd.	Derby
3	1	392176	Wm. Hines	Longton
3	14	392362	T. Furnival & Sons	Cobridge

APPENDIX B

Date		Parcel No.	Patent No.	Factory, Retailer Wholesaler, etc	Place
	3	18	392388–9	John Rose & Co.	Coalport
	4	5	392403	T. C. Brown–Westhead, Moore & Co.	Hanley
	8	5	392590	W. T. Copeland & Sons	Stoke
	8	12	392621	The Worcester Royal Porcelain Co. Ltd.	Worcester
	9	3	392626	Powell, Bishop & Stonier	Hanley
	9	4	392627	E. F. Bodley & Son	Longport
	9	5	392628–30	Hall & Read	Hanley
	9	11	392652	Davenports Ltd.	Longport
	10	17	392693	Gildea & Walker	Burslem
	12	3	392725	Holmes, Plant & Maydew	Burslem
	13	6	392760	Moore & Co.	Longton
	13	17	392809	T. & R. Boote	Burslem
	16	1	392855	Blair & Co.	Longton
	17	3	392888	W. H. Grindley & Co.	Tunstall
	23	8	393099	E. F. Bodley & Son	Longport
	23	10	393102–3	W. T. Copeland & Sons	Stoke
	24	1	393107	Sampson Bridgwood & Son	Longton
	24	2	393108–9	Wm. Brownfield & Sons	Cobridge
	25	3	393177	The Brownhills Pottery Co.	Tunstall
	26	8	393258	Wm. Lowe	Longton
	27	8	393298	G. W. Turner & Sons	Tunstall
	29	6	393310	Wm. Brownfield & Sons	Cobridge
	29	7	393311–2	W. H. Grindley & Co.	Tunstall
	30	1	393323	E. F. Bodley & Son	Longport
	30	12	393362	Wedgwood & Co.	Tunstall
	31	14	393413	Minton, Hollins & Co.	Stoke
Feb	1	3	393418	Sampson Bridgwood & Son	Longton
	1	17	393474	E. J. D. Bodley	Burslem
	2	4	393495	S. Hancock	Stoke
	2	17	393539	Wedgwood & Co.	Tuhstall
	3	3	393548	Mintons	Stoke
	5	2	393647	J. Holdcroft	Longton
	6	1	393668	Wood, Hines & Winkle	Hanley

APPENDIX B

Date	Parcel No.	Patent No.	Factory, Retailer Wholesaler, etc	Place
7	4	393714	Hawley & Co.	Longton
7	5	393715	Mountford & Thomas	Hanley
9	9	393979	E. J. D. Bodley	Burslem
12	3	394086	Dunn, Bennett & Co.	Hanley
14	3	394185	W. H. Grindley & Co.	Tunstall
15	5	394215	J. H. Davis	Hanley
17	13	394371	G. W. Turner & Sons	Tunstall
19	1	394374	W. A. Adderley	Longton
20	13	394443	Davenports Ltd.	Longport
20	17	394448	Gildea & Walker	Burslem
21	3	394452	Geo. Jones & Sons	Stoke
22	6	394556–61	Hall & Read	Hanley
22	20	394599	The Worcester Royal Porcelain Co. Ltd.	Worcester
22	21	394600	The Old Hall Earthenware Co.	Hanley
24	12	394676	Josiah Wedgwood & Sons	Etruria
24	13	394677	The Worcester Royal Porcelain Co. Ltd.	Worcester
26	6	394687	Williamson & Sons	Longton
28	3	394765	Thos. Till & Sons	Burslem
Mar 8	5	395284	M. Massey	Hanley
8	20	395316–7	E. F. Bodley & Son	Longport
14	3	395560	The Derby Porcelain Co. Ltd.	Derby
15	3	395622	T. Furnival & Sons	Cobridge
16	6	395688	J. Broadhurst	Fenton
17	8	395703	Mintons	Stoke
20	3	395818	E. A. Wood	Hanley
20	4	395819	Josiah Wedgwood & Sons	Etruria
24	3	396056	Sampson Bridgwood & Son	Longton
30	1	396200–1	Mintons	Stoke
30	9	396245	Minton, Hollins & Co.	Stoke
Apr 2	3	396313	T. & E. L. Poulson	Castleford
3	3	396316	E. Warburton	Longton

APPENDIX B

Date	Parcel No.	Patent No.	Factory, Retailer Wholesaler, etc	Place
6	14	396576	G. & J. Hobson	Burslem
10	1	396648	Banks & Thorley	Hanley
19	3	397090	R. H. Plant & Co.	Longton
21	1	397227	J. F. Wileman & Co.	Fenton
24	7	397311	G. L. Ashworth & Bros.	Hanley
25	14	397376	Pratt & Simpson	Fenton
27	17	397512	C. Littler & Co.	Hanley
27	18	397513	J. H. Davis	Hanley
27	19	397514	Powell, Bishop & Stonier	Hanley
May 2	4	397609–11	T. C. Brown–Westhead, Moore & Co.	Hanley
5	4	397751	Whittaker, Edge & Co.	Hanley
7	8	397819	S. Fielding & Co.	Stoke
8	6	397829–30	T. G. & F. Booth	Tunstall
11	5	398059	R. H. Plant & Co.	Longton
16	12	398280	T. A. Simpson	Stoke
22	11	398425	Powell, Bishop & Stonier	Hanley
22	12	398426	Burns, Oates	London
23	7	398436	T. G. & F. Booth	Tunstall
23	8	398437–8	E. A. Wood	Hanley
24	3	398479	The Brownhills Pottery Co.	Tunstall
25	4	398519	W. A. Adderley	Longton
28	2	398577–80	O. G. Blunden	Poling
31	17	398784	Wardle & Co.	Hanley
June 2	9	398849–55	Minton, Hollins & Co.	Stoke
4	8	398877–8	Clementson Bros.	Hanley
8	2	399068	H. Alcock & Co.	Cobridge
9	2	399135–6	Sampson Bridgwood & Son	Longton
9	6	399143	Mintons	Stoke
11	2	399147	F. W. Grove & J. Stark	Longton
11	8	399161	J. Matthews	Weston-s'-Mare
11	9	399162	idem	Weston-s'-Mare

APPENDIX B

Date	Parcel No.	Patent No.	Factory, Retailer Wholesaler, etc	Place
13	3	399319	Belfield & Co.	Preston-pans
13	7	399336	Pratt & Simpson	Stoke
14	2	399367–70	F. W. Grove & J. Stark	Longton
18	11	399554	John Tams	Longton
18	12	399555–9	Wm. Brownfield & Sons	Cobridge
20	3	399640	T. & R. Boote	Burslem
20	4	399641	Mintons	Stoke
20	16	399675	W. & E. Corn	Burslem
21	22	399822	Wardle & Co.	Hanley
23	4	399875	Josiah Wedgwood & Sons	Etruria
25	5	399891	Ford & Riley	Burslem
25	10	399897–8	Wm. Brownfield & Sons	Cobridge
July 2	4	400146	Edge, Malkin & Co.	Burslem
3	3	400176	J. Aynsley & Sons	Longton
3	4	400177	Moore Bros.	Longton
4	7	400348	Wm. Brownfield & Sons	Cobridge
5	6	400367	F. W. Grove & J. Stark	Longton
5	19	400462	T. Furnival & Sons	Cobridge
5	21	400464	Owen, Raby & Co.	Longport
6	2	400467	Blackhurst & Bourne	Burslem
10	9	400582	Ambrose Wood	Hanley
10	11	400583–4	J. Macintyre & Co.	Burslem
11	1	400596	Josiah Wedgwood & Sons	Etruria
19	4	400941	Davenports Ltd.	Longport
19	21	400994	Geo. Jones & Sons	Stoke
20	11	401035	Hollinshead & Kirkham	Tunstall
21	3	401040	Bridgett & Bates	Longton
23	3	401087	Josiah Wedgwood & Sons	Etruria
26	1	401296	W. A. Adderley	Longton
27	4	401410	T. C. Brown–Westhead, Moore & Co.	Hanley
27	13	401426–7	Wm. Bennett	Hanley
30	10	401553	Wm. Brownfield & Sons	Cobridge
31	3	401593	T. & R. Boote	Burslem

APPENDIX B

Date	Parcel No.	Patent No.	Factory, Retailer Wholesaler, etc	Place
Aug 1	3	401623	Wagstaff & Brunt	Longton
1	4	401624	Geo. Jones & Sons	Stoke
1	9	401653	T. C. Brown–Westhead, Moore & Co.	Hanley
2	3	401663–4	Davenports Ltd.	Longport
3	17	401769	E. J. Bodley	Burslem
8	9	401842	J. & E. Ridgway	Stoke
9	15	401897–9	Haviland & Co.	France and London
17	5	402346	E. J. D. Bodley	Burslem
20	8	402514	The Worcester Royal Porcelain Co. Ltd.	Worcester
22	1	402560–1	The Brownhills Pottery Co.	Tunstall
23	2	402625–6	Grove & Cope	Hanley
24	12	402736	Mountford & Thomas	Hanley
25	11	402839	Wm. Brownfield & Sons	Cobridge
29	3	402950	J. Aynsley & Sons	Longton
31	6	403110	W. & E. Corn	Burslem
31	7	403111	J. F. Wileman & Co.	Fenton
Sept 1	10	403204	S. Fielding & Co.	Stoke
5	3	403298–9	Wm. Brownfield & Sons	Cobridge
7	4	403486	The Derby Crown Porcelain Co. Ltd.	Derby
7	19	403513–4	Powell, Bishop & Stonier	Hanley
11	4	403665	Josiah Wedgwood & Sons	Etruria
13	17	403802–3	H. Aynsley & Co.	Longton
14	1	403805–6	W. & T. Adams	Tunstall
14	2	403807–9	Mintons	Stoke
17	14	403978	The Derby Crown Porcelain Co. Ltd.	Derby
20	12	404171–5	Hall & Read	Hanley
20	13	404176	The Derby Crown Porcelain Co. Ltd.	Derby

APPENDIX B

	Date	Parcel No.	Patent No.	Factory, Retailer Wholesaler, etc	Place
	21	4	404196	T. C. Brown–Westhead, Moore & Co.	Hanley
	24	9	404317	Jones & Hopkinson	Hanley
	25	4	404328	F. W. Grove & J. Stark	Longton
	25	5	404329–30	Sampson Bridgwood & Son	Longton
	27	21	404466	Meigh & Forester	Longton
	28	4	404473	Blair & Co.	Longton
	28	5	404474	E. J. D. Bodley	Burslem
	29	4	404571	Sampson Bridgwood & Son	Longton
Oct	2	15	404643	Mellor, Taylor & Co.	Burslem
	2	22	404652–3	Meigh & Forester	Longton
	4	4	404745	Sampson Bridgwood & Son	Longton
	4	5	404746	Whittaker, Edge & Co.	Hanley
	4	24	404809	The Worcester Royal Porcelain Co. Ltd.	Worcester
	6	2	404870	W. H. Grindley & Co.	Tunstall
	8	1	404900	Hollinson & Goodall	Longton
	8	2	404901–2	T. G. & F. Booth	Tunstall
	8	3	404903–5	Hall & Read	Hanley
	9	9	405016–8	A. Bevington & Co.	Hanley
	11	2	405215	Wittmann & Roth	London
	12	13	405336	Bridgetts & Bates	Longton
	13	3	405341	Wood & Son	Burslem
	13	11	405363–4	Wm. Brownfield & Sons	Cobridge
	17	5	405466	The New Wharf Pottery Co.	Burslem
	17	6	405467–8	Hall & Read	Hanley
	20	3	405724	W. A. Adderley	Longton
	20	4	405725–9	Wm. Brownfield & Sons	Cobridge
	23	6	405855	J. Dimmock & Co.	Hanley
	24	11	405946–8	Minton, Hollins & Co.	Stoke
	25	17	406032–3	Taylor, Tunnicliffe & Co.	Hanley
	26	7	406043	Jones & Hopkinson	Hanley
	27	1	406046	The Brownhills Pottery Co.	Tunstall

APPENDIX B

Date	Parcel No.	Patent No.	Factory, Retailer Wholesaler, etc	Place
30	2	406140	J. Marshall & Co.	Bo'ness, Scotland
30	3	406141	The New Wharf Pottery Co.	Burslem
30	17	406187	J. Robinson	Burslem
Nov 1	1	406223	A. Bevington & Co.	Hanley
1	25	406370	Wood, Hines & Winkle	Hanley
1	26	406371	S. Fielding & Co.	Stoke
1	27	406372	Davenports Ltd.	Longport
2	19	406464–9	The Worcester Royal Porcelain Co. Ltd.	Worcester
5	13	406511	H. Alcock & Co.	Cobridge
6	3	406516	E. & C. Challinor	Fenton
7	2	406561	W. & E. Corn	Burslem
10	9	406781	Taylor, Tunnicliffe & Co.	Hanley
10	10	406782	Wm. Brownfield & Sons	Cobridge
13	10	406875	T. G. & F. Booth	Tunstall
14	3	406893	Stonier, Hollinshead & Oliver	Hanley
15	17	407063	T. Furnival & Sons	Cobridge
17	2	407155	The Derby Crown Porcelain Co. Ltd.	Derby
21	3	407333	F. J. Emery	Burslem
22	3	407385	S. Fielding & Co.	Stoke
23	7	407587–8	Minton, Hollins & Co.	Stoke
24	3	407601	Powell, Bishop & Stonier	Hanley
26	2	407623	W. A. Adderley	Longton
26	3	407624	Sampson Bridgwood & Son	Longton
28	12	407805–10	The Worcester Royal Porcelain Co. Ltd.	Worcester
Dec 1	3	407913	idem	Worcester
3	10	407943	James Wilson	Longton
5	2	408035	Malkin, Edge & Co.	Burslem
5	3	408036	The Derby Crown Porcelain Co. Ltd.	Derby

APPENDIX B

Date	Parcel No.	Patent No.	Factory, Retailer Wholesaler, etc	Place
8	8	408136	J. F. Wileman & Co.	Fenton
14	4	408288	The Brownhills Pottery Co.	Tunstall
15	13	408356	T. G. & F. Booth	Tunstall
15	14	408357	Hollinson & Goodall	Longton
29	4	408849	Powell, Bishop & Stonier	Hanley

Bibliography

(in order of date of publication)

The Ceramic Art of Great Britain. L. Jewitt (Virtue & Co., revised ed., 1883)

English Ceramic Circle Transactions. (English Porcelain Circle, 1928–31); 1928–

Nantgarw Porcelain. W. D. John (Ceramic Book Co., 1948)

Longton Hall Porcelain. Dr. Bernard Watney (Faber & Faber, 1957)

Swansea Porcelain. W. D. John (Ceramic Book Co., 1957)

The Pinxton China Factory. C. L. Exley (Mr & Mrs Coke-Steel, 1963)

Encyclopaedia of British Pottery & Porcelain Marks. G. Godden. (Barrie & Jenkins 1964 and later editions)

Royal Doulton 1815–1965. Desmond Eyles (Royal Doulton, 1965)

Hull Pottery. John Bartlett & Derek Brooks (Kingston Upon Hull Museums Bulletin, September 1970)

The Illustrated Guide to Liverpool Herculaneum Pottery. Prof. A. Smith (Barrie & Jenkins, 1970)

Northern Ceramic Society. (Newsletters & Journals, 1971–)

The Illustrated Guide to Victorian Parian China. C. & D. Shinn (Barrie & Jenkins, 1971)

Derby Porcelain. Franklin A. Barrett & Arthur L. Thorpe (Faber & Faber, 1971)

Bulletins of the Scottish Pottery Society, 1972–

English Delftware. F. H. Garner & Michael Archer (Faber & Faber, revised ed. 1972)

English Blue and White Porcelain of the 18th Century. Dr. Bernard Watney (Faber & Faber, revised ed., 1973)

The Potteries of Tyneside. R. C. Bell & M.A.V. Gill. (Laing Art Gallery & Museum, 1973)

Royal Worcester Porcelain. H. Sandon (Barrie & Jenkins, 1973)

Sunderland Ware. J. T. Shaw (County Borough of Sunderland Public Libraries, Museum and Art Gallery 4th ed., 1973)

William De Morgan. Catalogue of Pottery. Roger Pinkham (Victoria & Albert Museum, 1973)

Yorkshire Pots & Potteries. Heather Lawrence (David & Charles, 1974)

Lowestoft Porcelain in Norwich Castle Museum. Sheenah Smith (Vol. I. Blue & White, Vol.II Polychrome, 1975 & 1986)

The Story of Wedgwood. Alison Kelly (Josiah Wedgwood & Sons Ltd., revised ed., 1975)

Royal Crown Derby. J. Twitchett & B. Bailey (Barrie & Jenkins, 1976)

Bo'ness Potteries. (Exhibition at Kenneil Museum: Falkirk Museums Publication, 1977)

Chelsea Porcelain at Williamsburg. John Austin (Colonial Williamsburg Foundation, Va., U.S.A., 1977)

A Collectors' History of British Pottery. Griselda Lewis. (Antique Collectors' Club, 2nd ed. 1977)

Mason Porcelain & Ironstone. R. G. Haggar & Elizabeth Adams (Faber & Faber, 1977)

Flight & Barr Worcester Porcelain. H. Sandon (Antique Collectors' Club, 1978)

Royal Doulton Figures. D. Eyles & R. Dennis (Royal Doulton, 1978)

Creamware. Donald Towner (Faber & Faber, 1978)

Scottish East Coast Potteries 1750–1840. Patrick McVeigh (John Donald, 1979)

Staffordshire Porcelain 1740–1851. (Northern Ceramic Society Exhibition: City Museum & Art Gallery, Stoke-on-Trent, 1979)

Della Robbia Pottery Birkenhead. (Williamson Art Gallery &
   Museum [David Hilhouse], 1980)
Derby Porcelain. John Twitchett (Barrie & Jenkins, 1980)
Wedgwood of Etruria & Barlaston Exhibition. (City Museum & Art
   Gallery, Stoke-on-Trent, 1980)
Caughley & Worcester Porcelains 1775–1800. G. Godden (Antique
   Collectors' Club, revised ed., 1981)
Coalport & Coalbrookdale Porcelains. G. Godden (Antique
   Collectors' Club, new ed., 1981)
Daniel, H. & R. M. Berthoud (Micawber Publications, 1981)
English Transfer-Printed Pottery & Porcelain. C. Williams-Wood
   (Faber & Faber, 1981)
Chamberlain Worcester. G. A. Godden. (Barrie & Jenkins, 1982)
English Brown Stoneware 1670–1900. Adrian Oswald, R. J. C.
   Hildyard & R. G. Hughes (Faber & Faber, 1982)
Rockingham Pottery & Porcelain. Alwyn & Angela Cox (Faber &
   Faber, 1983)
Hand Painted Gray's Pottery. (Exhibition: Stoke-on-Trent [Paul
   Niblett], 1983)
Spode-Copeland 1733–1983. (Exhibition: R. Copeland & A.
   Townsend: City Museum & Art Gallery, Stoke-on-Trent, 1983)
Staffordshire Porcelain. Edited by G. Godden (Granada, 1983)
Goss & other crested china. Nicholas Pine (Shire Publications, 1984)
Ridgway Porcelains. G. Godden. (Antique Collectors' Club, 1985)
Encyclopaedia of Pottery & Porcelain. Elizabeth Cameron (Faber &
   Faber, 1986)
Torquay Pottery Mark Book. Deena Patrick (Torquay Pottery
   Collectors' Society, 1986)
Chelsea Porcelain. Elizabeth Adams (Barrie & Jenkins, 1987)
Neale Pottery & Porcelain. Diana Edwards (Barrie & Jenkins, 1987)
New Hall. D. Holgate (Faber & Faber, 1987)
The Royal Potteries of Weston-super-Mare. (Woodspring Museum
   Publication [Sharon Poole], 1987)

Scottish Spongware. G. Cruickshank (Scottish Pottery Studies, 1982)

Encyclopaedia of British Porcelain Manufacturers. G. Godden
(Barrie & Jenkins, 1988)

Adam Notes. Dr. D. A. Furniss (private circulation, 1989)

Davenport. T. A. Lockett & G. Godden (Barrie & Jenkins, 1989)

Potters. E. Cooper & E. Lewenstein (The Craftsmen Potters
Association of Great Britain, 8th ed., 1989)

Worcester Blue and White Porcelain. L. Branyan, N. French & J.
Sandon (Barrie & Jenkins, revised ed., 1989)

Dynamic Design 1940–90. Kathy Niblett (City Museum & Art
Gallery, Stoke-on-Trent, 1990)

Glimpses of Glasgow's Pottery Tradition 1800–1900. (Exhibition:
Christie's of Scotland Ltd., 1990)

Dictionary of Minton. P. Atterbury & M. Batkin (Antique Collectors'
Club, 1990)

Longton Potters 1700–1865. Rodney-Hampson (City Museum & Art
Gallery, Stoke-on-Trent, 1990)

Derby Porcelain Figures 1750–1848. Peter Bradshaw (Faber &
Faber, 1990)

Bow Porcelain. E. Adams & D. Redstone (Faber & Faber, revised ed.,
1991)

The Dictionary of Worcester Porcelain Vol. I. T. Sandon
(Woodbridge Collectors' Club, 1993)

Spode & Copeland Marks. Robert Copeland (Studio Vista, 1993)